AFRICAN HISTORICAL DICTIONARIES
Edited by Jon Woronoff

Historical Dictionary
of
SIERRA LEONE

by

CYRIL P. FORAY

African Historical Dictionaries, No. 12

The Scarecrow Press, Inc.
Metuchen, N.J. & London
1977

Library of Congress Cataloging in Publication Data

Foray, Cyril P   1934-
    Historical dictionary of Sierra Leone.

    (African historical dictionaries ; no. 12)
    Bibliography: p.
    1. Sierra Leone--History--Dictionaries.
I. Title. II. Series.
DT516.5.F6   966'.4'003   77-3645
ISBN 0-8108-1035-2

TO MY PARENTS
MARY AND MICHAEL.

CONTENTS

EDITOR'S FOREWORD

Sierra Leone is one of Africa's most intriguing countries inasmuch as it, like neighboring Liberia, was established as a home for former slaves. This has created a certain dichotomy not only in the ethnic origin of the population, but also between the more urban--and urbane--Creoles in the Colony, and the more rural, tribalized units in the Protectorate. It is also intriguing in that, as opposed to Liberia, political ascendency gradually slipped out of the fingers of the Creole "elite" into the hands of the Protectorate Africans. After a number of years of independence, a de facto single party situation emerged and since 1973 political power has been wielded by only one party.

Given this heritage, it is quite natural that this historical dictionary should go into considerable detail on the different populations of the country and members of the earlier, and present ruling groups, from chiefs to colonizers, to administrators and pastors, to politicians and educators, without forgetting the military men. This biographical aspect has received very close attention from the author, C. P. Foray, often writing from personal knowledge. In addition to providing a very comprehensive "who's who," this dictionary contains other useful sections as well as an up-to-date general bibliography and chronology.

In the case of our Sierra Leone volume, we are pleased to have as author a person who is active as a historian and is presently head of the History Department at Fourah Bay College, Sierra Leone. Mr. Foray's particular research interests are the history of the Sierra Leone Parliament and a biography of Sir Milton Margai. In addition, he has periodically been a historical figure in his own right, born and bred in the country, studying at the college whose faculty he now serves on, elected to Parliament, appointed minister of foreign affairs and then health, and also detained under two governments.

Jon Woronoff
Series Editor

ACKNOWLEDGMENTS

My thanks are due to the following persons for kindly granting me permission to make use of materials in their published and/or unpublished works on Sierra Leone: the Rev. Father Hamelberg, C. S. Sp., of the Sacred Heart Parish, Freetown; the Rev. P. J. Bart-Williams of St. Philips Parish, Freetown; Mr. C. H. Fyfe, Centre of African Studies, University of Edinburgh, U. K.: Professor J. D. Hargreaves, Department of History, University of Aberdeen, U. K.: Dr. A. P. Kup, Department of History, Simon Fraser University, British Columbia, Canada; Associate Professor John Cartwright, Department of Political Science, University of Western Ontario, Canada; Dr. Leo Spitzer, Department of History, Dartmouth College, USA; and the following individuals from the University of Sierra Leone: Dr. A. T. Porter, vice-chancellor; Professor E. D. Jones, principal of Fourah Bay College; Professor N. A. Cox-George, Department of Economics, Fourah Bay College; Professor John Peterson, formerly of Fourah Bay College; Dr. A. J. G. Wyse and Dr. Cecil M. Fyle, History Department, Fourah Bay College; Mr. J. S. Thompson, assistant librarian, Fourah Bay College Library; Mr. A. J. Lasite, vice principal, Sierra Leone Grammar School, Freetown; and Mr. Farid R. Anthony of Freetown, barrister and solicitor of the Supreme Courts of Sierra Leone and the Gambia.

I also wish to thank Dr. H. M. Joko Smart, of the Department of Law, Fourah Bay College, and chairman, Public Archives Committee, for giving me permission to gain access to the Public Archives and to use materials therein; and Mr. Herbert Johnson of the Sierra Leone Daily Mail for allowing me to use information contained in the Daily Mail Year Books.

To Messrs. J. G. Edowu Hyde of the Institute of African

Studies, Fourah Bay College, and George S. Anthony, vice principal, Milton Margai Teachers College, Freetown, a special word of thanks for their kind help and advice in helping me prepare the manuscript; my gratitude is extended also to Mr. William Johnson, master and registrar of the Supreme Court, Freetown, and to Miss A. King of the Law Library, Freetown, for putting at my disposal information on the judiciary; and to all those too numerous to mention by name, whose help was so useful in the preparation of this work. Finally, my sincere apologies go to all those whose names I have inadvertently omitted in this work. The faults and shortcomings are, needless to add, entirely my responsibility.

Cyril P. Foray,
Department of History,
Fourah Bay College,
  University of Sierra Leone,
Freetown.
April, 1976

LIST OF ABBREVIATIONS

ACTEA	Association for Teacher Education in Africa
AMA	American Missionary Association
APC	All People's Congress
ATO	Amalgamated Teachers Organisation
AWMS	Annie Walsh Memorial School
BP	British Petroleum
CMS	Church Missionary Society
CSSP	Congregatio Spiritus Sancti (Congregation of the Holy Ghost; also known as the Holy Ghost Fathers)
DC	District Commissioner
DPC	Democratic People's Congress
EUB(C)	Evangelical United Brethren (in Christ)
FBC	Fourah Bay College
FSSG	Freetown Secondary School for Girls
IPP	Independent People's Party
KPM	Kono Progressive Movement
MOW	Ministry of Works
NCBWA	National Congress of British West Africa
NCCSL(NC)	National Council of the Colony of Sierra Leone
NRC	National Reformation Council
NUC	Njala University College
P & T	Posts and Telecommunications

PC	Paramount Chief
PCCH	Princess Christian Cottage Hospital
PCMH	Princess Christian Maternity Hospital
PEPU	Protectorate Educational Progressive Union
QC	Queen's Counsel
RDP	Radical Democratic Party
RSLMF	Royal [later, Republic of] Sierra Leone Military Forces
SEPA	Science Educational Programme for Africa
SJ	Society of Jesus (order of Jesuit priests)
SL	Sierra Leone
SLBS	Sierra Leone Broadcasting Service
SLEC	Sierra Leone Electricity Corporation
SLIM	Sierra Leone Independence Movement
SLPIM	Sierra Leone Progressive Independence Movement
SLPP	Sierra Leone People's Party
SLPRC	Sierra Leone Petroleum Refinery Company
SLTU	Sierra Leone Teachers' Union
SMA	Society of African Missions
SOS	Sierra Leone Organisation Society
SPCK	Society for the Propagation of Christian Knowledge
UDP	United Democratic Party
UPP	United Progressive Party
USL	University of Sierra Leone
YWCA	Young Women's Christian Association

CHRONOLOGY

ca. 1400   Baga, Temne and Yalunka arrived in Sierra Leone.

1446   The coast of Sierra Leone sighted by Portuguese expedition under command of Alvaro Fernandes after it had crossed the River Casamance.

1448   Dinis Dias passed Cape Verde and reached Sierra Leone.

1462   Pedro da Cintra (Sintra) reached Sierra Leone and mapped capes, rivers and islands, and gave name Serra Lyoa.

1466   Portuguese royal charter established administration in Cape Verde and Guinea.

1482   Portuguese built shortlived fort on River Sierra Leone.

1517   Trade between Portuguese merchants in Cape Verde and Sierra Leone prohibited by Portuguese authorities.

1533   Diocese of Cape Verde and Guinea established.

1550s   1500 slaves shipped annually from Guinea to Portugal. Mane invaders south of Sierra Leone move northwards.

1562   Sir John Hawkins visited Sierra Leone and obtained 300 slaves.

1465   Hawkins' second visit to Sierra Leone; landed at Tagrin.

1567-8   Hawkins' third visit to Sierra Leone during which he took part in the conflicts between two Mane kings. He seized and took away 250 slaves.

1580   Sir Francis Drake called at Sierra Leone and carved his name on a rock near the watering-place.

1582   Edward Fenton spent several weeks on the River Sierra Leone on his way to Brazil.

late 1500s   Tobacco smoking in pipes introduced in West Africa.

1592   A Patent of Special Licence granted to Thomas Gregory, Thomas Pope, and others to trade in Sierra Leone.

ca. 1600   Temne, Northern Bullom and Mane merged. Susu surrender Port Loko to Temne.

1605   Jesuit priest Father Balthazar Barreira arrived in Sierra Leone to start a mission.

ca. 1606   Dutch, Flemish and Portuguese traders in Sierra Leone.

1607   William Keeling arrived in Sierra Leone with three ships.

1618   The Company of Adventurers of London Trading to Africa started operations in Sierra Leone.

1620s   About 3000 slaves shipped annually from Guinea to Portugal.

1630   Formation of the Company of Merchants Trading to Guinea with a monopoly from Cape Blanco to Cape of Good Hope and with exclusive rights to import African goods into England.

1631   A Charter granted to Sir Richard Young and other adventurers to trade in Sierra Leone.

1662   Fort built at Tasso Island by the English Company of Royal Adventurers.

1663   English factory built at Sherbro by the Company of Merchants to Guinea.

1664   Dutch Admiral de Ruyter attacked and destroyed English fort on Tasso Island and carved his name on a rock at the watering-place.

1672   English fort on Bunce Island built by the Royal African Company (formerly Royal Adventurers).

1683   French pirate Jean Hamlin, disguised as an English man-of-war, captured 17 English and Dutch ships off Sierra Leone.

1688   Factory built at York Island by Royal African Company.

1699   Slaves shipped from Guinea required to be baptized.

1701   Catechism made compulsory for all slaves in Guinea.

1750   The Company of Merchants Trading to Africa started operations in Sierra Leone.

1758	Three London partners trading privately signed a treaty with Bai Samma, king of North Bulom, to ensure supply of timber and slaves.
1766	The same three London partners signed a treaty with King Sumana, a vassal of Suri, king of Sherbro.
1768	The Yalunka pushed out of Futa Jalon built a fortress town at Falaba.
1772-93	French established a factory on Gambia Island.
1787	Arrival of some 400 freed-slave colonists and 60 Europeans from England. Grant of land by King Tom for the settlers. Granville Town founded.
1788	Grant of land by King Tom in 1787 ratified by King Naimbana.
1789	The new settlement attacked by Temne and destroyed.
1790-1	Formation of St. George's Bay Company, later called the Sierra Leone Company, which assumed responsibility for the settlement.
1792	Arrival of 1190 Negroes from Nova Scotia and 119 Europeans from England. Freetown founded.
1793	Arrival in Freetown of first Kroomen.
1794	James Watt and Matthew Winterbottom set out from Freetown on a mission to Timbo and Labe. First Freetown printing press, sent out by the Sierra Leone Company, was set up in July. French squadron attacked Freetown.
1796	Governor moved residence from the waterfront to Fort Thornton.
1799	Sierra Leone Company granted a royal charter; governor-in-council given legislative powers. Freetown constituted a corporation with mayor and aldermen. Sierra Leone Peninsula granted by charter to Sierra Leone Company. Insurrection of Nova Scotians.
1800	Arrival of 550 Maroons and a detachment of the King's Regiment.
1801	Temne and Bullom attacked Colony. Attack repulsed. First Sierra Leone Gazette published.

1802   Fresh but abortive attack on Colony by Temne and Bullom.

1804   First Church Missionary Society's missionaries, the Rev.
            Melchior Renner and the Rev. Peter Hartwig, arrived
            in Sierra Leone.

1807   British Parliament declared slave trade illegal.
            Territory west of Freetown acquired by Sierra Leone
            Company.   Act passed transferring the rights of the
            Company to the Crown.

1808   Sierra Leone became a Crown Colony.   Possessions of
            the Sierra Leone Company transferred to the Crown.
            New series of the Gazette issued.

1808-15   Some 6000 slaves recaptured by the British naval
            squadron released in Sierra Leone.

1809   Leicester, the first village for recaptives established.
            Title of Gazette changed to The African Herald in January.

1811   Census of Freetown taken--population 1900
            Arrival of the first chief justice of the Colony, Robert
            Thorpe, appointed in 1808.
            Arrival of the first Wesleyan missionary from Europe,
            the Rev. George Warren.
            Wilberforce village founded as Cabenda or New Cabenda.

1812   Regent formerly Hogbrook Village and Kissy village
            formed.

1814   Sir Charles MacCarthy assumed reins of government
            of Colony as lieutenant governor.
            Christian Institution founded by the CMS to train local
            teachers and missionaries.

1815   Temne organized a secret society to recover Port Loko
            from Susu Chief Brima Konkuri.

1816   Gloucester village founded.   Sir Charles MacCarthy became governor of Sierra Leone.

1817   Colony divided into parishes.   Leopold village formed.
            New series of Gazette under the title of The Royal Gazette and Sierra Leone Advertiser issued in August.

1818   The Isles de Los ceded to Britain.
            Bathurst and Charlotte villages founded.

1819   Court of Mixed Commission established in Freetown to
            try slave cases.   Arrival of 85 men from Barbados.

Kent, York, Wellington and Hastings villages formed.
Three Companies of Royal African Corps disbanded.
Arrival of first group of West Indian troops.
Maporto and Robump (now Waterloo and Hastings) acquired by Colony.

1820   Banana Islands acquired by Britain.

1821   The Gambia and the Gold Coast made dependencies of
            Sierra Leone, forming the British West African set-
            tlements with governor in Freetown.
            Brian O'Beirne sent to the Futa Jalon to promote Sierra
            Leone's trade.

1822   Major Laing sent on a trade and diplomatic mission to
            the Scarcies and Falaba.
            Walls and roof of Maroon Church completed.

1824   Governor Sir Charles MacCarthy killed in Ashanti War
            in the Gold Coast.
            Bunce, Tasso and Tombo Islands, with one mile of
            north bank of river, acquired by Britain.

1825   Southern bank of Camaranca to the Gallinas River,
            known as Turner's Peninsula, and Bacca Loko or Port
            Loko and the Island of Matacong acquired by Britain
            by means of treaty between Governor Sir Charles
            Turner and native chiefs.

1826   Governor Turner set out on an expedition to Sherbro;
            died in Freetown.

1827   The Colony villages formed into divisions, or districts.
            New settlements established at Allen Town, Calmont
            and Grassfield. Kaffu Bulom District and Island of
            Bulama acquired by Britain.
            The Christian Institution refounded at Fourah Bay as
            Fourah Bay College.

1828   St. George's Cathedral Church opened for Divine Ser-
            vice.

1829   Murray Town and Aberdeen Villages founded.

1831-41   War between the Temne and Loko.

1832   Cobolo War or expedition against the Akus at Cobolo on
            the Ribi River.

1836   Government House, Fort Thornton, transferred from
            Ordinance Department to the Colonial government.

1837   Groundnuts to the value of £13 exported from Sierra
            Leone for the first time.

1841   Niger expedition under naval command accompanied by
            two missionaries, the Rev. James Frederick Schön
            and the Rev. Samuel Adjayi Crowther, set out for
            Nigeria. "Mendi Mission" started.

1842   Some recaptives emigrated to Abeokuta from Sierra
            Leone.

1845   William Fergusson, first British governor of African
            ancestry, became governor of Sierra Leone.
            CMS Grammar School founded in Freetown.

1847   Loko Masama and Kafu Bulom territories acquired by
            Britain.

1849   Female Institution opened by the CMS.

1850   The Gold Coast provided with Executive and Legislative
            councils and separated from Sierra Leone.

1852   Sierra Leone constituted a diocese in communion with
            the Church of England. First Anglican bishop of
            Sierra Leone, the Rt. Rev. O. E. Vidal, arrived
            in Freetown. St. George's Parish Church declared
            a cathedral.

1854   Buxton Church, Freetown, opened.

1854-5   Expedition to Malageah.

1855   American United Brethren in Christ started work in
            Sierra Leone.

1858   Apostolic Vicariate of Sierra Leone established under
            Monsignor de Marion Bresillac, founder of the Society
            of African Missions.

1858-9   Expedition to the Great Scarcies River; Kambia de-
            stroyed by the British.

1859   Arrival in Freetown of Mgr. Bresillac.

1860   Prince Alfred, Queen Victoria's son, landed in Free-
            town.
            Yoni attacked Magbele and destroyed CMS mission.

1861   Native Church Pastorate established.
            Koya war with the British. Bendu, parts of Koya and
            Bagru territories, Sherbro and Turtle Islands an-
            nexed to Sierra Leone Colony.

1863   Charter establishing executive and legislative councils
            in Sierra Leone.

1864	Samuel Adjayi Crowther consecrated Bishop of the West African countries beyond British jurisdiction. Arrival of Father Blanchet C. S. Sp. to establish Holy Ghost Fathers mission in Sierra Leone. St. Edward's primary school founded.
1865	First Industrial Exhibition held in Freetown.
1866	West African Settlements re-established with governor of Sierra Leone as governor-in-chief and a separate Legislative Council for Sierra Leone. Nuns of the Order of St. Joseph of Cluny arrived in Freetown. St. Joseph's Convent founded.
1870	New series of the Gazette under the title, The Sierra Leone Royal Gazette, issued in January.
1872	Diplomatic mission led by Dr. Blyden sent to Falaba. Retrocession of portion of British Koya.
1873	Blyden's diplomatic mission to Timbo. Gbanya, Kpa-Mendi chief, sent a contingent of warriors to assist the British in Ashanti war.
1874	Wesleyan Boys High School opened in Freetown. Lagos put under the governor of the Gold Coast; Sierra Leone separated.
1875	Governor Rowe's expedition to Sherbro.
1876	Fourah Bay College affiliated to the University of Durham, England.
1877	CMS Female Institution renamed Annie Walsh Memorial School.
1880	Wesleyan Female Institution founded in Freetown.
1880-4	Trade wars in the hinterland of Sierra Leone.
1882	Board of Education established in Sierra Leone. Gallinas territory acquired by Britain. Anglo-French convention on northern rivers boundary. The Island of Matacong ceded to France.
1883	Administrator F. F. Pinkett's expedition to Sherbro. Krim country annexed.
1884	War in Gallinas country. Leopold Educational Institute opened in Freetown.
1885	Yoni attacked Government House at Songo.

Boundary between Sierra Leone and Liberia defined.

1886   Direct telegraphic communications established between Freetown and London.
Sierra Leone and Liberia boundary agreement ratified.

1887   Queen Victoria's Golden Jubilee and the Colony's centenary celebrations held in Freetown.
Wilberforce Memorial Hall opened.
British offensive against the Yoni.
Robari captured and destroyed.

1888   Major Festing's mission to Almami Samodu, king of the Sofas.
Governor Hay's expedition to Krim country.

1889   Anglo-French convention on boundaries of Guinea and Sierra Leone.

1890   Sierra Leone Frontier Police Force established.
Local mail service established.
Steamer Service to Sherbro started.
British jurisdiction imposed on Imperri country.

1890s   Arrival of Syrian traders in Sierra Leone.
African Methodist Episcopal Missions opened at Mange and Magbele.

1891   Department of Native Affairs established.

1891-2   Tambi expeditions.

1893   Freetown Municipal Council created.
British sovereignty asserted over Port Loko.
Small (or Little) Scarcies territory brought under British jurisdiction.
Expedition against the Sofas and Waiima Incident.

1894-96   Governor Cardew undertook three extensive tours of the hinterland.

1895   Samuel Lewis awarded a knighthood.

1895-1914 Sierra Leone Railway constructed.   Pendembu terminal reached.

1895   Anglo-French agreement on the boundary of Sierra Leone.

1896   British Protectorate proclaimed over hinterland of Sierra Leone.

1897   Queen Victoria's Diamond Jubilee celebrated in Freetown.
Work commenced on Victoria Park, Freetown.

1898   Hut tax imposed in the Sierra Leone Protectorate.   In-
        surrection against the tax.
        A West African regiment formed in Sierra Leone.
        St. George's Cathedral Church disestablished.

1899   Sierra Leone government railway opened.
        Muslim School opened at Foulah Town.

1900   Harford Girls School, Moyamba, founded.

1901   Ordinance passed constituting the Sierra Leone Battalion
        of the West African Frontier Force.

1904   Anglo French convention on Sierra Leone/Guinea bound-
        aries.
        Albert Academy School for boys opened in Freetown by
        the Evangelical Brethren in Christ (EUBC) Mission.

1906   Bo Government School opened.
        Moa Barracks constructed.

1907   Court Messenger Force formally constituted by ordi-
        nance.

1910   Duke of Connaught visited Sierra Leone.

1911   Frontier with Liberia agreed.
        Collegiate School founded in Freetown.

1912   West Africa Currency Board constituted.

1916   Railway Workers Union Formed.
        Sierra Leone troops in the Cameroons.

1919   Anti-Syrian Riots; Strike of railway workers.
        Sierra Leone Bar Association formed.

1920   Congress of British West Africa formed.

1922   St. Edward's Secondary School founded.

1923   New Constitution for Sierra Leone.

1924   First three elected members of the Legislative Council
        took their seats alongside 11 official and seven
        nominated unofficial members.

1925   Visit of Edward, Prince of Wales.   Prince of Wales
        School opened in Freetown by the Sierra Leone
        Government.

1926   Geological survey of the country taken.
        Strike of railway workers.

1927   Domestic slavery abolished in Sierra Leone.

1930s   Ordinances introducing Native Administrations in the
            Protectorate.

1931   Diamonds discovered in Sierra Leone.
            Haidara War.
            Census of Sierra Leone taken--population 1,768,840.

1934   Wired broadcasting introduced into Sierra Leone.

1937   Ahmaddiya missionaries opened mission in Sierra Leone.

1938   West African Youth League formed.

1939   First Sierra Leone Roman Catholic priest, the Rev.
            E. J. Hamelberg, ordained.
            Airport built at Hastings.

1941   Death of the Rev. Cornelius Mulcahy.

1942-6   West African troops served in Burma.

1943   Two African unofficial members appointed to Executive
            Council.

1946   District councils and Protectorate Assembly set up.
            Chief Commissioner of Protectorate appointed.

1947   Governor Sir Hubert Stevenson's constitutional proposals
            publicized.
            First recorded earth tremor in Sierra Leone.

1949   Sierra Leone Produce Marketing Board (SLPMB) formed.
            Department of Cooperatives established.

1950   National Council of the Colony of Sierra Leone's
            (NCCSL) Colony Rural Area Council established.
            Catholic Vicariate became Diocese of Freetown and Bo
            with the Rev. Ambrose Kelly as first bishop.

1951   Sierra Leone Peoples Party (SLPP) formed.
            New constitution introduced and general elections held.
            Double-decker buses requisitioned for use by Road
            Transport Department.

1952   Motion for assumption of portfolios by unofficial mem-
            bers of the executive council introduced into Legisla-
            tive Council.
            Death of the Rt. Rev. Ambrose Kelly.

1953   Dr. Margai became leader of government business.
            Six African ministers appointed to the government.

Christ the King College opened at Bo by Catholic Mission.

1954   Formal opening of Queen Elizabeth II Quay.
          Government House, Fort Thornton, rebuilt.
          Dr. Margai accorded title of chief minister.
          Keith-Lucas commission appointed.

1955   Riots in Freetown following labor unrest.

1956   Legislative Council renamed House of Representatives.
          Franchise extended and representation increased.
          Chiefdom disturbances in the provinces.
          United Progressive Party (UPP) formed.

1957   General Elections held.
          Erection of the Catholic Diocese of Makeni.

1958   Further constitutional changes introduced an All-African
              Executive Council.
          Peoples National Party (PNP) formed.

1959   Dr. Margai awarded a knighthood.
          Formation of United Front Coalition.
          Bo Town Council created.

1960   Sir Milton Margai appointed prime minister with an All-
              African Cabinet.
          Fourah Bay College constituted into the University Col-
              lege of Sierra Leone.
          The All People's Congress (APC) Party formed.
          Paramount Hotel formally opened in Freetown.

1961   Sierra Leone achieved independence on April 27, with
              dominion status and membership in the British Com-
              monwealth.
          Visit of Her Majesty Queen Elizabeth II and the Duke of
              Edinburgh.

1962   General elections to parliament.

1963   Grant of Freedom of Entry into the City of Freetown,
              to the 1st. Battalion, the Royal Sierra Leone Regi-
              ment.
          Njala University College founded.
          First Sierra Leone governor-general, Sir Henry Light-
              foot Boston, appointed.

1964   Death of Sir Milton Margai; Albert Margai became
              prime minister.
          Siaka Stevens elected mayor of Freetown.
          First students enrolled at Njala University College.

Bank of Sierra Leone established; Decimal currency
introduced.

1965   Death of I. T. A. Wallace-Johnson.
Free Trade Area Pact signed between Sierra Leone,
Guinea, Liberia and Ivory Coast.
Visit of Sir Dauda Jawara, prime minister of Gambia.

1967   General elections held. Siaka Stevens appointed prime
minister.
Military rule established. City Council and Rural Areas
Council both suspended.
National Development Bank opened.

1968   Civilian rule re-established and Siaka Stevens reappointed
as prime minister. National government formed.

1969   Death of Sir Henry Lightfoot Boston.
Visit of President Kaunda of Zambia.
University of Sierra Leone established.
Sierra Leone became a non-permanent member of the
UN Security Council.

1970   Freetown City Council reconstituted.
National Government dissolved.
New Catholic Diocese of Kenema created.
First Sierra Leone Catholic bishop, the Rt. Rev. Josie
Henry Ganda, appointed bishop of Kenema.
Freetown City Council reconstituted.
Catholic Archdiocese of Sierra Leone created, with
Bishop Bronsnahan as first archbishop. The Arch-
diocese constitutes the Diocese of Freetown and Bo,
the Diocese of Makeni, and the Diocese of Kenema.

1971   Changeover to right side-of-the-road traffic.
Bishop Ganda consecrated in Kenema.
Sierra Leone became a republic and Mr. Justice
C. O. E. Cole sworn in as first president of the
Republic; Siaka Stevens assumed office as executive
president.
Brig. John Bangura, Maj. E. S. Momoh, Capt. Jawara
and Lt. Kolugbonda executed for attempting to over-
throw the government illegally.

1972   Visit to Sierra Leone of Haile Selassie, emperor of
Ethiopia.
National Insurance Company formed.
Fidel Castro of Cuba visited Sierra Leone.

1973   General elections to Parliament.
Mano River Union Declaration signed.

1974   National census--population 3. 5 million.

1975   Hurricane disaster.
            Execution of six civilians and two soldiers for attempting
                to overthrow the government illegally.

1976   Visit of Princess Pahlavi of Iran.
            President Stevens took oath of office for second term.
            Sierra Leone host to the All Africa Conference of
                Labour Ministers.
            Bridge across the Mano River linking Sierra Leone with
                Liberia formally declared open.
            First bus service between Freetown and Monrovia in-
                augurated by the Road Transport Corporation.

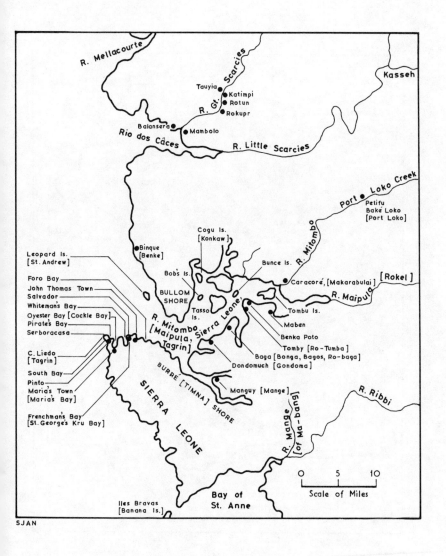

SJAN

MAP 1. Important places known and mentioned in 16th- and 17th-century reports on the Sierra Leone River and neighboring territories. (Modern names are given in brackets in some instances.)

xxvii

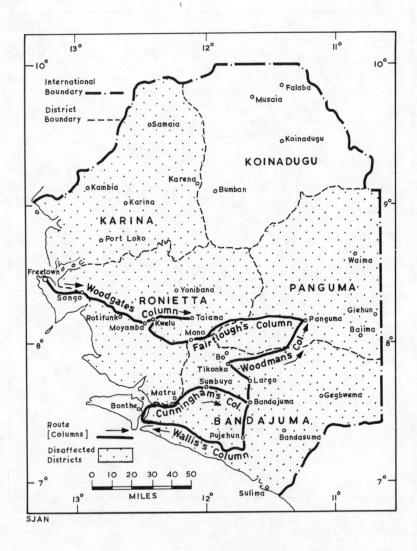

MAP 2. The five administrative districts of the Protectorate (1896) and routes of military expeditions to some disaffected areas in the 1898 Hut Tax War.

MAP 3.   Tribal divisions.

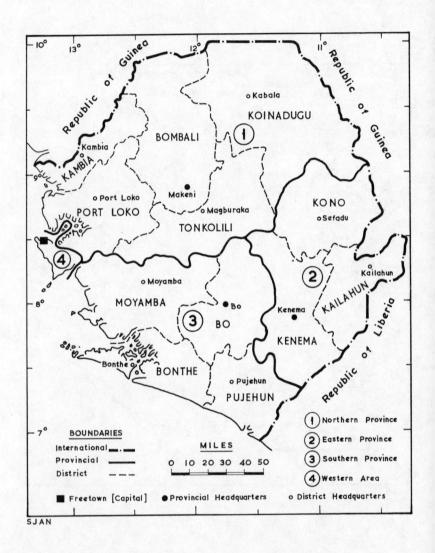

MAP 4.   Present-day administrative divisions.

INTRODUCTION

By African standards Sierra Leone is a small country. With a total area of some 28,000 square miles, a coastline of over 200 miles and with only two immediate neighbors, Sierra Leone in the African setting is in some ways exceptional. Sandwiched, as it were, between the republics of Guinea and Liberia, the country appears almost to exist by sufferance of its larger neighbours.

Sierra Leone today consists of the former Colony and the former Protectorate. The former Colony embraced the Sierra Leone Peninsula, ceded by treaty of Temne chiefs and acquired by a chartered company in the 1780s for the rehabilitation of persons displaced by the Atlantic slave trade. It also included Bonthe on the Sherbro Island and a number of adjacent territories, Turner's Peninsula, and a number of small islands. Subsequently Turner's Peninsula, some coastal strips and a number of islands previously part of the Colony were administered as part of the Protectorate.

The former Colony--i.e., the Sierra Leone Peninsula plus the Banana and Plantain islands (minus the other pieces of coastal territory and other islands)--is now referred to as the Western Area, and consists of some 270 square miles of territory. It includes Freetown and its rural environs.

The former Protectorate, over 27,500 square miles, consisted of the hinterland bounded in the north and northeast by the Republic of Guinea, in the east and southeast by the Republic of Liberia, and in the west and southwest by the Atlantic Ocean. It now consists of three provinces, Northern, Southern, and Eastern, divided into 12 districts, subdivided further into about 150 chiefdoms. The Northern Province embraces Kambia, Koinadugu, Port Loko, Bombali and Tonkolili districts; the Southern Province consists of

Moyamba, Bo, Bonthe and Pujehun districts; and the Eastern Province
is comprised of Kenema, Kailahun and Kono districts.

In colonial times the distinction between Colony and Protectorate, if not always clear, was nonetheless real, particularly in
terms of the legal status of the respective inhabitants. The people
in the Colony were regarded in law as British subjects and residents
of the United Kingdom, and in theory were entitled to all the rights
of, say, the English people themselves, while the people of the Protectorate were described as "British protected persons." Although
the Colony, in origin a home for the victims of the Atlantic slave
trade, contained virtually all the major tribal groups of the West
African coast (including Sierra Leone), in practice it came to be regarded as the home of the Creoles, a term used to describe the
descendants of the early settlers--Nova Scotians, Maroons, liberated
Africans (or recaptives)--in contradistinction to the inhabitants of the
hinterland, the Mende, Temne, Limba, Kono and other peoples.

Both the former Colony and the former Protectorate now constitute the independent state of Sierra Leone: the one, detribalized,
Westernized, predominantly, if not sincerely, Christian; the other,
more tribal, less Western, to a large extent animist or Muslim (although the adherence to Islam of these latter has largely been nominal). The broad distinction between Creoles and non-Creoles has
over the decades become somewhat blurred as more and more tribal
peoples from the outlying areas have become educated and acquired
Western habits and ways of thought. There has also taken place a
gradual process of national integration, facilitated by improved systems of communication, education and social mobility.

Geographical factors have however played an opposing role in
creating divisions in the country. The Southern Province is for the
most part within the heavy rain forest belt and the Northern Province
is to a large extent savannah, a situation caused by precipitation.
These geographical conditions have also determined the agricultural
pursuits and ways of life of the people.

English is the official language of Sierra Leone, but a patois,
Krio, is the lingua franca. There are in addition some 15 tribal
languages and a wide variety of dialects.

Sierra Leone rises gradually from a low coastal belt characterized by mangrove swamps and the estuaries of some seven major
rivers--the Bum (or Sewa), the Rokel (or Seli), the Moa, the Jong
(or Taia), the Little Scarcies (or Kaba), the Great Scarcies (or
Kolente) and the Mano.   Major agricultural products of the rain forest include cocoa, coffee, cola nuts, palm oil and kernels, ginger,
rice and cassava.   The north, savannah area produces mostly cattle
and peanuts and in places palm oil and kernels.   As a result of
mechanical methods however there has been an increase in rice cultivation in the north, particularly in the boli lands.

The important towns include Freetown, which is the capital,
Bo, Kenema, Makeni, Sefadu, Lunsar, Moyamba, Port Loko, Kambia,
Kabala, Bonthe, and Kailahun.   There are two major harbors, Freetown and Pepel, the latter used for the export of iron ore.   There
is an international airport at Lungi (Freetown) and some half dozen
small air strips elsewhere in the country.

Mineral products include diamonds, which account for over
40 per cent of the country's export trade, and iron ore, bauxite and
rutile.

The climate of Sierra Leone is tropical, characterized by
high humidity.   There are two major seasons, the dry season,
roughly November to April, and the rainy season, roughly from May
to October.   The greatest rainfall is experienced in the months of
July and August.   Tornadoes occur mostly in the months of April,
May, September and October.   Between December and March, a dry
easterly wind, the harmattan, blows.

In the 15th century European sovereigns led by those of Spain
and Portugal, patronized a number of voyages aimed among other
things at discovering the unknown parts of the world and at finding
a sea route to India.   Among the first Europeans to reach the West
Coast of Africa were the Portuguese.   The name Sierra Leone owes
its origin to Portuguese explorers--the earliest of whom, Alvaro
Fernandez, arrived in what is now Freetown harbor in 1447.   It is
generally agreed that the name itself was coined by another of the
Portuguese adventurers, Pedro Da Cintra, who visited the shores of

the country in 1462 and mapped a number of important landmarks
and called the country Serra Lyoa--"Lion Mountain. "

Three possible explanations have been put forward for the
name Sierra Leone: that the area was so called because of its
ragged and wild appearance; that from the tops of the misty mountains "thunder and lightning perpetually flashes"; and that the land
was infested with lions, whose roar could be heard by the Portuguese sailors. Of these the first is the most probable. Pacheco
Pereira, writing between 1505 and 1508, had this to say: "Many
people think that the name Serra Lyoa was given because many
lions were to be found in that part, but that is wrong. It is because de Sintra ... when he saw a land so rough and wild, called
it Lyoa. That is the only reason and no other explanation is true
because he told me this himself. "

This happened in 1462. Since then the name Sierra Leone
has been applied in three ways: to the mountainous area surrounding the Freetown Peninsula which was cited by the Portuguese in
the middle decades of the 15th century; to the piece of territory
some 20 miles square ceded by treaty between Temne chiefs and a
chartered company and acquired in 1787 as a home of the first settlers; and to the geographical and political entity that forms the republic of today.

It has been suggested that the earliest inhabitants of the
country were the Limba and the Capez (or Sape). The former still
comprise the third largest tribal group in Sierra Leone today; the
latter, now absorbed into other groups, were described by the
English explorer John Ogilby in the 1680s as the most polite nation
in all Guinea. The Capez may also have been the progenitors of
the Sherbro Bullom people of today who still occupy the coastal
strips of Sierra Leone.

From about the early decades of the 16th century onwards
the Limba and the Capez or Sape became victims of successive
waves of invasion by the Mane, who entered the country from the
east and northeast and by the Temne, who migrated from Guinea
into Sierra Leone from the north. The Mende (descendants of the

Mane) now occupy most of the southern areas of the country (i.e.,
the South and Eastern provinces) while the Temne occupy roughly
one-third of the Northern Province, which is also the home of the
Limba. Other tribal groups in Sierra Leone, the Kono and Vai in
particular, also hail from the Mane. By the early decades of the
17th century, the Mane invaders were indistinguishable from the
naturales--the locally born--and had become assimilated into the
existing societies. Manuel Alvares, who lived and worked as a
Jesuit missionary in Sierra Leone between 1607 and 1617, wrote in
1616, "It is difficult to speak of the Mane of Sierra Leone because
of their assimilation into the life there. Such genuine Mane about
whom one could speak are few and fast disappearing."

The middle decades of the 16th century witnessed attempts
by European traders to settle along the West Coast of Africa in
fortified trading stations. This process marked a departure from
earlier practice. Hitherto, visits had been made by traders who
plied the coast purchasing local merchandise, ivory, gold, slaves,
etc. with European manufactured goods, rum, tobacco, arms and
ammunition, etc. The Portuguese appear to have taken the lead
in establishing fortified trading stations along the West Coast. They
were soon followed by others, including the French, Dutch, and
Brandenburgers; the British were somewhat late in joining the venture. Their appearance became noticeable in the late 16th century
when they built factories and forts on Sherbro, Bunce and Tasso
islands. A number of European-chartered companies made use of
the services of resident agents in Sierra Leone. These companies
enjoyed monopolies in the coastal trade until their position was
threatened and effectively challenged by an influx of private ship-
owners and traders.

The quest for labor to work in the New World ushered in
the period of the Atlantic slave trade which lasted for four centuries. The West Coast of Africa proved particularly fertile in its
supply of human cargo and Sierra Leone with its harbor facilities
and well-populated adjacent territories provided ideal conditions for
trade in goods and slaves. Slaves were either captured by local

slave dealers, African, European or mulatto, or as prisoners of
war might be sold into slavery by local chieftains in return for
European goods, particularly rum and firearms.

A combination of factors, economic, philanthropic, religious
and social, led to demands, first in Britain, for the abolition of
the slave trade and the occasion soon presented itself for the abolitionists to acquire legal sanction and judicial blessing for their
anti-slavery activities.   A certain Britisher, David Lisle, on re-
tiring from Barbados in the West Indies, returned to England accompanied by his slave, Jonathan Strong, as a house servant.
Strong soon escaped from his master, ran into difficulties, fell ill
and got stranded.   Granville Sharp, one of the great protagonists of
abolition, by chance saw Strong at a London hospital and became an
acquaintance.   This was in 1765.   Strong was soon recaptured by
Lisle, who sold him for £10 to a John Kerr, then on his way back
to Jamaica in the West Indies.   Kerr had Strong bound, caged and
stored on board his ship.   Strong got in touch with Sharp, through
whose good offices an injunction was issued restraining Kerr from
keeping Strong in custody and granting Strong conditional freedom of
movement ashore.   In 1772 another slave, James Somerset, about
to be taken back to the West Indies, was able to avail himself of
Sharp's services.   Sharp obtained a writ of habeas corpus on Somerset's behalf from William Murray Mansfield, the then Chief Justice of England.

Chief Justice Mansfield's decision in effect asserted that a
runaway slave could not be forcibly sent back from Britain to the
plantations, on the grounds that slavery as an institution was unknown in the laws of England.

The result of this decision was to aggravate the "black
poor" problem in England by the large influx of slaves from the
West Indies and elsewhere into Britain.   The Poor Law authorities
in England were thus faced with a new problem and a committee
was set up for the relief of the black poor.   Whilst this committee
addressed itself to the problem of relief, a certain Dr. Henry
Smeathman, who had lived for about three years in the vicinity of

Sierra Leone, strongly proposed Sierra Leone as a suitable settlement for them.

Smeathman's proposals were accepted and contributions from
individuals like Sharp made possible the repatriation to Sierra Leone
of the first settlers.   The British government also manifested some
interest in the venture by providing transport and subsistence for the
settlers during their first few months in Sierra Leone.

In May 1787 the first settlers arrived in Sierra Leone.   By
means of treaty a parcel of land some 10 miles in length along the
coast and to a depth of 10 miles inland was ceded by Temne chiefs
in return for some £60 worth of goods--largely rum, tobacco,
arms, and ammunition.   This piece of territory was at first called
the Province of Freedom by Sharp, who intended it to be self-
governing.   Accordingly a system was devised which made it possible for all adults to take part in the government of the settlement.
The system known as frankpledge was similar to a system practiced
in ancient Israel and in England at the time of King Alfred.

The settlement was divided equally into tithings and hundreds.
A tithing consisted of a group of 10 families.   Each tithing elected
on a yearly basis a leader known as a tithingman.   Every 10 tithingmen in their turn yearly elected a hundredor and together the tithingmen and hundredors governed the settlement.

The first few years of the settlement were difficult.   Inclem-
ent weather (the first settlers arrived in May just at the beginning
of the rainy season), disease, attacks from neighboring hostile
tribes and a number of other problems combined to thwart the efforts of the settlers and to delude the hopes of Sharp.   In the circumstances Sharp resorted to the formation of a company.   The
Saint George's Bay Company (shortly thereafter called the Sierra
Leone Company) was formed in 1790 to take control of the settlement.   In July 1791 the Company was granted a charter, and took
over Sharp's responsibilities.   The period of May 1787 to July 1791
can with justification be referred to as the period of the proprietor-
ship of Granville Sharp.

The year 1792 saw a change in the fortunes of the settle-

ment. In January of that year, some 1200 freed slaves arrived in
Sierra Leone from Nova Scotia. These freedmen had taken part
as British Loyalists in the War of Independence and the American
victory had forced them to seek their fortunes elsewhere. They
had been sent to Nova Scotia where it was hoped they could settle
as farmers owning their own land. However, as a result of dis-
appointments and frustrations in Nova Scotia, they sent a protest
mission led by Thomas Peters to Britain to seek redress. With
the blessings of the British Government, the Sierra Leone Company
was able to make arrangements for the transfer of the Nova Scotians to Sierra Leone.

Neither the transfer of responsibility from Sharp to the
Company nor the arrival of the Nova Scotians put an end to the
problems of the settlers. Relationships between the Nova Scotians
and the Company's directors were more often than not far from
cordial. The period of charter Company government, 1791 to
1807, witnessed a number of problems, most of them of a local
nature, but some created by the stresses in Europe caused by the
French revolutionary and Napoleonic wars. Lack of adequate funds
was a perennial problem. In September 1794 the settlement was
attacked by a French naval squadron, which inflicted considerable
damage to property. In the process of reconstruction practically
all avenues for raising money were explored. Some of them, like
quit rents, provoked serious internal trouble and resistance without
relieving the financial crisis. In 1796 the annual revenue from
quit rents was estimated at about £200.

In 1799 the Crown, at the Company's request, granted a
new charter which reduced the opportunities for self-government
and vested power almost exclusively in the Company and its directors. At this point the Nova Scotians rose up in arms. In addition to their grievances over the imposition of quit rents they now
found themselves deprived of any say, such as they had previously
through the election of tithingmen and hundredors, in the government of the Colony. Reinforced by other dissidents, the Nova
Scotians almost overwhelmed the Company's forces but for the

timely arrival in Freetown of some 550 Maroons and a detachment
of the Royal African Corps.   The Maroons were runaway slaves who
for decades had eked out a living by means of guerrilla warfare in
the mountains in Jamaica.   When they finally surrendered to the
government of Jamaica they were sent to Halifax, Nova Scotia.   The
climate in Nova Scotia did not appeal to the Maroons, who petitioned
influential and sympathetic British members of Parliament to effect
their transfer to a more hospitable climate.   So some 550 Maroons
were dispatched to Freetown, arriving on September 30, 1800.   The
arrival of the Maroons and of the detachment of the Royal African
Corps turned the scales in favor of the Company against the Nova
Scotian insurgents.   The rebellion was suppressed and the ringleaders punished.

From about 1800 the British Parliament voted annual subsidies as grants-in-aid for the Colony's civil establishment and defence.   Still, financial problems, threats of insurrection from within, and fears of attack from without continued to plague the Company, and to prevent it from thriving as a commercial venture,
even if its better aims--the suppression of slavery and the "civilizing" mission--held considerable promise for the future.

Towards the end of 1807 the Company gave up its political
functions to the British Crown.   On the recommendation of a Committee of the Privy Council, the Colony was transformed into a
Crown Colony on January 1, 1808.   The directors of the now de-
funct Sierra Leone Company sought ways of continuing to exert influence, if not control, over the Colony's affairs by founding in
1807 what was called the African Institution, which from time to
time offered advice and made recommendations (particularly for
appointments) to the British government in matters relating to
Sierra Leone.

The British Parliament had in March 1807 passed an act
making it illegal for British subjects to participate in the slave
trade, effective May 1 of that year.   Having declared slavery illegal, the British government set about its suppression with the
aid of an unrivaled naval power.   The Admiralty Court established

in Freetown was effectively used to stamp out the slave trade on
the West African Coast.   Slaves set free from slave ships were
brought to Freetown where, as recaptives (or liberated Africans),
they joined the somewhat motley group of settlers.

The population of the Colony at the end of the first decade
of the 19th century consisted of the survivors of the original settlers who had arrived in 1787, plus Nova Scotians, Maroons, recaptives, and numbers of tribal immigrants from neighboring terri-
tories--notably, Temne, Madingoe, Susu, Mende, Foulah and Kru.
The tribal immigrants initially and for the most part had areas
within the Colony specifically delineated for their settlement.   (The
terms settlers and liberated Africans were often used, respectively,
to mean inhabitants of the Colony--including the 1787 arrivals, Nova
Scotians, and Maroons--and the recaptives, that is those who were
captured on the slave ships by British naval vessels and who in
fact did not get to the New World.)

The large number of recaptives flooding the streets of Freetown created serious problems for the administration.   An attempt
to solve the problem by a system of apprenticing recaptives to settlers proved inadequate and unsatisfactory.   A more effective solution to the problem was sought in the establishment of rural settlements around Freetown and in the encouragement of emigration to
the Gambia.   Three of these rural villages were first established
at Leicester in 1809, Cabenda in 1811 (in 1816 called Wilberforce),
and Regent in 1812.   Between 1812 and 1820, more rural villages
were established: Kissy in 1812, Gloucester in 1816, Leopold in
1817, Bathurst in 1818 (in 1825 Leopold and Bathurst were amalgamated and thereafter called Bathurst), Charlotte in 1818, York
in 1819, and Kent in 1819.   Waterloo, in 1819, and Hastings, in
1819, were built primarily to accommodate soldiers disbanded from
the Royal African Corps and the 4th West India Regiment, but were
soon crowded by an influx of liberated Africans.

The recaptives also received special attention from the
Church Missionary Society (CMS), which, in alliance with the
British Government and with funds from the British treasury, set

about providing educational and other facilities for the recaptives in
the rural communities. It was out of this arrangement that the
Christian Institution was formed in 1816. In 1827 the CMS founded
Fourah Bay College for the training of African clergymen. Later
in 1876 Fourah Bay College was affiliated to the University of Durham in England, whose degrees it conferred until 1969. In 1845
a secondary school for boys, the Grammar School, was established
by the CMS, followed in 1849 by a girls' secondary school, later
the Annie Walsh Memorial School.

Over the decades and certainly by the 1850s the descendants
of settlers and liberated Africans were able to produce a society
which in spite of initial heterogeneity was showing signs of integration and cohesion. Thus in 1853, the British Parliament, recog-
nizing the social trends in the Sierra Leone Colony, declared liberated Africans, for legal purposes, to be British subjects--a much
sought-after nomenclature at the time--thereby granting them equality
of status before the law with Nova Scotians and early settlers. By
the 1850s then, Creole society, detribalized, Afro-European in outlook, predominantly Christian in religion, had come into being. It
was the Creoles who from the middle decades of the 19th century,
from the Gambia to the Congo (now Zaïre) and even beyond, fulfilled in no small measure the aspirations of the founders of the
Colony who had hoped that "the Colony of Sierra Leone would not
only permit the displaced persons of the Atlantic slave trade to
evolve a society of their own, but might prove an agency for the social and spiritual regeneration of the whole Negro World." As
teachers, missionaries, traders, administrators, artisans and the
like, the Creoles measured the coastal length and in some cases
the interior breadth of West Africa, performing, again in accordance
with the hopes of the founders of the Colony "the honorable office of
introducing to a vast country long detained in barbarism, the blessings of Industry and civilisation ... and of importing ... the light
of Religion, Truth and the Security of the comforts of civilised Society." On the merits of the civilization so imparted and its effects on the societies affected there is considerable difference of

opinion. Suffice it to say that in the second half of the 19th century, Sierra Leone was considered worthy of emulation by other
West African territories in almost all aspects of life, thanks to the
exertions of the Creoles.

Nor did the Creoles confine themselves to West Africa.
They invaded British universities, particularly Edinburgh, London
and St. Andrews. By 1858 two Sierra Leoneans, William Brough-
ton Davies and James (Africanus) Horton, had qualified as members
of the Royal College of Surgeons, London, and then as M. D. s in
1859 at St. Andrews and Edinburgh respectively. As early as 1821
a Sierra Leonean, William Henry Savage, had acquired legal qualifications in England. John Thorpe entered University College, London, in 1832, studied natural philosophy and law, and, as the first
Sierra Leonean to acquire a university education, returned home to
establish a private practice.

On June 24, 1864, Samuel Adjai Crowther, a recaptive, was
consecrated in Canterbury Cathedral as bishop of the West African
countries beyond British jurisdiction. In business and in public life,
men such as John Ezzidio, Abraham Spencer Hebron, Malama
Thomas, William Christopher Betts, Afred James Shorunkeh-Sawyerr, John H. Malamah Thomas and others carved an enviable
name for themselves. Perhaps as a fitting testimony to the achievements of the Creoles, one of their number, Samuel Lewis, was
awarded a knighthood by Queen Victoria in the New Year Honors,
1896. This honor marked the climax of Lewis' career but in a
sense it also marked the climax of Creole achievement in the 19th
century. From 1896 Creole fortunes in Sierra Leone appeared to
be on the wane. In that year the history of the Colony of Sierra
Leone entered a completely new phase with the declaration of the
Protectorate.

As Creole society became more prosperous and enterprising,
quite a few ventured into the Sierra Leone hinterland in quest of
larger fortunes. This incursion created a number of problems.
Not the least was the question of redress if a British subject suffered injuries or damages in territories not under British jurisdic-

tion. The result was that from about the 1880s there were repeated demands by some Creole spokesmen for the extension of
British influence and control over the neighboring areas by the annexation of more territory. Early in the 19th century and thereafter from time to time some adventurous governors, such as
Charles Turner, Neil Campbell, N. W. Macdonald, Stephen James
Hill, and Samuel Rowe, had made attempts to extend the territorial
area of the Colony by signing with chiefs treaties of friendship or
of "cession of territory" to the British Crown. These efforts were
at times grudgingly applauded, often repudiated and rarely officially
approved either by the Colonial Office, the War Office or the Foreign Office in London. What these treaties meant to the chiefs was
not always clear. From the 1870s onwards, however, and thanks to
a change of attitude in Whitehall, various attempts were made by
the Colonial administration in Freetown either to extend the limits
of the Colony or to exercise more effective control over the hinterland. The policy was in some ways clumsy and unimaginative, at
times resulting in unforeseen financial expenditure and military expeditions. The methods adopted (including the old system of paying
stipends to chiefs) were described by Samuel Lewis as the humiliating policy "of going about peace begging in the neighboring districts and paying a lot of money" to do it. These moves if ineffective and costly, were dictated by the need for trade which presupposed peace and stability in the hinterland as well as by defense
considerations aimed at preventing sudden and unforeseen attacks on
the Colony proper. Towards the end of the 19th century and particularly after the Berlin Conference (1884-1885), a variety of motives prompted European powers to embark upon an almost feverish
acquisition of territory in West Africa and elsewhere on the continent and the principle of "effective occupation" was enunciated,
ushering in the period of the "scramble."

Some ten years after the Berlin Conference Col. (later Sir)
Frederick Cardew was appointed governor of Sierra Leone. By
this time France and Britain had conveniently demarcated, though
somewhat vaguely, what they called their respective "spheres of in-

fluence" in the areas now covered by Guinea and Sierra Leone.
This meant that each Power gave but did not always honor assurances to recognize the other's "rights" over the area so de-
limited.   Cardew, by the time of his appointment as governor of
Sierra Leone, had already acquired experience in Zululand and
elsewhere in the Colonial service and at 55 showed no signs of fa-
tigue or weariness. His six years as governor between 1894 and
1900 saw him on three extensive tours of the hinterland, covering
over 2000 miles and spending in all over 150 days away from his
headquarters in Freetown. During and even before Cardew's term
of office, friction with the French over boundary lines of "spheres
of influence" was becoming a problem. Moreover the Sofa warriors
of Samori (or Samadu) were making incessant raids into territory
within both "spheres of influence," particularly in the north and
northeast areas of the Colony of Sierra Leone. The British administration in Freetown entertained fears lest the French in their
attempts to contain Samori encroached on territory within the British sphere; the French in their turn harbored similar fears. The
British were also determined to put an end to the slave trade and
to the internecine tribal wars in the hinterland.

In 1893 French and British forces, which had been sent to
Kono country against Samori, inadvertently or through treachery
opened fire on each other, each mistaking the other for Samori's
Sofas. There were heavy casualties on both sides. The French
after some delay agreed to pay £9000 as compensation to the British Government. This affair, known as the Waiima Incident, made
it all the more necessary to demarcate proper boundaries between
French and British "spheres of influence."

All these factors prompted the introduction and enactment of
an order-in-council of August 28, 1895, which simply stated that
"the Crown had acquired jurisdiction in foreign countries adjoining
the Colony." A year later on August 31, 1896, by what was referred to as "best for the interests of the people," a Protectorate
was declared covering an area of about 27,000 square miles over
the territory within the British "sphere of influence."

Cardew had during his three tours of the hinterland, tried to explain his intentions and policies to the chiefs he met. There is evidence that some chiefs, fearful of hostile and powerful neighbors, either did welcome an understanding with the British or did not seem adverse to having friendly relations with them. It is however far from certain what the chiefs understood by the term "protectorate." The term itself was vague and imprecise. It had been used but not defined at the Berlin Conference. Given the somewhat elastic nature of the term and the circumstances in which a protectorate in Sierra Leone was declared, it would seem that the British governor and the chiefs each had their own views about the new arrangements. The basis for misunderstanding, if not conflict, was latent at the outset.

Once the Protectorate was declared a number of important questions arose. How was the area to be administered; which system of law was to operate; how was the protectorate administration to be financed? The answers were far from simple. The 1895 order-in-council had asserted that the Legislative Council of Sierra Leone had the same authority to enact laws for the Protectorate as it had for the Colony. How the Legislative Council had acquired such power was by no means clear. A series of ordinances passed in 1896 and 1897 made provisions for the administration of the Protectorate, which was divided into five districts--Karene, Ronietta, Bandajuma, Panguma and Koinadugu. The last two were farthest from Freetown in the east and northeast respectively. In each district an official called the district commissioner (DC) was responsible for administration and for a host of other duties. In many ways the DC was almost omnicompetent and since travel and communications were so slow and difficult the DC became in practice a local governor. Prior to the declaration of the Protectorate some chiefs had been styled as "king" or "queen." Such chiefs were after the declaration given the designation, "paramount chief" (PC), the title of king or queen being reserved only for the British sovereign. In theory the DC was expected to share his powers with the chiefs, a provision rarely observed in practice.

The Ordinance of September 1896 had made provision for three courts of law in each district. (1) The native courts, over which the chiefs and tribal elders presided, dealt with matters relating to tribal law and custom. (2) Courts presided over by the chiefs and DCs jointly dealt with situations which might arise out of the coalescence of two cultures and two systems of law. (3) Courts over which only the DC had jurisdiction. These courts dealt with such offenses as slave-trade as well as with cases involving non-natives. The DC referred capital charges to the Supreme Court in Freetown.

The administration of the Protectorate and the policing of the frontiers cost a considerable amount of money, estimated at about one-fifth of the total revenue of Sierra Leone. Cardew decided to defray the costs from taxes imposed directly in the Protectorate. Precedents in Zululand and elsewhere came readily to his fertile mind. So in addition to taxes on stores and spirits, Cardew decided to levy a tax on huts or houses in the Protectorate at ten shillings on houses with four or more rooms and five shillings on houses with fewer than four rooms, to come into effect on January 1, 1898. Chiefs were saddled with the responsibility of collecting within their chiefdoms and the DCs were to collect from chiefs within the district.

Cardew's enthusiasm for directly taxing the Protectorate at that stage was not shared by the Colonial Office in London. The Colonial Office viewed the imposition of the tax as somewhat premature and held the belief that it might likely provoke opposition if not active resistance. Cardew, though unwilling to concede that his hut tax was likely to stir opposition, had towards the end of 1897 come to realize that he had not fully appreciated the problems involved in collecting the tax. He therefore modified his original plan of assessment, exempted the more remote districts of Panguma and Koinadugu and imposed a flat rate of five shillings per house irrespective of the number of rooms.

During his tours of the hinterland Cardew had tried to explain, apparently without success, his tax proposals to the chiefs.

The governor assumed that the chiefs had no objection, or mistook their silence--engendered by unwillingness to contradict--for consent.   The chiefs on their part were convinced that the payment of taxes to a foreign power which had not subdued them meant the same as divesting themselves of their people's rights and authority-- a feat immeasurably beyond their competence.   A number of chiefs sent petitions and letters of protest against the tax to the governor, but Cardew, who by then had come to associate all forms of protest with the intrigues of what he called "agitators" and "pettifogging lawyers" (in Cardew's vocabulary these epithets were synonyms for Creoles), refused to countenance the petitions and protests.

In Karene district an influential chief, Bai Bureh, could not be persuaded to pay the tax and convinced or bullied neighboring chiefs into similar refusal.   In Ronietta, the DC reported to the governor that "there was a disposition on the part of the majority of the chiefs to make no effort to pay the tax and that the Mabanta and Bagru districts were in a very disturbed state."   In Bandajuma, the DC arrested and detained a number of chiefs who protested that five shillings was too high and that they could not pay.   Chiefs also learned that no such tax was being imposed in the Colony.   This fact not only enraged them further and strengthened their resolve not to pay, but reinforced their belief in the unfairness of the tax. They came to regard the tax both as a capricious exaction and as a pointer to what the future held in store.

In spite of the petitions, protests and intelligence reports-- or because of them--Cardew insisted on collecting the tax and by force, if necessary.   The outrages with which the Frontier Police set about forcibly collecting the tax merely heaped more fuel on an already smoldering fire.   There was open revolt in large areas of the Protectorate.   In Mende-speaking areas there was a rejection of everybody and of everything British and alien, black or white, accompanied in places by indiscriminate slaughter of persons and wanton expropriation of property.   In the North, Bai Bureh conducted his anti-tax campaign against the British with skill and discipline which contrasted sharply with the Mende performance.   With-

in a few weeks virtually the whole Protectorate was involved.
Casualties on both sides were high.   Eventually the insurrection
was suppressed by force of arms and the leaders punished.   Ninety-
six "rebels," or freedom fighters, were hanged and three prominent
chiefs, Bai Bureh, Nyahaguha and Be Sherbro were sent into exile
to the Gold Coast.

One of the remarkable features of the 1898 rising was the
spontaneity and the concerted manner--both attributed to the widespread influence of the poro secret society--with which it broke out.
Sierra Leone, unlike some other areas on the West Coast, had no
large, centralized, effectively organized political unit.   The Kpa
Mende Confederacy, corresponding roughly to parts of today's
Moyamba and Bo districts, was the nearest thing to a large organized political unit.   The Kpa Mende Confederacy was however
united less by loyalty or obedience to a suzerain, than by the at-
tractive influence and power of the Wunde secret society.   At any
rate Madam Yoko, who exercised nominal, if occasionally effective,
authority in Kpa Mende country, remained loyal to the British
cause, although there were serious outbreaks at Taiama and its
environs in which a number of American missionaries lost their
lives.

A royal commissioner, Sir David Chalmers, was sent out
from London to investigate the causes of the disturbances and to
make appropriate recommendations.   He ascribed the causes of the
rising to the imposition of the hut tax and put the blame on Cardew's impetuosity.   He pointed out that the government had rashly
resorted to force as a reply to opposition to the tax in a situation
where perhaps artful persuasion, and tactful good humor might have
averted the disaster.   He warned further that "though military men
have some valuable qualifications for service as Colonial governors
and district officers" (an obvious reference with veiled contempt
to Cardew's military background) "there is danger in allowing their
influence and ideas to be paramount.   It is perhaps natural," he
concluded, "that if exact obedience by the people under their care
is not instantaneous, men of military training consider an immediate

resort to compulsion by force the inevitable consequence." He expressed the view that the arrest and detention of chiefs had no legal
basis and felt that subsequent military operations into some disaffected areas were at best mere punitive reprisals, quite unjustifi-
able in scale and severity and obnoxiously futile in terms of the
aims they purported to serve.

After recommending a general amnesty, the Royal Commissioner proposed the abolition of the Hut Tax, a drastic reduction
and if possible disbandment of the Frontier Police Force, the res-
toration of the powers and authority of chiefs, a modification of the
duties of district commissioners, and government financial assistance
to missionaries.

The Colonial Office however upheld Cardew's submissions in
reply to Chalmers report and politely rejected the Royal Commissioner's more radical recommendations. The hut tax was allowed
to continue. Cardew himself stayed on as governor until 1900,
when he was succeeded by Sir Charles King-Harman.

In 1895, a year before the formal declaration of the Protectorate, it had been decided to construct a railway from Freetown across the country eastwards. The aim was to make the interior more accessible but equally important it was hoped that the
railway would make it possible to tap more effectively the economic
resources of the hinterland. It also became increasingly clear that
British presence in the hinterland if it was to be meaningful and
productive could not be sustained solely by force of arms. It was
decided that a policy of appeasement should be adopted towards the
chiefs.

The Colonial government had for some years previously made
provision for sons of chiefs to be educated in Freetown schools.
The products apparently did not fit into the Colonial scheme of
things (as Freetown schools were accused of imparting "bookish"
education) and did not conform with the colonialist concept of an
educated African. In these circumstances Bo Government School
was established to educate sons and nominees of chiefs. The
chiefs, still suspicious of British intentions, sent in the first few

years more nominees than sons. From among them it was hoped
a future class of educated chiefs could be recruited.

The Colonial authorities in establishing the Bo School took
care to prevent the boys from acquiring what was referred to as
"European education" and were equally at pains to discourage the
boys from cultivating what was described as "Western habits."
There was in fact a deliberate attempt to foster tribal life in the
school. Later when it became clear that education could not be
tribalized, an attempt was made, if somewhat unsuccessfully, to
pattern the school on the English public school system. The Bo
School curriculum and prospectus of 1905, whatever their merits,
unnecessarily delayed the emergence of educated Protectorate Africans who could effectively challenge the Creoles in the bid for national leadership when the opportunity arose. For nearly three
decades the Bo School had no secondary department. Those pupils
willing and able to pursue their studies at the post-primary level
were compelled to attend Freetown schools; the numbers were
negligibly few. And so it happened that the first three heads of
government of the country have been products of mission schools.
The Bo School experiment also tended to exacerbate the cleavages
between Colony and Protectorate and to intensify and polarize the
constitutional conflicts of the immediate post-World War II years.
It was not until the 1940s that the Bo School was permitted to pursue courses in arts and science, which facilitated the admission
of its pupils to institutions of higher learning at home and overseas.
Happily the Bo School today compares very favorably with the best
schools in the country.

A major policy change affecting the Protectorate was the introduction in 1946 of district councils, local government bodies
where representatives from chiefdoms in a district could sit with
central government officials to determine how local taxes and
government subventions could best be spent and to tackle a wide
variety of matters and problems affecting the district. A Protectorate Assembly was also established in 1946. It was somewhat
ephemeral, but during its brief existence, the Protectorate Assem-

bly--a quasi-representative body, consisting of leading chiefs, distinguished provincials, and Creole observers--provided a useful channel for discussing matters affecting the Protectorate and gave vocal expression to the mute aspirations of the Protectorate people. The Protectorate Assembly met annually in Bo under the presidency of the chief commissioner of the Protectorate, a very senior official in the colonial hierarchy. He shouldered responsibility in a general way for the administration and development of the Protectorate, subject of course to the overall authority of the governor. It has been suggested with some justification, if not with complete accuracy, that the creation of the post of the chief commissioner of the Protectorate with headquarters in Bo appeared to bring into being a dualism in the government of Sierra Leone, one kind for the Protectorate, another for the Colony.

The post-World War II period witnessed the introduction by the British Government of new constitutions in the West African Colonies. In Sierra Leone constitutional developments could be traced back into the early 19th century. After the failure of Granville Sharp's experiment in self-government and of the enterprise in a commercial company, Sierra Leone was administered from 1808 by a governor assisted by a council. Thomas Perronet Thompson, the first governor so appointed, changed the name Freetown, on the grounds that it had been "perverted to the purposes of insubordination and rebellion" and adopted instead Georgetown. He issued a new currency in pounds, shillings and pence, in place of dollars and cents, which he believed savored somewhat of American revolutionary ideas and republicanism. The governor's council was all-embracing in its functions, serving both as a legislative and executive council. The governor-in-council acted as a court of appeal until 1811 when the first chief justice, Robert Thorpe, appointed by the Crown in 1808, took office in Freetown. The council also carried out municipal duties and served as a king of "Native Authority" for the Colony's rural environs. In 1821 a new charter increased the governor's council to nine members, two of whom were resident in the Gold Coast, since the governor in Sierra

Leone was at the time responsible for all the British West African
dependencies. A new charter or constitution of May 1863 created
two distinct councils, the Legislative and the Executive. The Executive Council consisted of the governor, the chief justice, the queen's
advocate, the colonial secretary and the officer commanding the
troops. The Legislative Council included the executive and a minority of members appointed by the governor with the approval of
the secretary of state. In appointing unofficial members the governor was instructed to take into consideration "the wishes of the
more intelligent portion of the community."

The 1863 constitution remained, with slight modifications in
essentials, the basic instrument of government until 1924. The
1924 constitution, also known as the Slater Constitution, made provision for some kind of Protectorate representation and for the election for the first time in Sierra Leone of three unofficial members
to the Legislative Council. There were in addition 11 official members and seven nominated unofficials, three of whom were paramount chiefs representing in almost amorphous fashion, Protectorate
interests. This constitution remained virtually unchanged until
1951. In 1951 the constitutional arrangements projected in 1947 by
Governor Sir Hubert Stevenson were finally implemented, after
heated and violent debate between leaders of Colony and Protectorate
interests. The 1951 Constitution introduced a Legislative Council
of 30 members, excluding the governor, who presided, and a vice-
president who might or might not be a member. It consisted of
seven ex-officio members. These were the colonial secretary, the
chief commissioner of the Protectorate, the attorney-general (a
post created in 1896 after the abolition of the post of queen's advocate), the financial secretary, the director of medical and sanitary
services, the director of education, and the director of agriculture.
It also included seven unofficial members elected directly to represent the seven districts of the Colony. The franchise in the Colony
was based on adult suffrage with literacy and property qualifications. There were in addition, 14 members indirectly elected to
represent the Protectorate; 12 of them were elected through dis-

trict councils which served as electoral colleges and two by the
Protectorate Assembly.   The remaining two unofficial members
were nominated by the governor to represent trade and commercial
interests.   In 1952 a number of unofficial members of the Legislative Council were allocated ministerial portfolios and given responsibility for certain government departments.   Further constitutional
changes were introduced by the Sierra Leone (House of Representatives) Order-in-Council of November 29, 1956, which made provision for an enlarged legislature after the first general election,
scheduled to be held in 1957.   Provision was made for a House of
Representatives (which replaced the Legislative Council) of 57 members constituted as follows: a speaker (not an elected member),
four ex-officio members, 51 elected members, and two nominated
members (with no voting rights).   Fourteen of the 51 elected members represented the Colony, 25 represented the Protectorate, and
the remaining 12 who were paramount chiefs represented the 12
district councils of the Protectorate.

In 1960 at the Constitutional Conference held at Lancaster
House, London, a new constitution was devised for Sierra Leone
which ushered the country into independence and dominion status in
April 1961.   This independence constitution made provision for a
governor-general, a prime minister, an all-Sierra Leonean cabinet
with responsibilities for all aspects of national life, external affairs, defense, budgetary autonomy and so on.   It also contained
clauses safeguarding human rights, individual freedoms and the position of paramount chiefs.

In Part II of the 1961 Constitution, which dealt with legislation and procedure in parliament, provision was made for "entrenched clauses" and for the method of amending or removing them
by Section 43--itself an entrenched clause.   The entrenched clauses
included all clauses dealing with protection of fundamental human
rights and freedoms of the individual.   Section 43 (i) stated that
no amendment to any of the entrenched clauses could be made "...
unless the bill has been passed by the House of Representatives in
two successive sessions, there having been a dissolution of Parlia-

ment between the first and second of those sessions." Section 43
(ii) further provided that "A bill or an Act of Parliament under this
section shall not be passed by the House of Representatives in any
session unless at the final vote thereon in that session it is supported by the votes of not less than two-thirds of all the members
of the House." A redistribution of seats shortly before the 1967
general elections increased the membership of the House to 66 ordinary members and 12 paramount chief members, or 78 in all.

In 1967 a republican constitution was devised to change
Sierra Leone from a monarchical to a republican form of government. The republican constitution made provision for a ceremonial
president to replace the governor-general and enabled the prime
minister to appoint as ministers not more than three persons who
were not members of Parliament, and made the position of attorney-
general ministerial. The 1967 Constitution repeated the provisions
relating to entrenched clauses and was in essentials like the 1961
Constitution. The 1967 Constitution remained a dead letter after
the elections of 1967 until it was revived in curious circumstances
in 1971. On April 19, 1971, Sierra Leone became a republic. The
provisions of the 1971 Constitution were virtually the same as those
of 1967, the deputy speaker of the House certified "that the Bill introduced on the 19th day of April, 1971, is the same bill as was
passed on the 25th day of January, 1967, with only such alterations
as are necessary owing to the time that has elapsed since 1967."

The constitutional changes in Sierra Leone had been made
possible by the great changes which occurred in the world at large
after the strains of World War II. Britain and France, the largest
imperial powers, had emerged from the war victorious but ex-
hausted. Large numbers of African soldiers from colonial territories had participated in the war. These on their return home
agitated for a wide variety of reforms and concessions. They were
in most cases avowedly hostile to traditional authority and covertly
irreconcilable to continued colonial domination. In parts of the
country their demonstrations and intrigues culminated in the removal from office of some chiefs, while at the national level they

represented a manifestation of popular discontent. The ex-servicemen were in a kind of undeclared alliance with the Protectorate-
educated elite which had emerged over the decades. An impressive
number of male Protectorate youths had gone through the Bo School.
An appreciable number had also made their way to Freetown
Schools, the CMS Grammar School (1845), the Methodist Boys
High School (1874), the Albert Academy (1905), St. Edwards (1922),
the Prince of Wales (1925). Some had proceeded overseas to acquire knowledge of the coveted and learned professions of medicine
and law. Milton Augustus Strieby Margal returned to Sierra Leone
in the late twenties, James Callay Massally in the thirties, John
Karefa Smart in the forties, Momoh Conteh in the fifties--all qualified in the field of medicine. In law, Albert Margai, Arthur Massally, Banja Tejan-Sie, I. B. Taylor-Kamara, and S. T. Navo
returned in the late forties and early fifties as barristers-at-law.
In the field of education, the Caulker brothers, Richard and Solomon, the Sumners, W. H. Fitzjohn, and F. S. Anthony returned
from the United States armed with university degrees and diplomas.

Thus in the post-World War II period, this educated Protectorate elite challenged Creole pretensions, Colonial domination
and initially at any rate the entrenched position of traditional authority. Such organizations as PEPU and SOS were founded and
sponsored by this group. In the debates on the proposed Stevenson
Constitution of 1947 this group effectively rebutted Creole claims to
superior knowledge and challenged, if less effectively, the Colonial
administration's contention that the chiefs and traditional rulers
were the true and only representatives of Protectorate interests.

Thanks to Sir Milton's sensible, if perhaps tardy, approach
to politics, a kind of compromise was affected between the Protectorate-educated elite and the traditional rulers, which assumed
political form and expression in the creation of the Sierra Leone
People's Party. The SLPP was in fact a coalescence of the Protectorate-educated elite and traditional authority with enlightened and
imaginative Creole leadership as exemplified by Lamina Sankoh,
H. E. B. John, and the Rev. Harry Sawyerr.

The more intransigent Creoles found succor not only in the ranks of the Settlers' Descendants Union but sought political power through the National Council led by Dr. Bright. Dr. Bright and his National Council were afraid of Protectorate domination and what it might do to their cherished traditions and ways of life. In retrospect Dr. Bright's fears, if couched in unrestrained language and expressed in the form of unrealistic demands, were not unfounded.

Sir Milton Margai became leader of government business in 1951, later premier and then prime minister. He went on to consolidate his leadership of his party and of the country at large. By exercizing patience and statesmanship he succeeded in allaying the worst fears of his more irreconcilable opponents. He proved to be extremely tolerant; he was free from vanity and dishonesty. If forced occasionally to resort to unconventional methods, he soon made amends and made his peace with propriety. Often he boasted that his greatest ambition was to make Sierra Leone a model country. That boast was to a large extent justified. In April 1964 he died peacefully in his bed, a rare achievement among African political leaders. He was the first African head of government in the newly emergent Africa so to die--one might add the only one so far.

His two successors, Sir Albert Margai (1964-7) and Mr. S. P. Stevens (1968-), introduced in their various ways a different style of leadership and presented sharp contrasts to and deviations from Sir Milton's practice and approach. Sir Albert threatened to introduce a republican form of government based on a "democratic one party state." Caught in a cruel dilemma between the principles and beliefs of a British-trained lawyer and the instincts and ambitions of an African politician, Sir Albert destroyed himself and in a sense his party too. In March 1967 a general election was held in Sierra Leone, the issues--republicanism and the one-party state. For the first time in emergent black Africa an opposition party, the APC, won the elections. Deprived of the fruits of victory by the NRC, a military regime, the APC and its leader Stevens were kept in political cold storage for the

year 1967-1968.   By means of a counter-coup the APC was swept
back into power amid popular enthusiasm and great expectations.
Once in power, and provoked by a series of disturbances and political crises the APC reacted with ruthless determination and un-
precedented political chicanery.   Where the SLPP and Sir Albert had
tended to use words, the APC preferred "positive action"; where
the SLPP had at best merely threatened, the APC with few threats,
implemented their plans.   By 1971 the APC had transformed Sierra
Leone into a republic, with little respect for legal technicalities or
constitutional propriety.   In 1973 by means of "consultation" and
"selection" in largely uncontested elections, the party established
virtual monopoly over political power in Sierra Leone.

THE DICTIONARY

ACKIM, ELI.   One of the Nova Scotian immigrants to Sierra Leone
in 1792.   Although the Nova Scotians on arrival complained of
several disabilities and of breaches of promises, some, like
Ackim, made a fortune in their new home, lived in style and
spent money somewhat lavishly.   In 1796 Ackim was appointed
by the Sierra Leone Company as assistant apothecary.   He acquired considerable property in Freetown and owned the bulk of
land later acquired by the Crown as a settlement for Krumen.
Ackim died in reduced circumstances in 1835.

ADAMS, S. A. SOLADE, 1919- .   Educationist and administrator;
principal, Milton Margai Teachers College, Goderich, Freetown.
Mr. Adams was born on January 6, 1919, and was educated at
Buxton and Regent Amalgamated schools, the Government Model
School, the CMS Grammar School, Fourah Bay College (Univer-
sity of Durham), Freetown; King's College, University of Durham,
Newcastle-on-Tyne; and at Teachers College, Columbia University,
New York.   After a distinguished career as a schoolmaster, Mr.
Adams was appointed in September 1961 as vice-principal, Freetown Training College for Teachers (later Milton Margai Teachers
College), and in March 1965 became the first Sierra Leonean
principal of the College.   A prominent public figure, Mr. Adams
has held a number of positions in organizations and committees
including membership of the Joint Committee for Teachers (until 1971), the Board of Education, Ministry of Education (now de-
funct), the Text book Committee, Ministry of Education and the
National Committee of the West African Examinations Council.

AFRICAN AND SIERRA LEONE WEEKLY ADVERTISER (1855-1861).
A newspaper founded in Freetown in 1855 under the auspices of
the Church Missionary Society (CMS), printed and published by
Moses Henry Davies, an Aku from Hastings village.   Its aim
was to raise the moral standards of the community.   It published
local and foreign news, advertisements and government notices.

AFRICAN INTERPRETER AND ADVOCATE (1866-1869).   A newspaper founded in Freetown in 1866 by an Afro-West Indian,
F. A. Belgrave, a protégé of William Rainy whose mouthpiece
the newspaper became until it stopped publication in 1869.

THE AFRICAN STANDARD (1938-1945).   Newspaper founded in 1938
by I. T. A. Wallace-Johnson to represent the views of the West

1

African Youth League. To curtail and stem the widespread influence of the <u>Standard</u>, the Colonial Office authorized the Sierra
Leone Government in 1939 to introduce legislation to control "undesirable publications. " The laws against sedition were also
made to assume wider applicability in the hope that "a moderate
stiffening up of the Sierra Leone law might prove an effective
check to newspapers under the influence of Mr. Wallace-Johnson. "

AFZELIUS, ADAM. A pupil of Charles Linnaeus, Afzelius was the
third Swedenborgian Swede to be employed by the Sierra Leone
Company. He produced the first systematic botanical work on
West African flora. Afzelius arrived in Freetown in May 1792.
He cultivated two gardens, one at the waterfront and the other
at Susan's Bay. His first botanical work was published as an
annex to the Sierra Leone Company's official report of 1794.
His gardens were destroyed by a French naval squadron which
attacked Freetown in September 1794 and he addressed a letter
dated November 15, 1794, to the Swedish ambassador in London
describing the attack. He continued his work after the attack
and in May 1796 went to London to classify his discoveries. It
was he who identified an indigenous variety of coffee on Leicester peak and encouraged its cultivation. The Afzelia Africana or
Konta, a fine hardwood, derives its name from Adam Afzelius.

THE AGENCY AND MERCANTILE, SHIPPING, AGRICULTURAL,
ADVERTISING AND GENERAL REPORTER (1884-1887). A periodical published by J. E. Gooding with emphasis on advertisements.

AKAR, JOHN JOSEPH, 1927-1975. Broadcaster, short-story writer,
actor, playwright and journalist. Born on May 20, 1927, at
Rotifunk, Bompeh Chiefdom, Moyamba district. Educated at
EUB Day School, Rotifunk; the Albert Academy, Freetown; and
Otterbein College and the University of California, Berkeley, in
the USA; and at the London School of Economics. Appointed head
of programmes, Sierra Leone Broadcasting Service (SLBS) in
1957, and director of broadcasting, Sierra Leone, in 1960. Composer of the national anthem of Sierra Leone (1961). Appointed
Sierra Leone's ambassador to the United States, 1969-1971.
Died in Jamaica in 1975.

AKU EXPEDITION see MILITARY EXPEDITIONS (1)

ALIKALI see TEMNE

ALL PEOPLE'S CONGRESS [APC]. Political party first launched by
S. P. Stevens as an Elections Before Independence Movement
(EBIM) in July 1960 and as a protest against the United Front
Coalition. Two months later the formation of a new party was
announced--the All People's Congress, with Stevens as leader.
The leaders of the new party, Stevens, Secretary General C. A.
Kamara-Taylor, M. O. Bash Taqi, S. I. Koroma, S. A. T.

Koroma, Kande Mansaray, Badarr Koroma, and S. A. Fofana were northerners. But the party was at its inception almost a continuation of the People's National Party (PNP). Virtually all its leaders had been members (some in responsible positions) of or sympathizers with the PNP. Its political slogan, "elections before independence," had been the chant of the PNP. Its dislike of the United Front Coalition had been shared by large numbers in the PNP, particularly by those who felt that the United Front was at best an elaborate pretense at a national government, at worst a tricky device to keep the SLPP indefinitely in power. The APC's support of non-alignment had been a cardinal principle in the PNP's projected foreign policy. The APC's distrust of foreign bases had been proclaimed by the PNP. But there were differences and as time progressed the similarities gave way to the differences.

The APC was at its inception essentially a northern people's party (a name that was actually suggested but rejected). Its leadership with few exceptions was drawn largely from the lower levels of the educational, social and economic ladder. If some had been exposed to outside influences few had traveled out of the country. While some had links with traditional ruling houses few had sympathy or love for traditional authority. The party adopted as its symbol the red sun and as its motto "Now or Never," manifesting a determined spirit but revealing a desperate mood. Regarding itself as the party of the "common people," the APC professed a vague socialism, asserting as its goal "a welfare state based upon a socialist pattern of society in which all citizens regardless of class, tribe, colour or creed, shall have equal opportunity and where there shall be no exploitation of man by man, tribe by tribe or class by class."

The APC represents in many ways a radical party. But as the only party in the country to emerge from opposition to government there were bound to be sharp contrasts between its theoretical declarations in opposition and its practical performance in government. Within a year of its formation the APC won remarkable success in the annual Freetown City Council elections held in November 1960, securing two of the three seats with impressive margins and narrowly losing the third by only 27 votes. On the eve of independence in 1961, the SLPP government accused the APC leadership of attempts to wreck the celebrations by violence and sabotage and sent some 43 leaders to detention after declaring a state of emergency. After his release from detention Mr. Stevens, as national leader of the party, issued the following statement emphasizing his party's willingness to be law-abiding and rebutting firmly but politely the government's charges of subversion: "Independence having become an accomplished fact and the Government having given the assurance of General elections in 1962, the APC calls upon all its members to maintain the Party policy line of (a) full respect for law and order (b) constitutional and lawful procedure in all matters. The APC has never stood for violence, sabotage or unconstitutional action...."

In the 1962 general election the APC in alliance with

SLPIM won 20 seats out of 62 and thereafter became the official opposition party in parliament. Continued successes in
Freetown City Council elections between 1960 and 1964 led to
the appointment of Siaka Stevens as mayor of Freetown. By
1966 the APC was in virtual control of the entire North, the
entire Western Area and Kono District. The party's opposition
to Sir Albert's projected one-party state and republican constitution won support for the APC, particularly among Creole intellectuals. In the 1967 elections the party made history by becoming the first opposition party in independent Black Africa to
win a general election, capturing 32 out of 66 seats as against
the SLPP's 28 and the Independents' 6. Deprived of the fruits
of victory by the National Reformation Council military regime,
the APC finally assumed the reins of government in 1968. A
series of by-elections in 1968-69 increased its strength in parliament to 53. Armed with overwhelming numerical strength
the APC in 1971 introduced, with little legal propriety, a republican system of government in Sierra Leone. It buttressed
its political power by winning virtually all 98 seats in parliament in the elections held in 1973. Today the APC is the
only party represented in parliament, a de facto though not
de jure one-party-state situation.

ALLDRIDGE, THOMAS JOSHUA, I.S.O., F.R.G.S. Traveling
commissioner and author. Arrived in Sierra Leone from
Britain in 1871 and for several years served as agent for
Messrs. Randall and Fisher at York Island and then joined
government service. Appointed first as traveling commissioner by the government in about 1890, Alldridge succeeded Garret
as district commissioner of Sherbro, in 1893. In 1894 he accompanied Governor Cardew on the Governor's first tour of the
hinterland. Alldridge saw much of the fighting and disturbances
during the 1898 Hut Tax War. He published two books on
Sierra Leone, The Sherbro and Its Hinterland (1901) and A
Transformed Colony, Sierra Leone (1910).

ALLEN, WILLIAM. Member of the African Institution (London),
founded in 1807 to promote African education, trade and agriculture and to eradicate the slave trade. Allen had considerable
sympathy for the early settlers of the Sierra Leone Colony and
championed their cause in the columns of the Philanthropist.
He drew up plans for the establishment of model villages in the
eastern districts of the colony. Each villager was to own a
six-roomed cottage with cowshed and pigstye, grow some of
his own food and cultivate cash crops like coffee or cotton
which were to be marketed to England through the village
manager. The first of these model villages, built in 1827,
was called Allen Town after William Allen. Through his instrumentality Governor Doherty was instructed by the British
Government to annul a treaty of 1836 signed at Magbele making
provision for the surrender of fugitives to their masters, a
provision stigmatized by its opponents, including Allen, as an
attempt to revive and encourage slavery.

ALVARES, MANUEL, S.J., 1580-1619. A Jesuit missionary priest
in Sierra Leone where he worked for an unbroken spell of ten
years (1607-1617). For the first two years he was companion
to Father Balthasar Barreira and continued alone after the latter's departure in 1609. He worked among the people of the
Sierra Leone Peninsula and among the "Buloms" and the "Lagos" (probably Lokos). Father Alvares's Descripção geo-
graphica da provincia da Serra Leoa [Geographical Sketch of
the Province of Sierra Leone] was published in 1616. From
him we learn that the Quojas (Koyas) were already in Sierra
Leone by the first decade of the 17th century and from him we
learn that by the end of the 16th century the Mane invaders had
to a large extent been assimilated into the various groups they
had met in Sierra Leone. Alvares wrote, "It is difficult to
speak of the Mane of Sierra Leone because of their assimilation into the life there. Such genuine Mane about whom one
could speak are few and fast disappearing." Information about
the Mane contribution to--as opposed to the destruction of--
Sape civilization is derived from Alvares who observed that in
the technique of iron-working the Mane were in advance of the
Sape. He wrote "of the mechanic arts they [the Mane] have
not a single office with the exception of iron smiths and in the
understanding of this they far surpass the naturals of Sierra
Leone."

ALVARES VELHO. A Portuguese trader who established his headquarters for eight years in Sierra Leone. It was from Alvares
Velho that Valentim Fernandes writing in 1507 mainly derived
his information about Sierra Leone.

AMALGAMATED TEACHERS ORGANISATION. Formed in April
1948 in Freetown, the outcome of the merger of two unions--
the Sierra Leone Teachers Union (Colony only) and the Sierra
Leone Protectorate Teachers Union. In 1963 at a special con-
ference held in Bo, it was decided to change the name of the
Union from Amalgamated Teachers Organisation to Sierra Leone
Teachers Union. When the union was registered in 1969 as
SLTU the foundation date was given as September 9, 1950.
(See also SLTU under TRADE UNIONS.)

AMARA, ALIMAMY, of Foulah Town. An Aku recaptive landed
in Freetown in the 1830s and settled in Grassfields, west of
Freetown, where he embraced Islam. Amara was elected head
of the Muslim Community at Foulah Town in 1875. In 1891 he
became one of the proponents of the revival of the Aku Kingship which had been vacant since 1880. With other Aku leaders
Amara took part in the installation of a new Aku King in 1891.

AMERICAN MISSIONARY ASSOCIATION [AMA] see MENDI MIS-
SION

ANDERSON, ISAAC. Arrived in Sierra Leone from Nova Scotia in
1792 and became one of the leading spokesmen for the Nova

Scotians in Freetown. In 1793 Anderson along with a colleague, Cato Perkins, was elected to present a petition to the
directors of the Sierra Leone Company in London on behalf of
the Nova Scotians. The petition detailed grievances against the
Company and particularly against the new governor, William
Dawes. Anderson stayed in Britain for six months and returned
to Freetown crestfallen, and with grievances unredressed. In
December 1796 he was elected a hundredor and became a determined opponent of quit rents declared payable in July 1796
by Zachary Macaulay, the governor of the Colony. Anderson
was one of the ringleaders of the Nova Scotian rebellion in
1799 against the payment of quit rents and a host of other
grievances. The rebellion was crushed and Anderson was found
guilty of sending the governor an anonymous threatening letter,
at the time a capital offense, and was hanged.

ANDRE, BARTHOLOMEW. The most influential Portuguese trader
on the Sierra Leone River in the first decade of the 17th century. He also had extensive trading posts down the West Coast
of Africa. About 1602 Andre successfully prevented the Dutch
from building a fort on the River by threatening Don Felipe,
King of Sierra Leone, with the transfer of his own trade elsewhere if the King allowed the Dutch to carry out their project.
Thus thwarted the Dutch returned to their factory at Cape
Mount, where Andre soon effected their murder.

ANTHONY, F. S., 1910- . Educationist and politician. Born
September 15, 1910. Educated at the Albert Academy, at
Fourah Bay College, Freetown, and at Hampton Institute and
Cornell University, USA. Tutor at Bunumbu Teachers College, 1944-48, principal of Taiama Secondary School, 1960-67,
and principal of Leona Secondary School, Bo. One of the first
trained Sierra Leonean agriculturists. One of the leading
spokesmen for the Protectorate-educated elite in the political
controversies of the post-World War II period. Founder member of the Sierra Leone Organisation Society (SOS) and official
of the Protectorate Teachers' Union later to become through a
merger first the Amalgamated Teachers Organisation (ATO) and
subsequently the Sierra Leone Teachers Union (SLTU). With
A. M. Margai, Anthony was author of a "Memorandum to the
Secretary of State for the Colonies on the New Constitution,"
Sessional Paper No. 48 of 1948. Author also of miscellaneous
publications on education, agriculture and community development. Returned as member of parliament for Pujehun West
Constituency, 1967. Appointed minister of agriculture and
natural resources, 1968; resident minister, Eastern Province,
1969-1972.

ANTONIO, PA. Claiming descent from the Portuguese, Pa Antonio,
described as having "a brazen crucifix suspended from his
neck" was an Afro-Portuguese who as late as 1821 ruled over
one of the villages in Port Loko. Though his chiefdom was
small, his power and authority were nonetheless real and ef-

fective. Pa Antonio, like his predecessors, Lopez, Jerome, Thoma and others, represented the same trend on the Upper Guinea Coast from the late 17th through the early 19th centuries--the political and economic dominance of the Afro-Portuguese.

APPLETON, Maj. WILLIAM. Officer commanding troops, and acting governor of Sierra Leone 1815.

THE ARTISAN (1884-1888; 1892-1899). Newspaper founded by S. H. A. Case in 1884 to represent the views of the Mechanics' Alliance or Trade Union organized also by Case to protect the interests of artisans in the Colony. After the collapse of the Mechanics' Alliance, The Artisan continued as a mouthpiece of Case until 1888. It reappeared as an occasional paper from 1892 until 1899.

ASHMORE, ABRAHAM. Last governor of the Province of Freedom. Ashmore was later arrested by Falconbridge on charges of slave-dealing. Kept in custody on board ship for five days Ashmore was subsequently released for lack of sufficient evidence.

ATKINS, JOHN. Visited Sierra Leone in 1721. On April 7, 1721, Surgeon John Atkins called on Signor Joseph--traditionally considered the first African missionary to Sierra Leone who had arrived in 1715--at Kissy. Atkins observed that Signor Joseph was "a generous and good-natured Christian Negro, who had lately removed with his people some miles up the River. With his old buildings we wooded our ship." He also referred to coconut trees although he did not state clearly that they grew in the Sierra Leone Peninsula: "The shores hereabouts," he wrote, "like those of Sweden, are rocky, and without any cover of Earth almost yet produce large trees, the roots spreading on the surface. The Chief of them are the palm, the cocoa and the cotton-trees." Atkins discovered that Africans on the West Coast at the time wanted improved firearms, observing that the market required "a better sort of firearms." From him we learn that the African trader of the time "never cares to treat with dry lips"--a reference to the practice of offering to Africans a small quantity of liquor--or a "dash" as it later came to be known--as an indispensable preliminary to trade. The breakdown of law and order and the consequent lack of security caused by the ravages of the slave trade were remarked upon by Atkins when he observed that people on the Coast at the time "never care to walk even a mile from home without firearms."

THE AURORA (1918-ca. 1925). A newspaper published by H. C. Bankole-Bright, The Aurora was regarded by officialdom as the most hostile and acrimonious in the Colony. It adopted a particularly violent posture in its denunciations of Syrians after the anti-Syrian riots of 1919. From 1920 onwards Aurora ap-

peared to have put across the views of the National Congress
of British West Africa (NCBWA).

AWUNOR-RENNER see RENNER, WILLIAM

AZZOLINI, the Most Rev. AUGUSTUS. As Monsignor Azzolini, he
led the first batch of Italian missionaries, the Xaverians, to
Sierra Leone in 1950. The Xaverians concentrated their missionary efforts on the northern province where a diocese was
erected as the Roman Catholic diocese of Makeni with Bishop
Azzolini as first bishop in 1962.

- B -

BADGER, the Rev. HENRY, 1815-1877. Chairman and general
superintendent of the Methodist Mission in Sierra Leone (1846-
1847). The Rev. Badger arrived in Freetown on November 19,
1837, and, with the Rev. Dove, put Methodism in Sierra Leone
on firmer foundations. He succeeded Dove as chairman and
general superintendent in 1846. The next year he returned to
England and was appointed by the Methodist Conference in 1848
as general superintendent of the Gambia mission. Badger died
in England on December 24, 1877.

BAGRU EXPEDITION see MILITARY EXPEDITIONS (4)

BANGURA, FAMA-JOKA. Educated at the United Methodist Church
School, Taiama, the Freetown Secondary School for Girls,
Fourah Bay College, the Queen's University Belfast, and at Oxford University, Mrs. Bangura is Sierra Leone's most prominent woman career diplomat. She has been deputy secretary,
Ministry of External Affairs, and chairman of the United Nations Fourth Committee which deals with decolonization, non-
self-governing territories and trust territories.

BANGURA, Brig. JOHN. Educated at Bo Government School and at
the British military Academy of Sandhurst, the first Sierra
Leonean Sandhurst-trained officer. Bangura was arrested and
detained in 1967 on charges of mutiny. He was released in the
same year and sent to a diplomatic post at the Sierra Leone
embassy in Washington. He abandoned his diplomatic assign-
ment and went to Guinea in a bid to overthrow the National
Reformation Council military regime. After the overthrow of
the NRC by the rank and file of the Sierra Leone Military
forces, Bangura was recalled to head an interim government
and for about a week between April and May 1968 he was effective head of the government of Sierra Leone. He was most
instrumental in ensuring the return of Siaka Stevens as prime
minister of a civilian regime in 1968. In March 1971, John
Bangura, with other senior officers, was arrested on charges
of mutiny and treason, in an attempt to overthrow the government by unlawful means. Convicted and sentenced to death he

was executed by hanging with three other senior officers at Pademba Road Prisons, Freetown in 1971.

BANGURA, SAMUEL LANSANA, 1930- . Governor, Bank of Sierra Leone. Born at Yele on June 7, 1930. After attending the SDA Mission School, Yele, and Bo Government School, Samuel Bangura read economics at Hull University, England, where he graduated in 1957 and attended Queen's College, Oxford, in 1958/9. He joined the Sierra Leone government service as administrative officer and from 1959 to 1962 served first as assistant and later as district commissioner of Bonthe. From 1962 to 1964 he was attached to the Ministry of Finance where he rose to the rank of deputy financial secretary. He was appointed permanent secretary, Development Office (1964 to 1966), and transferred to the Bank of Sierra Leone June 1, 1966, as deputy governor. In November 1970 he was appointed governor of the Bank of Sierra Leone.

BANK OF SIERRA LEONE. Founded and created by the Bank of Sierra Leone Act 1963. Section 5 of that Act laid down in broad outline the major junctions of the bank as: to issue legal tender currency in Sierra Leone and to maintain external reserves in order to safeguard the international value of the currency; to act as banker and financial adviser to the government; and to promote monetary stability and a sound financial structure. The Bank of Sierra Leone (Amendment) Act 1970 Section 5 made the following provisions the bank's main functions--to promote monetary stability and sound financial structure and to promote credit and exchange conditions conducive to the balanced growth of the economy. The Act of 1970 also stipulated that the bank should at all times maintain reserves of not less than the value of three months' imports as recorded in the three preceding years. The bank issued its own notes and coins for the first time on August 4, 1964. The Bank of Sierra Leone has its headquarters office in Freetown and a branch office in Kenema.

BANKOLE-BRIGHT, HERBERT CHRISTIAN, 1883-1958. Medical practitioner, politician and journalist. Born of Sierra Leone parentage at Okrika, Nigeria, on August 23, 1883. Educated at the Wesleyan (later Methodist) Boys High School, Freetown, and at Edinburgh University where he qualified in medicine in 1910. He returned home to Freetown and set up private practice. He was one of the founders of the National Council of British West Africa (NCBWA). In March 1920 as Sierra Leone's representative at the Accra Conference of the NCBWA, "Bankie," as he was popularly called, read a paper entitled "Sanitary and Medical Reforms with Special Reference to Segregation Systems and the Position of the African Medical Practitioner in the Government Service." Later in that year he played the role of spokesman and secretary-general of the Congress delegation to London.

In 1924 Bankole-Bright was elected second urban member to the Legislative Council. His open support of and sympathy for the railway workers who went on strike in 1926 provoked some senior colonial administrators into unleashing most unwarranted attacks on Dr. Bankole-Bright and his fellow Creoles. There was in fact a threat, never carried out, to suspend the Slater Constitution. The Governor himself, if unwilling to sanction the premature destruction of his own handiwork, was irked enough to observe that "... the harm that demagogues of the type of Dr. Bankole-Bright and Mr. Betts can, and undoubtedly do cause, is to some extent mitigated rather than accentuated by their membership on the Council. Their sense of responsibility as legislators is, it is true, painfully low, but it is occasionally discernible...." Bankole-Bright and Beoku-Betts, fondly described as the "Double B's," dominated Freetown politics during parts of the twenties and thirties. Described spitefully, if inaccurately at the time, by one Colonial official as "not very successful practitioners of medicine and law," they were also accused by officialdom of having fanned "racial hatred and defied so far as they dared all discipline, law and order, making an invidious attempt to stir up disaffection through the nominated Protectorate chiefs." They were political allies initially but when Beoku-Betts in the late thirties accepted an MBE and a magistracy the relationship was severely strained, perhaps severed.

An oligarchist rather than a democrat, Bankole-Bright had little faith in the wisdom of the masses and was genuinely alarmed by the introduction of grass roots politics in Sierra Leone. He saw in the formation and activities of Wallace-Johnson's Youth League a dangerous threat to his position, to his own style of politics and to his own way of life. And so Dr. Bankole-Bright, hitherto the scourge of the administration, made a volte face, came to the rescue of the government and actually seconded three bills in 1939 aimed at stifling individual freedoms and at destroying the West African Youth League.

In 1951 Bankole-Bright was again returned to the Legislative Council as member for Freetown Central, and assumed the role of leader of the opposition. The council as constituted in 1951 had been enlarged by the provisions of the Stevenson Constitution of 1947, the implementation of which had been delayed by the unwillingness of both Colony and Protectorate spokesmen to accept some of its provisions. Bankole-Bright resorted to unrestrained rhetoric in his condemnation of the attempts to give a majority of seats in the council to the Protectorate representatives, whom he described as foreigners. If his description was technically and legally accurate his politics were somewhat faulty. In 1957 his party, the National Council of the Colony of Sierra Leone, lost all its seats with its deposits as well in the general elections. In the last years of his life he concentrated on politics and journalism at the expense of his medical practice. He was proprietor and editor of two newspapers, The Evening Despatch and The Aurora. He died in 1958 in somewhat reduced circumstances and was buried in Freetown.

BANYA, SAMA SIAMA, 1930- . Medical practitioner and civic
leader. Born on June 10, 1930, and educated at Bo Government School, the Prince of Wales School, Freetown, the University of Bristol, England, and at the West London Hospital,
London. One of the most enterprising and successful private
medical practitioners in Sierra Leone. Founder and proprietor
of the Nongowa Clinic and the Emma Thompson Nursing Home
in Kenema, a private hospital formally opened in April 1972.
In his student days in Britain, Dr. Banya was in the forefront
in student politics and served for a number of years as honorary
secretary of the Sierra Leone Students Union. He was also one
of the six conveners of a meeting which led to the formation of
the Anglo-Sierra Leone Society in the United Kingdom in 1962.
Appointed government medical officer in 1963, he served in Bo,
Kenema, Njala and Makeni before going into private practice.
Banya was arrested and detained under public emergency regulations at Mafanta and Pademba Road prisons in 1968; his release came in 1969.

BARBOT, JEAN. In 1678 Barbot was agent-général of the French
Royal Company of Africa with headquarters in Paris. Later,
for religious reasons, he became a refugee in England. He
wrote a "Description of the Coasts of North and South Guinea"
etc., mentioning the Sierra Leone estuary in some detail, warning his readers that the spring at the watering-place was not always healthy.

BARCLAYS BANK OF SIERRA LEONE LTD. First opened in Freetown in 1917 as a branch of Barclays Bank DCO (renamed Barclays Bank International Ltd.), a subsidiary of Barclays Bank
Ltd., one of the United Kingdom's "Big Five" banks. Barclays
Bank of Sierra Leone was incorporated in Freetown on March
15, 1971, and it took over effective April 1, 1971, the assets,
liabilities, rights and obligations of Barclays Bank DCO. The
Bank has provincial branches in Bo, Kenema, Makeni, Koidu
Town, Lunsar, Moyamba and Kabala. In addition it has agen-
cies at Magburaka and Yenegema.

BARREIRA, the Rev. BALTHASAR, S.J., 1538-1612. The most
outstanding of the Jesuit pioneer missionaries in West Africa
in the 16th century. The scene of his labors included the Congo and Angola (1580-1594) and "Guinea"--i.e. from Senegal to
Sierra Leone (1604-1612). At over 60 years of age and single-
handedly Barreira founded a promising mission in Sierra Leone,
then part of the Ecclesiastical Province of Cape Verde, with
headquarters on the island of Santiago. As leader of the mission to Guinea, Barreira traveled in slow stages down the
coast and arrived in Sierra Leone on September 25, 1605. His
plan was to transfer the headquarters of the mission of Guinea
from the island of Santiago to the mainland and preferably to
appoint as sole patron King Philip III of Spain who alone sub-
sidized the mission. The Jesuit Mission in Sierra Leone

came to an abrupt end in 1617 and the mission to Guinea was
abandoned in 1653.

    Barreira's reports to his superiors in Europe con-
stitute valuable source material for the study of the early
history and ethnography of West Africa and of Sierra Leone
in particular. They were published in his life time and
translated into Latin as well as a few European languages.
Writing in 1607 Barreira asserted that the Mane had arrived in the hinterland of Sierra Leone about 60 years
earlier, thus putting the date of the invasions roughly between 1540 and 1560. He also testified to the presence of
the Quojas (Coyas, Koyas) in Sierra Leone during his stay
between 1605 and 1609. From him we learn that the Sape
or Capeo or Capez were skillful, artistic and highly intelligent, but he felt that they had "weak and effeminate
minds"--a fact which may well have contributed to their
conquest and subjection by the more aggressive and virile
Mane. Barreira returned to Santiago in 1609 where he
died in 1612.

BARTHOLOMEW ROBERTS see ROBERTS, BARTHOLOMEW

BAWOLOME, CHIEF see MBAWOLOME

BE [Bey] SHERBRO of Yonnie (also, Gbana Lewis). Overlord of
    the whole of Sherbro; grandson of Kong Kuba, King of Sherbro
    who, under the name of Benka or Banka, signed with other
    chiefs a treaty on September 24, 1825, with Governor Sir
    Charles Turner, ceding what is known as Turner's Peninsula
    to the British. Kong Kuba's grandson, who had assumed the
    name Gbana (Kpana) Lewis (possibly derived from the name of
    slave dealer, Louis or Lewis, who had lived in the area in the
    1850s) became Be Sherbro of Yoni possibly in the 1870s. On
    November 18, 1882, Turner's treaty of 1825 was revived and
    Be Sherbro was able to secure a stipend from the British
    Government claiming it as successor of his grandfather. In
    1896 Be Sherbro, as suzerain of Sherbro, presided over the
    installation ceremonies of the new Sokong of Imperri. After
    the declaration of the Protectorate in 1896, along with other
    chiefs, he traveled to Freetown in February 1897 to protest
    to Governor Cardew against the Protectorate ordinance.
    Cardew, while insisting that the chiefs had to abide by the
    provisions of the ordinance, assured Be Sherbro that the
    ordinance would not affect him, as his territories were already
    within the Colony. On his return home, Be Sherbro, far from
    pleased with the governor's assurances, organized a boycott
    of European and Creole trade by means of the poro. Because
    of these activities an ordinance was drafted to detain him if
    and when necessary. Another ordinance was passed making the

use of poro to prohibit or obstruct trade a criminal offense.
When the Hut Tax War broke out in 1898, Be Sherbro was believed to be one of the moving spirits behind the insurrection.
He was summoned to Freetown and jailed on arrival in May
1898 without any charge proved against him.   He, along with
Bai Bureh and Nyagua, was deported to the Gold Coast on July
30, 1899.   Be Sherbro was however allowed to return home in
1905.

BECKLES, the Rt. Rev. EDWARD HYNDMAN.   Bishop of Sierra
   Leone (1860-1870); served as a parish priest in the West
   Indies before succeeding Bowen as Bishop of Sierra Leone in
   1860, where he implemented Venn's plan for a Native Church
   pastorate in 1861.   The last Bishop to serve on the Legislative
   Council, Beckles denounced the war against Koya which had
   broken out in 1861 as un-Christian, arguing that the chiefs had
   signed the treaty of cession against their will (the Bishop had
   himself been a signatory to the treaty as a witness).   Beckles
   fell out with Governor Hill, with whom he exchanged sharp letters, in one of which the Bishop said the governor would be
   answerable to a Higher Power, which he defined as God.   In
   1863 a new Charter or Constitution was promulgated in Sierra
   Leone and for the first time the Bishop of Sierra Leone was excluded from membership of the legislative council, thanks to
   Beckles' intractability.   Within his diocese the Bishop did little
   to discourage factiousness and conflicts, spending most of his
   time abroad either in England or in Madeira.   (In 1868 he had
   spent over four of his eight years out of his diocese.)   Threatened with loss of his colonial salary, Beckles returned to a
   new house at Bishopscourt, bought in his absence from proceeds of the colonial bishopric fund.   Early in 1869 Beckles
   was on his travels again ostensibly visiting the Gambia, but in
   actual fact returning to England.   By 1870 the Bishop had spent
   six years out of ten away from his diocese.   Deprived of his
   colonial salary since 1869, the trustees of the Colonial Bishoprics Fund decided on a similar measure.   Finding himself in
   this untenable situation the Bishop reduced himself in status,
   sought refuge in a rectory in Kent and drew some comfort from
   the patronage of Berkely Chapel, Mayfair.

BENDU EXPEDITION see MILITARY EXPEDITIONS (3)

BENKA-COKER, HANNAH, 1900-1952.   One of Sierra Leone's leading female educators.   She was co-founder of Osora or the
   Freetown Secondary School for Girls (FSSG) 1926 and first
   Sierra Leonean principal of the School (1938-1952).   The buildings which house the school at Brookfields were constructed in
   1952 largely through the determination and exertions of Mrs.
   Benka-Coker.   She died in the same year shortly after the
   formal opening of the new buildings.

BENKA-COKER, Sir SALAKO, 1900-1966. Chief justice of Sierra
   Leone (1960-1963). Sir Salako was born on June 16, 1900.
   He was educated at the CMS Grammar School, and at Fourah
   Bay College, where he graduated in 1918. He worked as a
   mercantile clerk from 1919 to 1921 and then proceeded to Britain to study law. He was called to the Bar at the Middle Temple in 1926; was in private practice in the Gambia, 1926-1935,
   and in Sierra Leone, 1935-1943. In 1943 he was appointed
   Crown counsel and in 1953 he became solicitor-general. He
   acted as attorney-general in 1954-1955 and again in mid-1956.
   He was appointed acting puisne judge in 1957 and puisne judge
   in 1958. In 1960 he was appointed chief justice and awarded
   a knighthood in 1961. He acted as governor-general in 1961
   and again in mid-1964. He was elected honorary bencher,
   Honourable Society of the Middle Temple 1962. He died in
   1966.

BEOKU-BETTS, Sir ERNEST S., 1895-1957. One of the first
   three to be elected in 1924 to the legislative council of Sierra
   Leone, where he served as first urban member. Sir Ernest
   was the first Sierra Leonean puisne judge (1945), first Sierra
   Leonean West African Court of Appeal judge (1946) and first
   vice-president of the Legislative Council (1953). He was born
   on March 15, 1895, and educated at the Leopold Educational Institute, at Fourah Bay College (Durham University), and at the
   University of London. He was called to the Bar in 1917; and
   served first as member of the Freetown City Council (1919-
   1926) and then as mayor of Freetown (1925-26). Beoku-Betts
   and Bankole-Bright (q.v.), the "Double B's" as they were fondly called, dominated Freetown politics in the twenties and early
   thirties and were a constant source of embarrassment to the
   Colonial administration. In 1937, however, Beoku-Betts quit
   politics for the bench and was appointed police magistrate. A
   keen sportsman, Beoku-Betts was for several years president
   of the Sierra Leone Football and Cricket Associations. For
   his distinguished service he was awarded a knighthood by Queen
   Elizabeth in 1957, the second Sierra Leonean to be so honored.
   He died later in the same year.

BERESFORD-STOOKE, Sir GEORGE. Governor of Sierra Leone
   (1948-1953). Sir George Beresford-Stooke arrived in Freetown
   in September 1948 to succeed Sir Hubert Stevenson as governor
   of Sierra Leone. Stevenson's projected constitution of 1947
   was finally implemented after protracted debate and in modified
   form in April 1951. Beresford-Stooke tried hard to effect understanding, if not cooperation among the various political
   groups in Sierra Leone--Creoles, chiefs and the Protectorate-
   educated elites--but he displayed considerable sympathy for the
   political claims and aspirations of the last group vis-à-vis the
   chiefs. He urged upon the Secretary of State for the Colonies
   the need to broaden the basis of political participation for the
   Protectorate masses in general and for the educated Protectorate elites in particular.

In a confidential dispatch to the Colonial Office in January 1949, Sir George observed that "when framing a new constitution, particular attention should be paid to the necessity of providing adequate opportunity for expression of the opinion of the common people in general and the educated classes in particular. ... It would be a mistake to overlook the claims to representation put forward by the educated classes in the Protectorate.... The Chief Commissioner has told me that under the [proposed] new constitution, as the proposals now stand, it is unlikely that commoners would be elected to the Legislative Council from more than two out of the [12] districts. The reason for this is that the District Councils (acting as electoral colleges for Legislative Council elections) are dominated by the Paramount Chiefs who, holding as they do both executive and judicial powers, are in a position to exert very considerable influence." The modifications in Stevenson's proposals were effected largely through Governor Beresford-Stooke's representations and exertions. In spite of the governor's pleas about eight chiefs were returned by the 12 district councils. Now in retirement in England, Sir George has continued to manifest a great deal of interest in Sierra Leone and he is a very active member of the Anglo-Sierra Leonean Society.

BERKELEY, GEORGE. Governor of Sierra Leone, 1873-1874. Berkeley arrived in Freetown on August 28, 1873, to govern Sierra Leone. Though a major source of the Colony's revenue and trade, the Sherbro had for decades been treated with neglect. One of Governor Berkeley's assignments in Sierra Leone was to visit the Sherbro, study its problems and make appropriate recommendations. At Bonthe on February 10, 1874, the Governor entered into treaties with chiefs of the Boom, Small Boom, Bagru, Imperri and other territories, by which the chiefs undertook to refrain from waging war and to submit disputes to the governor of Sierra Leone for mediation and arbitration. Berkeley's report on and recommendations for Sherbro were favorably received at the Colonial Office, which approved the provisions of the treaties of February 1874, the establishment of bonding warehouses, as well as the extension of criminal jurisdiction aimed at minimizing delay and expenses involved in referring cases to Freetown. A new charter of July 24, 1874, disestablished the government of the West African Settlements and created separate governments for the Gold Coast and Lagos territories.

Berkeley considered but rejected Hennessey's plans to transfer the seat of government of Sierra Leone from Freetown to the hills. He also did not think it appropriate to introduce municipal institutions in Freetown, even if such institutions had existed in practice in Freetown for decades. Faced with a deficit, but unwilling to revive direct taxes, Berkeley was forced to raise increased revenue by imposing heavy wharfage duties and by levying additional export duties particularly on agricultural products. Appointed governor to the Leeward Islands, Berkeley departed from Sierra Leone on August 14, 1874.

BINNS REPORT (1949). Report of the Commission of Enquiry submitted in March 1949 by the sole commissioner, Mr. A. L. Binns, into the conditions of service of teachers appointed by the governor with the following terms of reference: "(i) to examine Scale I, as set out on page 4 of Sessional Paper No. 9 of 1948, and to make recommendations regarding the qualifications to be demanded as normal condition of entry to this scale and the posts to which this scale should apply; (ii) in the light of the recommendations made in connection with the first terms of reference to examine the other scales set out in Sessional Paper No. 9 of 1948 and to make recommendations; and (iii) to make recommendations for the establishment of an appropriate organization for consultation between teachers, employers and Government on all matters affecting the terms and conditions of service of teachers.

BISHOPS (ANGLICAN) OF SIERRA LEONE. C. E. Vidal 1852-1854; J. W. Weekes 1855-1857; J. Bowen 1857-1860; E. H. Beckles 1860-1869; H. Cheetham 1870-1881; E. Graham Ingham 1883-1897; J. Taylor Smith 1897-1901; E. H. Elwin 1902-1909; J. Walmsley 1910-1922; G. W. Wright 1923-1936; J. L. C. Horstead 1936-1961; M. N. C. O. Scott 1961- .

BISHOPSCOURT. Official residence of the Anglican bishops of Sierra Leone, situated at Fourah Bay in the East End of Freetown. The property--formerly belonging to Judge John Carr and including a mansion called the "Retreat" with vast grounds --was acquired (1867) with money from the Colonial Bishoprics Fund during the episcopate of Bishop Beckles. Part of the grounds was later used to build the Princess Cottage Christian Hospital--now the Princess Christian Maternity Hospital.

BIYI, ESU see GEORGE, CLAUDE

BLACKALL, Maj. SAMUEL WENSLEY. Governor of Sierra Leone, 1862-1867. On November 12, 1862, Blackall arrived in Freetown to take office as governor of Sierra Leone. A new charter dated May 27, 1863, revoking the letters patent of July 5, 1799, October 17, 1821, and February 17, 1846, and proclaimed in Freetown on July 21, 1863, introduced constitutional changes in the Colony. The Governor's Council, which had hitherto served as an all-purpose body, was divided into an Executive Council and a Legislative Council. The Executive Council had as its members the governor, the chief justice, the queen's advocate, the colonial secretary, and the officer commanding the troops. The Legislative Council consisted of the Executive Council and a number of members (about four in 1863) appointed by the governor and approved by the secretary of state.

    In appointing unofficial members the Governor was instructed to take into consideration "the wishes of the more intelligent portion of the community." Accordingly Blackall asked the most influential merchants in the Colony to choose a nomi-

nee. John Ezzidio, a Nupe recaptive, won 23 votes against
John Levi, a European trader's 13 votes. The Governor,
somewhat disappointed at the outcome, reluctantly accepted
Ezzidio and in a dispatch to the Duke of Newcastle, Secretary
of State, pointed out that "... the result is not unsatisfactory
though no doubt a more educated representative than Ezzidio
could have readily been selected...." He then suggested that
Levi be considered for membership in the Legislative Council
unless the Secretary of State felt that "the official predominance
would be too seriously lessened by such an addition...." The
Secretary of State apparently believed it would, and the Governor's request was turned down.

     In 1863 Blackall paid a visit to Liberia to examine that
republic's claims to the Gallinas and made arrangements for
the boundary commission to meet in Monrovia. Unwilling to
accept Liberia's questionable claims, the Governor advised and
the Colonial office concurred, that the British should adopt a
non-committal attitude, neither accepting nor rejecting Liberia's
claims. After a visit to Sherbro in 1863, Blackall recommended
the imposition of customs duties to raise revenue for increased
administrative expenses. In the Colony itself the Governor introduced a number of reforms aimed at maximizing efficiency.
The Secretariat was divided into the Colonial Secretary's and
Colonial Treasurer's offices, each with its own administrative
and clerical staff. The Colonial Secretary's duties became essentially administrative; the Colonial Treasurer's, fiscal.

     A special auditor was appointed to audit accounts locally
before submission to London. The Customs Department was
also reorganized. Oxen introduced from Madeira as beasts of
burden did not thrive well and the scheme was given up as un-
economical. The Police force was reorganized; it replaced the
militia and it was put under the command of an inspector-general. Blackall's other schemes for the Colony included new
harbor installations and a piped water-supply system. His proposal to abolish juries in civil cases, as contained in the new
Supreme Court Ordinance of 1866, which allowed trial by jury
only in criminal cases, provoked protests and petitions in Freetown. The Colonial Office reluctantly approved the ordinance.
In November 1867 Blackall left Sierra Leone to take up appointment as governor of Queensland, Australia.

BLANCHET, the Rev. EDWARD, C. S. SP. Born in the Duchy of
     Savoy, in 1825; studied for the priesthood at the feet of Francis
     Libermann, founder of a society for the evangelization of "Ne-
     groes, wherever they are to be found." Father Blanchet found-
     ed the Holy Ghost Fathers' Mission to Sierra Leone after serv-
     ing in Senegal, 1850-1856, and in the Gambia, 1856-1864. On
     his way home to France in 1859 he crossed a ship from which
     he learned of the ill-fated mission of Bishop Bresillac to Sier-
     ra Leone. He arrived in Freetown in February 1864 with a
     26-year-old priest companion, Father Joseph Koeberle. In
     Freetown, Father Blanchet's many successes and achievements
     were due in large part to the fact that he had become in the

words of his former mentor an "African with the Africans."
The ease with which he acquired land and property in the city,
the cordial relations with his workers and not least the rapid
progress of the school (St. Edward's) which he founded all
bore testimony to this. By 1868 Father Blanchet had completed the new residence for priests at Howe Street in six
months and at a cost of £900. But now his superb physique
began to show signs of strain. He was ordered to take a complete rest and he retreated to Goree island off Dakar. In 1879
he was reappointed head of the Mission to Sierra Leone.

There were two priests in Freetown when Father
Blanchet returned, Father Cosgrave from Ireland and Father
Lutz from France, who was to play in (1885-95) the role of
pioneer Holy Ghost Missionary in Southern Nigeria. For the
first four years the "Southern" Nigerian Mission was under the
jurisdiction of Freetown. By 1882 Sierra Leone had for the
first time six resident priests, and Father Blanchet decided to
extend his missionary activities to Monrovia, Liberia. Encouraged by the Liberian president, he himself in 1884 installed
the first missionaries in the Liberian capital. The Liberian
mission came to an abrupt end and the missionaries left Monrovia to start a new mission in Bonthe on Sherbro Island,
where Father Blanchet had already negotiated the purchase of
a plot of land and house. He had visited Bonthe way back in
1866. In November 1884 Father Blanchet laid the foundation
stone of the Catholic Cathedral in Freetown; the solemn blessing took place in October 1887. He himself supervised the
building operations. This church still serves as the Metro-
politan Catholic Cathedral of Sierra Leone. In 1890 the first
Catholic Mission in Conakry (Guinea) was founded from Freetown; that of Boffa had been founded in 1877 in the absence of
Father Blanchet. He retired from Sierra Leone in 1892 and
died on July 30, 1896, at Thies near Dakar (Senegal).

BLOOD, H. R. R. Colonial Secretary and acting governor of
    Sierra Leone, 1939, while Governor Jardine was on leave in
    England. As acting governor, Blood had to contend with the
    problem created for the administration by I. T. A. Wallace-
    Johnson and his Youth League. Blood, as colonial secretary,
    had previously proposed that "the way to neutralize Wallace-
    Johnson's effect was to appoint him to the Legislative Council
    and not to try to repress him by severe measures." Faced
    with disturbances and labor unrest, engendered for the most
    part by the Youth League, Blood rashly resorted to the very
    measures he had earlier wisely warned against, and requested
    the secretary of state's approval of legislation to enable the
    Sierra Leone government to deport Wallace-Johnson. While
    not acceding to Blood's request, the Colonial Office did make
    possible the introduction of legislation in Sierra Leone which
    effectively curtailed fundamental human freedoms and in the
    long run destroyed the Youth League.

BLYDEN, EDWARD WILMOT, 1832-1912. Scholar, diplomat,

author, statesman and educator, Blyden was born on August 3, 1832, at St. Thomas, Virgin Islands. Between 1842 and 1844 Blyden's family lived in Porto Bello, Venezuela. In May 1850 he went to the United States in an unsuccessful attempt to enter into a theological seminary. In December 1850 he emigrated to Liberia where he arrived in 1851 and for the next five decades served the young republic in various capacities. After studying at Alexander High School, Monrovia, he became editor of Liberian Herald (1855/6); a Presbyterian minister and principal of Alexander High School (1858); professor of classics at Liberia College (1862-1871); Liberian secretary of state (1864-66), combining politics with education; Liberian ambassador to the Court of St. James (i. e., Great Britain), 1877-1878 (and in 1905 Liberian minister plenipotentiary and envoy extraordinary to London and Paris), president of Liberia College (1880-1884), and minister of the interior (1880-1882).

In 1885, after an unsuccessful attempt at the Liberian presidency, Blyden made Sierra Leone his base, paying occasional visits to Liberia where he continued to play an important role in national affairs. He resigned from the Presbyterian church in September 1886 to become "minister of truth" and in 1887 he published his magnum opus, Christianity, Islam and the Negro Race. He traveled widely, paid eight visits to the United States and two to Lagos as well as visits to the Middle East. In Sierra Leone, where between 1872 and 1873 he served as government agent to the interior, he led diplomatic missions to Falaba in 1872 and to Timbo in 1873. From 1901 until 1906 he was appointed director of Mohammedan Education in Sierra Leone. Through the pages of the newspaper The Negro, founded in Freetown in 1872, which he edited, Blyden expressed his views on Islam and propounded his "doctrine of the interior." Blyden's views on these topics were controversial. He suggested that Christian missionary teaching, in contrast to Islam, tended to undermine rather than foster the African's self-reliance and originality. At other times he implied, if somewhat inconsistently, that Islam could, if purified, be used as a foundation for Christianity. Maintaining that Christian and European influence had already destroyed the Africans along the Coast he sought solace in the interior and subscribed to the view that "The Negro plays his real part/ Within Nigretia's virgin heart."

Blyden was one of the earliest advocates of a West African University where "African teachers from both hemispheres including Muslims from the interior would teach students not to copy European models but develop their own originality." And yet he supported the extension of British influence into the interior, in preference at any rate to French encroachment and suggested in the process (one of the first to do so) the construction of a railway to Falaba. In 1906 Blyden withdrew from active public life and lived "in retirement" until his death on February 7, 1912.

BLYDEN, EDWARD WILMOT, III. Educator, politician, and diplo-

mat.   Grandson of E. W. Blyden (see entry immediately
above).   Blyden was educated at the Wesleyan Boys High
School, Fourah Bay College (University of Durham), Freetown,
and Lincoln University and Harvard University, USA.   Head of
the Extra-Mural Department, Fourah Bay College (University
of Durham), 1953-1955.   In 1957 Blyden formed SLIM and became the movement's first leader.   After teaching at the University of Nigeria, Nsukka, in the early 1960s he was appointed
director of the Institute of African Studies at Fourah Bay College (1967-1971).   In 1971 he was appointed Sierra Leone's ambassador to the Soviet Union and in 1974 Sierra Leone's permanent representative at the U.N.

BOKARI BAMP.   Regent chief of Port Loko at the time of the Hut
Tax War (the Alikali of Port Loko was at the time paralyzed
and unable to perform his functions effectively).   On February
5, 1898, Captain Sharpe arrived at Port Loko in an attempt to
collect the hut tax from some 50 or 60 traders, mostly Creoles, who lived in Port Loko in houses rented from their local
landlords.   The traders told Sharpe that they had been warned
by their landlords against paying the tax.   They insisted that
the tax should be paid by their landlords and deducted from the
rents, pointing out that if they paid the tax, they could legally
claim ownership of the huts or houses.   Unimpressed by legal
technicalities, Sharpe explained the differences between rents
and taxes and sent for Bokari Bamp the regent chief.   Bokari
Bamp pointed out to Sharpe that he could not interfere in a
matter between landlords and tenants, and that tax collection
was beyond his province and authority.   He also told Sharpe
that he could do nothing without reference to Bai Forki his
suzerain.
    Sharpe immediately arrested and detained the traders
who refused to pay and once more tried to persuade Bokari
Bamp and his colleagues to submit.   Reluctantly the chiefs
agreed not to prevent the traders from paying and undertook not
to molest them in anyway.   But the traders, far from assured,
still refused to pay.   Thereupon Sharpe ordered the frontier
police to seize their shops, only to find that the goods had been
carefully removed.   Sharpe then imposed fines on 38 traders
for tax evasion and for contempt.   Still unable to convince the
chiefs, Sharpe arrested Bokari Bamp and four others, sen-
tencing them to prison terms varying from three to 15 months
at hard labor, and sent them to jail in Freetown.   The traders
then agreed to pay the tax and Sharpe remitted or reduced most
of the fines.

BOKARI BOMBOLI see KOMPA, BAI

BOKARI GOMNA (Governor).   An influential and powerful chief in
the hinterland, Bokari was of Mende and Vai ancestry.   He
laid claims to the chieftaincy of Gendama, whose ruler Jaia he
had been suspected of murdering.   In 1885, persuaded by
Governor Rowe and bribed by S. B. A. Macfoy, Bokari Gomna

agreed to keep open trade routes and not to molest chiefs and
their subjects under special protection of the governor of Sierra
Leone. He also agreed to maintain peace in the area. Bokari
Gomna's enemies, still distrustful of him, organized a <u>poro</u> to
destroy him. In 1887 Governor Hay, alarmed by reports of
imminent war in the Gallinas country, traveled to the area to
prevent the outbreak of hostilities. The chiefs agreed to destroy their stockades as an indication of their willingness to
keep the peace; the governor proposed to restore the Gallinas
kingship to a scion of the Massaquoi house of Gendama. Bokari
Gomna gave up his claims to Gendama. But his enemies, bent
on destroying him, rebuilt their stockades and sought allies in
Liberia. Bockari Gomna and his own allies once more decided
to blockade Sulima and Mano-Salijah, thereby contravening the
provisions of the 1885 agreements. Rowe called him to Freetown and to pacify the area passed an ordinance in 1888 deporting him to the Gambia. In 1891 Bokari was allowed to return to Sierra Leone. By then he had been certified as insane
and sent to Kissy where he died.

BOLOFARE, KING. A Mane king who ruled in the Port Loko area
in the 1650s. When Capuchins visited the area in 1654 they
found Afro-Portuguese in the township of Port Loko obedient
and suppliant to the Mane King Bolofare, who treated them
somewhat harshly and imposed arbitrary levies on their goods.
By the turn of the century and certainly by the 1720s this relationship between African rulers and Afro-Portuguese was reversed, with the African rulers finding themselves more often
than not at the mercy of the Afro-Portuguese. The Capuchins
succeeded in converting King Bolofare to Christianity. Thereafter Bolofare seems to have behaved more in conformity with
Christian precepts and to have refrained from arbitrary and
capricious actions.

BONGO, Chief of Mafwe. Chief of Mafwe in Lugbu at the time of
the hut tax. On January 3, 1898, Captain Carr, the district
commissioner in Bandajuma, assembled the chiefs to explain
the tax proposals. Carr gave the chiefs a week's grace at the
end of which the chiefs complained that five shillings per hut
was excessive and beyond their resources. The district commissioner promptly arrested and detained a number of chiefs
including Chief Bongo at Bandajuma until Bongo paid £5 for his
own town. He also agreed to persuade the other chiefs to comply with the district commissioner's tax demands. He was then
released and allowed to return to Mafwe. There after recount-
ing his deprivations in detention, he got the chiefs, albeit reluctantly, to pay the tax.

BOSTON, Sir H. J. LIGHTFOOT, 1898-1969. First Sierra Leonean
governor-general (1962-1969). Born in 1898; educated at Cathedral Boy's School, CMS Grammar School and Fourah Bay
College (University of Durham), Freetown. Entered Sierra
Leone government service in 1920 and worked at the Secre-

tariat and at the Treasury. In 1922 he proceeded to Britain
to study law and entered London University and Lincoln's Inn.
In 1925 he received an LL. B. and in 1926 was awarded the
Barstow Scholarship. On his return home he went into private
practice. In 1946 he was appointed police magistrate; in 1954
registrar general; in 1955 senior police magistrate and between
1945 and 1957 acted on several occasions as a judge. In October 1957 he was elected speaker of the House of Representatives, a post he held until 1962 when he was appointed governor-general. Relieved of his duties by the NRC in 1967 he
died two years later in Britain and was buried in Freetown.

BOWEN, the Rt. Rev. JOHN. Bishop of Sierra Leone 1857-1859.
Worked in Canada as a farmer and traveled for the CMS in the
Middle East before succeeding Weeks as bishop of Sierra Leone
in 1857. A linguist with an appreciable knowledge of Arabic,
Bowen was ahead of his times in his tolerance of and sympathy
for Islam. Bishop Bowen performed his episcopal functions
with great zeal and fervor. His first ordination ceremony was
made more memorable by the presence of David Livingstone,
who was traveling through Freetown in 1858. Bowen apparently had reservations about his clergy. He is credited with the
aphorism that it was the clergy not the climate that killed
bishops of Sierra Leone. (The first three, Vidal, Weeks and
Bowen died within seven years.) The Bishop Bowen Memorial
Fund was created to honor his memory and it yielded some
£50 annually. During his term of office as bishop of Sierra
Leone the piece of land now housing the Annie Walsh Memorial
School was bought in 1858 for £200 and the plan of the old
building with projecting wings and a veranda between was drawn
up by the bishop himself. Bowen contributed much to the development of the female institution (later the Annie Walsh Memorial School) but his attitude towards the "Fourah Bay Institution" was less imaginative. He felt the academic curriculum
of the Institution unsuitable for training village clergy, and reduced the number of students. The Institution was actually
closed until 1864 when it was reopened under the name "Fourah
Bay College," now generally used. Bowen died in 1859 a victim of yellow fever epidemic which claimed the lives of 106
Europeans, including the Roman Catholic bishop and five of his
missionary companions.

BOYLE, SYBLE. An Aku recaptive who combined the name of the
ship that recaptured him from slavery, the HMS Sybille, with
the name of his first master, the colonial surgeon Dr. Boyle,
to become Mr. Syble Boyle. He went into business and by the
1850s had become quite successful. In 1865 he was the leading exhibitor at the first International Exhibition held in Freetown. He was one of the sponsors of the newspaper The Negro
and, though a Methodist, a staunch supporter of the Native
Pastorate Grant. Boyle built himself a fashionable house at
Trelawney (now Lamina Sankoh) Street where he entertained
senior civil servants and leading businessmen, European and

African, on a grand scale. In 1870 he was appointed temporary member of the Legislative Council and in 1872 was given
a permanent seat on the Council until 1887 when he was replaced because of ill health.

BRESILLAC, Mgr. MELCHIOR DE MARION, 1813-1859. First
Catholic bishop of Sierra Leone and founder of the "Society of
African Missions" (SMA). Monsignor Bresillac had served as
a missionary in India (1842-1854) where he became a bishop;
he then volunteered to serve as a simple missionary in Africa.
Rome authorized him to found a "Society of Priests for the
Evangelization of Africa." Thus was born the Society of African Missions (SMA) on December 8, 1856, in Lyons, France.
The "Vicariate Apostolic of Sierra Leone" was set up on April
13, 1856, and Bresillac was named its bishop in June. At the
time Sierra Leone was part of the vast "Mission of Two
Guineas," entrusted to the congregation of the Holy Ghost
(CSSp), with headquarters in Dakar and with ill-defined limits
to the south along the coast beyond Gabon, and no limit inland
to the west. In November 1858 two priests and a lay helper
of the SMA set sail from Marseilles, bound for Freetown. They
arrived on January 12, 1859. The Spanish consul put his house
at their disposal. At their first Sunday service there were
thirty Catholics, mostly Europeans. They then visited the
governor, who promised them the "same protection as he gave
to other religious bodies."
    In March 1859 Monsignor Bresillac set out from Brest
with a priest companion and a lay brother. After a stop-over
at Dakar they arrived in Freetown on Saturday, May 14. The
city was paralyzed by an epidemic of yellow fever, the worst
in more than 25 years. The captain of the ship expressed mis-
givings about letting the Bishop and his companions go ashore
but the Biship insisted on being put on land to "share the misfortune of his children." The small band of SMA missionaries
started planning excursions into the interior of the country. On
June 2, 1859, the epidemic claimed its first SMA victim, then
another on the 5th and a third on the 13th. The Bishop himself succumbed on June 25, 1859, and was buried the next
morning as the last surviving member of the mission also lay
dying.

BREWA, LUSENI ALFRED MORLU, 1924-   . Lawyer and politician. Minister of foreign affairs 1968-1969. Born at Taiama
Kori Chiefdom, Moyamba District, on April 21, 1924. Educated at Bo Government School and at the Prince of Wales
School, Freetown; Northwestern University and University of
Chicago, in the USA, King's College (University of London) and
Lincoln's Inn. Called to the Bar in 1959, he returned home in
1960 and set up private practice. Elected unopposed member
of parliament for Moyamba North Constituency in 1962 as an
independent; re-elected for same constituency in March 1967
again as an independent. Appointed minister of external affairs, April 1968; minister of health, April 1969; attorney

general, April 1971. Retained his parliamentary seat unopposed in 1973; reappointed attorney general, and in 1974 minister of works.

BRIDGE, the Rev. JABEZ. Chairman and general superintendent of the Methodist Mission in Sierra Leone (1892-1895). He suggested the need for periodic official visits to the district by one of the secretaries of the Methodist Missionary Society in London. No such visit was paid during his chairmanship but his efforts led to the visit in 1901 of the Rev. W. H. Findlay, general secretary from the Methodist Mission House in London.

BRONSNAHAN, the Rt. Rev. THOMAS JOSEPH, C. S. Sp., 1905- Catholic bishop of Freetown and Bo, and archbishop of the Catholic Archdiocese of Sierra Leone. Born in Ireland in 1905; ordained a priest in 1929; missionary to Eastern Nigeria 1930-1952; vicar-general, Onitsha, 1950-1952. Appointed bishop of the Diocese of Freetown and Bo, 1952; consecrated bishop of Freetown and Bo in 1953, and consecrated first Roman Catholic archbishop of Sierra Leone 1971. Archbishop Bronsnahan's term of office is one of the most progressive and successful in the annals of the Catholic mission in Sierra Leone. Two buildings in particular, Spiritus House and Santanno House at Howe Street, are a monument to his foresight and exertions.

BULLEN, Capt. CHARLES. Commander of the HMS Wasp which, cruising along the coast, called at Freetown harbor in 1801. Captain Bullen took part in the attack on King Tom I, burned the King's towns and destroyed the King's territories between Freetown and the Cape. Later Bullen tried to mediate between the Temne chiefs and the Freetown government. When he sailed away on April 1, 1802, Bullen believed prematurely that he had succeeded in "making peace between the Colony and the Natives." The Temne renewed their attack on the Colony on April 11, 1802.

BULLOM (Bulom, or Sherbro). The Bullom are among the earliest inhabitants of Sierra Leone. Valentin Fernandes, writing in 1507, made the point that Sierra Leone was inhabited by Bullom and Temne, the former essentially a coastal people. It has been observed that in the southern sections of the Upper Guinea Coast "the single dominant element along the Coast were the Bulloms extending roughly between Cape Verga [Verde] and Cape Mount." By the end of the 16th century, the Temne, originally an inland people, had pushed their way towards the Coast and in the process had "cut the Bullom tribe into two parts." The northern branch today occupying parts of Kambia and Port Loko districts while retaining the name Bullom "was subsequently whittled down by Temne and Baga" and are now indistinguishable from the Temne and Susu with whom they are assimilated. The southern and larger branch are known today as Sherbro, a name which according to the Dutch surgeon Ol-

phert Dapper was derived from Selbore or Sherabola, a Mane
viceroy who imposed his rule on the naturales of Sierra Leone.
     The Sherbro now occupy most of the coastal area of
Sierra Leone between the Sierra Leone Peninsula and the estuary of the Bum River.   Sherbro chiefdoms extend inland for
about 20 to 30 miles and occupy parts of Bonthe, Bo and Moyamba districts.   The Sherbro have to a large extent been absorbed by the Mende, whose language and cultural traits they
have mostly adopted.   They appear to have no tradition of immigration into Sierra Leone and insist that they inhabited their
present homeland from time immemorial.   It has been suggested that they may have arrived in Sierra Leone by sea.
Largely a fishing folk, the Sherbro, though they cultivate rice,
consider cassava their staple.   They produce palm oil and kernels and process piassava for export.   They also manufacture
salt extracted from sea water.   The Sherbro originally seem to
have believed in matrilineal descent.   The kinship system based
on the matriclan or ram traces descent from female members
of the family.   The system has over the years shown signs of
a breakdown, and today the ram has become bilateral and can
and does include paternal and maternal relatives.   In some aspects of inheritance the matrilineal system still enjoys acceptance and the system survives through the transmission of the
Yom, although it is now little more than a family taboo.
     The Poro for men enjoys strong support among the
Sherbro, as does the Bundu for women.   Other societies or
associations include the Tuntu for both sexes with its greatly-
feared medicine the Kontogi; the Thoma for both sexes but from
which members of the Poro or Bundu are excluded; and the
Yassi, a healing association in some ways related to the Poro.
     The Sherbro made the first contacts with Europeans and
some of the leading families, the Tuckers, Caulkers, and
others, have European ancestors.   They enjoy a relatively high
percentage of literacy and when not animist are predominantly
Christian.

BUM KITTAM EXPEDITION   see   MILITARY EXPEDITIONS (7)

BUREH, Bai (or Kebalai or Kabba Lahai).   Warrior and traditional
     ruler.   Of Loko descent, Bai Bureh was born ca. 1840 (being
     considered about 50 or 60 in 1898) in the little village of
     Rokthenti on the Mabole River, a tributary of the Little Scar-
     cies, some 13 miles northwest of the present Makeni Town.
     Kebalai or Kabba Lahai had by means of military prowess and
     great organizing ability acquired chieftaincy in Kasse (Little
     Scarcies) and had assumed the title of Bai Bureh.   Since 1871
     Kasse had received a stipend from the British.   Bai Bureh
     honored his obligations as a stipendiary chief and on occasion
     referred disputes with his neighbors to the governor in Free-
     town for arbitration and mediation.   As Kabba Lahai or Ke-
     balai he had taken part in the wars between the Temne and
     Susu on the Scarcies in 1859.   In 1874-75 he was involved in
     war against the Susu and in 1889-1892 he opposed Karimu and

his Mureteis.   In 1892 he served with distinction with the
British expedition against Tambi.

The British had made one or two attempts to arrest
Bai Bureh for what they considered insubordination and each
time he had escaped. After one such attempt in 1894, Bai
Bureh, though still enjoying his stipend, kept aloof, and after
the Protectorate was declared in 1896 treated the district commissioner of Karene with reserve if not contempt. Once the
Protectorate was declared Governor Cardew decided to impose
what became known as the hut tax on huts or houses in the
Protectorate to help defray administrative expenses. Captain
Wilfred Stanley Sharpe, district commissioner of Karene, carrying out orders to collect the tax in his district, sent a letter
to Bai Bureh calling on him to collect the hut tax in his chiefdom beginning immediately. Bai Bureh's warriors prevented
the frontier lance corporal who took the letter from seeing Bai
Bureh, declaring that they had orders not to allow any government emissary to go through. The letter was therefore returned unopened. Sharpe's later contention (denied by the
lance-corporal) was that the lance-corporal had met Bai Bureh,
who refused to accept the letter and had sent him back with in-
sults and threats. Sharpe decided once more to arrest Bai
Bureh. Bai Bureh in his turn decided to resist the tax. From
February until his capture or surrender on November 16, 1898,
Bai Bureh was at war with the British. Between February and
March 1898 attempts to capture him or to force him to comply
with the tax proposals cost the British heavy casualties, eight
officers and several men killed and wounded.

Lt.-Col. Marshal, who took command at Port Loko on
April 1, 1898, described the operations against Bai Bureh as
involving "some of the most stubborn fighting that has been
seen in West Africa," pointing out that "no such continuity of
opposition had at any previous time been experienced on this
part of the coast." Bai Bureh made effective use of stockades
built of palm logs embedded in the ground buttressed with
laterite boulders and tied with creepers. The defenders lay
protected in trenches behind the stockades and fired through
loopholes. Large numbers of stockades were built close to
the road, on either side, invisible from the road, enabling the
defenders to fire at will and at times in concert. Marshall's
columns succeeded in destroying most of the stockades. They
also burned towns and villages, destroyed rice fields and crops,
and terrorized the inhabitants of the area. In all, by the end
of May 1898 Marshall's troops had destroyed some 97 towns
and villages, depriving Bai Bureh of reinforcements and food
supply. Still Bai Bureh evaded capture. Cardew offered £100
reward for his capture. Bai Bureh reciprocated in more generous terms by offering, it is said, a £500 reward for the
governor's head. In October three companies of the West
African Regiment (newly created by Col. E. R. P. Woodgate,
sent out by the British War Office to take charge of operations), commanded by Col. George Glengairn Cunningham, relieved the garrison at Karene. Bai Bureh finally surrendered

on November 16, 1898. The official version described his being pursued and captured by Sgt. B. Thomas; the unofficial
version described him as emerging from the bush with raised
hands shouting to the soldiers not to fire and declaring that the
war is over.

He was taken to Karene where he made attempts to escape or possibly attempts were made to rescue him. So in
February 1898 he was transferred to Freetown. Sharpe and
Cardew proposed that he should be tried for treason. The
Crown law officers pointed out that treason could be committed
only within Her Majesty's dominions or by Her Majesty's subjects within or without her dominions. The Protectorate they
maintained was, under the Foreign Jurisdiction Act, "foreign";
and therefore Bai Bureh could not be so charged. In the circumstances, Bai Bureh was detained by ordinance while Sir
David Chalmer's report was being studied by the secretary of
state, Chamberlain. Chamberlain recommended his release
but Acting-Governor Nathan urged not to risk future peace by
setting him free. Finally on July 30, 1899, Bai Bureh and
two other chiefs, Nyagua and Be Sherbro, were deported to
the then Gold Coast. He was allowed to return home in 1905
and to resume his chieftaincy until his death in about 1908.

BURTON, Sir R. F. Appointed British consul at Fernando Po in
the early 1860s. On his way to his new station Burton spent
three days in Freetown in September 1861. Author of Wander-
ings in West Africa from Liverpool to Fernando Po, (London,
1863, 2 vols.). In chapter five of the book, "Three days at
Sierra Leone," the author's disdain for the Colony was ex-
hibited in the use of the most uncharitable epithets about its
inhabitants and institutions. In a similar vein he gave evidence before the Select Committee of the House of Commons
on West Africa (1865) and used unrestrained language in his
denunciation of Sierra Leone and its inhabitants whom he characterized as failures--shiftless, troublesome and dishonest.
About the same time he addressed a meeting of the Anthropological Society in London at which he expressed wild senti-
ments against the Christian missionaries in West Africa and
asserted that Islam was the best and only answer to their
well-meaning blunders. Because of his experience and fame
as an explorer Burton's views on Africa and on Sierra Leone
in particular carried considerable weight at the British Colonial and Foreign offices in London.

BUXTON, Sir THOMAS FOWELL. One of the great English cham-
pions of abolition of the slave trade. Buxton believed that the
slave trade could best be supplanted by legitimate trade. He
therefore strongly supported British acquisition of land for
plantations and trading posts in West Africa, not in the interests of empire building but as grounds for training the African to engage in more peaceful and productive pursuits. In
1839 he published his The Slave Trade and Its Remedy. He
also founded the Society for the Civilisation of Africa, branches

of which were formed in Sierra Leone. Buxton Church on
Charles Street, Freetown, erected and opened in 1854, was
named after T. F. Buxton. Grateful recaptives also contributed
to Buxton's bust which was placed in St. George's Cathedral,
Freetown.

- C -

CABENDA. Village founded in 1811 by Acting Governor Lt. R.
Bones as a new home for 42 recaptives from Cabenda (Cabinda)
at the estuary of the Congo. The recaptives were resettled on
Devil's Hill or Signal Hill where a deserted Temne town was
revived and called Cabenda or New Cabenda. In 1816 Governor
Sir Charles MacCarthy renamed the village, Wilberforce.

CADAMOSTO, ALVISE DE. An Italian from Venice; one of the explorers at Prince Henry the Navigator's Court at Sagres, who
put their skill and knowledge of seafaring at the disposal of the
Portuguese rulers in the 15th century. Under Henry's patronage Cadamosto made a number of voyages to West Africa and
in 1456, sailed as far as the River Cassamance. In 1507 he
published his recollections of the West Coast of Africa in which
he made mention of Pedro da Sintra's visit to Sierra Leone in
1462, and gave reasons for the names Pedro gave to various
places on the Coast. The modern name Sierra Leone is a mix-
ture of Portuguese and Italian, a combination largely ascribable
to Cadamosto's influence.

CAMPBELL, Maj. HENRY DUNDAS. The governor of Sierra
Leone, 1835 to 1837, Major Campbell had served in the army
1814 to 1825 and after ten years' retirement, arrived in Freetown on February 13, 1835, to administer the government of
Sierra Leone as lieutenant-governor. He concentrated on improving the Liberated African Department which he considered
disorganized and inefficiently run. He also devoted much of
his time to improving the physical layout of Freetown--three
streets, Henry, Dundas and Campbell (all named after him)
were constructed in Grassfields, west of Freetown, and five
streets were laid out in Kru Town--and to ensuring a decent
standard of comportment and appearance of its inhabitants: appearing naked in public was declared an offense. It was during
Campbell's term of office that Fort Thornton in 1836 became
the official residence of the governor.
    He raised the efficiency of the Freetown constabulary,
now called police, by increasing its numbers from about 26 to
60 and by appointing a town inspector and three sub-inspectors,
all under the supervision of a head constable, appointed since
1827. Like his predecessor Findlay, Campbell in his upcountry
policy formulated what has been described as the "most comprehensive of early treaties to end civil war among the Susu
and Temne, to lay down rules for reciprocal surrender of offenders, criminals and domestic slaves and to provide by in-

creased customs a source of revenue to meet the cost of annual stipends. " These treaties, though approved by the Colonial Office, were not implemented until clauses dealing with
fugitives were revised.   The chiefs of the Scarcies meeting at
Magbele conferred on Campbell the Order of the Palm and Al-
ligator with the title of Abbas, "supposed by them, " he reported, "to be the highest rank a mortal can attain. "   At this
point the Colonial Office decided to recall the Abbas and on
June 13, 1837, Campbell returned to England.

CAMPBELL, Gen. Sir NEIL.   Governor of Sierra Leone (1826-
    1827).   Born in 1776, Campbell enlisted in the army in 1797
    as an ensign and became a major-general in 1825.   He arrived
    in Sierra Leone towards the end of 1826 to assume the reins
    of government.   Determined to reduce government expenditure
    to the minimum he continued Turner's austerity measures,
    turning his attention first to the problem of liberated Africans.
    His new scheme, known as the "Plan of January 1st, " substi-
    tuted cash payment for food and supplies hitherto given to re-
    captives on arrival.   The sum of three pence per day paid
    weekly in advance, for a maximum of six months, replaced the
    system of issuing rations of food and supplies.   Thereafter the
    recaptives were expected to make their own arrangements and
    provide for themselves.
        This policy increased circulation of money, gave added
    impetus to agricultural production and stimulated the economy.
    More important still it forced the recaptives to be independent.
    Unmarried women were taken care of for a maximum of three
    months.   If still unmarried at the end of that period, they
    were transferred to another village where bachelors might be
    in the majority.   Children were adopted by the old settlers un-
    til the age of 15.   Thereafter they would be released from the
    care of foster parents and given land to cultivate on their own.
    The rural communities of the liberated Africans were formed
    into districts with names descriptive of the area, as follows:
    (1) the Eastern or River districts consisted of Kissy, Welling-
    ton, Hastings, Waterloo, Calmont and Allen Town; (2) the
    Central or Mountain districts consisted of Wilberforce, Leices-
    ter, Gloucester, Regent, Bathurst, Charlotte, and Grassfield;
    and (3) the Western or Sea districts consisted of York, Kent
    and the Banana Islands.
        Campbell had his headquarters at Kissy, but effected
    improvements in Freetown, draining streets with gutters and
    laying out a new cemetery at Circular Road.   The governor
    also manifested an interest in the neighboring territories.   He
    revived trade with the Gallinas and made friends with Chiefs
    Harry and James Tucker and King Siaka.   He sent troops to
    Sherbro Island, visited Port Loko, ratified Turner's treaty,
    installed Fatima Brima as Alikali and prepared grounds in the
    town for the erection of a house for the governor.   Haunted by
    the guilt of Napoleon's escape from Elba (to which exile Camp-
    bell had been one of the official escorts), distrustful and sus-
    picious of his subordinates, his policies disapproved by Lon-

don, insecure and fidgety, Campbell succumbed to an attack of
fever and died at Government House, Freetown, on August 14,
1827.

CARDEW, Sir FREDERICK, 1839-1921. Governor of Sierra Leone
(1894-1900). Born in 1839 Cardew joined the Army in 1858.
He retired from the army in 1890 and was appointed resident
commissioner of Zululand in the same year, a post he held until 1894. Colonel Cardew arrived in Freetown on March 14,
1894, to succeed Fleming as governor of Sierra Leone in a
temporary capacity. In May 1894 he was awarded the CMG
and on December 3 of the same year he was appointed governor
and commander-in-chief of Sierra Leone. In June 1897 he was
knighted.

Early in the 19th century and thereafter from time to
time some of Cardew's predecessors as governors of Sierra
Leone had for a variety of reasons made attempts to extend
the territorial boundaries of the Sierra Leone Colony into the
vast adjoining hinterland. These efforts had rarely been officially approved by the Home Government in Britain. But
from the 1880s onwards and particularly during the governorship of Rowe and Hay, a more vigorous policy of expansion
was pursued and sanctioned by the Colonial Office. By the
1890s, when Cardew became governor, France and Britain had
demarcated, if somewhat imprecisely, what they called their
respective "spheres of influence" in the areas now occupied by
the republics of Sierra Leone and Guinea. This meant that
each power was willing, if not always readily able, to recognize
the other's "rights" within the areas so prescribed.

Cardew was entrusted with the responsibility of declaring
a protectorate over the British sphere of influence. At 55 his
robust health and vigorous energy were still unimpaired; he
neither drank nor smoked. An able administrator and hard-
working governor, his six years in Sierra Leone (1894-1900)
saw him on three extensive tours of the hinterland. His first
tour after barely two weeks in office took him from Freetown
on March 27, 1894, across Mende country to Panguma and
thence to Waiima in Kono country where he made provision for
the proper maintenance of the graves of Captain Lendy and other
illustrious victims of the Waiima tragedy of 1893. From Waiima, Cardew traveled to Falaba and returned to Freetown by way
of the Scarcies on May 17, 1894, spending slightly over six
weeks and covering some 600 to 700 miles. He set out from
Freetown on his second tour on January 30, 1895, and traveled
through Songo, Rotifunk, Bo, Segbwema and Kailahun. From
Kailahun he traveled through Kono, Koranko, Limba, Loko and
Temne countries and returned to Freetown by way of Kambia
and the Great Scarcies on April 5, 1895, covering in all some
600 miles.

The Governor's third tour of the hinterland was begun
on January 28, 1896. He traveled from Freetown by way of
the Rokel River through Kunike country to Tembi-Kunda, around
the source of the Niger. Thence he traveled southwards along

the Anglo-Liberian frontier to Kailahun. He traveled through
Luawa and Bombali to Taiama, Bandajuma and Mafwe and by
way of Bonthe to Freetown on April 5. On this third tour he
traveled some 675 miles. In all Cardew covered some 2000
miles and spent some 180 days from his headquarters in Freetown during the three tours of the hinterland.

During these tours Cardew had signed a few treaties
with chiefs and had tried to explain his policies and plans to
them. These policies and plans included the declaration of a
protectorate, taxation and the construction of a railway. The
railway, after preliminary surveys had been completed in 1895,
was started in January 1896. It was planned that the railway
would run through Mende country with branch lines radiating
eventually over the hinterland. It had a narrow 2' 6" gauge
and the first phase from Cline Town to Songo was estimated to
cost £150,000.

Cardew's plans for a protectorate were to a large extent incomprehensible to the majority, if not to all, of the
chiefs he met. Some chiefs had signed treaties of peace and
friendship with the British. Others had allegedly been signatories to treaties of cession of territory. Quite a few were,
as stipendiary chiefs, in the pay of the British. It was however far from certain what their understanding, if any, of a
protectorate really was, given the rather vague and somewhat
imprecise nature of the term itself at the time.

An Order of the Queen in Council made on August 24,
1895, under the Foreign Jurisdiction Act, 1890, had vested the
Sierra Leone Legislative Council with the same powers to make
laws for the projected Protectorate as it had for the Colony.
A series of ordinances passed by the Legislative Council in
1896 and 1897 established British jurisdiction over and made
provisions for the administration of the Protectorate. Samuel
Lewis in September 1896, speaking in the Legislative Council
on these ordinances, argued that no evidence existed to show
how the Legislative Council had acquired such legislative powers over the Protectorate and maintained that since the Protectorate had not been acquired by conquest, it would be ex-
pedient to state categorically that it had been done through the
consent of the chiefs--an equally difficult proposition in the circumstances.

For administrative purposes the Protectorate was divided
into five districts--Karene, Ronietta, Bandajuma, Panguma
and Koinadugu. A district commissioner responsible for administration and a host of other duties was appointed in each
district. The ordinances also made provision for three courts
of law. The cost of administering the Protectorate and of
policing its frontiers was estimated at about one-fifth of the
total revenue of Sierra Leone. Cardew decided to impose direct taxes in the Protectorate to help defray these costs, at
the rate of ten shillings for houses with four or more rooms
and five shillings on houses with fewer than four rooms. The
new tax was to come into effect on January 1, 1898. Chiefs
were to collect taxes within their chiefdoms and district com-

missioners were to collect taxes from chiefs within their districts.

A number of chiefs protested against the tax, partly because they felt it was too high, but more importantly because they believed that payment of a tax to a foreign power that had not conquered them, meant, in effect divesting themselves of their authority and sovereignty. Nor did the Colonial office share Cardew's enthusiasm for directly imposing a tax in the Protectorate at that juncture. Cardew, though unwilling to countenance the protests of the chiefs or to share the fears of his superiors in London, had towards the end of 1897 come to appreciate more fully some of the problems involved in the new arrangement. He therefore modified his original scheme, exempted the more remote districts of Panguma and Koinadugu, and imposed a flat rate of five shillings per house irrespective of the number of rooms.

The outrages with which the frontier police set about forcibly collecting the tax provoked more protests. There were open and spontaneous revolts over large areas of the hinterland. Casualties were high. Eventually the rising was suppressed by force of arms and the ringleaders punished. Some 96 "rebels" were hanged and three prominent chiefs, Bai Bureh, Be Sherbro, and Nyagua, were sent into exile to the Gold Coast.

A royal commissioner, Sir David Chalmers, was sent out from London to investigate the causes of the rising and to make recommendations. Sir David ascribed the causes of the Hut Tax War, as the rising became known, to the imposition of the hut tax and put the blame on the Governor's impetuosity. He recommended suspension, if not abolition, of the tax and suggested a drastic review of the powers and functions of the district commissioners. The Colonial office however supported Cardew's arguments and rejected the Royal Commissioner's more radical recommendations.

In the Colony itself, Governor Cardew encouraged agriculture by establishing a botanical station, the precursor of the Colonial Agriculture Department and of today's Ministry of Agriculture and Natural Resources. He sponsored annual agricultural shows, patronized by government individuals, which offered prizes for the best crops and best animals. Cardew also introduced, although on a small scale, a scheme of agricultural subsidies. Over the issue of the use of juries, he introduced ordinances which were interpreted by his critics as further encroachment on jury rights, a long-standing grievance in the Colony. In June 1898, an ordinance was passed empowering the attorney-general (the new title for the queen's advocate) to apply for a judge and assessors to try non-capital criminal cases. If a jury was used, however, the judge was authorized to over-rule its majority verdict if, on the weight of the evidence before him, he was satisfied that there had been a gross miscarriage of justice. In August 1898 another ordinance made provisions for the use of assessors even in capital offenses in cases arising in the Protectorate. As early as 1895 Cardew had crossed swords with Samuel Lewis over the Mokassi land

dispute case. Cardew's encounters with Lewis over legal matters in particular and his experiences with other Creoles in
government service led him to adopt a hostile attitude towards
Creoles. He came to the conclusion that no Creole was fit to
be head of a department and he increasingly resorted to the use
of uncharitable epithets in his reference to Creoles. This attitude, it has been suggested, may have adversely affected race
relations in the Colony.

   Cardew's governorship also marked the effective beginnings of the decline of Creole fortunes, particularly in government service. The Governor preferred European to Creole officers, a policy that was continued by his successors. It has
been estimated that in 1892, out of some 40 senior posts in
government service, Creoles held 18, nearly 50 per cent. In
1912, by contrast, out of 92 such posts in a rapidly expanding
service, Creoles held only 15--roughly 16 per cent; five of
these posts were abolished in 1917. This trend continued into
the post-World War II era when the figure was less than 1 per
cent. The process was only reversed by the popular demand
for Africanization in the decade before independence. Cardew
was succeeded in 1900 by Governor King-Harman.

CAREW, the Rt. Rev. BENJAMIN ALBERT, 1906- . First bishop
   of the United Methodist Autonomous Church in Sierra Leone
   (1973) and president of the United Christian Council (UCC)
   (1975). Born May 6, 1906, at Yandu, Kori Chiefdom, Moyamba District. Educated at Taiama United Methodist Church (UMC)
   Central School, at the Albert Academy and at Fourah Bay College, Freetown. Elected general superintendent of the Sierra
   Leone Conference in 1968; prior to becoming its president, between 1968 and 1974 he was vice-president of the United Christian Council (UCC) in Sierra Leone.

CASE, JOHN. English factor at Bunce Island in the 1680s. Case
   regularly complained about competition from other European nations particularly the Dutch and the French for trade in and
   around Bunce Island. In 1687 he reported that "a Dutch Inter-
   loper gott Teeth" (tusks) and in 1688 he wrote to his directors
   in London complaining that on his way to Rio Nunez he "was
   taken by a French man with foure of the Companye's vessells."
   From John Case's reports we know that the export of slaves
   from Sierra Leone had by the 1680s been considerably reduced.
   In 1682 he sent 118 captives to the New World, emphasizing that
   because of the shortage of trade goods even the 118 had been
   acquired with considerable strain.

   In May 1685 Case's Company at Bunce Island incurred
   losses amounting to £300. Case had paid a visit to Sherbro
   and on his return to Bunce was greeted with the customary gun
   salute. Some of the wads set fire to the thatched roofs and
   the blaze spread, causing much damage to Company property.

CASE, SAMUEL H. ATHANASIUS, 1845-1901. Builder, printer
   and journalist. Case was a Colony-born Popo descendant, a

stone-mason who became a clerk, and then reverted to his
original trade to become foreman in the Royal Engineers department at the military barracks. In July 1884 he and a
group of fellow artisans organized the Mechanics' Alliance, a
trade union aimed at improving their status and conditions of
labor. A regular contributor to the West African Reporter,
Case started to print and edit his own paper, The Artisan, in
1884. The Artisan poured scorn on the new-found African
consciousness, manifested in the assumption of African names
and the use of "African dress," which became the vogue in
Creole circles in Freetown in the 1880s. He ridiculed particularly members of a "Dress Reform Society" who adopted
names and forms of dress with which they had virtually no connection or acquaintance. After the dissolution of the Mechanics'
Alliance in 1886 The Artisan continued to appear irregularly
until 1888, when Case also started to print a few numbers of
The Commonwealth. In 1891 he brought out a short-lived weekly, The Trader. He also occasionally published The Artisan
until 1899. He died in 1901.

CAULKER, the Rev. R. E. KELFA, 1909-1975. Clergyman, educationist and diplomat. Born at Mambo, Kagboro Chiefdom,
Moyamba District, on March 14, 1909, and educated at the Albert Academy, Freetown, and at Otterbein College, at Oberlin
College Graduate School, and Teachers College, Columbia, in
the USA. Principal of Albert Academy 1939-1961. Sierra
Leone's first ambassador to the United States (1961-1963) and
permanent representative at the United Nations (1963-1964).
High commissioner for Sierra Leone at the Court of St. James
(i.e., Great Britain) (1964-1966) and ambassador to the Republic of Liberia (1969-1973). He died in Freetown in 1975.

CAULKER, the Rev. S. B., 1911-1960. Vice principal, dean of
the Faculty of Arts, warden of men students, senior lecturer
and head, Department of Philosophy at Fourah Bay College
(University of Durham) (1946-1960). Born at Mambo, Kagboro Chiefdom, in 1911. Educated at the Albert Academy,
Freetown, and at Otterbein College and the University of Chicago, USA. Appointed to Fourah Bay College in 1946 as a lecturer in philosophy. Died in an air crash at Dakar (Senegal) in
1960.

CAULKER MANUSCRIPT. A family history of the Caulkers and
the wars between two branches of the family. One branch,
headed by Thomas Stephen Caulker of the Plaintain Islands,
fought against another branch headed by Canreba Caulker of
Bompe. The Caulker Manuscript was written in the early
years of the 20th century by G. M. Domingo whose family had
intermarried with Thomas Stephen Caulker's family and whose
father had been Thomas Stephen Caulker's bugler at the Battle
of Bendy in the 1840s.

CHALMERS, Sir DAVID PATRICK. Royal Commissioner to Sierra

Leone 1898-1899 to investigate the causes of the Hut Tax War.
A Scottish barrister and retired Colonial judge, Chalmers had
served in various offices in West Africa in the years 1867-1878
including Sierra Leone, where he was queen's advocate 1873-4.
In 1878 he was appointed chief justice of British Guiana. While
in retirement he was in 1898-1899 appointed royal commissioner to Sierra Leone to investigate the causes of the 1898 Hut
Tax War and to make recommendations in a general way on how
the country should be administered and financed. Sir David
Chalmers arrived in Sierra Leone as royal commissioner on
July 18, 1898 and was accorded a hero's welcome by the Creoles, who hailed him as a savior from the tyranny of Governor
Cardew. His inquiry lasted for about four months and he took
evidence from over 270 witnesses. His final report dated January 21, 1899, filled 82 folio pages; the appendix containing evidence collected ran into 682 pages.

The Commissioner ascribed the causes of rising to the
imposition of the hut tax. He pointed out that the tax was re-
pugnant to the customs and feelings of the people and that the
methods of collection were harsh and unfamiliar. The diminu-
tion of the authority and power of chiefs, the Governor's arbitrary installation as chiefs persons who according to native law
and custom had no claim or right to the office, the threatened
compulsory appropriation of lands in the Protectorate as contained in the clauses of the first Protectorate Ordinance (although repealed)--all these the Commissioner submitted were
additional grievances which led to the revolt.

Sir David recommended a general amnesty and a halt to
all punitive expeditions to disaffected areas and asked for the
immediate repeal of the "Insurgents Detention Ordinance," 1898,
which empowered the governor by a simple order to arrest and
imprison without trial for an indefinite period persons who took
part or were suspected of having taken part in the disturbances.
Chalmers proposed that the judicial functions of the district
commissioners should be reviewed, that police posts or stations in the Protectorate should be abolished, and that the hut
tax itself should be discontinued. He also recommended that
the government should give financial assistance to the missionaries to promote their work in the interior.

Chalmers's report was a damaging denunciation of government policy. His antipathy towards Cardew may have jaundiced his views. His case was overstated and in instances un-
supported by adequate evidence. The report was sent to Governor Cardew for his comments and in a dispatch dated May 1,
1899, he answered the Commissioner point by point, stoutly
defending his policy and drawing conclusions that were dia-
metrically opposed to Sir David's. Chamberlain, at the Colonial Office, in a dispatch of July 7, 1899, while expressing
appreciation of the Royal Commissioner's work, upheld the
Governor's submissions and in effect rejected his own Commissioner's report. This rejection it has been observed may well
have marked a turning point in British policy towards Sierra
Leone and towards Creoles in particular, the beginnings of the

decline of whose fortunes in government service and in business
date back to the closing decade of the 19th century. Sir David
himself, worn out by his exertions, died in August 1899 almost
at the time when the secretary of state had made up his mind
to repudiate his report and reject his recommendations.

CHARLES, WALTER.   Appointed chief agent of the Royal African
   Company in Sierra Leone in 1726.   Faced with increasing competition from mulattoes in Sierra Leone and from Afro-Portuguese elsewhere, Charles embarked on a bold plan of action.
   He declared himself determined to take "effectual care while I
   stay in the country that no white black man shall make any
   figure here, above what the meanest natives do. " He then appealed to the African rulers to put the mulattoes in their proper
   place and to break their stranglehold on trade in Sierra Leone.
   Charles' challenge was taken up by José Lopez de Moura, the
   most powerful of the mulattoes in Sierra Leone and a dominant
   political figure in the country throughout the first half of the
   18th century.   Lopez and his associates, Jerome and Thomas,
   led a band of Africans to attack the company's factory on Bunce
   Island.   Charles was forced to scale the walls in retreat and
   to seek refuge elsewhere.   When he returned a few weeks later
   to collect papers and other company property, he discovered
   that Lopez had signed the company's death warrant by posting a
   notice at the watering place which stated that "the ships of all
   nations, English, French, Dutch, etc. shall have free liberty
   of trade in the river and the utmost safety except those belonging to the Royal African Company of England. " The company
   never fully recovered from this disaster in Sierra Leone.

CHAYTOR, DANIEL EMANUEL BABATUNJI, 1931- .   Dr. Chaytor
   was born April 13, 1931, and was educated at the Methodist
   Boys High School, the Prince of Wales School, Freetown, and
   at the universities of Aberdeen and London.   He is professor
   of zoology and director of the Institute of Marine Biology and
   Oceanography (1971-present), Fourah Bay College (USL).   He
   has also held the following positions: dean, Faculty of Basic
   Sciences (1965-1969), and vice principal (NUC) 1968-1969;
   visiting professor in biology at the Massachusetts Institute of
   Technology (1969-1971); consultant, American Council on Education Mission to Cuttington College, Republic of Liberia, 1968;
   consultant, UNESCO Mission to University of Liberia 1971; educational consultant to Peace Corps Education Training Programs
   in the Gambia (1970-71) and in Sierra Leone (1972-74), where
   he also served as program director; director, Teacher Education Materials Development Project of SEPA (1972 to the present); member, American Association for the Advancement of
   Science; vice president (1964-1965) and president, Sierra Leone
   Science Association (1974 to the present).   Professor Chaytor
   has published several papers on embryology, virology, zoology
   and education.   He is joint author and chairman of the Editorial
   Board of SEPA Handbook for Teachers 1974 and of SEPA
   Sourcebook for Science Teachers (1976).

CHEETHAM, the Rt. Rev. HENRY. Bishop of Sierra Leone 1870-
1881. A parish priest in Derbyshire England before his trans-
lation to the diocese of Sierra Leone as successor to bishop
Beckles. Cheetham put an end to dissension in his diocese by
introducing a number of conciliatory measures. He made provision for a uniform salary scale with marriage and children's
allowances for the clergy; he involved the laity in church work
by appointing them to church committees and issuing licenses
to some "lay helpers" to serve as catechists. To give security
to the poor and to encourage thrift and savings Bishop Cheetham
in 1873 opened a Penny Bank of his own. He also opened a library for lending books and a Cathedral Day School. Through
Bishop Cheetham's initiative, the Parent Committee of the CMS
agreed to admit to Fourah Bay College without denominational
test any student of good character who had fulfilled entry requirements. In 1876 the College was affiliated to the University of Durham, England. In the same year the CMS opened
missions in Bulom and Quiah territories. Cheetham went on
leave to England on June 13, 1881, and retired at the end of
the year.

CHIEF JUSTICES. Charles Studdard 1788; Dr. Robert Thorpe 1811;
Dr. Robert Goold Hogan 1816; Edward Fitzgerald 1817; Daniel
Molly Hamilton 1817; John William Bannister 1827; Sir John
William Jeffcott 1830; Robert Rankin 1833; John Carr 1861;
George French 1867; H. J. Huggins 1877; William Warren
Streeten 1880; Francis F. Pinkett 1882; Sir William H. Quayle-
Jones 1888; E. Bruce Hindle 1896; George Stallard 1898;
Crampton P. Smyly 1901; Arthur Hudson 1903; G. K. J. Pur-
cell 1911-1927; M. L. Tew 1929-1932; A. Webber 1933-1937;
Ambrose Henry Webb 1937-1939; E. Graham-Paul 1940-1945;
John H. Lucie-Smith 1946-1950; A. C. Smith 1951-1955; Paget
J. Bourke 1955-1957; V. R. Bairamain 1957-1960; Salako
Benka-Coker 1960-1963; Samuel Bankole Jones 1963-1966;
Gershon B. O. Collier 1967- ; Banja Tejan Sie 1967-1968;
C. O. E. Cole 1970- .

CHRISTIAN INSTITUTION. In 1814 the Church Missionary Society
acquired a piece of land on the southeast slope of Leicester
Mountain as a site for a Christian Institution. The Institution
opened by the CMS in 1816 was intended to provide opportunities for recaptive children to acquire knowledge of agriculture
and useful trades; the ablest were to be trained as teachers or
missionaries. The Rev. Leopold Butscher was put in charge.
In 1819 the Christian Institution was removed from Leicester
Mountain to Regent Village. Governor Sir Charles MacCarthy
hoped that the Christian Institution at Regent would develop into
a college where settler and recaptive children could pursue
courses of study leading to the learned professions. The high
mortality rate among the European missionaries made it difficult for the CMS to recruit staff for the Institution.
        There was in addition a corresponding shortage of pupils
and, in 1826, with only two on the roll, the Christian Institu-

tion was closed. Determined to revive it, the CMS brought
out a Bavarian missionary the Rev. Charles Haensel to take
charge. The buildings at Regent had deteriorated considerably;
the lowest estimated cost of repairs was put at £1,200. No
suitable site was immediately available. So the Rev. Haensel
reopened the Christian Institution in Freetown where, on April
3, 1827, he admitted his first pupil. At the beginning of 1828
Haensel reported to the CMS Committee that "The late Governor
Turner's estate on Fourah Bay, in the Sierra Leone river is to
be sold in small lots as they may be called for and we have a
tender of that part of it ... which would, with the water on
every other side, form a situation altogether secluded. The
buildings consist of the former dwelling-house, which is a stone
building, with a slated roof considerably out of repair but which
will admit of being fitted up at an expense of somewhat more
than £100, and will then answer the purposes of the Institution
until the number of the pupils shall exceed ten...." The property was acquired in about mid-1828 by the CMS for about
£320. Because of its new location, the Christian Institution
was renamed Fourah Bay Institution or College; its purpose to
train teachers and clergymen for the Anglican Church. (See
also FOURAH BAY COLLEGE.)

CHURCH MISSIONARY SOCIETY [CMS]. An association of evangelical churchmen founded in 1799 in London to send missions
abroad to convert people to Christianity. In 1813 the association formally assumed the name of Church Missionary Society
(CMS). Sierra Leone was one of its first areas of operation
and there, in cooperation with the British Government, the Society sent out missionaries initially to help with liberated Africans, or recaptives. In 1816 the CMS opened the Christian
Institution and in 1827, Fourah Bay College; the CMS Grammar
School followed in 1845 and then the Female Institution, 1849
(renamed in 1877 the Annie Walsh Memorial School). All were
firsts of their kind in black Africa. The Society sponsored a
number of other organizations and institutions and sent missions
not only into the hinterland of Sierra Leone but into the vast
extent of West Africa as well. Although English in origin, the
first missionaries sent out to Sierra Leone under the auspices
of the CMS were German nationals.

CHURCH OF GOD. Founded in Freetown at his house in Rawdon
Street by John McCormack, possibly on June 21, 1853. In doctrine it had close affinity with the Baptists but McCormack's
Church of God was separate from other churches in Freetown
and maintained connections with a congregation in London.
McCormack died in March 1865 but made provision in his will
for the building of a Church of God from the proceeds of the
sale of his property. The Church was built near the spring by
Regent Road and Frederick Street (in the late 1860s). In 1878
a branch of the Church of God was established at Senehun,
Chief Gbanya's town, by John Parker, a Mende recaptive.
Money for the building was contributed by friends of the Church

of God in England. In 1882 the Rev. Thomas Truscott of the
United Free Methodists took over the Church of God Mission at
Senehun.

CINTRA [Sintra], PEDRO DA. Portuguese navigator to whom Sierra Leone owes its name. Pedro da Cintra sailed down the
west coast of Africa, visited the shores of the country in 1462
and mapped a number of important landmarks. It was he who
called the country Serra Lyoa (Lion Mountain) because of its
ragged and wild appearance, it is thought.

CIVIL SERVICE COMMISSION, 1952-53 see SINKER/MOMOH
COMMISSION

CIVILIAN RULE COMMITTEE [CRC]. Formed in February 1968 by
the National Reformation Council (NRC) military regime. The
Committee was invited to deliberate and advise on "(i) the necessity for fresh general elections; (ii) if (i) above is in the
negative, the method of forming a National Government; if (i)
above is in the affirmative, the stages by which the hand-over
(to a civilian regime) should be effected; (iii) any other action
which the Civilian Rule Committee considers necessary to effect a peaceful hand-over." The Committee had barely concluded its deliberations when the NRC was overthrown in a
counter-coup in April, 1968.

CLARKE, HUGH MARSHALL, 1912- . Educator and administrator.
Born September 13, 1912. Educated at the Methodist Boys
High School, Fourah Bay College (University of Durham), Free-
town, and at Birmingham University, England. First principal,
Magburaka Government Boys Secondary School (1950); secretary,
Training and Recruitment (1958); first Sierra Leonean perma-
nent secretary, Ministry of Education (1960). Seconded to
UNICEF, Nigeria (1962); chairman, Commission of Inquiry into
the Civil Services etc. (Hugh Clark Commission) of Sierra
Leone (1970-1971).

CLARKE, ROBERT. Assistant colonial surgeon in Sierra Leone.
Author of Sierra Leone: Description of the Manners and Customs of the Liberated Africans; with observations upon the
Natural History of the Colony (London 1843) and of Sketches of
the Colony of Sierra Leone (1863).

CLARKSON, Lt. JOHN, R.N. Governor of Sierra Leone, March-
December, 1792. Younger brother of Thomas Clarkson, the
English philanthropist. Joined the Royal Navy at an early age
and saw service in the West Indies where his experiences led
him to question the morality of war and forced him into a premature breakaway from the Navy. He supported his brother's
activities for the abolition of the slave trade and manifested
keen interest in Granville Sharp's plans for the rehabilitation
of freed Negro slaves in "a Province of Freedom" in Sierra
Leone. He offered his services to the directors of the Sierra

Leone Company to go to Nova Scotia and transport prospective immigrants to Sierra Leone. Clarkson embarked for Nova Scotia in August 1791, collected some 1200 Nova Scotians, and in 16 ships set sail from Halifax in January 1792, arriving in Sierra Leone early in March that year with 1131 immigrants. The Sierra Leone Company appointed him their first governor and he took the oath of office on March 10. Clarkson's Nova Scotians founded a new settlement at the site of the original Granville Town and renamed the settlement Freetown. In August, the remaining survivors of settlers at the old Granville Town joined the Nova Scotians in Freetown. Regular streets were laid out which Clarkson named after the directors of the Sierra Leone Company. The Company's charter, or instrument of government of the new Colony, had made provision for a council of eight sharing equal powers, only a casting vote being reserved for the governor. "The present consequences," Clarkson pointed out in a dispatch to the directors, "are confusion and disorder.... Eight gentlemen, all invested with great power, each of them acting for himself, and none of them accountable to the other, form to be sure, a system of government as pregnant with contradictions and inconsistencies as can be imagined.... Nothing is done according to my views, and I have no authority to alter what I disapprove...." The directors responded by vesting all civil, military, commercial and political authority in Governor Clarkson and two councilors, a measure which considerably improved government in the colony. Clarkson returned to England at the end of December 1792. The reception from the directors was cordial but not warm. There was a feeling of suspicion and mistrust of Clarkson, who, if he had "saved the colony," had made unauthorized promises to the Nova Scotians which were an embarrassment to the Company. His demands for higher salaries, increased capital outlay, and reticence in reports could not be viewed without uneasiness. Clarkson in turn believed the directors to be unnecessarily frugal and cold-blooded. In April 1793 the Company dispensed with his services. He became a banker, helped to found the Society for the Promotion of Universal Peace, and died in 1828 a somewhat disappointed man.

CLARKSON PLANTATION. A square mile of land on Bulom Shore leased by Governor Clarkson and ceded by Bulom Chiefs to the Sierra Leone Company in 1792. The land, called "Clarkson Plantation," was acquired to cultivate sugarcane, cotton and rice as the soil around Freetown was unsuitable for such agricultural pursuits. James Watt, a former planter in Dominica was put in charge. As Clarkson Plantation showed signs of promise, a second square mile was leased to settle some Nova Scotians. Those who emigrated to Clarkson had first to give up all claims to town and country land in Freetown and had to pay rents at the rate of a bushel of rice per acre. These unattractive conditions provoked protests from hundredors and tythingmen. In the circumstances, new terms and conditions-- an annual rent of two shillings sixpence per acre payable after

two years' occupation--were drawn up but they proved equally
ineffective in attracting more immigrants to Clarkson. The
Plantation was for all practical purposes given up in 1796. In
December 1845 the square mile originally leased by Clarkson
was revived by Governor Fergusson. In 1846 Governor Macdonald sent Peter Wilson, nephew of Be Sherbro, nominal
suzerain of the Bulom Shore, as overseer to Clarkson. But
the Susu at Lungi attacked the Plantation and expelled the Governor's overseer. Macdonald's attempts to regain Clarkson by
dispatching a military expedition to the Bulom Shore were
thwarted by the Colonial Office, which instructed the governor
to give up the Plantation immediately.

CLARKSON'S PRAYER. Offered by Governor John Clarkson at the
time of his departure from Sierra Leone in December 1792, the
Prayer has over the years acquired almost divine attributes.
In a number of houses in Freetown and elsewhere in Sierra
Leone, Clarkson's Prayer is framed and prominently displayed.
It enjoys a veneration second perhaps only to the Bible.

CLINE, EMMANUEL. A Hausa recaptive who assumed the name
Cline after a German missionary. In the early 1830s Cline
went into business as a trader, investing his profits in real
estate. In 1835 he acquired land near Krutown, parceled it into lots and resold them. He continued over the next decade to
acquire more real property in Freetown and was listed in 1853
as one of the 19 biggest owners of land and houses in Freetown.
In 1846 he bought a piece of land in the east end of Freetown
at Fourah Bay and renamed it Cline Town. Cline died in 1858,
bequeathing to the Church Missionary Society land at Cline
Town to build a church.

COBOLO WAR see MILITARY EXPEDITIONS (1)

COCKILL, the Rev. WILLIAM R. Chairman and General Superintendent of the Methodist Church in Sierra Leone (1886-1891).
As chairman, Cockill put the fiscal and administrative organization of the Sierra Leone District on a very sound basis.

COCKLYN, Captain. Commanded a pirate ship formerly called the
Rising Sun. Cocklyn and his men arrived in the Sierra Leone
estuary possibly in 1718 and attacked and seized a ship belonging to a Signior Joseph. He paid them ransom with which they
replenished their food and ammunition supplies, settled in the
estuary and captured several other ships plying the river.

COELHO, FRANCISCO DE. Portuguese amber merchant who
traded on the Upper Guinea Coast from the 1640s onwards.
Coelho wrote of Dutch presence in Sierra Leone and of Dutch
interest in Sierra Leone trade when he stated that in the 1660s
there were eight or ten Dutchmen occupying two wooden houses
at Robaga on the Sierra Leone River. That was the period of
the Anglo-Dutch wars and Coelho mentioned that the two wooden

structures had been damaged in fights between the English and
Dutch. Although he had not seen it himself, he did in 1669
refer to an English factory at Tasso which the English had used
for "more than 60 years."

COELHO, LEMOS. Portuguese trader born at Balola on the Rio
Grande de Buba. Coelho paid regular visits to Sierra Leone
between 1646 and 1658. Writing in 1669 he referred to the
Mane invasions as a process in the past, dating it at "ninety
years ago." In addition to his own personal experiences he also collected information from Afro-Portuguese born in Sierra
Leone. He personally knew a Mane ruler called Sherabola, at
the time of Coelhos' acquaintance reputed to be 100 years old.
Coelho wrote charitably about the mulattoes on the Upper Guinea
Coast and made favorable comments about Africans who had
embraced Christianity. From him we learn of the Mandinka
and Fula flair for commerce. From him also we know that
arms and ammunition at the time on the list of goods prohibited by Portuguese officials were being sold by Portuguese
and Afro-Portuguese traders on the Upper Guinea Coast. So
also was paper.

COLE, CHRISTOPHER OKORO ELUATHAN EUSTACE, 1921- .
Chief justice of Sierra Leone. Born April 17, 1921, at Waterloo Village. Educated at Seventh Day Adventists School, Waterloo, Buxton Memorial School, and at the CMS Grammar School,
Freetown. He studied at the London School of Economics
where he graduated with an LL. B. degree and at the Middle
Temple where he was called to the Bar in 1946. He returned
to Sierra Leone and set up a private practice until 1951, when
he was appointed police magistrate. He was appointed acting
master and registrar of the Supreme Court in 1952. Later he
was appointed Crown counsel and subsequently promoted to solicitor-general. In December 1960 he was appointed a judge of
the Supreme Court and acted as chief justice of the Gambia in
1962. Between 1963 and 1967 he acted on several occasions as
Chief Justice of the Sierra Leone Supreme Court. In January
1967 he was appointed Sierra Leone's permanent representative
at the United Nations and ambassador to the United States of
America. In 1970 he was appointed chief justice and then acting governor-general in March 1971. He was sworn in on
April 19, 1971, as first president of the Republic of Sierra
Leone until further constitutional changes introduced an executive presidency three days later.

COLE, the Rev. JOHN AUGUSTUS ABAYOMI. Born at Ilorin, Nigeria, of Sierra Leone parentage; educated at Hastings under
A. B. C. Sibthorpe and at the CMS Grammar School, Freetown, Abayomi Cole (as he was popularly known) later worked
at Shenge for the Wesleyan and UBC missions. He proceeded
to the United States where he was ordained a minister of the
American Wesleyan Methodist Church. Whilst in the States he
published in 1886 a tract entitled The Revelations of the Secret

Orders of Western Africa--a treatise on the Poro and other
secret societies which he compared with the Freemasons. Interested in the medicinal aspects of herbs, he became a member of the National Association of Medical Herbalists of Great
Britain and set up business in Freetown as an eclectic practitioner. Tolerant of Islam and friendly with Muslims, Abayomi
Cole studied Arabic and contributed to the magazine Saturday
Ho! (1891-6) by writing a news-summary in Arabic for Muslim
readers. In 1893, after disagreement with his congregation,
Abayomi Cole farmed at "Beulah Hills" on the way to Leicester
where he also sold refreshments. The Rev. Abayomi Cole was
also author of The Interior of Sierra Leone; What Can It Teach
Us? (1887), Astrological Geomancy in Africa (1898), Hala Goloi
Mende Yiahu (First Book in the Mende Language) (1900), and
Trees, Herbs and Roots in West Africa (1906).

COLE (MASSAQUOI) J. B., 1925- . Journalist and politician.
    Born in 1925, Cole was educated at St. Anthony's Primary
    School and St. Edward's Secondary School, Freetown; at the
    London School of Journalism and at Indiana University, USA.
    He served in the Royal Navy during World War II and rose to
    the rank of petty officer. Secretary general of the Sierra
    Leone People's Party (SLPP), 1962-1971. Editor, Shekpendeh
    newspaper (1959-1961).

COLE, N. H. A., 1931- . Educator and author. Professor and
    head, Department of Botany, Fourah Bay College (USL). Fel-
    low, Linnean Society of London (FLS) 1964. Dr. Cole is au-
    thor of several scientific publications in learned journals. He
    is also the author of The Vegetation of Sierra Leone (1968) and
    is chairman, Representative Council and the Executive Commit-
    tee of SEPA.

COLERIDGE-TAYLOR, GEORGE ONYEAH, 1932- . First black
    president of the Durham Union Society and winner of the Robson
    Shield of the Durham Colleges for debating (1959). Born in
    Freetown on July 4, 1932. Educated at the Prince of Wales
    School, Freetown, at University College, Durham, and at the
    Australian National University, Canberra. First secretary,
    Sierra Leone Mission to the United Nations, New York 1964-
    1965; counselor at the Sierra Leone Embassy, Washington,
    1966-1967; acting high commissioner for Sierra Leone in Ni-
    geria, 1968-1969; deputy secretary, Ministry of External Af-
    fairs, Freetown 1968; permanent secretary, Ministry of Ex-
    ternal Affairs 1970-1973; seconded to the Mano River Union
    Secretariat, 1975.

COLLIER, GERSHON BERESFORD ONESIMUS. Lawyer, diplomat
    and author. Born in Freetown; educated at the CMS Grammar
    School, Fourah Bay College (University of Durham), the Middle
    Temple Inns of Court and at New York University. Sierra
    Leone's first ambassador and permanent representative to the
    United Nations, 1961-1963; 1964-1967; ambassador of Sierra

Leone to the United States 1963-1967. Appointed chief justice of Sierra Leone, 1967; professor at New York University 1967-1974; legal consultant, Freetown. Author of Sierra Leone; An Experiment in Democracy in an African Nation (1970).

COLUMBINE, Capt. EDWARD HENRY, R.N. Governor of Sierra Leone, 1810-1811. Appointed in 1808 as commissioner, with Ludlam and Dawes, to investigate the British West African settlements and to report on the slave trade. Columbine got subsequent instructions to travel to Sierra Leone and administer the government until a substantive governor was appointed. He was authorized to "study, observe and change such aspects of [his] predecessors' administration as [he saw] fit." He arrived in Freetown on February 10, 1810, and took the oath of office on the 12th. After a clash with a Mr. John Grant, who relying on the support of the military commanding officer had seriously challenged the new governor's authority, Columbine settled down to work. He revived the system of apprenticeship without solving the problem of the liberated Africans, who continued to troop into the rural communities around Freetown. His answer to the Colony's fiscal problems and to the prevailing inflation, was to slash government spending heavily and to increase agricultural production by encouraging farming, particularly in the rural areas. He also introduced an efficient system of accounting and insisted on regular weekly reports detailing the scope of government works, the number of employees and the amount of wages. To deal more effectively with the problem of the liberated Africans, Columbine appointed the second member of his council to assume responsibility for the new arrivals and to report to the governor on the "actual condition of these people; their disposal, health and the weekly expense of their maintenance." This new approach to the problem of the liberated Africans never got the blessings of the Home Government. Relentlessly victimized by the climate of Sierra Leone (he had lost his wife and daughter by the end of 1810), frustrated and unwell, he asked to be relieved of his duties. When no successor arrived Columbine discharged himself from the service in May 1811 and on his way back to England died at sea in June of the same year.

COMBER, PC Bai, Chief of Upper Bambara, Central Province. Nominated by the governor to represent the Protectorate in the legislative council in 1924. One of the first three paramount chiefs nominated under the provisions of the Slater Constitution to represent Protectorate interests.

COMMISSION ON THE CIVIL SERVICE, 1952-53 see SINKER/ MOMOH COMMISSION

COMMITTEE OF EDUCATED ABORIGINES [CEA]. The first articulate and effectively organized political association of the Protectorate. Formed in the early 1920s to voice the demands and aspirations of the Protectorate-educated elite and to repre-

sent in a general way the interests of the Protectorate at large.
Precursor of the Protectorate Educational Progressive Union
(PEPU).

COMPANY OF AFRICAN MERCHANTS. Incorporated in Liverpool
in 1863, the Company of African Merchants initially operated
further down the west coast of Africa and opened branches in
Sierra Leone in Freetown and Bendu in 1864. It operated in
Sierra Leone a little under a decade, winding up business in
the country in 1872.

CONTON, WILLIAM FARQUHAR, 1925-   . Educator and author.
Born on September 5, 1925, at Bathurst (Banjul), Gambia.
Educated at the CMS Grammar School, Freetown, and at the
Bible College, Swansea, Wales. Read history at St. John's
College, Durham, and was a lecturer in history at Fourah Bay
College, 1947-1953; headmaster, Accra High School 1953-60;
principal, Bo Government School, 1960-1962; principal, Prince
of Wales School, Freetown, 1962-1963; and chief education of-
ficer, Sierra Leone 1963-1969. Author of the novel, The Afri-
can (1960), and West Africa in History (1962, 1963, 2 vols.).
Retired from Sierra Leone government service and took up
appointment with UNESCO.

COTAY, ALEXANDER BAJULAIYE, 1913-   . Born in Freetown
on June 26, 1913. Educated at the Albert Academy and at the
Prince of Wales, Freetown, at Lincoln University and Northwestern University, USA; at University of Exeter, U.K., Lincoln's
Inn, London, and at King's Inns, Dublin. First Sierra Leonean
High commissioner for Sierra Leone and the Gambia in London, 1958-1959; editor of the Protectorate's first newspaper,
the Sierra Leone Observer, Bo, 1949-1955; editor of debates,
Sierra Leone House of Representatives, 1965-1967. Appointed
police magistrate, 1967-1969; senior police magistrate, 1970,
and principal police magistrate, 1971.

COUNTESS OF HUNTINGDON CONNECTION. Introduced into Sierra
Leone in 1792 by Nova Scotian immigrants. The Countess of
Huntingdon Connection had been introduced into Nova Scotia by
John Marrant, a freed Negro from South Carolina, after the
American Revolutionary War. Marrant died in 1791 and Cato
Perkins assumed leadership of the congregation in Nova Scotia,
assisted by William Ash, the leading preacher of the Connection.
Perkins and Ash were both headmen of Nova Scotian
groups during the trans-Atlantic voyage to Sierra Leone in 1792.
In Sierra Leone members of the Countess of Huntingdon Connection were regarded in official circles as dissenters and non-
conformists and soon their leaders formed the nucleus of opposition to the government of the Sierra Leone Company. Cato
Perkins was one of the delegates sent to London in 1793 by the
settlers with a petition of protest against Governor Dawes. The
refusal of the directors to countenance the petition drove Perkins and most Huntingdonians into further opposition to Company

government. In the 1800 settlers' rebellion, many Huntingdonians, though not Perkins himself, were active participants.
Ash died in 1801; Perkins, in 1805. Thereafter the mantle of
leadership of the sect in Sierra Leone fell on John Ellis, a
Maroon. The arrival in Sierra Leone of more freed slaves
after 1808 reinforced the ranks of the Huntingdonians and ensured the survival of the sect. John Ellis sent a letter to the
Huntingdonian Conference in England in 1825. The letter was
read aloud, the first piece of news of their brethren in Sierra
Leone since Perkins' visit in 1793. Outside Freetown and the
Western Area the Connection had a branch at Baoma, Bo District, some 160 miles by the then railway from Freetown and
in one or two other areas in the provinces.

COX COMMISSION OF INQUIRY. A Commission of Inquiry appointed on March 28, 1956, by Governor Sir Robert de Zouche
Hall, "to enquire into the causes of the recent disturbance...."
The disturbances referred to were known locally as the "strike"
and more generally described as "tax disturbances." They began in Maforki Chiefdom, Port Loko District, and spread to
other chiefdoms and districts in parts of the northern and
southern provinces. The commissioners were Sir Herbert Cox,
chairman; Mr. A. T. A. Beckley, Mr. A. J. Loveridge, Mr.
Justice S. P. J. Q. Thomas, members; and Mr. D. W. Tur-
berville, secretary. The commissioners presented their report
on July 19, 1956.

COX-GEORGE, N. A., 1915- . Sierra Leone's leading economist.
Born in Freetown on June 15, 1915, educated at the CMS Grammar School, Prince of Wales School, Freetown, and at the London School of Economics and Political Science, University of
London. Lecturer-in-charge, Department of Economics, Fourah
Bay College (University of Durham), 1946-1951; senior lecturer
and dean, Faculty of Economic Studies, Fourah Bay College,
1955-1961; professor and head, Department of Economics, University of Nigeria, Nsukka, 1961-1964; professor of political
economy, University of Sierra Leone, 1964-1965; director of the
Trade, Fiscal and Monetary Division, United Nations Economic
Commission for Africa, 1965-1967; chief of Trade Policies
Problems Section, United Nations Conference on Trade and Development (UNCTAD), 1967-1969; professor and head, Department of Economics, Fourah Bay College, University of Sierra
Leone, since 1969. Author of numerous articles and pamphlets
and two major books--Finance and Development in West Africa:
The Sierra Leone Experience (1961) and Studies in Finance and
Development; The Gold Coast (Ghana) Experience 1914-1960
(1973).

CRANKAPONE, RICHARD. One of the Nova Scotian immigrants into
Sierra Leone in 1792. It is said that, accompanied by three
other men, Crankapone travelled over 300 miles on foot from
St. John to Halifax to join other Nova Scotian immigrants. In
Sierra Leone Crankapone, with Abraham Smith and John Kiz-

zell, borrowed money to build a boat, The Three Friends, with
which they traded for cattle in the Northern Rivers. Crankapone, as marshal, effected the arrest of James Robertson and
Ansel Zizer, leaders of Nova Scotian opposition to the government of the Sierra Leone Company and who in September 1800
attempted illegally to assume the authority of governor and
council. When a new charter was granted to the settlement in
1800 constituting Sierra Leone a Colony, marshals were replaced by a sheriff, a European official; and Crankapone was
appointed under-sheriff. On November 18, 1801, the Temne,
in league with some Nova Scotian dissidents, attacked Fort
Thornton and Crankapone was killed fighting in defense of the
Fort and of the government.

CRAWFORD, Capt. R. E. COPLAND. A special service officer
sent to the Sulima area by the governor of Sierra Leone
in 1888 as acting-manager. He had at his disposal a force of
47 policemen and was instructed to use the force only for defense purposes. Crawford, determined to make his mark mili-
tarily, ignored his instructions, arrested chiefs, captured and
burned towns and on the whole pursued an aggressive policy in
the Pujehun, Sulima, Bahama and Lago areas. These moves
by the special service officer, though unofficially sanctioned
were privately a delight to the governor, pleased with the dis-
comfiture of "troublemakers" like Makaia of Lago.

At the Colonial Office itself, where the possibility of a
large expensive military expedition into the hinterland had been
under active consideration, Crawford's exploits were viewed
with relief, if suppressed approval. Governor Hay himself
traveled to the interior with reinforcements to enable Crawford
to bring Makaia of Lago to his knees. In a series of skirmishes,
Crawford's expedition, consisting of 75 policemen and over 800
"friendlies" supplied largely by Momo Jah, captured and destroyed a number of towns and stockades--strongholds of Makaia,
who was himself compelled to flee. His 600 captives were released by Crawford and sent back to their homes.

Back in the Sulima District Crawford fell ill. Accusing
his servant, Gbana Gombu of stealing, he had him tried by
ordeal and beaten by the police to extort a confession, he himself though seriously ill taking part in the flogging. In the process Gombu died. A coroner's jury at Bonthe passed a verdict
of manslaughter against Crawford, the policemen, and one
Robert Maister, an Afro-European trader for years in the Gallinas who was alleged to have abetted the crime. Though the
evidence of the cause of death was not conclusive the judge in
the Supreme Court in Freetown summed up against the accused.
The jury (two Europeans and a Creole majority) found Crawford
and Maister guilty of manslaughter--both were sentenced to a
year's imprisonment--and acquitted the policemen. Crawford's
conviction embittered race relations in the Colony, the Europeans attributing the jury verdict to racial prejudice. In Britain the Liberal opposition in the House of Commons exploited
the episode to discredit the government. The matter was taken

up by the British Press and by the Aborigines Protection Society, both denouncing Crawford's expeditions as aggressions of a harsh colonial administration.   Crawford's trial and conviction had undermined European faith in Sierra Leone juries and made possible the enactment of subsequent ordinances (the Jury Ordinance of 1890 excepted) which encroached further on jury rights.   Crawford, too ill to serve his sentence in Freetown, was sent to England where he was released on medical grounds.   A plea by his lawyer, Samuel Lewis, for a free pardon was rejected by the Home Secretary.   Maister was set free on instructions from the Colonial Office as no direct evidence had been adduced to confirm his actual involvement.

CREOLE.   The term Creole is generally used in some countries to designate persons of mixed racial origin.   In Sierra Leone over the years the term has acquired a variety of meanings.   Originally it was used to denote Colony-born children--i. e., descendants of Nova Scotians, Maroons and recaptives (or liberated Africans), who by the middle decades of the 19th Century had formed by a process of integration a discernibly cohesive group.   The term also came to refer to other persons (mostly tribal immigrants into the Colony) who had cultivated habits of the settlers (i. e., Nova Scotians and Maroons) and liberated Africans and had accepted their way of life.   By the 1870s the term Creole was exclusively used to mean settlers, liberated Africans, and their descendants, and was so used in the 1911 census.   By the 1930s the term was used to refer to persons who had acquired a number of Western attitudes and ways of thought and behavior, many of whom obtained Christian schooling and adopted Christian names.
          In the post-World War II period, debates over constitutional changes and the implementation of some constitutional provisions tended to inject an element of group or tribal consciousness into national politics which in many ways arrested, almost reversed, this trend.   The term Creole came to be increasingly used to refer to Colony-born persons--i. e., descendants of settlers and liberated Africans in contradistinction to "countrymen," the bulk of the country's tribal Africans, literate or illiterate, Christian, Muslim or Animist.
          The Creole are predominantly Christian but a small group, particularly in Foulah Town, Fourah Bay and Aberdeen, are Muslims.   They attach much importance to certain attainments, such as a high level of literacy, the acquisition of real estate, a career in law, medicine, the church or more recently in engineering.   And yet the Creoles, though Western in outlook, have not allowed such practices as Awujoh to fall into disuse.   Awujoh and similar observances are part and parcel of African traditional cultural systems with emphasis on ancestral veneration.   In these respects then, in the drive towards modernity and in the emphasis on achievement in the observance of traditional rites, there is a great deal in common between Creoles and educated tribal Africans.   It is therefore true to assert that the broad distinction between Creole and countryman rests

largely on what is increasingly becoming a myth. Education,
social mobility, intermarriage and above all the old system of
wardship have all contributed over the decades to blurr the distinction and to promote integration, no matter how slow.

In the middle decades of the 19th century the Creole of
Sierra Leone had acquired advantages over the bulk of tribal
Africans which enabled them to play leading roles in virtually
all aspects of the Colony's life. Creole ascendancy was in the
end destroyed by deliberate colonial policy and from about the
turn of the century Creole fortunes in Sierra Leone began to experience a downward trend. Today, although a minority group,
the Creole still enjoy an influence in national life out of all
proportion to their numbers. It is not too much to assert and
there is evidence to support the view, that British "liberalism"
in West Africa in contrast to British paternalism and British
connivance at racism in eastern, central and southern Africa
in colonial times, was dictated less by a British sense of fair
play than by Creole vigilance and intransigence in the 19th century.

The home of the Creole in Sierra Leone is in the western area (the former Colony)--Freetown and its rural environs--
approximate in size to the piece of territory acquired in 1787
by the British for the rehabilitation of victims of the Atlantic
slave trade. But almost from the inception of the colony, the
settlers and other groups whose descendants are called Creoles,
ventured into the hinterland, amassing wealth in some cases,
risking life and limb in others, and on the whole creating problems between the administration in Freetown and the chiefs of
the interior. When the Hut Tax War broke out in 1898 large
numbers of Creole were maimed or killed. In spite of such experiences the Creole continued to contribute in no small measure
to the spread of the blessings of industry and "civilized" life
among their brothers in the interior. Krio, the vernacular of
the Creole, is the lingua franca in Sierra Leone.

CROOKS, JOHN JOSEPH. Colonial secretary. Acting governor,
   1891-92, 1893, 1894. Author of A History of the Colony of
   Sierra Leone Western Africa and A Short History of Sierra
   Leone.

CROWTHER, J. C. O., 1893- . Born at Waterloo Village on May
   13, 1893. Educated at the Countess of Huntingdon Day School,
   Waterloo, and at the CMS Grammar School, Freetown. First
   member of the Rural Areas Council (1937) and first vice-president, Rural Areas Council. Parliamentarian for 24 continuous
   years in the Legislative Council, in the House of Representatives and in the Sierra Leone Parliament (1938-1962). In 1963,
   Crowther was made "honourable gentleman" for life in recognition of his long and devoted service in the national legislature.
   Appointed first chairman of the reconstituted Ports Authority in
   1964.

CROWTHER, the Rt. Rev. SAMUEL ADJAI, ca. 1806-1892. Bishop

of the Niger and of the West African Countries Beyond British
Juristiction (1864-1892). Born about 1806 at Oshogun, Yorubaland, in what is now Republic of Nigeria, Adjai started life as
a farmer, breeding poultry and cultivating yams, and made a
good job of it. During the Owu War of 1821-9, Adjai's town
was attacked, he and his family were captured and sold into
slavery. Put on board the Portuguese ship, the Esperanza
Feliz, for the trans-Atlantic voyage to America, Adjai was
rescued by two British warships and taken to Sierra Leone
where he was set free on June 17, 1822. On arrival in Freetown he was sent to Bathurst village where he avidly devoured
everything he was taught and within six months could read the
New Testament in English with ease. On December 11, 1825,
Adjai was received into the Christian Church and he took the
name of Samuel Crowther after a CMS benefactor. In 1826,
Samuel Adjai Crowther was taken to England by the missionaries
who sent him to a parochial school for a few months. When he
returned to Freetown, he was employed as a schoolteacher and
in 1827 was enrolled as a student at the Christian Institution,
renamed Fourah Bay Institution (or College) in 1828. From
Fourah Bay College, where he later became a tutor in 1834 under the Rev. G. H. Kissling, Crowther was sent first to Regent in 1829, and from there to Wellington to serve as a schoolteacher.

The Lander Brothers had in 1830 discovered the estuary
of the Niger. In 1837, on Fowell Buxton's initiative, a new
Society for the Civilisation of Africa was founded and expeditions were planned to the Niger. The first Niger expedition of
1842 was accompanied by two representatives of the CMS, the
Rev. J. F. Schon and Samuel Adjai Crowther. The European
death toll on the expedition (42 out of 150 in two months) was
disastrously high and Crowther reflecting on the situation noted
in his journal "I am reluctantly led to adopt the opinion that
Africa can chiefly be benefitted by her own children." The Rev.
Schon, impressed by Crowther's sincerity and ability, recommended him to the CMS for ordination as a priest to help in
the work of evangelizing his native land. Crowther was then
sent to the CMS College at Islington, received into deacon's
orders and ordained a priest on October 1, 1843. While in
England he published a Vocabulary of the Yoruba Language and
began to translate the New Testament into Yoruba. In 1845
Crowther returned to Yorubaland to help the Rev. Townsend establish a Christian mission at Abeokuta, where he was reunited
with his sisters and mother, whom he baptized using the Yoruba
version of the baptismal service which he had himself translated
from English.

Back in England in 1851 Crowther had the opportunity of
discussing the slave question with members of the royal family,
the Prime Minister and other civic and religious leaders.
Partly as a result of the representations he made, another Niger expedition was sent in 1854 and Crowther lost no time in
making useful contacts for the establishment of the Niger Mission. Equally important, he was able on this expedition to

prevail on a number of chiefs to give up slavery and other bar-
baric practices and some became Christians. He followed up
these early successes and during the Niger expeditions of 1857-
9 ensured the establishment of Christian missions at Onitsha
and Gbebe, effecting in the process a great deal of evangelization along the banks of the Niger.

In 1864 Crowther returned to England, this time to be
made a bishop of the Anglican Church. On June 29, 1864, the
Rev. Samuel Adjai Crowther was consecrated bishop of the Niger, the first African in modern times to be so elevated in the
ecclesiastical hierarchy. The University of Oxford conferred on
him an honorary Doctor of Divinity degree. Bishop Crowther,
bishop of the West African Countries Beyond British Jurisdiction, returned to his vast, unwieldy diocese. The intertribal
wars waged on. On one occasion the bishop was kidnapped but
he escaped. He continued to work diligently in the midst of
many difficulties and problems and died at Lagos on January 9,
1892, after nearly 60 years of continuous missionary work.

CUFFEE, Capt. PAUL. Son of a freed African father and an
American Indian mother, a pious Quaker, lived in New Bradford, Mass., where he did business with his own boats. In
1810, after hearing of the African Institution's plans, he visited
Sierra Leone in his brig, the Traveller. He spent a few months
in Sierra Leone and at the invitation of William Wilberforce and
William Allen he went to England. He returned to Freetown
at the end of 1811 and organized a cooperative trading society,
the "Friendly Society of Sierra Leone," to enable the settlers
by combined efforts to promote and improve agriculture, market
their produce overseas and put an end to the monopoly enjoyed
by European merchants. Cuffee also brought back with him
from England three schoolmasters and the Rev. George Warren
as missionaries sent out by the English Wesleyan Conference.
He returned to America in 1812 with plans to send to Sierra
Leone Americans of African descent, sturdy farmers, skilled
artisans, experienced businessmen, whose example, exertions
and expertise he hoped the settlers would emulate and thus be
inspired to enterprise and independence. He acquired a house
in Freetown as a manifestation of his permanent involvement
in the Colony and promised on his departure to return every
year with goods and new immigrants. Cuffee's plans for an
annual visit did not materialize but he came back to Sierra
Leone in February 1816 with a sawmill, merchandise, and 34
immigrants. He returned to America with African produce
which he sold at a loss. He died in 1817. His Friendly Society and his other admirable plans died with him.

CUMMINGS, IVOR GUSTAVUS, 1912- . Born December 10, 1912;
educated at Methodist Boys High School, Freetown, and at the
Whitgift Middle Foundation, Croydon. Served in the British
Home Service and Colonial Office, with the rank of principal,
mainly concerned with the organization of the Welfare and Students Department and responsible for coordination of recruit-

ment of Colonial Personnel for the War effort and their post-war rehabilitation. He was secretary, Secretary of State's Advisory Committee on the Welfare of Colonial People in the United Kingdom, and joint secretary, Sub-Committee of the Cabinet on Welfare of Overseas Students (1940-1951). Created OBE on the Prime Minister's List, June 1948, and awarded a coronation medal in 1952. Served in the Colonial Administrative Service as assistant director of Social Welfare and Community Development, Accra, Ghana (1952), and as deputy director of Recruitment and Training, Establishment Secretary's Office, Accra, Ghana. Administrative manager, Sierra Leone Selection Trust, Yengema, responsible for Training, Recruitment, Social Development and Personnel Services. Director of the Ghana Company and director of the Group (Duncan, Gilbey and Matheson) responsible for training and localization programes, and for public relations.

CUMMINGS-JOHN, AGATHA CONSTANCE. First woman in British West Africa to hold elective political office (1938) and, with Madam Ella Koblo Gulama and Mrs. Patience Richards, the first woman to be elected to the national legislature in 1957. First woman mayor of Freetown, 1966-67. Founder and first principal, Roosevelt School for Girls (1952).

CUNNINGHAM, Col. GEORGE GLENGAIRN. An experienced officer who had served in many parts of Africa, Cunningham arrived in Sierra Leone in April 1898, one of eight officers with eight sergeants sent out by the War Office to organize a West African Regiment and to help put down the 1898 rising in the Protectorate. On May 3, 1898, Cunningham, in command of a force of seven officers and 159 NCOs and men of the West India Regiment, arrived at Bonthe on Board the Countess of Derby with the object of relieving Bandajuma, which was heavily besieged. He sent a detachment of troops to Bandajuma which relieved the town on May 22. It was to Cunningham that the Rev. C. H. Goodman of Tikonko (the only surviver among the European missionaries who had been captured during the rising) was handed over unharmed. In October 1898 three companies of the newly formed West African Regiment commanded by Col. Cunningham relieved the garrison at Karene. When, at the cessation of hostilities, it was decided to march through the Protectorate "to show the flag," Cunningham was put in command of operations. Thus he is said to have commanded "the largest force yet seen in Sierra Leone; 995 troops under 56 officers with 4295 carriers."

CUTHBERT, JOHN. A Nova Scotian settler and a Baptist elder who was elected a hundredor in 1792 and also made marshall of Freetown with powers to summon juries and enforce writs. Cuthbert accompanied Dawes on leave in England in March 1794 but returned towards the end of the year in time for the French attack. Thereafter he became increasingly critical of government policies and measures. In the circumstances Governor

Ludlam refused to accept Cuthbert's election as a justice of the
peace in April 1800. This rejection merely helped to drive
Cuthbert into further opposition and he began to incite feeling
against the Governor. After the Nova Scotian rebellion of 1799-
1800, he was banished from the Colony for life although he had
himself not taken part in the fighting.

- D -

DA CINTRA see CINTRA, PEDRO DA

DAILY GUARDIAN (1933-1938; 1938-1958). A newspaper published
in Freetown. Through its pages Thomas Decker mounted his
crusade for Krio as a language in its own right.

D'ALMADA, ALVARES. A Portuguese mulatto from Santiago, Cape
Verde, who gave an eyewitness account of events on the Upper
Guinea Coast from the 1560s. In 1580 he went to Lisbon to advise and encourage the government of Portugal to colonize Sierra Leone. He collected a mass of information on the rivers of
Guinea. His work, published in 1594 and entitled Tratado breve
dos rios de Guine [Short Account of the Rivers of Guinea], was
a useful handbook giving an account of the history, customs and
secret societies of the Guinea Coast, the hospitality of the inhabitants and the fertility of the soil. D'Almada also described
the judicial systems and the political structure of the countries
on the Coast and his somewhat rosy picture may to a certain
extent have encouraged Philip III of Spain to send the first resident Christian missionary to Sierra Leone--the Jesuit priest
Balthasar Barreira. From D'Almada we learn that the Mane
invasions took place in the 1550s. He stated that he was told
that the original leader of the Mane forces was a woman whom
Mannuel Alvares referred to as "Mabete, Queen of Guinea."
D'Almada stated further that the Mane paid a tax called "Maref"
to a suzerain who dwelt inland "far behind."

DAPPER, OLPHERT [Offert]. A Dutch surgeon and geographer.
He wrote in 1666 a work entitled (as translated by John Ogilby), Africa, Being an Accurate Description of the Regions of
Egypt, Barbary, Libya, Billedulgerid, the Land of Negroes,
Guines, Aethiopia and the Abyssines with All the Adjacent Islands. He gave a detailed account of rivers, towns, peoples,
flora, fauna, rites, customs, language, wealth, religion, politics and government. Dapper described at length, probably
from information supplied by a Dutch trader, the poro secret
society and the tremendous influence it exercised, particularly
in the Sherbro-Cape Mount area. He also referred to a female
secret society, more social than political, where girls were
circumcised and trained for womanhood. On the Mane invasions he wrote that the second invasion from the south imposed
a viceroy called Selbore (Sherabola) upon the inhabitants of
Sierra Leone and he averred that the word Sherbro is derived

from Selbore (or Sherabola). From Dapper we learn that the
inhabitants of Quoja country acted as middlemen between the inland nations and the maritime regions, imposing duties on imports and exports.

DARAMY, Sheik BATU, 1924- . Commissioner of labour, 1959-
1961; deputy financial secretary, 1961-1963; financial secretary,
1963-1968. Charged with treason in 1968 and convicted and imprisoned in 1969, his sentence was suspended in 1972. He then
took up an appointment with the World Bank, 1973.

DAVIES, F. B., 1937- . Born on August 27, 1937. Educated
at the Albert Academy, Fourah Bay College (University of Durham), Freetown; Bonn University, Germany; and Liverpool University, England. One of Sierra Leone's most successful private medical practitioners. Founder and proprietor of Bonner
General Hospital, Freetown, in August 1974.

DAVIES, MOSES H. "Veteran of the Freetown press," in the 19th
century and the most inventive publisher. Moses founded and
edited the following newspapers: The African and Sierra Leone
Weekly Advertiser (1855-1861); The Free Press and Sierra Leone
Weekly Advertiser (1861-1865?); The Day-Spring and Sierra
Leone Reporter (1868-1873); and The Watchman and West African Record (1875-1886). He died in poverty at Cline Town in
1896.

DAVIES, P. R., 1911- . Born in Freetown on September 18, 1911.
Educated at the Bishop Crowther Memorial Day School, Government Model School, CMS Grammar School, Freetown, and
Gray's Inn, London. Acting master and registrar of the Supreme Court (1952-1966); acting puisne judge and then puisne
judge, 1966. Chancellor of the Anglican Diocese of Sierra
Leone and of the Province of West Africa (1969); justice of the
Appeal Court (1971), and speaker of the Sierra Leone Parliament (1973).

DAVIES, W. J. Popularly known as "Bully." One of the most
successful expatriate education officers in Sierra Leone. Principal of Prince of Wales School, Freetown (1937-1948); president of the City Council of Freetown 1944-1945; 1947-1948.

DAWES, Lt. WILLIAM. Governor of Sierra Leone, 1792-94; 1795-
96; 1801-03. Dawes arrived in Freetown in September to act
as member of Governor Clarkson's Council, constituted by
charter of the Sierra Leone Company in August 1792. He succeeded Clarkson as governor of Sierra Leone on December 31,
1792. Murmurs of grievance against the Company during Clarkson's tenure of office as governor were raised to a clamor
when Dawes took over. The settlers held the new Governor
responsible for their misfortunes and frustrations, and sent two
delegates to England in 1793 to make representations on their
behalf to the directors of the Company. The decision of the

directors to treat the complaints as unfounded merely served
to increase tensions in the Colony. In 1793 the Nova Scotians
rose up in arms. The rising was suppressed, some six of the
ringleaders were excluded from the colony, and a general amnesty was granted to the rest. In March 1794, because of ill-
health, Dawes returned to England. Recuperated, he returned
to Freetown in March 1795 and took charge of the government.
      Dawes and his council imposed the first direct tax in the
Colony when in October 1795 they passed a measure levying a
road tax on all adults, male and female, computed as equivalent to six days' annual labor or the payment of a fine in lieu.
In 1796, disappointed and frustrated, Dawes resigned the governorship for health reasons. In retirement, his administration,
which had been denounced and detested, was nostalgically recalled as a Golden Age. Assured by reports and convinced by
the directors, Dawes for a third time embarked for Freetown
on gubernatorial duties and arrived in January 1801 to take
charge of the Colony. Financially strengthened by the annual
grant-in-aid from the British government, the Governor and his
Council launched a newspaper, the Sierra Leone Gazette, in
February 1801. During Dawes' third term of office, the Temne,
led by King Tom II and in alliance with certain dissident Nova
Scotians, twice attacked the Colony--in November 1801 and in
April 1802. When Dawes finally gave up the governorship in
1803, he procured, on Wilberforce's recommendation, temporary employment on a Commission to report on the British West
African Settlements and on the slave trade. The commissioners completed their first report early in 1810 and made their
final submission in April 1811. Dawes died in 1836.

DAY, Capt. WILLIAM. Governor of Sierra Leone, 1803; 1805.
      Born in the West Indies, Capt. Day of the Royal Navy, arrived
in Freetown in February 1803 to succeed Dawes as governor of
Sierra Leone. Within his first six months, Day strengthened
the Colony's defense system against external attack by creating
an efficient corps of volunteers recruited from Maroons and
Nova Scotians, rebuilt Fort Thornton and installed a battery at
Falconbridge Point. Possibly to forestall King Tom II and his
allies on the Bulom Shore, he chose Jack Wilson of Yongru,
who had spent a year in England, sponsored by the Sierra Leone
Company, as King of Kafu Bulom with the title King George
Bana. Towards the end of 1803, Day left for England to appear before the parliamentary committee appointed to investigate the affairs of the Sierra Leone Company. Reappointed
governor by the grateful directors, Day returned to Freetown
in January, 1805. He then embarked on completion of the defenses at Fort Thornton and constructed fortifications at Wansey Hill, renamed Tower Hill. To foster agricultural development in the Colony, he cultivated a large sugar plantation east
of Freetown at what is now Fourah Bay. On November 4,
1805, his health seriously undermined by incessant stomach
trouble, Day died, the first governor to die in office, and was
buried in Freetown in the cemetery east of Fort Thornton.

THE DAY-SPRING AND SIERRA LEONE REPORTER (1868-1873).
Newspaper started in 1868 by M. H. Davies.

DECKER, THOMAS ALEXANDER LEIGHTON, 1916- . Born July
25, 1916. Educated at the CMS Grammar School and at Fourah
Bay College, Freetown. Editor of Daily Guardian for some
years until 1950. Joined Public Relations Department (now
Government Information Services, Ministry of Information and
Broadcasting), 1950. Appointed chief information officer, 1961,
and permanent secretary, Ministry of Information, 1963.
Charged with treason in 1968 and sentenced to death in 1969.
Reprieved and released after some three years in jail. Author
of "Counter Proposal for a New Constitution for Sierra Leone"
(1948), "Our Paramount Chiefs of the Sierra Leone Protectorate" (1948), Tales of the Forest (1968), Julius Caesar by
William Shakespeare translated into Krio and Udat Dikiap Fit,
a Krio Adaptation of "As You Like It." He is one of the best
known crusaders for Krio as a language in its own right and
one of the most distinguished authors in Krio.

DELEDUGU EXPEDITION see MILITARY EXPEDITIONS (14)

DEMBA, PA. A Temne chieftain whose town lay south of Granville Town II. In September 1794, after the French attack on
the settlement, Pa Demba provided accommodation for some
Nova Scotian victims of the attack. In 1814 when some Portu-
guese-speaking recaptives were settled in Pa Demba's Town,
it was renamed Portuguese Town. Pademba Road, Freetown
commemorates his name.

DEMOCRATIC PEOPLE'S CONGRESS [DPC]. Formed in July 1965,
after the dissolution of the SLPIM following Tamba Mbriwa's
defection to the SLPP and his subsequent re-election to the
paramount chieftaincy from which he had been deposed. The
DPC declared among its major aims the "radical improvement
in the political, economic and social conditions of the toiling
masses whose interests appear to be woefully neglected." Although it spoke vaguely of improving conditions of "the toiling
masses," the DPC was almost exclusively a Kono movement,
created more to show that in spite of the SLPIM's dissolution,
there was still active opposition in Kono to SLPP policies. By
1967 the DPC was in alliance with the APC and in the March
elections of that year won all five seats in Kono on the APC/
DPC ticket.

DE MOURA see MOURA, JOSE LOPEZ DE

DENHAM, Col. DIXON. Born in London in 1786. In 1811 Denham
joined the army as a volunteer, progressed through the ranks.
In 1821, with Clapperton and Oudney, he had traveled across
the Sahara from Tripoli to Lake Chad on a British govern-
ment-sponsored expedition to discover the sources of the Niger.
Appointed in 1826 as general superintendent of the liberated

Africans, Denham arrived in Sierra Leone on January 9, 1827.
Thwarted by Campbell, who distrusted him, Denham reorganized the villages upon Campbell's death. Wilberforce village,
virtually deserted, he patiently brought back to life, resettling
some of the old inhabitants at Pa Sandi, renamed Lumley.
Denham was appointed lieutenant-governor of Sierra Leone and
assumed office on May 5, 1828. Under his guidance roads and
bridges were constructed to facilitate travel to and from the
rural communities. Attacked by fever, he died on June 9, 1828.

DEPARTMENT OF NATIVE AFFAIRS. In about 1888, Governor Sir
J. S. Hay introduced administrative changes in the Colonial
Secretariat by separating the Aborigines Branch from the Secretariat and by appointing J. C. E. Parkes its superintendent.
In 1891 the new department, with Parkes as head and directly
under the governor's supervision, was renamed the Department
of Native Affairs. In 1896 Governor Cardew designated Parkes
as secretary for native affairs. But, with the formal declaration of the Protectorate in that year, the duties of the secretary
of the Department became limited as the new district commissioners in the Protectorate more often than not corresponded
directly with the Colonial Secretary or with the Governor himself. When Parkes died in August 1899 the Department ceased
to function.

DE RUYTER, Adm. MICHAEL. Admiral in command of the Dutch
fleet which called at Sierra Leone and dropped anchor at King
Jimmy Wharf on September 12, 1664. De Ruyter had his name
carved on a large rock at the watering-place. He then sailed
up river and attacked and seized an English fort on Tasso Island.

DOHERTY, Col. Sir RICHARD. Governor of Sierra Leone, 1837-
1840. Doherty enlisted in the army in 1803 and saw service in
the Caribbean. He was appointed to the 1st West India Regiment in 1827 and eight years later in 1835 was put in command
of the 89th Foot. Lt.-Col. Doherty arrived in Freetown on
June 15, 1837, and took office as governor of Sierra Leone.
As a result of representations made by the CMS and some
Christian groups about the increasing threat of Islam, Doherty
made proposals to the secretary of state to be authorized to
remove the Muslims at Fourah Bay to a safe distance away
from the Colony. A similar move was contemplated against
the Muslim community at Fulah Town, whose representatives
had indicated to the Governor their willingness, subject to certain conditions, to be removed to another locality. The Governor was authorized by the secretary of state to effect the removal of the Muslims who asked for three months' grace to
look for a suitable spot and to make the necessary arrangements. The removal, however, never came about.
    Difficulties experienced by liberated Africans and British
subjects who had settled in Quiah country led Governor Doherty
to suggest in a dispatch to Lord John Russell the purchase of

Quiah or part thereof as the best way of putting an end to "a source of constant embarrassment and annoyance to the government of the Colony"--a proposal that was implemented in 1861 when the British acquired part of Koya by means of a treaty of cession. Governor Doherty also questioned the whole system of stipends on the grounds that they were "not productive of any compensatory advantage, but were on the contrary and in fact attended with loss and injury to the interests of the government; the treaties themselves being ineffective and prejudicial."
These observations and criticisms made possible the formulation of a new comprehensive treaty policy in 1840 and 1841.
In 1839 the police destroyed a mosque at Fulah Town. Governor Doherty's hostile attitude towards Muslims who were the chief promoters of trade between the Colony and the interior, and his plans to limit the number of "strangers" in the colony were vigorously opposed by European merchants in Freetown who saw in the governor's policy a threat to their business interests. The settlers and recaptives on the other hand united in a common cause and, delighted at the prospect of eliminating alien competitors, supported the Governor. In 1841 Governor Doherty was transferred to Jamaica.

DOMINGO of Royema   see   SIGNIOR DOMINGO

DON PHILIP   see   FLANSIRE

DONNA, Chief. One of the Kisi Chiefs who, after the delimitation of the Sierra Leone/Liberian boundary in 1903, continued to raid British territory. In about October 1906, Chief Donna's warriors attacked some frontier police who were patrolling the east bank of the Mafessa River. A force commanded by Capt. Murray, with lieutenants Cooke and Gill, and consisting of about 80 frontier police was sent against Donna. The River Mafessa was flooded, and a "tie-tie" bridge was improvised. Chief Donna's men were taken by surprise at night and routed. Lt. C. G. C. Crooke, while crossing the tie-tie bridge in the darkness, fell into the flooded river and got drowned in spite of the gallant rescue efforts of three frontier police, corporals Momo Sento and Sumara Makka, and Pvt. Sorie Kailahun, who later received the thanks of the governor Sir Leslie Probyn and a special reward. The expedition raided and destroyed three of Donna's largest towns but Donna's warriors continued their raids and made it necessary for another expedition, commanded by Capt. Norman, assisted by Lt. Bill, to be sent against him. Norman's force encountered Donna's at Leha and in the fighting that ensued Norman was seriously wounded, some seven frontier police were hit and Lt. Bill was incapacitated. Early in January 1907 another company was dispatched against Donna, but because of the proximity of the French outpost no action was possible. In the middle of March, a column of six officers and 110 frontier police invaded Donna's territory and burned a number of towns. No further disturbance was reported thereafter.

DONOVAN, C. E. Director of education, 1946-1951--probably the
most controversial in the history of education in Sierra Leone.
Donovan had before coming to Sierra Leone served as deputy
director of education in Kenya. Because of his experience in
Kenya his "Revised Plan of Development of Education in Sierra
Leone" (1948) was greeted with suspicion and skepticism.
There was widespread feeling that the director's plan was inspired and influenced by white "settler" views and attitudes towards Africans. In particular his scheme to reorganize primary
and secondary education into a six-year primary course consisting of two infant classes and four standards and a seven-
year secondary school course leading to the school certificate
met with violent disapproval from informed Sierra Leoneans.
So also did his scheme for a "special intermediate type of
school" in the Protectorate which was to provide a three-year
course in standards V, VI, and VII and was designed to provide the necessary background for vocational training.

DOOMABEY, ALEXANDER PHILANDER. Son of Kong Doomabey,
Chief of Mando, Timble Chiefdom, Moyamba District. Alexander was educated by the United Brethren in Christ (UBC) missionaries, had worked for the mission as an accounts clerk and
was preparing to go into holy orders. He quarreled with the
missionaries and when the Hut Tax War broke out in 1898, decided to settle scores with them. He led the attack on the
mission house at Shenge and massacred the inmates. Alexander
was hanged, probably at Bonthe, in 1898/99 along with a number of chiefs who had organized resistance to the tax.

DORMAN, Sir MAURICE HENRY, 1912- . Born on August 7, 1912,
and educated at Sedbegh School and at Magdalene College, Cambridge. Worked in the colonial administration in a number of
countries, including Tangayika, Malta, the Gold Coast and Trinidad and Tobago. Appointed governor of Sierra Leone in 1956
and awarded KCMG in 1957. He was the last colonial governor
of Sierra Leone (1956-61) and the first governor-general of independent Sierra Leone (1961-62). In 1962 Sir Maurice was
appointed governor of Malta.

DORNELAS, ANDRE. A Portuguese trader of Cape Verde who
spent some fifty years on the Upper Guinea Coast--roughly between 1570 and 1625. He first visited Sierra Leone in 1574 and
paid a number of subsequent visits. He retired to Santiago in
1625 and wrote about his fifty years' experience on the coast.
In addition to his own eyewitness experiences, Dornelas got a
great deal of information from three Mane whom his father,
also a Cape Verde trader, had bought in Sierra Leone in 1560.
Dornelas personally witnessed the internecine strife among the
Mane after the conquest of the Sape. Of the inhabitants of
Sierra Leone he had this to say: "All these nations are called
in general 'Sape' in the same way as in Spain several nations
are called 'Spaniards'," although he did not suggest that 16th-
century Sierra Leone had the elements of a unitary state. He

gave an account of the origins of the Mane as handed down by
oral tradition.   Like other Portuguese commentators Dornelas
also paid tribute to the military prowess of the Mane, rating
them as better warriors than the Senegalese Wolofs, for whom
he had great respect.

"DOUBLE Bs" see BANKOLE-BRIGHT; BEOKU-BETTS

DOUGAN, ROBERT.   Acting governor of Sierra Leone in 1854 and
1855.   Queen's advocate 1853.   Dougan, an Afro-West Indian,
arrived in Freetown in 1822 and worked his way up to the posts
of queen's advocate and acting governor largely through a successful legal practice.   As acting governor he sanctioned, although he did not give prior permission for the disastrous expedition to Malaghea against Chief Baimba Mina Lahai.   As a
result Dougan was relieved of his duties.   He spent his last
days in private practice in Freetown where he died in 1871 in
considerably reduced circumstances.

DOVE, the Rev. THOMAS.   Chairman and general superintendent
of the Methodist Mission in Sierra Leone (1838-1845).   Although the Wesleyan Methodist Mission began to work in 1811,
it would appear that no chairmen and general superintendents
were appointed until 1838, when the Rev. Dove, who had already worked in the Gambia from 1833 to 1837, arrived to take
charge of the Wesleyan Mission in Sierra Leone.   In the 1830s
the mission's progress in the country had been obstructed by
squabbles within, among missionaries themselves or with their
congregations, or without, with other sects or with the government.   Thomas Dove's major contribution to Methodism in
Sierra Leone was to put an end to these squabbles and to in-
augurate an era of constructive work.   He restored peace and
harmony and opened new stations in Regent, Gloucester, Sussex,
Hamilton, York, Kent and Waterloo.   He rebuilt Soldier Town
Church as a dual purpose structure--a Church "Zion on the
Hill" and a mission house.   In 1842 he introduced a scheme
for training teachers there.   In 1843, at Dove's persuasion,
the Wesleyan Committee bought Kenneth Macaulay's mansion at
King Tom (originally built at a cost of £7000) for a mere 300
guineas, and transformed it into a training college.   He also
built the old Gibraltar Chapel at Kissy Street, which was replaced by the present Gibraltar Church in 1884.
        Before Dove's arrival in Sierra Leone, no recaptive ap-
pears to have established commercial links with England.   It
was Dove who "took hold of some who had business tact combined with straight-forwardness and introduced them to mercantile houses in England. "   One of the first beneficiaries was
John Ezzidio who went to England in 1842 and was introduced
by Dove to English businessmen as a good Methodist, a shrewd
businessman, and a creditworthy customer.   This made it possible for Ezzidio to order goods directly from England and to
compete effectively and on equal terms with his European rivals
in Sierra Leone.   The Sierra Leone Watchman--though short-

lived, the first private newspaper in the Colony--was founded
by Dove in 1842 to publish news, advertisements and articles;
this contributed immensely to raising the standard of journalism in Freetown. In 1846, the Rev. Thomas Dove left Sierra
Leone for good and after a brief stay at Gibraltar returned
home to England where he died December 15, 1859.

DOVE-EDWIN, GEORGE FREDERICK, 1896-1974. Born May 18,
     1896; educated at the CMS Grammar School, Freetown, and at
     Lincoln's Inn, London. Chairman of Commission of Inquiry
     into the Conduct of the 1967 General Elections in Sierra Leone
     (see next entry). Judge of the Appeal and Supreme Courts of
     Sierra Leone.

DOVE-EDWIN COMMISSION OF INQUIRY (1967). A Commission
     of Inquiry appointed by the National Reformation Council (NRC)
     military regime on May 22, 1967, "To inquire into the conduct
     of the last 'General Elections' held on the 17th and 21st days
     of March, 1967, and in particular to inquire into ... (i) the
     compilation and operation of the Register of Voters; (ii) the
     custody of Ballot Papers; (iii) the conduct of Political Parties;
     [and] (iv) the results of the aforesaid General Elections."
          Mr. Justice G. F. Dove-Edwin, Appeal Court judge,
     was appointed chairman of the Commission. The other mem-
     bers were Capt. T. W. Caulker (Royal Sierra Leone Military
     Forces) and Mr. T. M. Kessebeh (superintendent of police).
     The Commission sat from June 12 to August 10, 1967. It sub-
     mitted its report (in four volumes of 2374 pages) to the chair-
     man of the NRC on September 23, 1967, after taking evidence
     from 142 witnesses. In its statement on the Commission's re-
     port, the NRC concluded, "From the evidence of the Commis-
     sion of Inquiry ... the National Reformation Council is of the
     conviction that the Elections held under the conditions described
     in the Report of the Commission, parts of which have been
     quoted in this White Paper, were rigged and corrupt."

DOWDER, JAMES see JIMMY

DRAPE, WILLIAM. An Afro-West Indian printer, who founded the
     weekly newspaper The New Era in 1855 with the motto "To con-
     sult the welfare of the people is the first great law." Through
     the pages of the New Era, Drape poured scorn on Governor
     S. J. Hill and criticized some aspects of his administration.
     Hill in retaliation withdrew government notices from the paper.
     He also introduced an ordinance to curtail the freedom of the
     press. For a breach of the provisions of the ordinance Drape
     was fined £30 in 1858. The matter was taken up by Drape's
     representatives in England and awkward questions were asked in
     Parliament. As a result Hill was ordered to repeal the ordi-
     nance and to remit Drape's fine. In 1858, while the New Era
     was out of circulation as a result of Hill's ordinance, Drape
     brought out another paper, The Sierra Leone Spectator and West
     African Intelligencer; published by his brother Francis. Even-

tually Drape became a supporter of Governor Hill in the ever-
changing shift of political alliances in mid-19th-century Freetown.   Not for long, however, as Drape died in 1859 and the
New Era ceased publication altogether.

DRESS REFORM SOCIETY.   Founded in 1887 as an outward manifestation of a new ethnic consciousness which swept through
Freetown social circles in the 1880s.   Its members included
J. H. Spaine, E. W. Blyden, Claudius May and A. E. Tuboku-
Metzger.   Members of the society adopted forms of dress--
loose flowing garments--to emphasize "their separate racial
identity."   A similar trend was discernible in the rejection of
"foreign" surnames in preference for those that sounded African.
Metzger hyphenated his name to Tuboku-Metzger; Claude George,
author of the Rise of British West Africa (1904), became Esu
Biyi; Isaac Augustus Johnson renamed himself Algerine Kefallah
Sankoh, and so on.   The attitudes of members of the Dress
Reform Society were by no means universally shared.   S. H. A.
Case in The Artisan poked fun at the antics of members of the
society and wives and girlfriends refused to put on what they
regarded as unfashionable, if not inelegant, forms of dress.

DUBOIS, Mrs. ISAAC see FALCONBRIDGE, Mrs. ANNA MARIA

- E -

EARLY DAWN (ca. 1855-1894).   Probably the first newspaper to
be published in the hinterland of Sierra Leone; founded by the
American Missionary Association (AMA) at Mano Bagru or at
Mo Tappan in the mid-1850s.   It stopped publication for some
years but was revived in 1883 as a monthly paper and edited
by the Rev. J. A. Evans, an Afro-American missionary, until
it finally disappeared in 1894.

EASMON, MACORMACK CHARLES FARRELL, 1890-1973.   Born
on April 11, 1890.   Educated at the CMS Grammar School,
Freetown, St. Paul's Preparatory School, Colet Court, London,
and at London University, where he qualified in medicine.   Appointed medical officer, government of Sierra Leone, 1913-
1942, and senior medical officer, 1942-1945, when he retired
on pension.   He was re-engaged as temporary medical officer
in 1949, a post he held for quite a while.   He saw active service in World War I in the Cameroons.   A founding member,
1922, and later chairman of the Sierra Leone Branch of the
British Medical Association.   Chairman, Mining Wages Board
1947; chairman, Maritime and Waterfront Wages Board, 1948;
chairman, Monument and Relics Commission, and president,
Arts and Crafts Society, 1960.   Member and later chairman of
the Sierra Leone Society.

EASMON, RAYMOND SARIF.   Medical practitioner and one of the
country's most promiment public-spirited figures.   Educated at

the Prince of Wales School, Freetown, and at King's College
(Durham University), Newcastle-Upon-Tyne, England.   Chairman of the Civilian Rule Committee (1968).   Novelist and playwright: author of the plays, Dear Parent and Ogre (London,
1964), and The New Patriots (London, 1965), and of the novel,
The Burnt-Out Marriage (London, 1967).   Arrested and detained
under public emergency regulations in 1970 and released in
1971.

EDNEY, the Rev. JAMES.   Chairman and general superintendent of
the Methodist Mission in Sierra Leone (1850-1855).   Born near
Bath, England, in 1799 and ordained a minister of the Wesleyan
Methodist Church in 1828.   After serving in the Caribbean for
nearly 20 years he returned to England in 1847 and spent the
next three years in Cornwall before he was appointed general
superintendent and chairman of the Wesleyan Mission in Sierra
Leone.   The Rev. Edney arrived in Freetown on December 1,
1850, and for the next four years concentrated on the construction of Buxton Memorial Church at Charles Street.   Edney left
Sierra Leone for good on July 12, 1856, on grounds of health.

ELWIN, the Rt. Rev. EDMUND HENRY, 1872-1909.   Bishop of
Sierra Leone 1902-1909.   Vice-principal of Fourah Bay College,
appointed principal after the 1898 disturbances.   Elwin was consecrated bishop of Sierra Leone on January 25, 1902.   His
predecessor, Bishop Smith, had begun repairs to the Cathedral
but had left the work unfinished.   Bishop Elwin's first task was
to complete the work of reconstructing the Cathedral, which was
consecrated, for divine worship on December 23, 1907.
      Bishop Elwin opened new Anglican stations in the Pro-
tectorate, particularly in the Limba and Yalunka countries, and
traveled widely on visits, to these missions.   He also promoted
the Africanization of the clergy at a time when in other walks
of life in the Colony Africanization as a policy had been discredited and virtually abandoned.   Elwin founded the Clergy,
Widows and Orphans Aid Association on May 26, 1903, to help
the families of deceased clergymen of the diocese.   The Association did not long survive its founder.   The Lay Readers
Association, which he also founded, still functions effectively
however.   During his episcopacy, the Church House at Westmoreland (now Siaka Stevens) Street was bought by the Pastorate
Church in 1905 and in October the same year the bishop of
Sierra Leone was by an ordinance constituted a body corporate.
In March 1906 the formation of an Anglican Province of West
Africa was discussed at a conference of bishops held in Lagos
and Elwin was elected chairman of the Conference.   Bishop El-
win died on November 9, 1909, and was buried at Kissy Road
Cemetery, Freetown.

EQUIANO, OLAUDAH (also, Gustavus Vassa).   An Ibo sold in
slavery to the West Indies, Equiano after several vicissitudes
eventually made his way to England.   He learned to read and
write, became a Christian and in 1789 published his Interesting

Narrative. Equiano in his book wrote of the great possibilities Africa held for "legitimate" as opposed to the Atlantic slave trade; that if Africans were treated as customers rather than as goods vast profits could accrue to manufacturers. In 1787, thanks to the activities of men like Sharp and Clarkson, the British Government agreed to give assistance in fitting out an expedition to rehabilitate the first colonists in Sierra Leone. The comptroller of the Navy, Sir Charles Middleton (later Lord Barham), appointed Equiano commissary to the expedition. But Equiano soon quarreled with Irwin, the London Committee's agent, which led to his dismissal. He and 23 others were not given permission to sail. Later Equiano was granted £50 compensation by the Treasury.

THE ETHIOPIAN (1876-1877). A short-lived monthly newspaper which specialized in church news; founded in 1876, printed on the CMS Grammar School Press and edited by the Rev. James Quaker, principal of the school.

EZZIDIO, JOHN. A Nupe boy recaptured in Freetown from a slave ship in 1827 and apprenticed to a French shopkeeper, Jean Billaud, who gave him the names Isadore (later changed to Ezzidio) as a surname and John as a Christian name. Ezzidio served two other Europeans after Billaud's death, and then started on his own. He prospered in business, acquired a house and by 1850 was importing goods directly from England worth about £3000-£4000 per annum. In 1835 Ezzidio became a convert to Methodism and also, successively, exhorter, classleader and local preacher. In 1844 he became alderman and in 1845 mayor of Freetown. When a new charter was proclaimed in 1863, making provision for the election of an unofficial member of the newly created legislative council, Ezzidio was elected by his fellow merchants, the first liberated African to serve on the legislative council of Sierra Leone. In 1856, largely through his agency, land was acquired at the corner of Trelawney and Oxford streets for the erection of a large new Methodist Church to rival the Anglican Cathedral and in 1858 Governor Hill laid the foundation stone of Wesley Church.

As a leading member of the community, Ezzidio was actively involved in presenting petitions and protests both to the Colonial Office in London and to the governor in Freetown. In 1847, for instance when Governor Norman William Macdonald went to England on leave, Ezzidio was among some 600 signatories who petitioned the secretary of state for the Colonies not to let the somewhat high-handed and arrogant Governor return to the Colony. Again, in 1853, Ezzidio was among those heading some 550 names protesting to the secretary of state for the Colonies against Kennedy's two ordinances, one abolishing grand juries and requiring property qualifications for petty jurors, the other enacting the compulsory registration of alien children in the Colony before a police magistrate. Both ordinances were aimed at destroying the slave trade but both were interpreted by Ezzidio and other opponents as a loss of legal rights and as re-

strictions on imported labor respectively. The petitions were
rejected by the Colonial Office. When, in 1859, Ezzidio and
other prosperous recaptives formed the National Society of the
Liberated Africans and Their Descendants, the settlers responded by forming their own society, the Nova Scotian and
Maroon Descendants Association.

In 1864, Ezzidio, eager to promote the cause of
Methodism in Sierra Leone more effectively, wrote to London
asking for a European superintendent to relieve him of his
church duties. The result of his appeal was the Rev. Benjamin Tregaskis, with whom Ezzidio soon fell out. Tregaskis
saw Ezzidio not as a brother-in-Christ but as a rival who had
to be destroyed if he, Tregaskis, was to have his way. In the
Legislative Council, Ezzidio regularly voted in favor of the
government grant to the Native Pastorate of the Anglican
Church, which Tregaskis was determined to put an end to.
Tregaskis was equally determined to prevent the completion of
Wesley Church, which epitomized Ezzidio's contribution to
Methodism in Sierra Leone. In 1867 work on the building was
stopped. Ezzidio, losing money in business and failing in
health, went to England in 1870 for a rest. His health continued to deteriorate and when he returned to Freetown he had
to be carried ashore from the ship. With characteristic lack
of Christian charity, the Rev. Benjamin Tregaskis gloated over
his enemy's misfortune and even predicted his death. In October 1872 Ezzidio died, driven to an untimely grave (he was
probably slightly over 60) by the man whose presence in the
country he had himself sponsored.

- F -

FAIRTLOUGH, Capt. EDWARD CHARLES D'HEILLMER. Born in
    Ireland in 1868, commissioned from the Dublin Military Acad-
    emy in 1888 and joined the Sierra Leone Frontier Police in
    1894. Fairtlough was appointed district commissioner in Ro-
    nietta by Cardew after the formal declaration of the Protec-
    torate. In the subsequent fighting that broke out in the Pro-
    tectorate in protest against the imposition of the hut tax, Fairt-
    lough fought in his own district, Ronietta, and also in Panguma.
    In Ronietta he took part in the campaign against Bai Kompa of
    Koya, who, although refusing to pay the hut tax, later sent
    Fairtlough £ 30 tax money from his hiding-place. Fairtlough
    nevertheless deposed him and appointed Fula Mansa to act as
    chief of Koya. Fairtlough's arbitrary and harsh methods yield-
    ed by April 1898 over £ 2500 in tax payment, mostly in cash.
    He defended Kwelu, with the help of Fula Mansa's Yonis and
    Kongoma of Kwelu's warriors, sent his Yoni allies to storm
    Bunjema, and marched on to and captured Taiama. By June
    he had marched to the relief of Panguma where he arrived on
    the 23rd. After some four days fighting, reinforced by Cun-
    ningham's relief force, Panguma fell. Fairtlough returned to
    Kwelu, taking with him Nyagua of Panguma, whom he subse-

quently sent to Freetown. When the Hut Tax War was over,
Fairtlough addressed a report to Secretary of State Chamberlain, which the Secretary sent to the press in strong support of
Cardew, thereby provoking protests from the Chambers of Commerce at what was considered a breach of official impartiality.

FALCONBRIDGE, ALEXANDER. A ship's surgeon formerly engaged in the slave trade, Falconbridge repented his earlier activities and became a champion of abolition. Impressed by the
zeal of the new convert, the directors of the Sierra Leone Company appointed him as an agent. In 1781 he arrived in Sierra
Leone with instructions from the directors to relieve and rehabilitate those settlers dispersed and displaced through the
early misfortunes in the new settlement. He reassembled 48
of the dispersed settlers, former inhabitants of the first Granville Town, moved them two miles eastwards along the estuary
to Fourah Bay and there resettled them in a village of 17 huts
also renamed Granville Town. He stayed in Sierra Leone for
six months, calling on neighboring chieftains to effect new agreements. On two of these visits to Robana he was accompanied
by his wife, Anna Maria (see following entry). By mid-1791
Falconbridge returned to London to report to the directors who
decided to raise more money for the company.

    In February 1792 Falconbridge, again accompanied by
his wife, returned to Sierra Leone as commercial agent with
new employees of the company and their families in the Company's ships the Amy, the Harpy and the Lapwing. Falconbridge's lack of self-control and his addiction to drink became
too evident this time. He was held responsible for the company's failure to progress as expected and on the basis of reports and complaints, he was dismissed from the company's
service. Already somewhat estranged from his wife, unem-
ployed and hated, Falconbridge decided to drown his sorrows
in large quantities of alcohol. When he died in 1792, his wife
while accusing the directors of treachery for dismissing him
wrote that she did not regret his death.

FALCONBRIDGE, ANNA MARIA. Wife of Alexander Falconbridge,
agent of the Sierra Leone Company. After his death she married Isaac Dubois. She accompanied her first husband to Sierra Leone on two tours between 1791 and 1793. Her impressions were published (1st ed., 1794; 2d ed., 1802) in a book
entitled Narrative of Two Voyages to the River Sierra Leone
During the Years 1791-2-3, Performed by A. M. Falconbridge.
With a succinct account of the distresses and proceedings of
that settlement; a description of the Manners, Diversions, Arts,
Commerce, Cultivation, Custom, Punishments etc. And every
interesting particular relating to the Sierra Leone Company (reprinted in 1967). Unlike most of her contemporaries who approached the subject of Africa with preconceived ideas and who
wrote more to entertain than to explain, Mrs. Falconbridge's
narrative was objective and informative. Though not the first
Englishwoman to visit Sierra Leone, she was the first to pub-

lish her experiences in Sierra Leone in the form of a book.

FARAMA, Bai.   Elected king of the Koya Temne in 1793/4 in succession to Naimbana.   Bai Farama was approached by Prince
Bartholomew Naimbana to lend support to the French attack on
Freetown in September 1794.   Farama had his own grievances
against the Colony, in particular its providing a haven of refuge
for his dissident subjects and runaway slaves.   In November
1801, in league with King Tom II and in alliance with refugee
rebels from the Colony, Bai Farama's Koya Temne attacked
Fort Thornton in Freetown, killing some 30 people, including
women and children, before the attack was repulsed.   In July
1807 peace was restored between Farama and the Colony by
means of treaty which among other provisions promised him
watering dues (henceforth collected by the government of Sierra
Leone) and an annual present in recognition of his status as
landlord.

FASSALOKKO [Fassuluku], Chief.   A Kissi war-chief who lived at
Kunduma (in present-day Liberia) before the delimitation of the
Sierra Leone-Liberian boundary in 1903.   Chief Fassalokko paid
taxes to the British Government, but even then the Chief was
regarded by the British as refractory.   Between 1904 and 1905
the Kisis, inspired by Fassalokko, made a series of raids on
what was considered to be British territory in Sierra Leone.
On December 20, 1904, the Kisis invaded Sierra Leone and
captured the town of Bakidarra, taking as prisoners four men
and 40 women and children.   Chief Fassalokko's son who was
among the raiders was killed in the encounter.   On January 23,
1905, Fassalokko's warriors again attacked a number of towns
and villages in Sierra Leone, burning a few, plundering others,
and taking away a large number of captives.   With the consent
of the secretary of state for the Colonies and the Foreign Office in London the Sierra Leone Government approached the Liberian authorities on the subject of Fassalokko's raids.   The
Liberian Government agreed that some kind of punitive action
might produce a salutary effect.   An expedition was sent to the
area under the command of Major Palmer.   On May 7, 1905,
the force arrived at Kunduma and occupied it, using it as a
base for operations.   Some of Fassalokko's towns were destroyed, but the Chief himself escaped and fled into French
territory.

FAWUNDU of Mano [Kittam].   One of the signatories to the treaty
of October 21, 1883, ceding strips of coastal territory to the
British Crown, embracing parts of Krim and Messimah--Mano
areas.   By 1888 Fawundu appears to have changed his mind.
It was rumored that he was planning to attack or blockade Pujehun.   Capt. Copland Crawford, a special services officer
sent to Sulima, gave orders for Fawundu's arrest.   In the process six of Fawundu's supporters were killed.   He was arrested but subsequently released on Governor Hay's instructions,
partly because Crawford had no authority to arrest chiefs and

partly because of lack of evidence against him. On February 10, 1887, Fawundu and other chiefs signed a treaty with Governor Sir J. S. Hay, by which they undertook to destroy stockades and give up warfare. They also agreed to an arrangement for the election of a member of the Massaquoi house as ruler of Gendama pro tempore. Fawundu died about 1894 and was succeeded by his son, Francis Fawundu.

FENTON, Adm. EDWARD. Admiral Fenton, an Englishman in command of a fleet of four ships, arrived in Sierra Leone harbor in August 1582. Setting out from England and bound for Brazil, Fenton missed his landfall and landed at Cape Mount: steering windward again he sailed into the shallow waters of Cape St. Anne and finally arrived in the estuary of the River Sierra Leone on August 9. He spent several weeks on the Sierra Leone River. Fenton's fleet was visited by three white men then living in Sierra Leone, and although one of them was said to have been born in Venice, all three were called Portuguese by Fenton's men, a pointer to the fact of Portuguese monopoly of trade and Portuguese ascendancy in the country at the time. King Farama (or Farima), living then at Robaga, also called on Fenton. Another king, Fatinca of Bullom, though not calling on Fenton, sent the Admiral a present of a monkey and a tusk of ivory. The admiral in return wrote him a letter of thanks and appreciation and sent him one and a half yards of red broadcloth and ten pounds of powder, and a "Russian" smock and a "tuppeny looking-glass" for his queen.
Fenton's men made excursions into the hills of the peninsula where they saw three "turkey cocks" and two beasts "of a brown color with short tayles and round flat hornes as big as three year old bullocks very grosse and fat." They also found elephant droppings near Aberdeen point and were amazed to see "hens just as ours." Before leaving Sierra Leone, Fenton--following Drake who had carved his name on a rock at the watering-place--put up in Queen Elizabeth's name, a copper plate inscribed with his crest, his motto "rien sans Dieu," his initials and an epigraph.

FERGUSSON, WILLIAM. Governor of Sierra Leone, 1844-1845. An Afro-West Indian army doctor, commissioned in the Royal Africa Corps, Fergusson had been serving off and on in Sierra Leone since 1815. A graduate of the Royal College of Surgeons, Edinburgh, Fergusson had for a time served as colonial surgeon in Sierra Leone and had been in charge of the recaptive hospital reopened at Kissy. On two previous occasions, in September 1841 and in June 1844, he had served as acting governor of the Colony. In July 1844, shortly after Macdonald's departure, Fergusson was appointed governor of Sierra Leone. It was during Fergusson's tenure of office that the CMS established the Grammar School at Regent-Square, Freetown, in March 1845. In the same year the CMS laid the foundation stone of a new building at Cline Town to house Fourah Bay College. Fergusson gave an address at the cere-

mony and was reported to have broken down in tears when he
mentioned that on the very spot for the building stood a slave
factory forty years previously. In May 1845 Governor Fergusson authorized commissioners to sign treaties of peace and
friendship with chiefs at Kortaigh and at Malaghea by which the
chiefs agreed to put an end to the slave trade, to refrain from
warfare and to keep open the trade routes. On the Bulom
shore in December 1845, the Governor tried to settle a long-
standing dispute between the Bulom people and recaptives over
a piece of territory "ceded" in 1792 but for years unclaimed.
Fergusson reestablished the claims of the colony to the square-
mile piece of territory known as "Clarkson Plantation" on the
Bulom Shore. Shortly afterwards he fell ill, left Sierra Leone
on December 27, 1845, and died at sea on January 19, 1846.

FERNANDES, ALVARO. Commander of the Portuguese expedition
which sailed past the River Cassamance in 1446. Fernandes
was reputed to have been one of the first European explorers
to see the coast of Sierra Leone which 16 years later in 1462
was mapped by Pedro da Sintra.

FERNANDES, VALENTIM. A German from Moravia who settled
in Lisbon as a printer. Author of Description de la côte Occi-
dental d'Afrique (Senegal au Cap de Monte 1505-1510 (Description of the West African Coast, Senegal to Cape Mount).
One of the earliest European commentators on the west coast of
Africa, Fernandes got his information secondhand, mostly from
Alvaro Velho, a Portuguese merchant who had traded in Sierra
Leone for eight years, and from other Portuguese merchants
and adventurers. Writing in 1507 from such sources Fernandes
stated that the country (Sierra Leone) was inhabited by Bullom
and Temne, the former mostly in the maritime regions, the
latter in the hinterland; that each village was ruled by a chief
called Bee and that the Temne owed allegiance to a suzerain
called Obe Vrig. Fernandes also made mention of a people in
the "north" whom he identified as Capeos (Capez, Sape) for
whom grilled puppies (for each of which they were willing to
pay the Portuguese handsomely) were a great delicacy. Fernandes also commented on the artistic skills of the Sape, particularly their ivory carving.

FESTING, Maj. AUGUSTUS MORTON. A retired pay officer appointed by Governor Rowe in 1885 as one of his special service
officers. Described as an amateur poet with a smattering of
Arabic, Festing was wont to dress sometimes in Muslim robes
as a manifestation of his contempt for and lack of faith in attempts to introduce European habits into Africa. In 1886 Rowe
sent him on a mission to the Yoni after the latter had raided
Songo in November of the previous year. Fond of hearing his
own voice, Festing held the Yoni spell-bound, confessing as he
did that he had "talked incessantly for over 23 days. " In the
end subdued by his words they promised good behavior. In
1887 and in 1888 he traveled to Bumban in the Limba country,

where he visited Chief Suluku and made peace between the Chief
and the Sofas.   Thence he traveled to Heremako, the Sofa
camp, to meet Samori.   Ignoring his instructions, Festing
talked the Sofa leader into promising a treaty (which was not
consistent with his orders) as well as granting him a railway
concession which he sent to a business friend in Freetown.
On his return journey to Freetown he died of blackwater fever
in August 1888 and was buried in the centre of the town Sinin-
koro (now destroyed).   Six months after Festing's death Samori
signed a third treaty with the French.

FINCH, WILLIAM.   An English merchant who visited Sierra Leone
in August 1607.   He kept a journal and out of it he wrote his
Remembrances Touching Sierra Leone in August 1607, and the
Bay, Countrey, Inhabitants, Rites, Fruits and Commodities.
Finch's "Remembrances" were by far the most comprehensive
and complete of the early accounts of Sierra Leone.

FINDLAY, Lt.-Col. ALEXANDER.   Governor of Sierra Leone,
1830-1833.   On April 25, 1830 Lt.-Col. Findlay arrived in
Freetown from the Gambia to assume the reins of government
of Sierra Leone.   His three-year tenure was characterized by
conflicts and feuds with virtually all sections of the community.
He clashed first with the CMS, whose clergy in Sierra Leone
he believed were recruited from undesirable elements and who
he was convinced had gone into the church not from a sense of
vocation but as he put it "to live like gentlemen."   Findlay expressed great faith in the liberated Africans and in September
he wrote with optimism to London that he was "convinced from
[his] limited experience that by the manner in which the Liberated Africans generally conduct themselves ... they have acquired such habits of industry and order as in [his] opinion
qualify the major part of them to be left to their own unre-
stricted exertions."   For the Settlers however he had little
hope or sympathy, refusing to promote them and constantly accusing them of disloyalty and sedition.
        Concerned about the "great influence which the Mo-
hammedan Priests have over the Liberated Africans" Findlay issued orders restricting the movements of the liberated Africans, prohibiting the Islamic priests from settling in any of
the liberated African villages, and directing the liberated Africans "As far as their circumstances will admit to conform to
the European mode of dress."   Determined to put an end to
what he considered to be a Muslim threat to the Colony, Findlay in August 1830 issued orders forbidding worship of idols
and suppressing "superstitious practices."   This led to an
exodus of Muslim Aku from the Colony and their subsequent
rebellion, known as the Cobolo War (see MILITARY EXPEDI-
TIONS (1)).   After suppressing the rebellion the Governor
made attempts to charge the leaders with treason.   In the adjacent territories Findlay, and later Campbell, introduced what
has been called a new peace buying policy by concluding with
the traditional rulers "the most comprehensive of early treaties

to end Civil war among the Susu and Temne, to lay down rules
for reciprocal surrender of offenders, criminals and domestic
slaves, and to provide by increased Customs a source of revenue to meet the cost of annual stipends." After convicting Mc-
Cormack in a highhanded manner for libeling his, Findlay's,
son, which Findlay believed tantamount to libeling the government, anger in the Colony rose to fever heat. In July 1833
the Governor was recalled in circumstances that savored of dis-
grace and dismissal. McCormack was released and Findlay
made amends by paying him £1000 compensation.

FITZJOHN, the Rev. WILLIAM HENRY, 1915- . Churchman,
    educator, politician, and diplomat. Born on November 5, 1915,
    at Mattru Jong, Bonthe District. Educated at the Albert Acad-
    emy, Freetown, and Lincoln University and Teachers College,
    Columbia University, USA. Ordained minister of the Evangeli-
    cal United Brethren in Christ Church, in 1946. Acting princi-
    pal, Albert Academy, 1946-1949; lecturer at Fourah Bay Col-
    lege, 1950-1959. Elected to the legislative council in 1951 as
    member for Moyamba District electoral college. Re-elected to
    the House of Representatives in 1957 as member for Moyamba
    North constituency, but resigned his seat in the same year.
    Sierra Leone's first ambassador to the United States, 1959-
    1961; high commissioner to the United Kingdom, 1961-1964;
    high commissioner to Nigeria, 1972. Author of Chief Gbondo
    (1974) and Ambassador of Christ and Caesar (1975), auto-
    biographies.

FIVE PASTORS CASE (1891-1894). A celebrated case in the an-
    nals of the Anglican Church in Sierra Leone. The case in-
    volved Bishop Ingham and the Church Committee on the one
    hand and five pastors--the Rev. M. Taylor of Waterloo, the
    Rev. G. I. Macaulay of Kissy, the Rev. S. G. Hazeley of
    Wellington, the Rev. Moses Pearce of Christ Church, Padem-
    ba Road, and the Rev. H. P. Thompson of Bengueme--on the
    other. The case arose out of the refusal of the five pastors
    to sign the "Articles of Arrangement" or the new constitution
    drawn up by Bishop Ingham in 1890. (See INGHAM.)

FLANSIRE. King of the Folgias during the first half of the 17th
    century. In a series of raids Flansire was able to conquer the
    whole coastal area westward of the Sierra Leone River and to
    appoint viceroys in his new territories. One of these viceroys
    whom he appointed further south was called Selbore (or Sel-
    boere or Sherabola). The viceroys appointed by Flansire in
    the Gallinas area conspired and rebelled against him. After
    much fighting, they asserted their independence and divided
    Flansire's territories among themselves. Assisted by his
    eldest son Flamburre, Flansire temporarily restored his au-
    thority over the rebellious vassals. By 1670 Flamburre, who
    had succeeded his father, was baptized by the Portuguese mis-
    sionaries and renamed Don Philip.

FLEMING, Sir FRANCIS, 1842-1922. Governor of Sierra Leone,
1892-1894. Born in 1842, entered the Colonial service in 1869,
and served in various capacities in Mauritius, the Seychelles,
the Caribbean and in Hong Kong. Appointed governor of Sierra
Leone in 1892, he arrived in Freetown in May of that year and
took the oath of office. He was the first governor who con-
sciously tried, by revising the Standing Orders of the Council,
to transform the Legislative Council from a mere committee to
a political assembly. During his tenure, proceedings of the
Council assumed the form of parliamentary debates and the ri-
gid distinction between "official" and "unofficial" members became somewhat blurred. Fleming's policy up-country, which
he visited only once, was considerably influenced by the views
of J. C. E. Parkes, head of the Department of Native Affairs.
Fleming revived the civil service entrance examination and
favored local promotions. In February 1893, the Freetown
Municipality Ordinance was passed, ushering a new phase in
the city's history. In November 1892, the first serious strike
in the Colony took place at the barracks over wages. But the
Governor contained the strikers and the matter was amicably
settled. The Sierra Leone Times applauded him as the most
popular governor since Hennessy. Towards the end of 1893 he
reluctantly sanctioned a military expedition against the Sofas,
which led to the tragedy at Waiima in December 1893 (see
MILITARY EXPEDITIONS (12)). Early in 1894 Fleming returned ill to England.

FORAY, CYRIL PATRICK, 1934-   . Minister of Foreign Affairs,
1969-1971. Born March 16, 1934; educated at our Lady of
Victories School, Gerihum, Sacred Heart School, Serabu, St.
Columba's School, Moyamba, and St. Edwards' Secondary
School, Freetown. Entered Fourah Bay College (University of
Durham), Freetown, in 1952; then proceeded to St. Cuthbert's
Society, Durham University, England, where he took a degree
in modern history, 1957; post-graduate diploma in education,
1958; assistant master and senior assistant master St. Edward's
Secondary School, 1958-1962; worked for British Petroleum
(West Africa) Ltd., 1962-1964; lecturer, Njala University Col-
lege; post-graduate student at African Studies Centre, University of California, Los Angeles (USA), 1965-1967; detained by
NRC military regime, 1967; lecturer at Fourah Bay College,
1968-1969. Elected member of Parliament for Bo Town I
Constituency, March 1969; appointed minister of external affairs, April 1969, and minister of health, May 1971. In September 1971 relieved of duties as cabinet minister; lecturer,
Department of History, Fourah Bay College, University of Sierra Leone; detained under emergency regulations August-October
1974.

FORAY VONG. Chief of Taiama in the 1890s and signatory to the
Treaty of Friendship with Governor Hay, signed at Taiama on
January 3, 1891. Foray Vong was one of the chiefs who re-
sisted the hut tax. He was held responsible for the killing of

two American missionaries, the Rev. and Mrs. L. A. McGrew, at Taiama during the 1898 Hut Tax War. Foray Vong was subsequently convicted and executed at Kwelu after the cessation of hostilities.

FORKI, Bai. Chief of Maforki, Port Loko, in the Karene District in the 1890s. In 1897, a year after the Protectorate was declared, Capt. Cave-Browne-Cave, acting for Capt. Wilfred Stanley Sharpe as district commissioner of Karene, invited Paramount chiefs in the district to Karene, to receive their new insignia of office--a gold-headed staff. Bai Forki of Maforki failed to turn up. Cave-Browne-Cave dispatched a force of frontier police to bring him to Karene, by force if need be. Bai Forki was put under arrest but his people at Port Loko rallied and rescued him from the police. (A Port Loko headman was later fined for taking part in this rescue operation.) In 1898 when the Hut Tax War broke out, Bai Forki supported Bai Bureh, because, it was alleged, of the outrages of the troops who had destroyed some of his towns. He also blockaded the road to Falaba. Col. John Willoughby Marshall, in command at Port Loko, marched through Maforki Chiefdom, destroying more of Bai Forki's towns. After the defeat of his forces Bai Forki surrendered, bringing the hut tax military operations in the Karene district to a close. Sharpe sentenced him to 15 years' imprisonment at hard labor. Governor Cardew confirmed the sentence, but the sentence was disallowed after the publication of the law officer's report on Bai Bureh. Bai Forki was however detained in Freetown where Maj. Nathan, acting governor in the absence of Cardew, kept him until his country was considered peaceful enough. (His Successors in the Maforki Chiefdom, Port Loko District, also held the title Bai Forki.)

FORNA, A. G. SEMBU, 1932- . Minister of finance (1970-1971). Born at Penlap near Makeni on April 11, 1932. Educated at the Binkolo Boys School, Rogbane Day School, Koyeima Government School and the Bo Government School. He entered Fourah Bay College in 1952 and subsequently won a UNESCO fellowship to study fundamental education in India. He then proceeded to Britain to study diamond valuation under the auspices of the Anglo-American Corporation. Before joining this firm, Forna worked in the Sierra Leone Civil Service as assistant social development officer from 1955-1958. He worked for the Diamond Corporation West Africa Ltd. from 1962 to 1967. In 1967 he was elected member of Parliament for the Bombali South constituency. In April 1969, he was appointed minister of transport and communications and in September 1970, minister of finance. He has also held the portfolios of agriculture and natural resources, health, and tourism and cultural affairs. He was returned to Parliament unopposed in the general election of 1973.

FORNA, M. S. , 1935-1975. Minister of finance (1968-1970).

Born in 1935; educated at EUB Primary School Moyamba, the Bo Government School, and at the University of Aberdeen, where he qualified as a medical doctor. He returned home, worked briefly in the Ministry of Health, joined the army as medical officer with the rank of captain and finally went into private practice. In 1967 he was elected to Parliament as member for Tonkolili West constituency. Detained by the NRC from July to November 1967; in 1968 he was appointed minister of finance and acted as prime minister on several occasions between 1968 and 1970. In 1970 September he was detained under the emergency regulations and his parliamentary seat was subsequently declared vacant. Released from detention in 1973, he went into business. In July 1974 he was arrested and charged with treason. In July 1975 he was executed at Pademba Road Prison.

FORSTER, LATI-HYDE. Principal, Annie Walsh Memorial School 1961-1975, after serving as vice-principal of the school from 1955-1961. First Sierra Leonean woman B.A. graduate of Fourah Bay College (University of Durham), 1938. Retired as principal of Annie Walsh Memorial School in 1975.

FOURAH BAY COLLEGE [FBC]. Originally the CMS Christian Institution refounded as Fourah Bay College, or Institution, in Freetown in 1827 for the training of Anglican clergymen; affiliated to the University of Durham, England, in 1876. In 1918 the Wesleyan Methodist Society became associated with the CMS in the management and work of the College and a council representing both societies was set up. Ten years later the government of Sierra Leone established a normal course at the college for the training of primary school teachers. In 1945, the Methodist Women's Teacher Training College was absorbed into Fourah Bay College. In 1943 the Elliot Commission on Higher Education in West Africa visited the College and a minority of the commissioners recommended the continued existence of the College. During World War II FBC was housed at Mabang in the Moyamba District. After the war it was transferred to its present site on Mount Aureol in Freetown. In May 1950 the Sierra Leone government established a new council for FBC representing all sections of the country. By then the CMS had indicated that it could no longer run the College as a private institution or from its own resources.

In 1954 Sir John Fulton was appointed to head a commission to make recommendations "on a long-term policy for Fourah Bay College." On the recommendation of the Fulton Commission, the Sierra Leone government assumed full responsibility for the College. Degree courses in science and diploma courses in engineering were introduced in addition to the courses in arts and economic studies offered. In 1965, degree courses in civil, mechanical and electrical engineering were started at the College. These developments necessitated the removal in 1959 of the Teacher Training Department from FBC, which then became by the grant of a royal charter, the

University College of Sierra Leone. In 1966 FBC became a
constituent College of the University of Sierra Leone (USL) set
up by the University of Sierra Leone Act of 1967, which brought
to an end the almost century-long connection with Durham University. In 1969 the last set of FBC students took Durham degrees. Thereafter FBC conferred USL degrees. The College
now has a student population of over 1000 drawn from a large
number of countries in Africa and elsewhere.

FRAZER, Capt. ALEXANDER MACLEAN. A Royal African Corps
officer, he arrived in Sierra Leone on January 12, 1830, and
held office as acting governor until April 25. As acting governor, Frazer was also acting commissary judge. Over-con-
scious of his seniority and insistent on his exercise of authority,
Frazer quarrelled with other members of the court of Mixed
Commission. Six slave ships carrying 1200 recaptives lay an-
chored in the harbor while Frazer and his colleagues argued
about rights and procedure, until April 1830 when Lt.-Col.
Alexander Findlay arrived from the Gambia to take over the
reins of government. Findlay declared Frazer's acts illegal,
a whole year was spent on partisan politics, brawls and duels
until Findlay finally succeeded in sending Frazer back home.
Frazer returned in 1832 to continue to create problems for
Findlay until Findlay then left the colony in 1833.

THE FREE PRESS AND SIERRA LEONE WEEKLY ADVERTISER
    (1861-1865). Newspaper founded and published by Moses Henry
Davies.

FREETOWN. Capital of the Republic of Sierra Leone: population
250,000; founded in 1792. Initially the home of freed slaves,
Nova Scotians, Maroons and liberated Africans, Freetown's
population now includes large numbers of tribal immigrants
from the interior. In September 1794 the town was attacked
and destroyed by a French naval squadron. Rebuilt, it was
again attacked in 1801 and 1802 by neighboring Temne in alliance with some dissident Nova Scotians. Between 1821 and
1827 Freetown became the administrative headquarters of the
British West African Settlements. The Gold Coast was separated in 1827. In 1843 the Gold Coast was once more placed
under the governor of Sierra Leone in Freetown and the Gambia
was separated. The Gold Coast was again separated in 1850.
In 1866 the Gold Coast and Lagos were placed under the governor of Sierra Leone and in 1874 Lagos and the Gold Coast became separate governments.
        Because of its first-class natural harbor, the port was
used by ships plying the west coast of Africa. After the abolition of the slave trade by the British Parliament in 1807,
Freetown became the base of operations for the British naval
squadron against slave ships as well as the seat of the Mixed
Commission Courts (q.v.). In both world wars Freetown was
used by the British as a naval base. Freetown was fancifully
described, particularly in the second half of the 19th century,

as the "Athens of West Africa."

THE FREETOWN EXPRESS AND CHRISTIAN OBSERVER (1882-
     1884). Newspaper founded by J. E. Gooding, nephew of M. H.
Davies by marriage, and incorporating The West African Chron-
icle and Gooding's Advertising Journal, established in 1872.

FRONTIER POLICE   see   SIERRA LEONE POLICE

FULA MANSA. (Successive holders of title in Yoni, Tonkolili Dis-
     trict.) After the 1725 jihad in Futa Jalon, Muslim adventurers,
Fula, Mandinka and Susu sought their fortunes elsewhere. Some
moved towards the coastal areas; others moved into the central
and eastern Sudan. A few established dynasties in the areas
into which they moved. In the hinterland of Sierra Leone, a
Fula mansa (or king) became ruler in Yoni country among the
Temne in the second half of the 18th century. About 1786 we
are told that "A Foulah Mohamedan from the Futa country,
journeyed into the Mendi country, and, residing there, in time
became wealthy and renowned for the efficacy of his charms,
which were reputed to have more power than any other medicine man in that part of the country in which he resided. For
this reason they styled him Foulah Mansa, or the Foulah King,
and marrying many wives, he soon became allied to most of
the principal chiefs of the country and the owner of many slaves.
At his death his eldest son, adopting his name, took to war as
his occupation, and conquered a vast extent of country now
known as Yonnie district and bounded on the east by various
Timanee districts, on the south by the Mendi, Bompeh and
Sherbro countries and north and west by the Quiah and Masi-
merah districts."
     One of these Fula Mansa, a staunch and loyal supporter
of the British, was made acting chief of Koya in 1898 in place
of Bai Kompa, whom the British deposed. The Fula Mansa
also took part as an ally of the British in the hut tax military
operations in Ronietta district. In one of the campaigns at
Bunjema the Fula Mansa was killed.

FYFE, C. H. The leading historian of Sierra Leone. Author of,
     among other works, the monumental (773-page) A History of
Sierra Leone (1962), A Short History of Sierra Leone (1962),
The Sierra Leone Inheritance (1964), and Africanus Horton:
West African Scientist and Patriot (1972), and editor of E. W.
Blyden's Christianity, Islam and the Negro Race (1968). Mr.
Fyfe has also written several articles on Sierra Leone and
African history in learned journals the world over. He served
as government archivist in Sierra Leone from 1950 to 1952 and
is now reader in African history at the Centre of African Stud-
ies, University of Edinburgh.

FYLE, CLIFFORD NELSON. Educator and author. Born in Free-
     town, educated at the Methodist Boys High School, Fourah Bay
College (University of Durham), Freetown, Hatfield College,

Durham University, England, University of Leeds, England, and
the University of Indiana and the University of California at
Los Angeles, USA. Acting head, Department of English,
Fourah Bay College, and external examiner in English language,
University of Ibadan, Nigeria, since 1973. Fyle wrote the national anthem of Sierra Leone and a number of short stories,
including "Of All Things Visible and Invisible" (1960), "Stray
Lad" (1962), and "Hunted" (1962). Also the author of children's books, including Tough, Ugly Weeds (1966), Tommy and
the Mango (1966), and The Farm That Went Mad (1971). Fyle
wrote pedagogic texts as well, related to the development of
good reading and writing skills in English among students of
developing countries.

- G -

GABBIDON, STEPHEN. A Maroon who prospered in business in
Freetown in the early decades of the 19th century. In 1815
with Samuel Thorpe, another Maroon, Gabbidon arrived in London on a mission of protest against some of Governor Maxwell's measures. By 1822 Gabbidon was appointed sheriff, refusing in 1825 the post of mayor because his trade kept him
away often from the capital. Acting in concert with his trade
partner, Savage, whom in 1828 he recommended in vain to the
Colonial Office for the post of king's advocate, Gabbidon put
forward suggestions to help the settlers believe that the government existed for their benefit rather than for that of others.
Among other things he recommended the establishment of a
chamber of commerce to serve as an advisory body, and perhaps administer the Colony's revenue. In 1831, Governor Findlay strengthened the Freetown garrison by raising a militia, appointing, in an effort to mollify the settlers, Gabbidon as major
and two others as lieutenants. Gabbidon and Savage, on December 30, 1825, signed a treaty with Amura of Forekaria, king
of Moribia, for lease of the island of Matacong. Kenneth Macaulay as acting governor thwarted these moves by securing
their withdrawal from the island and its cession to the colony.
  Gabbidon was prosperous enough to pay a number of
business trips to England but when he died in 1839, his substantial properties in Water, George and Trelawney streets of
Freetown had to be sold to cover his debts.

GALLINAS see KONO AND VAI

GANDA, the Most Rev. JOSEPH HENRY, 1932- . First Mende
Catholic priest and first Sierra Leonean Catholic bishop. Born
at Serabu, Bumpe Chiefdom, Bo District, and educated at the
Sacred Heart School Serabu, St. Edward's Secondary School,
Freetown, Bigard Memorial Seminary, Enugu, Nigeria, St.
Peter's College, Rome, and Claver House, London. Ordained
a priest in Bo--the first ordination ceremony ever of a Catho-
lic priest in Sierra Leone--on April 9, 1961, and consecrated

a Catholic bishop at Kenema on February 21, 1971, also a first
for Sierra Leone. Worked in Moyamba Parish, 1962-1966, and
in Blama Parish, 1966. Lecturer at the Catholic Training College, Bo, and director of the Catechetical Centre for the diocese of Freetown and Bo, 1968-1969. Parish priest of Kenema
1969 and first bishop of the newly created diocese of Kenema,
1970.

GBANA, LEWIS see BE SHERBRO

GBANKA of Yoni. A powerful warrior; son of a Yoni Temne father
and a Kpa Mende mother. Gbanka fought many wars in Temne
country, particularly against the territories of Marampa, Masimera, Malal, and Kholifa. He also conducted a number of successful campaigns against the Kpa Mende but later changed
sides and allied with them against the Yoni. His campaigns
against some chiefs considered refractory by the British won
him the support and friendship of the governor. However, in
1888 Gbanka was imprisoned in Freetown for attacking territories within British jurisdiction or territories whose rulers
had signed treaties with the British. On his release in 1894,
he returned to Yonibana and although he had no right or claim
to the chieftaincy of Yoni made up his mind to become the next
Fula Mansa. With the support of the British he got himself installed as Fula Mansa of Yoni in 1898. When the Hut Tax War
broke out in 1898, Gbanka as Fula Mansa fought as an ally of
the British, who also made him acting chief of Koya. He was
killed at Bunjema in 1898. (See also FULA MANSA.)

GBANYA of Senehun. A powerful Mende chief who ruled the Upper
Bagru area between the 1850s and 1875. He had helped British
forces during the Koya expedition in 1861 and had also sent a
small contingent of men to serve on the British expedition
against the Ashanti during the Ashanti invasion in December
1872 of the British Gold Coast Protectorate. Gbanya supported
George Stephen Caulker in the wars against the latter's cousin
John Caulker in 1875. In December 1875, Gbanya, with the
Caulkers, signed a treaty of peace with the British. He died
in 1878 and was succeeded by his widow, Madam Yoko.

GBERRI [Gberry] of Gbonge [Imperri]. One of the chiefs who
signed treaties of peace and friendship with the British on
February 6, 1880. He quarreled with and fought a war against
Chief Seppe, a Bumpe. Chief Gberry won the support of Mr.
Laborde, acting civil commandant in the Sherbro who, with few
exceptions, viewed these wars as trade wars in which coastal
chiefs were ranged against chiefs of the interior.

GBOW [Kpow] of Talia. One of the influential warrior chiefs who
before the formal declaration of the Protectorate actively resisted the extension of British influence into the hinterland.
He aimed at paralyzing trade in the Sierra Leone Colony by
organizing a boycott of Creole and European traders operating

in his part of the country. He also tried to disrupt the communications system of the Sierra Leone government. Early in
April 1883, Gbow and his warriors attacked the territories of
Chief W. E. Tucker, occupied a number of villages, and destroyed others. They then blockaded trade along the Boom and
Kittam rivers, threatened to attack the customs post at Tama-
lay, and finally seized money from a constable which was meant
to pay the Sierra Leone police stationed at Barmany.

An expedition commanded by Acting Governor F. F.
Pinkett left Freetown on April 12 for Sherbro to put an end to
Gbow's exploits. Also a reward of £50 was offered for his arrest. Some of his stockaded towns were destroyed, he himself
escaped, but four of his able lieutenants--Bi (or Be) Yormah,
Gangarah, Congofoh and Langabai--were arrested and detained
as political prisoners in Freetown, an ordinance to that effect
having been passed on July 18, 1883. Gangarah died in detention.

Capt. A. E. Havelock, the governor, traveled to
Sherbro in October to make an on-the-spot inquiry into the circumstances of the arrest and detention of the three survivors.
As a result of his inquiries, Bi Yormah and Langabai were released on the instructions of the secretary of state. Congofoh
was tried in the Supreme Court in November and convicted.
Gbow, still at large, rebuilt his fortifications. There was
strictly speaking no legal basis for these arrests, detentions
and trials as these men were not under British jurisdiction,
even if, admittedly they did raid territory within British jurisdiction. Governor Havelock on October 21, 1883, signed
treaties of "cession" of territory with the chiefs of Krim country. As a result the government issued a proclamation in November 1883 that, effective January 1, 1884, Sulymah, Manoh
Salijah, and Combraya (or Kittam Point) would become customs
ports.

GBUJAMA, SHIRLEY YEMA, 1936- . Born in 1936. Educated at
Harford School for Girls, Moyamba, Fourah Bay College, and
the State University of New York. Taught at Harford School
and worked at Bank of Sierra Leone as research officer, 1966-
1972. Promoted Senior Research Officer, 1967, and later became head of the Domestic Economy Division. Appointed Sierra Leone's first woman ambassador 1972, accredited to Ethiopia.

GENDA, Lt.-Col. A. P. First chairman of the National Reformation Council (NRC) military regime, 1967. On his way home
to assume office, Genda was summarily removed from the
chairmanship on the grounds (it was rumored) that he was determined to hand over power to the party that had won the general elections in March 1967. He was requested to disembark
at Las Palmas and to wait for further instructions. In effect
Genda was head of government and head of state of Sierra
Leone from March 23-30, 1967. Appointed Sierra Leone's ambassador to Liberia, 1967-1968; deputy force commander, 1968;

Sierra Leone's high commissioner to London, 1968-1969, and
Sierra Leone's ambassador to Moscow, 1969-1970. He now
lives in London.

GEORGE, CLAUDE (also, Esu Biyi). Author and educator. One
of the earliest indigenous Sierra Leonean writers. After obtain-
ing a Durham degree from Fourah Bay College, he taught for a
while, then joined government service and rose to be a senior
clerk at the Secretariat. In 1902, following the practice which
had become fashionable among some Creoles in the last two
decades of the 19th century, he changed his name to Esu Biyi.
Digging among official records and other written sources, he
published The Rise of British West Africa in 1904. A second
edition came out in 1968. The book, dedicated to Sir Alfred
Jones, covered the period 1787-1827. The subtitle of the book
indicated it included "the early history of The Colony of Sierra
Leone, The Gambia, Lagos, Gold Coast etc. with a brief account of climate, the growth of education, commerce and religion and a comprehensive history of the Bananas and Baunce
Islands, and sketches of the constitution."

GODMAN, the Rev. MATTHEW, 1816-1881. Chairman and general
superintendent of the Methodist Mission in Sierra Leone, 1877-
1881. Born in England in 1816 Godman became a convert to
Methodism in 1834. In 1877 he was appointed chairman of the
Sierra Leone District after serving in the Gambia and in Cape
Colony, South Africa. As chairman in Sierra Leone he sought
and obtained the Missionary Committee's approval to open mission stations in the hinterland. As a result of Godman's exertions, Methodist mission stations were opened at Mokelleh on
the Bagru in 1878, at Forekaria in 1880 and at Mabang on the
Ribi in the same year. On January 1, 1880, the Wesleyan Female Institution was established in Freetown by a private company, whose members though drawn from various denominations,
were predominantly Wesleyans. The Rev. Godman, who was in
the chair on the opening day, had emphasized the need for another girl's secondary school to serve the educational needs of
the community. It was publicly acknowledged at the ceremony
that the scheme owed its success to Rev. Godman's zeal and
patience. He retired from Sierra Leone in 1882 and died on
June 25, 1887.

GOVERNORS (to 1961) AND GOVERNORS-GENERAL (1961-1971) OF
SIERRA LEONE. 1792 Lt. John Clarkson; 1792-93 Lt. William
Dawes, R.N.; 1794-95 Zachary Macauley; 1795-96 Dawes; 1796-
99 Macauley; 1799 John Gray; 1799-1800 Thomas Ludlam; 1800
Gray; 1801-03 Dawes; 1803 Capt. William Day, R.N.; 1803-05
Ludlam; 1805 Day; 1806-08 Ludlam; 1808-10 Lt. T. P. Thomp-
son, R.N.; 1810-11 Capt. E. H. Columbine, R.N.; 1811-14
Lt. Col. C. W. Maxwell; 1814-24 Col. Sir Charles McCarthy;
1825-26 Maj.-Gen. Sir Neil Campbell, C.B.; 1828 Lt. Col.
Dixon Denam; 1830-33 Col. A. Findlay; 1833-34 Maj. O. Tem-
ple; 1835-37 Maj. H. D. Campbell; 1837-40 Lt. Col. R. Do-

herty; 1840-41 Sir John Jeremie, Kt.; 1842-44 Col. G. Macdonald; 1844-45 Staff-Surgeon Fergusson; 1846-52 N. W. Macdonald; 1852-54 Capt. A. E. Kennedy; 1854-62 Col. S. J. Hill;
1862-68 Maj. S. W. Blackhall; 1868-72 Sir Arthur Kennedy,
C.B.; 1872-73 J. P. Hennessey, C.M.G.; 1873 R. W. Keate;
1873-74 G. Berkeley; 1875-77 C. H. Kortright; 1877 Sir Samuel
Rowe, K.C.M.G.; 1881-84 Capt. A. E. Havelock, K.C.M.G.;
1885-88 Rowe; 1888-91 Capt. Sir James Hay, K.C.M.G.; 1892-
94 Sir Francis Fleming, K.C.M.G.; 1894-1900 Col. Sir Freder-
ick Cardew, K.C.M.G.; 1900-04 Sir C. A. King-Harman,
K.C.M.G.; 1904-11 Sir Leslie Probyn, K.C.M.G.; 1911-16
Sir Edward Mereweather, K.C.M.G.; 1916-22 R. J. Wilkinson,
C.M.G.; 1922-27 Sir Ransford Slater, K.C.M.G., C.B.E.;
1927-31 Brig.-Gen. Sir J. A. Byrne, K.C.M.G., K.B.E.,
C.B.; 1931-34 Sir Arnold Hudson, K.C.M.G.; 1934-37 Sir
Henry Moore, K.C.M.G.; 1937-41 Sir Douglas Jardine,
K.C.M.G., O.B.E.; 1941-48 Sir Hubert Stevenson, K.C.M.G.,
O.B.E., M.C.; 1948-53 Sir George Beresford Stooke,
K.C.M.G.; 1953-56 Sir Robert de Zouche Hall, K.C.M.G.;
1956-61 Sir Maurice H. Dorman, K.C.M.G.; 1961 April-62
Sir Maurice H. Dorman, K.C.M.G.; 1962-69 Sir Henry Ligh-
foot-Boston, G.C.M.G.; 1969-71 Sir Banja Tejan-Sie.

GRANT, MARCUS C., 1909- . Born in Macdonald Village, Waterloo District, in 1909 and educated at the Church of England
School, Bathurst Village, the CMS Grammar School and the Albert Academy, Freetown. Grant started life as a clerk in a
lawyer's office where he worked for 13 years; he served in the
Public Works Department and finally, through the efforts of
Wallace-Johnson, joined the Trade Union Movement and became
general secretary of the Artisans and Allied Workers Union.
In February 1955 Grant led a general strike in Freetown of all
daily wage employees of Public Works, Electricity, Railway,
and Sanitary and Waterworks departments, commercial employees, civilians of the Admiralty and Imperial departments, private contractors, and others, for higher wages. In a prior
public notice posted and signed by Grant (as "Workers' representative") explaining the strike, he said, "... It is to be appreciated that the undermentioned action for which we have now
resolved is not done maliciously with a view to break contract
of service with Departments of any description, nor will such
action be intended to deprive the inhabitants of this Colony and
Protectorate of Sierra Leone, but that such action is borne of
extreme circumstances over which we have no control. Please
observe this as Notice served upon your undertaking and/or
Department and on you and on your management of affairs that
three days after ... this notice ... there will be a General
Strike when all tools will be down until further notice. Dated
this 5th day of February, 1955...."
        The government appointed Sir John Shaw as chairman of
a commission of enquiry into the strike and the accompanying
riots and looting. Grant gave evidence for 15 hours before the
commission and submitted reasons for his refusal to accept ar-

bitration and to resort to strike action. The most important
reason he gave was government's unwillingness to accept the
workers' demand for a ten pence increase in wages and its refusal to pay above sixpence. Strike casualties, all of which
occurred on February 11 and 12, were as follows: 1 policeman and 17 civilians killed; 61 police and 60 civilians wounded.

Hardly had the strike been called off when the formation
of a political party, the Sierra Leone Labour Party, was announced. Marcus Grant was one of the moving spirits and held
the position of joint national secretary of the party. Although
Grant maintained in his evidence before the Shaw Commission
that the formation of the party had long been planned and had
little or nothing to do with the industrial unrest, the timing was
suspicious. At any rate the party itself initially enjoyed much
support and sympathy because it was widely believed that Grant
and, ipso facto the workers, had had a raw deal at the Commission's hands. The party's popularity was however short-
lived and it ceased to exist after its debacle in the 1957 general
elections.

In May 1962, Grant was elected as an independent member of Parliament for the Waterloo District constituency. After
consultations with his constituents he was authorized to declare
for a party and he took his seat in Parliament as a Sierra
Leone People's Party member.

For some 26 years Grant was general secretary of the
Artisans and Allied Workers Union which meanwhile changed its
name to the Artisans, Ministry of Works and General Workers
Union. Largely because of political pressure (his new party
connection did not have the blessing of the bulk of his union
membership) Grant resigned from the Artisans and Allied Workers Union in 1964. He then became general secretary of the
Maritime and Waterfront Workers Union which was affiliated to
the Sierra Leone Labour Congress. This connection made it
possible for Mr. Grant to become the President of the Sierra
Leone Labour Congress. Following the withdrawal of the Maritime and Waterfront Workers Union from the Labour Congress,
he resigned his presidency of the Congress in 1973. The Maritime and Waterfront Workers Union, of which he is still general secretary, then became affiliated with the Sierra Leone
Council of Labour.

GRANT, WILLIAM, ca. 1830-1882. One of the most successful
businessmen and one of the most distinguished Sierra Leoneans
in the 19th century. Member of the Legislative Council (1870-
1882) and from 1874 the senior African Unofficial member.
One of the sponsors of the newspaper The Negro and proprietor
of The West African Reporter. Staunchly religious and a good
churchman, Grant consistently supported the Native Church
Pastorate Grant. He was also a champion of British annexation of territories adjacent to the Colony. As one of the chief
promoters of agriculture, Grant in 1880 established an estate
called Rowesville (in honor of Governor Rowe) on which he cultivated rice, sugarcane and cocoa. Born in Freetown about

1830 of liberated African parentage, a self-educated man, with much intellect, strong character and singular determination (he was nicknamed "Independent Grant") Grant, like some of his very able contemporaries, died in his prime in 1882.

GRANVILLE TOWN I.   Town founded in May 1787 and called after Granville Sharp by the first settlers.   The town was located between the watering place and today's State House.   This town was attacked and destroyed by the Temne in December, 1789.

GRANVILLE TOWN II.   Founded in 1791 by Alexander Falconbridge an agent of the Sierra Leone Company sent out to rescue the settlers dispersed from the first Granville Town.   Falconbridge assembled some 48 of the survivors and moved them two miles eastwards near Fourah Bay and there built Granville Town II, a village of 17 huts abandoned as haunted by evil spirits.   The residents of Granville Town I were allowed to resettle in Freetown, the name given to the new town founded by the Nova Scotians who arrived in 1792.

GRAY JOHN.   Member of Governor's Council, accountant of the Sierra Leone Company and later commercial agent of the Company.   In 1795 Gray visited parts of the Kamaranka and Bompe rivers in an effort to promote trade with the Colony.   Encouraged by what he saw, he planned (but never carried out) an expedition to the Mediterranean through Timbuktu and the Sahara desert.   In Freetown, Gray successfully cultivated coffee on some 20 acres on his farm to the east of town (the site of the present Bishopscourt).   Later he resigned his membership in the Governor's Council and took to slave trading.   He forfeited his farm in consequence and died at Bassia in 1807.   On two occasions, in 1799 and in 1800, Gray acted for short periods as governor of Sierra Leone.

GULAMA, PC ELLA KOBLO.   Born at Moyamba, educated at Harford School for Girls, Moyamba, and at the Women Teachers' Training College, Wilberforce.   First Sierra Leonean woman member of the cabinet and the first woman to take a seat in the national legislature.   Elected paramount chief of Kaiyamba Chiefdom, Moyamba District, 1953.   Elected to the House of Representatives 1957, re-elected member of Parliament, 1962, and appointed minister without portfolio and a member of the cabinet, 1964.   She has also held the following positions: member of Scholarships Advisory Committee, president of Sierra Leone Women's Federation, and member of the Sierra Leone Library Board.

GULAMA, PC JULIUS.   One of the few educated chiefs in the then Protectorate in the post-World War II period who appreciated the need for alliance and cooperation between traditional rulers and the educated elite of the Protectorate.   Only paramount chief member of the Sierra Leone Organisation Society (SOS) and the Society's honorary president.   One of the moving spirits behind the formation of the SLPP.   Chief Gulama died in 1952.

- H -

HAENSEL, the Rev. CHARLES LEWIS FREDERICK.   A Bavarian
   missionary from the Basel Missionary Institution sent out by
   the CMS in January 1827 to revive the Christian Institution.
   On April 3, 1827, the Rev. Haensel reopened the Christian
   Institution in Freetown and received his first pupil.   He became
   the first principal of Fourah Bay College when the Christian Institution was transferred to Cline Town and renamed Fourah
   Bay Institution, or College, at the beginning of 1828.

HAIDARA CONTORFILI see MILITARY EXPEDITIONS (15)

HAMELBERG, the Rev. EDWARD, C. S. Sp. , 1915- . Born
   August 11, 1915, educated at St. Edward's primary and secondary schools, Freetown; studied for the priesthood in France and
   ordained the first Sierra Leonean Roman Catholic priest in 1939.
   Awarded Bronze Cross for bravery on April 2, 1932, by the
   then Governor Sir Arnold Hudson.   He also won the Royal Hu-
   mane Society Award for gallantry in the same year.   Tutor at
   St. Edward's Secondary School, 1942-1947; 1958-1969.   First
   principal of the Catholic Training College (CTC) Bo; parish
   priest, Sacred Heart Parish, Freetown.

HAMILTON-HAZELEY, LOTTIE ELIZA AMY, 1909-1972.   One of
   Sierra Leone's leading female educators.   Teacher at Osora
   School, the Freetown Secondary School for Girls (FSSG), 1927-
   1955, where she rose to the post of vice-principal, 1952-1955.
   First principal of the Magburaka Government Secondary School
   for Girls, 1956-1966.   Principal of the Young Women's Christian Association (YWCA) Vocational Institute, Freetown, 1966;
   president of the Sierra Leone YWCA and Education Secretary
   for the All African Conference of Churches, with headquarters
   at Ibadan, Nigeria, 1966-1971.   She died on February 20, 1972,
   and was buried in Freetown.

HARGREAVES, J. D.   One of the best-known historians of Sierra
   Leone and of West Africa.   Author of "A Life of Sir Samuel
   Lewis" (1958) and of several articles on Sierra Leone in various learned journals.   The "partition of West Africa" is Professor Hargreaves' major interest in African History and he
   has published three substantial volumes on the topic.   From
   1952-1954, Hargreaves was senior lecturer and head of the
   Department of History at FBC (University of Durham), and
   editor of Sierra Leone Studies, the journal of the Sierra Leone
   Society.   He now is a professor of history at the University of
   Aberdeen.

HARRIS, J. M.   Author of Annexations to Sierra Leone and Their
   Influence on British Trade with West Africa (1883; reprinted

1975). A Jewish tailor from Chatham, England, who came out to Sierra Leone to trade in 1855. He set up business first on Yelbana Island in the Sherbro estuary. By 1860 he was prosperous enough to open a factory at Sulymah (Sulima) in the Gallinas country. The Liberian government, laying claims to the Gallinas, seized Harris's ships for violating their customs regulations and towed them off to Monrovia. Harris demanded redress and appealed to the governor of Sierra Leone, Col. S. J. Hill, who sent a gunboat to retrieve the ships. When the Liberian authorities refused to surrender them, the captain of the gunboat seized the ships and brought them back. Since boundaries between Liberia and Sierra Leone were not clearly demarcated, it was decided to appoint a boundary commission to settle the limits of Liberian jurisdiction.

Harris, while resisting Liberian government claims to the Gallinas and adjacent territories, was far from enthusiastic about extending British jurisdiction over the area, although he maintained that his successful rebuttal of Liberian pretensions left "the country open and available for future annexation to Great Britain." At any rate, when in 1882, Governor Turner's treaty of 1825 was revived and ratified, Harris predicted that the "annexation of the country is proclaimed under conditions which will stir up strife where he has long labored successfully to appease it, and which are calculated only to provide a revenue for the distant Colony of Sierra Leone without conferring any benefit on the country or the trade which is to contribute that revenue." Harris, who had become a member of the Poro Society and married into the ruling house of Juring, exercised considerable sway in the Gallinas and neighboring countries. Before the annexation in 1882, he had lived outside customs areas and could trade unfettered by customs regulations. Annexation implied for Harris a reduction in the margin of profits, even if it meant greater security and added protection. He therefore found himself in the uneasy position where he welcomed British protection but refused to accept the obligations.

In June 1883 he published a brochure entitled "Annexations to Sierra Leone, etc." in which he tried to appeal to British public opinion against what he considered to be ill-advised policies of the Colonial government in West Africa, particularly in the establishment of customs ports in the territories neighboring the Sierra Leone Colony. He also proffered advice based on his own long experience as a merchant on the West Coast of Africa. Harris died in 1909.

HAVELOCK, ARTHUR EDWARD. Governor of Sierra Leone, 1881-1884. Born in 1844, Havelock, after an army career in the years 1862-1877, served in the Colonial administration in Fiji, Nevis, St. Lucia and the Seychelles. In 1881 he was appointed governor of Sierra Leone and arrived in the Colony on June 27. Before taking up the governorship, Havelock was one of the commissioners sent to Paris in May 1881 to negotiate with the French about the Northern Rivers boundary. The sequel was the convention, very favorable to the French, signed on June

28, 1882, which the French government nonetheless failed to ratify. The British government however accepted the terms of the convention both in principle and in practice, and thereby lost the Northern Rivers and the island of Matacong to Sierra Leone.

In January 1882 Havelock was appointed British consul to the Republic of Liberia. Shortly afterwards he traveled to Monrovia to examine the validity of certain claims made by some British traders in the Gallinas against the Republic of Liberia. He then negotiated the settlement of a boundary between Sierra Leone and Liberia which was to solve the perennial problem of the areas of jurisdiction of both territories. On March 30, 1882, the stretch of Gallinas territory bordering on the Atlantic Ocean for half a mile from high water mark as far south as the Mano river was "ceded" to Britain. The Governor also signed a treaty with King Jaia of Gallinas and with the chiefs of Gallinas, Gbemah and Mano.

In 1882 Havelock, accompanied by a gunboat and a force of Sierra Leone constabulary, went to Mattru Jong to obtain satisfaction for an injury alleged to have been done by some chiefs to Mr. Laborde, the civil commandant at Sherbro. The expedition destroyed some huts in Mattru and returned to Freetown. Accused of fomenting trouble in the area, Chief Lahsaru was arrested and detained. In November 1882 Havelock signed treaties with Chief Tucker and with the chiefs and sub-chiefs of Bulom and Shebar which revived Governor Turner's treaty of 1825.

The Governor returned to Sierra Leone from leave of absence in August 1883 and in October traveled to Sherbro to investigate charges against Chief Gbow's lieutenants, Bi Yormah, Gangarah, Kongofoh and Langabai, which had led to their arrest and detention. On the 21st the governor signed agreements with the chiefs of Krim country by which a portion of Krim country ruled by Zorokong, Fawundu and others was "ceded" to Britain. Consequently a proclamation was issued declaring that with effect from January 1, 1884, Sulima, Mano Salija and Combraya (or Kittam Point) would become customs posts within Sierra Leone. Havelock left for England on September 9, 1884.

HAWKINS, Sir JOHN. Paid three visits to the West Coast of Africa (including Sierra Leone) in 1562, 1564 and 1567. He was the earliest contemporary European observer of the Mane invasions who has gone on record. From Hawkins we learn that a people whom he called "Sumboses" had arrived in the River Sherbro in 1561. He took part in the conflicts between two Mane kings, Sasena and Shere, in 1567-8. The latter he described as "king of Sierra Leone," at whose request he agreed to help drive away Sasena and Seterama, two other Mane rulers who had entrenched and fortified themselves at a place called Bonga on the southern tip of the Sierra Leone channel. Hawkins' willingness to help Serre was based on the condition that Hawkins obtain as many slaves as a result of the wars

as he wanted, a bargain which, from Hawkins' account, was
not fully honored by Serre once Sasena had been dislodged.
After losing quite a few of his men in the encounter, Hawkins
seized and took away 250 slaves.   One of his crew suggested
however that Serre had told Hawkins to proceed to the River
Cess to collect his captives, a move which Hawkins did not undertake.   Hawkins initially got his slaves by attacking villages
and seizing slaves already purchased by the Portuguese.   Subsequently when he discovered that such methods were no longer
efficacious he made alliances with the local warrior chiefs for
the supply of captives.   After his third voyage in 1567 Hawkins
was reputed to be one of the wealthiest men in England.

HAY, Sir JAMES SHAW.   Acting governor of the West African set-
    tlements, 1886-1887; governor of Sierra Leone, 1888-1891.
    Born in 1839, Hay joined the British Army (1858-67), rising
    to the rank of Captain.   He saw military service in India dur-
    ing the latter part of the mutiny.   Between 1875 and about 1881
    he served in the colonial government of the Gold Coast and held
    colonial appointments in Mauritius between 1875-1885.   In 1885
    Hay was appointed administrator of the Gambia and in 1886-7
    he acted as governor of the West African settlements.   He was
    awarded the CMG in 1887 and a knighthood in 1889.
        By exercising ruthless economy in governmental expendi-
    ture, Governor Hay considerably reduced the Colony's budgetary
    deficits, gradually liquidated the Imperial Government loan of
    1877, and by 1891 had succeeded in making a hitherto virtually
    bankrupt Colony solvent.   He introduced a number of adminis-
    trative changes to ensure greater efficiency and reestablished
    the Colonial Secretariat and Treasury (amalgamated in 1887) as
    independent departments in 1889.   Hay granted justiceships of
    the peace somewhat liberally, not only in Freetown but in the
    villages and in the Sherbro.   Though he finally rejected the
    popular plea for the restoration of trial by jury, he passed a
    jury ordinance in 1890 which added literacy to property owner-
    ship as a qualification for service as a juror.   In addition the
    ordinance gave the police magistrate, not the sheriff, the pow-
    ers to appoint jurors, reduced the right of challenge and sub-
    stituted the principle of unanimity for the two-thirds' majority
    rule.   A municipality ordinance, making provision for a city
    council was drafted in 1890 but not implemented.
        Hay established the Aborigines Branch of the Secretariat
    as an independent department directly under the governor and
    appointed J. E. C. Parkes as its superintendent.   With the as-
    sistance of Superintendent Parkes' Department (renamed in 1891
    the Department of Native Affairs), the governor in 1888 devised
    a plan to foster the Colony's trade with the hinterland by en-
    suring greater protection for the areas that yielded the bulk of
    produce.   A network of roads was projected, connecting the
    river heads and forming a frontier roughly parallel to the coast
    some thirty miles inland.   This enclave was to be patrolled by
    a paramilitary police force and toured by two traveling com-
    missioners who would promote peace among the neighboring

chiefs and ensure stability. A manager (the former title of
commandant was dropped in 1888) was put in charge of the
"Sulima District," with headquarters in Bonthe. A police
headquarters was also established at Bandajuma near Pujehun.
Between 1888 and 1889, Hay dispatched two military expeditions against Makaiah of Largo (November 1888) and Darwah
of Wondeh (March 1889), whose warlike pursuits were impeding
trade in the Gallinas area.

During his governorshop, Hay made a number of tours
of the hinterland signing an impressive number of treaties of
peace and friendship with chiefs and settling disputes. In January 1887 he traveled to Bonthe Sherbro and held meetings with
the chiefs of Imperri, Jong, Bagroo and Sherbro districts and
appealed to them to give up war, disperse their warriors and
destroy war stockades. In March 1888 he sent Major Festing
to Bumban to prevail on the chiefs to maintain peace and to
keep open the trade routes to the Colony. On December 22,
1888, the Governor left Freetown on a tour of various districts
of the hinterland, signing treaties with chiefs; he returned to
Freetown on January 24, 1889. From February 14 to April 13,
1889, Hay again went on a tour of the territories in the north
and southeast districts of the Colony, covering some 300 miles
by land and 250 miles by water. In March and April 1890,
shortly after his return from leave in England, the Governor
toured the Sherbro, Port Loko and Great Scarcies districts.
On October 24, 1890, by means of a proclamation, the Sierra
Leone government decided to exercise active jurisdiction over
Imperri country to put a stop to an increase of murders in that
territory. Hay then proceeded to Sherbro to meet with the Imperri chiefs and to inform them of government's intentions.
From Sherbro he went on a tour of the surrounding districts,
visiting Lavanah, Sulimah, Mano Salija, Fairo, Bandajuma,
Pujehun and others, and returned to Bonthe by way of Mattru
Jong in January 1891. Towards the end of February 1891 Hay
left Freetown and by way of Port Loko visited the Kunike,
Marampa and Masimera districts, returning by way of Ribbi on
April 9, 1891. On April 21, 1891, he went on leave and was
appointed to Barbados.

HEARD, BETSY. Educated in England she ruled as chief at Bereira
up the rivers. Miss Heard supplied information about medicinal
herbs to the Colony government. Later she supported Governor
Dawes against King Tom II and refugee rebels from the Colony.

HEDDLE, C. W. M. Son of a British father and an African mother.
Pioneer in Sierra Leone in the groundnut and palm kernel trade,
which he first exported in 1837 and in 1846 respectively. Referred to at times as a "merchant prince," Heddle was the
most prosperous merchant in the Colony. He was appointed to
the Legislative Council in 1845. In 1847 he prevailed upon
Governor N. W. Macdonald to extend British sovereignty over
a quarter-mile wide strip of territory around the Bulom Shore,
as a preemptive bid against French encroachment. When Judge

John Carr went on leave in 1848. Heddle, though not trained as
a lawyer, was appointed by Governor Macdonald to act as judge.
In 1851 the Mercantile Association was formed in Freetown,
with Heddle as its first chairman. He was also very instrumental in the institution of a mail packet service between Britain and Freetown in 1852. In 1867 he was appointed a member
of the newly constituted Board of Health. He retired in 1870
and went to France, leaving first his nephew and then his son
as agents of his vast commercial empire.

HENNESSEY, JOHN POPE. Governor of Sierra Leone, 1872-1873.
An Irishman and a Roman Catholic, Hennessey was born in
1834; he arrived in Freetown on February 27, 1872, to become
governor of Sierra Leone. Within two days after his arrival
an ordinance making provision for inquests by coroners was
passed enabling the governor to appoint coroners for the Colony.
Preferring to play the role of champion of oppressed people
wherever they may be, and irrespective of color or creed,
Hennessey enthusiastically set about abolishing all forms of direct taxation. A series of ordinances passed between March
and August 22, 1872, abolished the house and land tax, the road
tax, market dues and ad valorem duties, leaving only specific
duties on spirits, tobacco and ammunition, as the main sources
of revenue. These sweeping changes, if "disliked," were "tol-
erated" by the Colonial Office, while in Freetown they evoked
the wildest enthusiasm. Hennessey was popularly hailed as a
liberator and August 22, "Pope Hennessey Day," was observed
as a public holiday to commemmorate the abolition of the taxes.
     There was however one influential voice of dissent, the
Rev. James (later Bishop Johnson) who saw in the abolition of
taxes not relief but deprivation, since for him the ordinances
had removed the peoples' rights of tax-paying citizens. A few
months after the governor's departure from Sierra Leone it
was observed at the Colonial Office that "... the hopes of a
buoyant revenue at one time entertained as a consequence of
Mr. Pope Hennessey's financial policy have not as yet been
fulfilled. The Governor writing on the 17th November reports
the probability of a large deficit at the close of the year 1873."
In fact there was a deficit at the end of the year, the first in
nearly a quarter century.
     Hennessey was also long remembered and honored in
Freetown for his toleration of Islam. On occasions the Governor attended Muslim religious services in person at Fourah
Bay. Islam, hitherto regarded by most of his predecessors
as a threat and a danger to the Colony's Christian and civilizing
mission, he treated as useful to the Colony's commercial and
social interests. In recognition of Muslim learning and of the
usefulness of Arabic as a medium of communication with some
chiefs in the interior, he appointed Mohamed Sanusi as government Arabic writer. Influenced by Blyden's views that Christian missionary education was destructive of the African spirit
of self-reliance and originality, Hennessey embraced the "doctrine of the interior." In the hinterland where Islam not Chris-

tianity was the dominant religion, the Governor and Blyden sought "the genuine specimens of the Negro-Race beyond the Settlements" in contrast to the Christian missionary-educated people of the Colony who were "though not bad ... very inferior." Together they journeyed to the north, Hennessey as far as Kambia and Blyden to Timbo, where he signed a treaty with the chiefs.

There was an element of ambivalence in Hennessey's as in Blyden's attitude towards Christian-educated Africans. While denouncing products of the Christian educational system as corrupt and not self-reliant, Hennessey advocated the replacement of Europeans by educated Creoles in the government service, suggesting in the process that self-government be introduced into the Colony with the minimum of delay. Pope Hennessey left Sierra Leone for England on February 21, 1873. When news of his death reached Freetown 20 years later, there was general mourning. The citizens, mostly non-Catholic had a Requiem Mass offered at the Catholic Pro-Cathedral in Freetown for the repose of his soul and a funeral oration was delivered at the Wilberforce Memorial Hall.

HILL, Col. Sir STEPHEN JOHN. Governor of Sierra Leone, 1854-1862. Born in 1809, Hill joined the army in 1825 and became a lieutenant-colonel in 1854. He saw service in the West Indies and in the Gambia and in 1857 was appointed governor of the Gold Coast. Between December 27, 1854, and January 16, 1855, Lt.-Col. Hill administered the government of Sierra Leone. Doubts about the legality of his authority to govern Sierra Leone during that short period necessitated the enactment of an ordinance on July 30, 1855, to indemnify him and others acting on his instructions for acts done during his three-weeks' administration. On September 18, 1855, Hill returned to Sierra Leone from leave of absence and took the oath of office as governor. To introduce long-needed reforms in the judicial system he passed an ordinance simplifying and reorganizing the judiciary. One Supreme Court was created, incorporating the existing courts of Recorder, Quarter Sessions and Chancery, and to allay fears and suspicions of interference by the administration, members of Council no longer sat as assistant judges.

A master of the Supreme Court was appointed. An Ordinance of June 7, 1861, authorized the appointment of a sheriff of the Colony on a permanent basis and in 1862, partly as a result of a squabble between the Governor and the acting chief justice, the offices of queen's advocate and police magistrate were made separate. Hill's attempts to gag the press in Sierra Leone by passing an ordinance to regulate the press were thwarted by the Colonial Office, which repealed the ordinance by order-in-council and directed the Governor to publish the order of repeal. During his term of office, partly as a result of popular protests and equally important thanks to his prejudices, the policy of appointing Afro-West Indians to high office in Sierra Leone was discontinued by the British government. To make provision for an accurate and up-to-date registry of titles to land, and of births, deaths, baptisms, burials, marriages, etc., in the Colony, an ordinance was enacted on February 9, 1857, establishing a Registry Office for the purpose in Freetown and creating the office of registrar-general (to be appointed by the governor). On April 14, 1859, an ordinance was passed authorizing the officer administering Sierra Leone to grant licences for marriage in the Colony without publishing banns. An ordinance passed on December 14, 1855, made provisions for the maintenance and repair of roads and highways by levying a fee of one shilling and sixpence per annum on all inhabitants of the Colony between the ages of 16 and 60, with a penalty of six days' labor on the roads in default of payment. A new militia ordinance of December 29, 1860, laid down that the force should be called out once every month instead of for 20 days in the year as stated by the ordinance of 1856.

Up-country, Hill's aggressive policy involved the Colony in a series of expensive military expeditions particularly to the Scarcies and the Sherbro areas. The Governor also signed a number of treaties of peace and friendship with chiefs, by which the chiefs agreed to abolish the slave trade, to keep the roads and trade routes open and peaceful, to desist from warfare, and to recognize the right of the government to demand the surrender of offenders who were British subjects for trial in Colony courts. Hill annexed Koya, Bendu, and Bulama in 1861. On July 22, 1862, he left the Colony.

HOLMES, Lt. H. J. Commander of the detachment of the Royal West African Frontier Force, consisting of 34 men sent against Haidara Contorfili's forces at Bubuya in 1931. Holmes was killed in the brief encounter but Haidara's forces were annihilated.

HORSTEAD, the Rt. Rev. JAMES LAWRENCE CECIL, 1898- . Bishop of Sierra Leone, 1936-1961; archbishop of West Africa, 1955-1961. Born February 16, 1898, educated at St. John's College, Durham University, where he read mathematics and theology; ordained a Deacon in 1923 and priest in 1924. From 1923 to 1926 Horstead was curate of St. Margaret's rectory, Durham; in 1926-36, principal of Fourah Bay College; and in 1929-36, canon missioner.

The Rev. Canon J. L. C. Horstead was consecrated bishop of Sierra Leone in 1936 at a time when it has been observed Sierra Leone was experiencing "a spiritually declining situation." To arrest the trend Horstead invited Bishop A. M. Celsthrope from Nigeria in 1938 to conduct a "Campaign of Revival" in Freetown. The Campaign, described as a great success, gave the Sierra Leone Anglican Church "a fresh lease of spiritual life." The stresses of World War II, the increased emphasis on material things engendered by a wave of secularism, leading to spiritual and moral degeneracy, created new problems for Bishop Horstead. It became increasingly difficult to attract suitable men to the ministry of the church: the prob-

lem still exists.   In April 1951, the Anglican Province of West
Africa was inaugurated in Freetown and Bishop Vining was consecrated the first archbishop.   When he died he was succeeded
by J. L. C. Horstead who became the second Anglican archbishop of West Africa in 1955.

Archbishop Horstead, it has been observed, "always
stood for the best in worship and intellectual proficiency
wherever he went. " He organized vacation courses for Mission school teachers and weekend courses for church workers
in the Protectorate, which improved efficiency.   In the last
years of his bishopric, Horstead, who had previously acquired
notoriety in Anglican circles for negotiating the sale of the
Grammar School building to the Freetown City Council decided
to build Cathedral House at Gloucester Street, Freetown.   The
building, which houses among other things the Sierra Leone
Diocesan Bookshop and the Mano River Union Secretariat, is a
magnificent monument to Horstead's episcopacy and a testimony
to his vision.   In mid-July 1961 Archbishop and Mrs. Horstead
retired and took leave of Sierra Leone where they had served
faithfully and well for nearly 30 years.

HORTON, JAMES AFRICANUS BEALE, 1835-1883.   Scientist,
patriot and author.   Born on June 1, 1835, at Gloucester Village, Freetown, educated at the CMS Grammar School, Freetown, Fourah Bay College, King's College, London, where he
received the M. R. C. S. , and at Edinburgh University where he
received the M. D. degree.   On September 5, 1859, Horton
was commissioned as an officer in the British Army to serve
in West Africa with the rank of staff-assistant surgeon, equivalent to the military rank of lieutenant.   He was sent to the then
British Gold Coast in the latter part of 1859.   In 1862 he published a six-page pamphlet entitled "Geological Constitution of
Ashanti, Gold Coast" and took part in the Anglo-Ashanti War of
1863-64.   He also saw service in the Gambia.

Inspired by the spirit of nationalism Horton became increasingly interested in the independence of West Africa.   He
published his views on the subject in his Political Economy of
British West Africa in 1865 and developed his ideas more fully
in West African Countries and Peoples, British and Native with
the Requirements Necessary for Establishing that Self-Government Recommended by the Committee of the House of Commons
1865; And a Vindication of the African Race, published in 1868.
His other publications included works on West African medicine, climatology, entomology, diseases and politics, which
appeared in the 1860s and 70s.   Horton returned to Freetown
in 1881 and lived in Horton Hall, his impressive mansion at
Gloucester Street.   He had been one of the earliest advocates
of a West African University and, although Fourah Bay College
was affiliated to Durham University in 1876, the move did not
quite fulfill Horton's aspirations for a West African University.
In retirement he played a leading role in civic life, champion-
ing the establishment of a Commercial Bank of West Africa, the
development of the Sierra Leone Native Pastorate and a host of

other projects. He died on October 5, 1883, and was buried
at Circular Road Cemetery in Freetown.

HUDSON, Sir ARNOLD. Governor of Sierra Leone, 1931-1934.
One of the most popular colonial administrators in the country's history. Fondly referred to in the Colony as the "Sun-
shine Governor," Hudson pioneered broadcasting in Sierra Leone
and in West Africa when he introduced the rediffusion service
in Freetown in 1934.

HUMPHREY, the Rev. W. J. CMS Secretary and principal of
Fourah Bay College. At the outbreak of the Hut Tax War in
1898, the Rev. Humphrey set out from Freetown for Port Loko
to ensure the safety of three missionaries at Rogberi. Though
captured and detained, the missionaries were in fact safe and
unmolested. On his way, Humphrey was killed by warriors--
against Bai Bureh's wishes and instructions. Those responsible for the crime were executed on Bai Bureh's orders.

HUT TAX WAR   see   MILITARY EXPEDITIONS (13)

HYDE, ADESANYA KWAMINA, 1915- . Born September 4, 1915,
at Murray Town, Freetown. Educated at the CMS Grammar
School and at the Methodist Boys High School, Freetown. He
worked at the Public Works Department after leaving school.
In 1941 he enlisted in the Royal Air Force and served as navigator in the Bomber Command in Europe; he was demobilized
in 1947. Appointed to Colonial administrative service as administrative officer. Promoted to permanent secretary, Ministry of Health, Sierra Leone, in 1961 and provincial secretary,
Southern Province, in June 1962. In 1967 he became Secretary
General I in the NRC military regime. In 1968 he was appointed Sierra Leone's ambassador to the United States. He
returned home and took up appointment with the Sierra Leone
Diamond Mining Company in 1969.

- I -

INDEPENDENCE DAY. April 27th. Sierra Leone's "National
Day." On April 27, 1961, Sierra Leone achieved independence
and became a member of the Commonwealth and of the United
Nations.

THE INDEPENDENT (1873-1878). Newspaper published by James
Taylor, a staunch Wesleyan and a shopkeeper of Aku parentage.
The Independent became the mouthpiece of the Rev. Benjamin
Tregaskis. Through its pages Taylor and Tregaskis attacked
the newspaper The Negro until it stopped publication, and vili-
fied Blyden, its editor, until he retired to Monrovia.

INDEPENDENT PROGRESSIVE PARTY [IPP]. Formed between December 1959 and January 1960 as a result of a breach within

UPP ranks.   Protesting against what they called the "auto-
cratic rule" of the UPP leader, Mr. C. B. Rogers-Wright,
UPP members of the House of Representatives--Valesius Neale-
Caulker, Dickson-Thomas, and J. B. Wilson--broke away to
form the Independent Progressive Party.   They chose Neale-
Caulker as their leader, with G. Dickson Thomas as secretary.
Essentially a parliamentary grouping, the party drew its support largely from the personal following its members had in
their constituencies.   Lacking any organizational structure or
party policy, the IPP was a short-lived affair.   Soon its members joined either the SLPP or the APC.

INGHAM, the Rt. Rev. ERNEST GRAHAM.   Bishop of Sierra Leone,
1881-1896.   Brought up in Bermuda, consecrated as bishop in
the Chapel Royal, Whitehall, Ingham arrived in Sierra Leone in
March 1883 to succeed Bishop Cheetham.   His 15 years' work
(the longest episcopal tenure in 19th-century Sierra Leone) was
marred by a long controversy known as the Five Pastors Case.
The 1852 constitution of the Sierra Leone Church, which had
been projected by Venn, its articles dated March 1853, did not
come into force until 1861.   The salient feature had been the
provision "That the charge and superintendence of the native
pastors and Christian congregations which have been, or may
hereafter be, raised through the instrumentality of the Society's
Mission in Sierra Leone, be placed under the Bishop of Sierra
Leone, assisted by a council and by a church committee.   And
that arrangements be proposed for providing the native pastors
with a suitable income from local resources, and also for giving them a status assimilated to that of the incumbents at
home."   In 1879 the exercise of this authority by bishop and
council who had withdrawn a pastor's license for immorality and
drunkenness had been questioned.   In the process it had been
shown that the articles had no legal validity, the inference being that the pastors in Sierra Leone were not legally subject to
local discipline.   In 1887 Bishop Ingham and the Church Council, acting in accordance with powers conferred on them by the
"invalid" constitution, ordered the transfer of the Rev. Moses
Taylor from Waterloo where he had worked for 20 years.   On
refusal, Ingham withdrew Taylor's license.   Making use of the
provisions of the same 1852 constitution, the Rev. Taylor appealed to the Archbishop of Canterbury, who upheld Taylor's
right of appeal and who maintained, since the articles had no
legal basis, that the Sierra Leone clergymen had the same
status as those in England.   Thus thwarted, Ingham reinstated
Taylor.
        But worse was to follow.   In 1890 the chief justice ex-
pressed the view that by law the governor was dean of the
chapter of the Cathedral and that the bishop had no power to
interfere with the services--Ingham disliked and disapproved of
surpliced choirs and choral services.   Fortunately for the bishop the chief justice's opinion was rejected as incorrect by the
Colonial Office.   Elated by this victory, Ingham reinforced his
control over the Cathedral by creating two canons.   He and a

church committee drew up a new constitution aimed at making
the pastors subject to local discipline. The "Articles of Arrangement" (the new constitution) were approved in March 1890.
In 1891 the pastors were required to sign them. Five pastors,
the Rev. Moses Taylor of Waterloo, the Rev. G. I. Macaulay
of Kissy, the Rev. S. G. Hazeley of Wellington, the Rev.
Moses Pearce of Christ Church, Pademba Road, and the Rev.
H. P. Thompson of Benguema, refused to be signatories to the
new articles, preferring to continue with the constitution they
had been appointed under. Ingham promptly withdrew their licenses and prevailed upon the CMS to eject them from their
parishes, still vested in the Society in trust for the Sierra
Leone Church. Legal action had to be resorted to to effect the
ejection.
    Meanwhile the Rev. Nathaniel Boston on the Bulom Shore,
at loggerheads with the Sierra Leone Church Missionary Association, which had assumed responsibility for mission stations,
and restrained by a court injunction from carrying out his functions as a priest, was accused of immorality by Ingham, who
proposed to preside over the case in the bishop's court. Ingham's right to hear cases was challenged by Lewis, Boston's
counsel, and the supreme court ruled that the bishop's jurisdiction extended only to ecclesiastical not criminal cases. The
case of the five pastors dragged on with embarrassing publicity,
dividing congregations for and against them. In the end Lewis
on a legal technicality got judgment in favor of one of the pastors against the CMS. The episode did irreparable damage to
the Anglican Church in Sierra Leone, destroyed the filial bonds
between the Colony and the CMS, and provoked Ingham to lose
faith in "native agents" produced in the colony and to search
for Afro-West Indian clergy to work up-country.
    In 1894 Ingham published his Sierra Leone After a Hun-
dred Years, drawing heavily from Governor Clarkson's diary,
from reports of the Sierra Leone Company, and from early
mission records. Ingham's century, if disappointing, was far
from unprogressive. In 1892 Bishop Ingham completed and
opened Cottage Hospital, called Princess Christian Cottage Hospital after Her Royal Highness. Mrs. Ingham, wife of the
bishop, was the prime mover of the project. In 1889 he had
reopened the Cathedral School at Howe Street and in 1895 he
raised money in England for the construction of a technical
school on the adjacent piece of land. Ingham resigned in 1896
and in the same year the Sierra Leone Church was disestablished.

- J -

JAIA of Gendama. Succeeded Prince Mana of Gendama in 1872.
    In return for stipends, Jaia signed a treaty on March 30, 1882,
    with Governor A. E. Havelock "ceding" a half-mile strip of
    coastal territory as far as the Mano river, including Sulima and
    Mano Salijah to the British. He was murdered about 1884 or 85.

JARDINE, Sir DOUGLAS. Governor of Sierra Leone, 1937-1941.
One of the Colony's most unpopular governors, Sir Jardine was
confronted with the problem of Wallace-Johnson and his Youth
League and the Governor's attempts to contain them were
thwarted almost at every turn. More disturbing still, details
of the Governor's confidential and secret dispatches to London
as well as of other government secret documents were published in Freetown papers, particularly in Wallace-Johnson's
African Standard. One such dispatch which provoked a public
outcry showed that the Governor had minuted that an African
workman and his wife could live comfortably on 15 shillings a
month and that labor was cheap and plentiful. Mass meetings
were organized and petitions drawn up not only requesting the
Governor's immediate recall but demanding "his exclusion from
any colony inhabited by peoples of African descent." To put
an end to these embarrassments and to what Jardine called
"Creole agitation," six bills were introduced into the Legislative Council in May 1939 (after consultations with Jardine then
on leave in England and with the blessings of the Colonial Office) as follows: the undesirable British subjects control bill
(frequently referred to simply as the "deportation bill"); the
sedition bill; the undesirable publications bill; the incitement to
disaffection bill; the trade union bill; and the trade disputes
(arbitration and inquiry) bill.
    The introduction of these bills provoked further protests
and there was such a threat to the maintenance of law and order that the government made a special request for a warship
to be stationed in Freetown harbor. The Youth League organized a protest march said to involve 15,000 or more to Government House, where the Legislative Council sat. Governor Jardine, embarrassed by these moves and bitter against Wallace-
Johnson for inciting civil strife, nevertheless tried to under-
stand, perhaps even to sympathize with the Creoles. The bills
were passed in spite of the protests (or because of them).
Wallace-Johnson was still at large but on September 1, 1939,
he was arrested and charged with criminal libel. Wallace-
Johnson's arrest dealt a fatal blow to the Youth League and all
it stood for, in actual and potential terms, thanks to Governor
Jardine's efforts and hostility.

JAVOUHEY, Saint ANNE MARIE, 1779-1851. Foundress of the
Missionary Society of Women (1807) with religious vows known
as the Sisters of St. Joseph of Cluny from the town in France
of its first foundation. Under Saint Javouhey's personal supervision members of the society undertook work in the French
colonies. She took the initiative to take a group of young
Africans to France to be trained as priests. She foresaw that
this was the final solution to the evangelization of Africa. By
1843, three had completed their studies and returned to their
native Senegal.
    On a tour of inspection of West Africa she arrived in
the Gambia where she met Sir Charles McCarthy, who as governor of all the British West African settlements had his head-

quarters in Freetown. McCarthy, a French nobleman by birth, invited her to visit Sierra Leone and gave her a free hand to organize the government hospital in Freetown. She arrived in Freetown in March 1823 accompanied by Florence, a Fulani Christian maid. An epidemic of yellow fever broke out and put her organizing ability and stamina to a severe test. At the end she was herself laid low by the plague. She was nursed back to health by the faithful Florence with the aid of local herbs of which the latter had some knowledge. Mother Javouhey left Freetown with regret in September 1823. In 1866 the first group of Sisters of St. Joseph of Cluny arrived in Freetown, followed since then by many others. Today they number about forty, among them three Sierra Leoneans, dedicated to work in schools and social welfare. Mother Javouhey is now one of the saints of the Catholic Church.

JEREMIE, Sir JOHN. Governor of Sierra Leone, 1840-1841. A lawyer by profession, Jeremie was appointed in 1824 as chief justice of St. Lucia, a post he held until 1830. A determined abolitionist his appointment in 1832 as public prosecutor of Mauritius exposed him to the hostility of the slave-owning interests on the island and when he arrived at Port Louis he had to be provided with a military guard for protection. Attacked by a mob in the streets, he was advised to return to England. He went back to Mauritius in 1833 and thereupon fell out with the judges, whom he accused of being interested in slave trading and resigned. Appointed to a judgeship in Ceylon in 1836, he was while there presented by his co-abolitionists with a large silver candelabrum for his championship of Negro freedom.

In October 1840 Jeremie was appointed Governor of Sierra Leone and knighted in November of the same year. He arrived in Sierra Leone on December 16, 1840, to take up duties--the first civilian governor of the Colony appointed by the Crown. Following Governor Turner's precedent, Jeremie intervened in a chieftaincy dispute at Port Loko in support of a candidate who would promote trade with the Colony. He installed as alikali of Port Loko, on February 13, 1841, Moriba Kindo of the Bangura Family. It was arranged that after him and so alternately in the future, a Kamara scion of Fatima Brima's House should succeed. After declaring the conventions with governors Findlay and Campbell in 1831 and 1836 null and void, Jeremie signed new treaties with the chiefs, who agreed to suppress the slave trade and to promote legitimate trade with the Colony. The Governor paid the chiefs' arrears of stipends. For the Colony itself he had a number of schemes including cotton cultivation, an internal postal service and a savings bank. The successful implementation of these schemes was thwarted by Jeremie's death on April 23, 1841 after barely four months in office, the last governor to die in Sierra Leone.

JIMMY [Jemmy] (or James Dowder), King. Temne ruler who suc-

ceeded King Tom I as King of the watering-place in 1788. As
James Dowder, he had been one of the signatories (by putting
his mark) to Capt. John Taylor's treaty of August 22, 1788,
which is regarded as the legal foundation of the Colony of Sierra Leone. King Jimmy had a number of grievances against the
new settlement and against its inhabitants, the settlers. Outraged by attacks on his subjects by ships calling at the harbor
and incited by slave-dealers against the settlement, King Jimmy
attacked and destroyed Granville Town, the capital of the Province of Freedom as the settlement was then called, in December 1789. When the settlement was rebuilt and after King
Naimbana's death in 1793, King Jimmy was appointed by Bai
Farama, his suzerain, to act as the Colony's landlord. King
Jimmy died in 1796 and was succeeded by Pa Kokelly who took
the name of King Tom.

JOHN, H. E. B., 1916-1970. Born May 9, 1916, in Freetown.
Educated at St. George's Cathedral Day School, the CMS Grammar School, Fourah Bay College (University of Durham), Freetown, and at St. John's College, Durham University, England,
where he obtained an honors degree in modern history. Assistant, and later senior assistant master at the Sierra Leone
Grammar School. Foundation member of the Sierra Leone People's Party and its first secretary-general (1951-1958). Member of the Fulton Commission on Higher Education in Sierra
Leone, 1954. Elected to the Sierra Leone House of Representatives as first member for Freetown West constituency in
the general elections of 1957. Appointed minister of education
(1957-1962). He lost his seat in the legislature in the 1962
general elections and was appointed a director of the Diamond
Corporation West Africa (Dicorwaf) Ltd. He died in 1970.

JOHNSON, the Rt. Rev. THOMAS SYLVESTER CLAUDIUS, 1873-
1955. Born September 23, 1873. Educated at the CMS Gram-
mar School, and at Fourah Bay College, Freetown. Head-
master Dan Street Mohammedan School, 1896-1898; diocesan
inspector of schools, 1911-1932; tutor and later senior tutor,
Fourah Bay College, 1911-1932; principal, CMS Grammar
School, 1933-1936. First assistant Anglican bishop of Sierra
Leone, 1936-1948. Chairman of Interim Council of Fourah Bay
College, 1948-1949; Author of The Story of a Mission (1949).
One of the greatest religious leaders in Sierra Leone's history.

JONES, D. RADCLIFFE. One of the most successful and popular
medical practitioners in Sierra Leone. His patients included
all races and men and women from all walks of life. So popular was Dr. Jones and so appreciative was the community of
his efforts and services, that after his death funds were raised
by the public to erect a full-length statue of him in the Taylor-
Cummings Gardens near the Cotton Tree--the first in Freetown
and in the country. He died at sea on August 12, 1950.

JONES, E. D., 1925- . Born January 6, 1925, in Freetown.

Educated at Holy Trinity School, CMS Grammar School, Fourah
Bay College (University of Durham), Corpus Christi College,
Oxford, and Durham University, England. Since 1964 profes-
sor and head, Department of English, Fourah Bay College
(USL). Fullbright research and Smith Mundt grant tenable at
the Folger Shakespeare Library, Washington, D. C., 1960-1961.
Folger research fellowships, 1962, 1964, 1968, 1969. Visiting
professor at University of Leeds, England, University of British
Columbia, Canada, and the Universities of Sheffield and Kent,
England, in the 1960s and 70s. Commonwealth fellow, Univer-
sity of Toronto, 1970-1971. Fellow of the Royal Society of
Arts. Jones is Sierra Leone's leading Shakespearean scholar
and one of Africa's best known critics of literature. Professor Jones' major works include The Way to Write Successful
Letters (1962), Othello's Countrymen; A Study of Africa in the
Elizabethan and Jacobean Drama (1965), The Elizabethan Image
of Africa (1971), and The Writings of Wole Soyinka (1973).
He contributed to the volume, The Teaching of English Literature Overseas (1963), edited with R. Ridout, Adjustments: An
Anthology of African and Western Writing (1965), and edited
with Christopher Fyfe, Freetown; A Symposium (1968); he is
editor of African Literature Today.

JONES, the Rev. E. N. (later, Laminah Sankoh). Clergyman,
writer, politician. Born E. N. Jones, but later changed his
name to Laminah Sankoh. Educated at the CMS Grammar
School, at Fourah Bay College (University of Durham), and at
Oxford University. His father, a Sierra Leonean who had made
good in business in the Gambia, wished his son to go into the
ministry. E. N. Jones was ordained a minister of the Church
of England. One of the most sincere and ardent advocates of
national reconciliation and unity, the Rev. Jones quit the church,
sacrificing the assured status and sure means of livelihood of
a clergyman for the problematical and at times unsafe game of
politics. In 1949 he founded the People's Party which attracted
a number of liberal Creoles and Protectorate Africans. He also founded and edited a newspaper, The African Vanguard.
When the SLPP was formed in 1951, Laminah Sankoh merged
his party with it and transferred his proprietory rights over
the Vanguard to the SLPP. In the first national election of
officers held by the party in 1951, Laminah Sankoh was appointed second vice president. In the heated and protracted
debates between Colony and Protectorate spokesmen over constitutional changes, he took sides solidly with the Protectorate
Africans. His political stance as well as his earlier apostasy
lost him considerable support and sympathy among a number
of Creoles. He unsuccessfully contested the 1951 elections to
the Legislative Council as an SLPP candidate for a Freetown
constituency. Thereafter his political and other fortunes appeared to be on the decline. Disappointed by the attitude of
some of his new colleagues in the SLPP and distrusted by his
own people, the Creoles, Laminah Sankoh died--a martyr for
the cause of national unity--in Freetown in 1953 and was buried

at the Ascension Town Cemetery.

JONES, Sir SAMUEL BANKOLE, 1911- . Born August 23, 1911.
Educated at the Methodist Boys High School, 1922-1928, and at
Fourah Bay College, Freetown, 1929-1932. Law student in
Britain 1934-1938; called to the Bar in 1938. Returned home
to Sierra Leone and set up private practice, 1938-1949; ap-
pointed police magistrate, 1949-1958; acting puisne judge, 1958-
1960; puisne judge, 1960, and chief justice in 1964; president,
Sierra Leone Court of Appeal, 1965; and awarded a knighthood
in 1965. In 1969 he was installed as chancellor of the Univer-
sity of Sierra Leone. He retired from the chancellorship in
January 1972 and from the presidency of the Court of Appeal in
March 1972.

JONES, W. S. MARCUS, 1926- . Educator, lawyer and author.
Senior lecturer in law, Fourah Bay College (USL). Author of
The Legal Order, Contemporary Social Change and the Develop-
ment of Law in Sierra Leone, and the 647-page Leading
Cases in Sierra Leone (1975). Born on July 3, 1926. Edu-
cated at the Prince of Wales School, Freetown, the London
School of Economics and Political Science (London University),
the University of Birmingham, England, and Yale University,
USA.

JONG RIVER EXPEDITION see MILITARY EXPEDITIONS (6)

JOSEPH, SIGNIOR see SIGNIOR JOSEPH

JUXON-SMITH, A. T., 1931- . Chairman, National Reformation
Council military regime and brigadier and force commander
(RSLMF), 1967-1968. Born in 1931; educated at the Methodist
Boys High School, Freetown, and at the British Military Acad-
emy of Sandhurst. Succeeded A. P. Genda as chairman of the
NRC in 1967. Overthrown in a counter-coup in 1968. Arrested,
detained, and charged with treason, 1968; convicted and sen-
tenced to death in 1969 and reprieved in 1972.

- K -

KABBA LAHAI see BUREH, Bai

KABBAH SEI [CABBAH SEH]. A Mende war-chief of Mando, Upper
Moa in the 1880s. He was born at Potolu about 1840. In 1880
he rebuilt Potolu and from 1880-1890 he was sole ruler of the
area. Kabbah Sei inaugurated a society in the early 1880s
which he called Tukpay (Tukpei) meaning "push ahead," aimed
at consolidating his power and authority over the four chiefdoms of Mando, Dia, Malema and Guma. Tukpay was in addition an offensive and defensive alliance to repel invaders.
After Kabbah Sei had effectively established himself in Mando,
he decided to abandon his earlier aggressive leanings for more

peaceful pursuits, acting as mediator and peacemaker between
neighboring warring chiefs. On March 30, 1890 he signed a
treaty of friendship with the British.
    When Mbawolomeh invaded his territories and occupied
one of his towns, Giehun in Guma Chiefdom, Kabbah Sei, with
the assistance of the Tukpay (Tukpei) society, drove him away
without completely defeating him. Mbawolomeh continued his
exploits and attacked Fabunde's (a treaty chief's) towns. Unfortunately the British authorities were informed (possibly by
Kabbah Sei's enemies) and were willing to believe that Mbawolomeh was either an ally of Kabbah Sei or was acting in col-
lusion with him. In September 1896 Major Fairtlough, after
dispersing Mbawolomeh's warriors, moved against Kabbah Sei,
destroyed his town and confiscated his property. Kabbah Sei
fled westwards towards Freetown. He was captured, taken to
Freetown and confined as a political prisoner, in spite of his
protests and professions of innocence. His chiefdom was divided between Nyagua and Kai Lundo. In 1898 he was released
from prison. When the Hut Tax War broke out later in the
year, he refused to fight against the British and gave all the
assistance he could to the garrison at Panguma.

KAFARI, Bai. Successive holders of title in Tane Chiefdom,
    Tonkolili district.

KAFURA of Kenema. In Kisi country, in the 1890s and 1900s,
    Kafura was one of the leading chiefs hostile to British presence
    and British rule in the hinterland of Sierra Leone. In about
    1897 Kafura took a solemn oath to destroy the Frontier Police
    outpost at Korumba and made two serious but abortive at-
    tempts to do so, killing two frontier policemen in the process.
    Between June 10 and July 4, 1905, a large number of Kisi
    chiefs assembled at Wulade to hold consultations with British
    officials about the final settlement of the country and to take
    concerted action against Kafura and his alies. Kafura was re-
    moved from his chieftaincy and he was replaced by more ame-
    nable chiefs.

KAI LUNDO of Luawa. Born about 1845 at Mano Semabu in the
    Wonde country across the Moa River. At about the age of 18
    he set out from home to enlist as a trumpeter under Nyangbe
    of Mendekelema, near Small Bo (Blama). Within a few years
    Kai Lundo became a warrior. He won fame, acquired wealth,
    returned to his homeland and built a town which he called Ma-
    findo, after a town in Njaluahun chiefdom which he had visited.
    He fought with Ndawa against Benya of Blama in the Kpove war.
    Subsequently Kai Lundo had disagreements with Ndawa, a dis-
    agreement which led to the Kanga goi (war of rebellion) be-
    tween the two warriors. Kai Lundo succeeded in driving
    Ndawa away from his territory. As a result of his victory
    over Ndawa, the chiefs in the surrounding country swore al-
    legiance to him, thereby recognizing him as suzerain of Luawa.
    Thereafter Kai Lundo consolidated his position by distributing

slaves and spoils of war among his sub-chiefs. In the early
1880s he built a new town on the site of Sakalu, calling it
Kailahun or Kai's Town, in the most central part of his dominions. His new chiefdom consisted of what is now Luawa,
the three Kisi chiefdoms within the British sphere of influence,
the Wunde, Mafisa and Kama chiefdoms in what is now the Republic of Guinea and Kisi Teng, part of which is now in the Republic of Liberia. On April 7, 1890, Kai Lundo signed a treaty
of friendship with Governor Sir S. J. Hay through T. J. Alldridge, who visited him again in 1891. The frontier with Liberia divided Kai Kundo's chiefdom between the British sphere
of influence and Liberia. When he died on April 7, 1895, Governor Cardew recognized his speaker Fabundeh as his successor.

KAI SAMBA I, PC. Of Nongowa Chiefdom, Kenema District (1902-
1955). One of the country's most enlightened and progressive
chiefs. Born on July 1, 1902. Educated at Bo Government
School; joined the civil service and worked in the provincial administration 1924-1942; elected paramount chief of Nongowa
Chiefdom, Kenema District, 1942. Assessor of the Supreme
Court, 1942. Member of the Legislative Council, 1948-1951.
Awarded King's Medal for Chiefs, 1950. One of the few chiefs
who opposed participation of paramount chiefs in national politics as supporters of a political party, on the grounds that the
party system would seriously erode the traditional authority
and position of chiefs as fathers of their people. In conformity
with his views Chief Kai Samba refrained from contesting the
1951 elections to the Legislative Council. He died on January
3, 1955.

KAI SAMBA, K. I., 1931- . Lawyer and politician and son of
PC Kai Samba I. Kutubu Ibrahim Kai Samba was born at
Pendembu, Kailahun District on March 6, 1931. Educated at
Bo School, Fourah Bay College (University of Durham), King's
College (Durham University), Newcastle-on-Tyne, and Gray's
Inn, London. First elected to Parliament in 1962 as member
for Kenema Central. Appointed minister of agriculture and
natural resources (1964-1967). Re-elected to Parliament in
March, 1967-1973. He was one of the independents whose re-
fusal to support Sir Albert Margai, after the general elections
of 1967, led to the downfall of Sir Albert as prime minister
and to the loss of political power by his party, the SLPP.
The letter dated March 21, 1967, addressed to the governor-
general, Sir Henry Lightfoot-Boston, and signed by Kai Samba,
L. A. M. Brewah, J. B. Francis and P. J. Williams, ran as
follows: "Sir, We the above-mentioned having been elected to
Parliament at the recent General Election do hereby declare
ourselves to take our seats in the said Parliament as Independent Members. We would like it to be known to the People
of Sierra Leone that we shall at all appropriate times co-
operate in whatever measure may be deemed necessary in the
national interest with any of the two Political Parties which

commands the majority of members in the House, provided that
in the case of the Sierra Leone People's Party the present
leader of that Party, Sir Albert Margai, resigns the Premiership and his leadership of that Party. "

KALLON, MAIGORE CHRISTIAN, 1927- . Minister of foreign affairs, 1965-67. Born at Jojoima, Kailahun District. Educated
at Bunumbu Central School, Bo Government School, and the
University of Pennsylvania, where he studied public finance.
Elected member of the House of Representatives for Kailahun
West in May 1957; appointed parliamentary secretary, Ministry
of Health; resigned in 1958 to join the People's National Party
(PNP) as organizing secretary; appointed government whip and
leader of the House 1962; appointed minister of the interior
1964 and minister of foreign affairs in November 1965. Re-
elected, unopposed, as member of Parliament for Kailahun
West, March 1967; lost seat as a result of an election petition;
returned in the bye-election held in 1968 as member of Parliament for Kailahun West; in voluntary exile in Liberia since
1968.

KAMANDA of Bauya. A Mende Chief who ruled Bauya in the 1880s.
A rival of Madam Yoko of Senehun (later of Moyamba) for
hegemony in the Upper Bumpe River Area, Kamanda was believed to be secretly in alliance with the Yoni who invaded and
destroyed Senehun, Madam Yoko's chiefdom headquarters about
August 1886. A British force consisting of 200 men of the 1st
West India Regiment, a small naval detachment, and 50 police
was sent against the Yoni, who were easily put to flight and
the ring leaders rounded up. Kamanda and six leading warriors were deported to Elmina in the then Gold Coast towards
the end of the year.

KAMARA-TAYLOR, CHRISTIAN ALUSINE, 1917- . Prime minister 1975; minister of finance, 1971-1975. Born on June 3,
1917, at Kai-Hanta, Tonko Limba Chiefdom, Kambia District.
Educated at the Methodist Boys High School, Freetown, and at
the School of Accountancy in London where he obtained a diploma in business methods. Worked as a clerk for the Sierra
Leone Development Company and joined the Sierra Leone Regiment, rising to the rank of sergeant and saw service in Burma
during World War II. After demobilization he joined the United
Africa Company and became secretary to the general manager
and public relations officer. "C.A.," as he is popularly called,
then went into politics and became the first secretary-general
of the All People's Congress, when that party was formed in
1960. In 1962 he was elected to Parliament as member for the
Kambia, East constituency. He retained his seat in the 1967
general election and after the return to civilian rule in 1968 he
was appointed minister of mines, lands and labour. Following
a cabinet reshuffle in 1971, he was appointed minister of finance and in a subsequent cabinet reshuffle in 1975 was appointed prime minister and minister of the interior.

KANTA, ALEXANDER BEY. King of Koya, 1859-1872. Koya country at one time included the peninsula of Sierra Leone but,
since the establishment of the Colony in 1787, the peninsula had
ceased to be part of Koya. Temne oral tradition maintains
that a curse was laid on the Koya kingship as a punishment for
the loss of the peninsula to the Colony. When Bai Farama died
no new king of Koya was crowned and the country was put under
the effective control of Momodu Bundu of Foredugu (on the Rokel), whose mother had been Naimbana's daughter. Through
the good offices of John McCormach (in Temne tradition, "old
Chief Mohomok"), the Koya kingship was revived with the installation in 1859 of Bai Farama's youngest son who took the
title of Bai (or Bey) Kanta. Alexander Fitzjames, queen's advocate and acting governor at the time, gave the government's
blessing by bestowing his own Christian name on the new King
who then became known as Alexander Bey Kanta.

In March 1861 Alexander Bey Kanta got into difficulties
with Governor Col. S. J. Hill when some of his subjects plundered a trader at Tombo Island within British jurisdiction.
Alexander Bey Kanta was asked to pay £500 as compensation
for the outrage. Unable to raise such a sum, he was forced
to lease a strip of Koya country (about ten miles in width from
Waterloo and Calmont creeks to the Quiah River [or Creek] and
some 16 miles in length from the River Sierra Leone to the
Ribbi River) to the Colony, at an annual rent of £100. He was
told and did believe that the territory was leased. The treaty
he put his mark to however declared the territory "ceded" to
Britain. When conditions returned to normal in Koya, Hill declared the "leased" or "ceded" territory British. In October
1861 there were fresh disturbances in what had then become
British Koya. A factory belonging to one Mr. Jolly was attacked and plundered. Troops were dispatched to the area on
December 2. During the operations Maj. William Hill and some
officers and men of the 2nd West India Regiment were wounded
and one sergeant killed.

Bey Kanta was held responsible for the disturbances and
after the cessation of hostilities Governor Hill decided that he
should no longer reside in British Koya. Hill annexed two important Koya towns of Robaga and Ro Bana and suspended Bey
Kanta's annual stipend until full compensation was paid to Jolly
for property lost. On January 29, 1872, the British Government signed a treaty retroceding a portion of British Koya to
Bey Kanta and his chiefs, with the British reserving the right
of resumption if and when the need arose. In all between 1859
and 1872 Bey Kanta entered into four treaties with the British--
on June 24, 1859; April 2, 1861; February 1, 1862; and January
29, 1872. Alexander Bey Kanta died shortly after the treaty of
retrocession in 1872 and the Koya kingship was held in abeyance
until 1890.

KAREFA-SMART, JOHN MUSSELMAN, 1915- . Sierra Leone's
first minister of foreign affairs, 1961-1964. Born June 17,
1915, at Rotifunk Bompeh Chiefdom, Moyamba District. Edu-

cated at E. U. B. School, Rotifunk, Albert Academy, Freetown,
Fourah Bay College (University of Durham); Otterbein College,
U. S. A.; McGill University, Canada and at Harvard University.
Licentiate of the Medical Council of Canada; member of the
College of Physicians and Surgeons, Alberta; fellow of the Royal
Society of Tropical Medicine and Hygiene.   Served as medical
officer in the Royal Canadian Army during World War II; served
as missionary doctor, Rotifunk hospital.   Appointed regional
medical officer for WHO West Africa Region and worked in Monrovia, Lagos and Brazaville.   Taught at Ibadan University College where he was also dean of the Medical School.   President
of Sierra Leone Ex-Servicemen's Association.   Elected to Sierra Leone House of Representatives in May, 1957, as member
for Tonkolili, West constituency; appointed minister of lands,
mines and labour, 1957-1960; minister of lands and surveys
with special responsibility for external affairs and defense,
1960; Sierra Leone's first minister of external affairs, 1961-
64.   Founding member of United Democratic Party, 1970; arrested and detained under emergency regulations, 1970.   Appointed professor of international public health at Harvard, 1971.

KARIMU of Moria (or Samaia).   Karimu was an ambitious Susu
warrior and chief of Samaia on the upper reaches of the Small
Scarcies.   He aimed at carving an empire for himself out of
the surrounding territories.   In the 1880s he waged war against
the Limba of Upper Sanda.   Karimu's forces consisted of bands
of Muriteis, or rebels, recruited mostly from run-away slaves.
Bands of muriteis roamed about the country, waging war and
constructing "egois," or war camps, and fortifications into
which they retired when attacked.
        Karimu's boys had built one of these egois at Tambi (or
Tembe), a town west of the Little Scarcies River on the borders of the Susu and Limba country.   Soluku of Bumban, the
Limba chief, appealed to the British for help against Karimu's
muriteis at Tambi.   Three expeditions were dispatched to Tambi, the first on April 22, 1891; the second on March 14, 1892;
and the third on March 28, 1892.   The first two of these expeditions were unsuccessful.   The third achieved its objective.
Tambi was destroyed and burned to the ground.   Karimu and
his warriors were dispersed and he and a large number of his
supporters retired into the French "sphere of influence."

KEBALI see BUREH, Bai

KEITH-LUCAS COMMISSION OR ELECTORAL COMMISSION.   A
commission appointed by the governor of Sierra Leone on July
1, 1954, to consider and advice on electroal reform in Sierra
Leone.   The chairman was Bryan Keith-Lucas of Nuffield College, Oxford, and the other members were the Hon. Dr. H. C.
Bankole-Bright, then Leader of the Opposition in the legislature, and A. T. A. Beckley, PC Kai Samba I, Y. D. Sisay,
and B. Tejan Sie, supporters of the government.   The commission's terms of reference were as follows: "To examine

the present electoral system (including the franchise) of the
Legislative Council and local government bodies in the Colony
and Protectorate and to report on the desirability of enlarging
the electoral franchise in the Colony and of extending the electoral system in the Colony to the Protectorate (or to any part
or parts thereof) with or without variations and to make recommendations. "
        Later it was ruled that these terms of reference were
not applicable to the election of paramount chiefs or tribal authorities.   The Commission presented its report on September
9, 1954.   The general elections of May 1957 were held in practically all essentials on the basis of the recommendations of the
Keith Lucas Commission.

KELLY, the Rt. Rev. AMBROSE, CSSP.   Vicar Apostolic of Sierra
    Leone, 1937-1950.   First Catholic bishop of the diocese of
    Freetown and Bo, 1950-1952.   Bishop Kelly died in Freetown
    in 1952 and was buried at Kissy Road Cemetery.

KENNEDY, Sir ARTHUR EDWARD.   Governor of Sierra Leone,
    1852-54, 1868-72.   Served in the army 1827-1848 and was an
    Irish Poor Law commissioner from 1849-1851.   At the age
    of 41 Kennedy was appointed governor of the Gambia but was
    transferred instead to Sierra Leone, where he arrived on Octo-
    ber 12, 1852, to serve as governor.   On arrival he found ad-
    ministrative standards--hardly ever appreciable--to be critically
    low, thanks to the highhanded methods of his predecessor.   Be-
    fore Kennedy's term of office, problems had arisen over the
    exercise of British jurisdiction over British subjects outside the
    Colony.   These problems had also provoked queries about the
    legal stutus of liberated Africans.   The Crown law officers had
    held that liberated Africans resident in Sierra Leone were not
    British subjects and consequently were not included in treaties
    with chiefs making provision for reciprocal surrender of crimi-
    nals and for delivery of British subjects for trial in the Colony.
    A solution suggested to Kennedy's predecessor by the Colonial
    office was that treaties should be so worded as to include Lib-
    erated Africans.   The formula ran thus "... criminals being
    British subjects or liberated Africans" or "British subjects or
    others resident in Sierra Leone. "   Clearly the formula was
    not as efficacious as it was meant to be.   So on August 20,
    1853, the British Parliament passed an act declaring Liberated
    Africans "natural-born subjects of Her Majesty," from the
    moment of their arrival in the Colony.
        To put an end to the traffic in domestic slaves Kennedy
    passed an Ordinance on December 7, 1853, making provision
    for the better protection of alien children.   To prevent what
    appeared to be indefensible acquittals in cases involving slave
    traffickers, he proposed amendments to the jury ordinance,
    abolished grand juries and imposed property qualifications for
    petty jurors.   Another ordinance removed the need for un-
    animity in jury verdicts by allowing the courts to accept as
    valid the verdict of the majority of jurors.   These measures

raised storms of protest in the Colony, where petitions against
the ordinances were sent to, but rejected by, the Colonial Office. In 1853 and 1854 the Governor entered into treaties with
chiefs, whose additional clauses enabled British cruisers to detain and search slave ships operating in waters within the chiefs
territories.

To improve the standard of administration and supervision in the rural areas, the Governor issued fresh instructions
on January 9, 1854, for the guidance of district managers. An
ordinance of August 8, 1854 (amending the Ordinance of April
1851) was passed imposing a tax on lands and houses in the
Colony. (It was repealed in 1872.) He started a scheme for
dispensing free medical service to the poor. The old and destitute were also given small sums of money out of government
coffers on Saturday, and would parade through the streets begging for alms at private houses. Thus came into being the
"Saturday militias" as they came to be called, who have since
formed a permanent feature of the freetown Saturday scene.
Up-country, Kennedy in 1853 questioned the whole policy of stipends, advised a change from paying goods assessed in devalu-
ated "bars" to payment of money, and proposed that on the
death of an incumbent signatory chief, the payment of stipends
should be terminated. His suggestions were accepted at the
Colonial Office but were not followed by his successors in Sierra Leone. In May 1853 Kennedy, following precedent, intervened in a Port Loko chieftaincy election dispute to ensure the
installation of a candidate who was unquestionably pro-British,
requesting the chiefs to elect the new alikali with the minimum
of delay but under no circumstances "to give their support or
influence to any candidate--observing a strict neutrality...."

On October 13, 1854, Kennedy left Sierra Leone for
service in Australia but returned four years later on February
18, 1868, to become governor of the Colony for a second time.
During his second term of office, the governor sponsored a
number of diplomatic missions to the interior following precedents of 1821 and 1841. In 1869 he dispatched Winwood Reade
to Falaba, Solima and the Niger and in 1869 and 1872 sent Dr.
E. W. Blyden to Falaba and Timbo respectively. In 1869 he
advised British withdrawal from Koya on the grounds that it
had become "unnecessary, impolitic and expensive to maintain
it," an advice that was implemented in 1872 shortly after his
final departure from Sierra Leone. He also withdrew for
similar reasons a garrison of troops from Sherbro in 1870.
In a move to strengthen their attachment to the British Crown,
Kennedy in April 1869 entertained a large number of chiefs at
Government House at what was called a durbar. In the Colony,
to put through a more efficient system of registration and taxation of Crown lands, the Governor in 1869 set up a land Court
and appointed a surveyor, but since records were not properly
kept it was difficult to make the tax productive. A loan of
£60,000 for the construction of public buildings was floated by
ordinance on March 17, 1871. In two years (1871-73) £50,000
was raised. The loan was finally repaid in June 1898. An

ordinance of January 4, 1872, introduced a public water supply
system to Freetown.   Earlier in April 1868, the Governor had
started competitive examinations for recruiting junior clerk-
ships, hitherto filled by Governor's patronage, into the civil
service.   He put an end to the holding of Legislative Council
debates in secret and ordered the printing and publication of
bills after first reading.   By adopting strict disciplinary measures including improvements in the police force, Kennedy considerably reduced the prison population of the Colony.   In January 1872 Kennedy left Sierra Leone for good to take up appointment in Hong Kong.

KESEBE SURI of Rotifunk.   After the defeat of the Loko by the
Temne in the 1840s, Loko refugees, led by Suri Kesebe, a
powerful warrior moved southwestwards and enlisted as fighters
for Canreba Caulker of Bompe, who repaid their services by
offering them land at Rotifunk to settle.   In 1878 Suri Kesebe
allowed the UBC Women's Missionary Association to open a
mission at Rotifunk.   During the Yoni War (1885-7) the Loko
Chief became a useful ally of the British by sending a number
of "friendlies" to reinforce Col. Sir Francis de Winton's expeditionary force against the Yoni (1886-7).   Kesebe took advantage of his friendship with the British to extend his territory and authority at the expense of the Yoni.   (See MILITARY
EXPEDITIONS (8).)   When he died in 1897 he was succeeded
by his son, Santigi Bundu.

KIKONKEH EXPEDITION   see   MILITARY EXPEDITIONS (5)

KING, ROBERT GRANVILLE OJUMIRI, 1906- .   Minister of fi-
nance (1964-1967).   Born at Campbell Town, Waterloo Rural
District, on November 11, 1906.   Educated at Free Church
School, Waterloo, Government Model School and at the CMS
Grammar School, Freetown.   Taught for many years and later
became headmaster of Newton Rural School.   Elected to the
House of Representatives as member for British Koya elec-
toral district in 1957.   Appointed parliamentary secretary,
Ministry of Education and Social Welfare and Communications,
1957-1961; minister of development, 1961-1964 and minister
of finance, 1964-1967.   Appointed chairman of the Sierra Leone
State Lottery in 1973.

KING, VICTOR EDWARD, 1908- .   Educator and author.   Dr.
King was born on February 13, 1908, and educated at Kissy
School, Samaria School, Government Model School, CMS
Grammar School, Fourah Bay College (University of Durham),
Freetown, Yale University, and London University.   Between
1929 and 1944 he taught at the Methodist Boys High School,
the CMS Grammar School and at Fourah Bay College.   In 1948
he was appointed headmaster, Koyema Government Central
School.   Thereafter he joined the Sierra Leone government
service and from 1952-1961 he was education officer, senior
education officer, senior inspector of schools, and acting

deputy director of education. From 1961-1964 he was visiting
professor of African studies and of psychology at Shaw University in North Carolina and at State University of New York at
New Paltz. He became the first principal (1964-65) of Freetown Teachers College, and from 1965 to 1969 he was professor of education and dean of the Faculty of Education, Njala
University College (USL). In 1970 he was appointed principal
lecturer and head, Department of Education, Milton Margai
Teachers College.

KING-HARMAN, Sir CHARLES ANTHONY. Governor of Sierra
Leone, 1900-1904. Succeeded Cardew as governor in 1900
after serving for some 30 years in the colonial administration
in the West Indies. The plan for a West African Frontier
Force (WAFF), later Royal West African Frontier Force
(RWAFF), was implemented during King-Harman's governorship. He decided to transform the Sierra Leone battalion of
the West African Frontier Force (as the Frontier Police came
to be called) into an essentially military body, by relieving the
Frontiers of police duties (which were taken over by court messengers) and putting them into barracks.
　　Distrustful of Creoles as much as his predecessor, he
continued to bar them from the administration of the Protectorate. He did however, on representations made by Creoles
up-country, introduce a circuit court under a puisne judge to
curb the "crude and peculiar procedure" district commissioners
in the Protectorate were wont to employ the court cases.
　　Hill Station, an area between Wilberforce and Regent
villages, was specifically reserved for European occupation
during King-Harman's tenure. He proposed a railway to the
reserved area some eight or nine thousand feet above sea level
and the construction of about 100 houses to accommodate government European officers. The line would go from Water Street
Station along Westmoreland and Sanders streets, through Brookfields, up to Wilberforce and through Wilberforce barracks to
Hill Station. At King-Harman's suggestion, money for the capital outlay of Hill Station, railway and houses was to be acquired from the loan capital for the Sierra Leone railway--a
measure which increased the loan capital to £1,250,000 (including £39,000 for the Hill railway and £47,000 for the
houses). The houses were sent out prefabricated from England
and the project, begun in 1902, was put into operation in 1904
with the opening of the railway and the completion of the first
houses. In 1904 King-Harman left Sierra Leone to take up appointment as high commissioner for Cyprus.

KISI. The Kisi, who occupy only three chiefdoms in Kailahun District, in the Eastern Province of Sierra Leone, live in larger
numbers in the republics of Guinea and Liberia. Kisi tradition
states that they came from the Upper Niger before 1600 and
pushed the Limba westwards. After 1600 the Kisi were in turn
attacked by the Koranko, who pushed them into the areas they
now occupy. Linguistically the Kisi are closely related to the

Sherbro and Krim, although they are separated by large tracts of Mende territory. Culturally the Kisi in Sierra Leone have acquired many Mende traits and an appreciable number are Mende-speaking. Neither Islam nor Christianity has made much progress among them.

KNIGHT, the Rev. CHARLES, c.1805-1879. First African chairman and general superintendent of the Methodist Mission in Sierra Leone (1874-1876). Recaptured from a slave ship and brought to Freetown in 1822, Charles Knight, an Ibo, was brought up at Gloucester Village, went through elementary school and got employment as a shopkeeper in Freetown before becoming a school teacher. When in 1840 some English Quakers agreed to sponsor and pay for two recaptive teachers at the Borough Road School London, the Sierra Leone Wesleyans selected Charles Knight and Joseph May. On his return home Knight was made an assistant missionary in 1844 with the title of "Reverend" and in December 1848 he was ordained a full minister of the Wesleyan Church. He served with distinction in virtually all the circuits of Sierra Leone and the Gambia. In 1874 he succeeded Tregaskis as chairman and general Superintendent. He fell ill in August 1877, was made a supernumerary and died on December 14, 1879.

KOBLO, PC Bai PATHBANA, 1912-   . Traditional ruler and minister of government. One of the few literate paramount chiefs who made a great impact in the colonial legislature and a leading spokesman for Protectorate interests in the legislative council. Born on September 22, 1912, at Marampa, Marampa Masimera Chiefdom, Port Loko District. Educated at Bo Government School and at St. Edward's Secondary School, Freetown. Elected paramount chief in 1943. Member of Protectorate Assembly 1946-1955. Appointed to the Executive Council in 1949. Elected member of House of Representatives for Port Loko District (1957-62); returned in 1967 and again in 1973 as member of Parliament for the district. Appointed minister without portfolio, 1959-1962 and 1968 to the present.

KOELLE, the Rev. S. W. CMS missionary to Sierra Leone who came out in 1847 to teach Greek, Hebrew and Arabic at the Fourah Bay Institution, or College, and stayed until 1855. He is the author of Narrative of an Expedition into Vy Country of West Africa and the Discovery of a System of Syllabic Writing Recently Invented by the Natives of the Vy Tribe (1849), Outlines of a Grammar of the Vei Language Together with a Vei-English Vocabulary (1853), and Polygotta Africana; or A Comparative Vocabulary of Nearly 300 Words and Phrases in More Than 100 Distinct African Languages (1854). The Rev. Koelle compiled the Polygotta from information supplied by recaptives landed in Sierra Leone from countries ranging from Mozambique to Senegal.

KOMPA, Bai (also Bokari Bomboli; also William Rowe) [but see

following entry]. Chief of Koya in the 1880s and 1890s. In
his younger days he had served a prison sentence in 1857 in
Freetown for kidnapping. In the late 1870s he had assisted
Governor Rowe on his tours of the hinterland, and assumed the
Governor's name in admiration. When fighting broke out again
in Koya, Bai Kompa was arrested and kept for a while in custody. In 1890 the Koya Kingship, vacant since 1872, was revived. Bokari Bomboli was elected king and he took the title
of Bai Kompa. When the hut tax was levied in Ronietta he was
one of the chiefs accused of resisting the tax. Capt. H. G.
Warren, assistant inspector at Kwelu, was sent to arrest him
for inciting resistance and intimidating loyal chiefs. He moved
to Romangi, one of his villages, where Warren, after trying
forcibly to remove him, had doubts about the legality of this
action, not sure whether Romangi was within the Colony or the
Protectorate and so let him go. Bai Kompa complained to
Governor Cardew about Warren's conduct towards him but was
told to comply with orders, collect the tax and report to Capt.
Moore at Kwelu. On failing to report at Kwelu, Bai Kompa
was accused by Chief Charles Smart of organizing resistance
and of being in league with Bai Bureh of Kasse. Early in
March 1898 Moore, with a force of 40 Frontier Police and
helped by Chief Charles Smart, set out in search of Bai Kompa.
The force burned villages and killed several of Bai Kompa's
subjects without capturing him and returned to Kwelu crestfallen.
Eventually from his retreat sent £30 tax money. He was however deposed and replaced by Fula Mansa to act as chief of
Koya. Bai Kompa died shortly after the 1898 rising was suppressed. (The above individual's successors also held the
title, Bai Kompa, in Koya chiefdom, Port Loko District.)

KOMPA, PC Bai [but see preceding entry]. Nominated to represent the Protectorate in the Legislative Council in 1924. One
of the first three paramount chiefs nominated under the provisions of the Slater Constitution to represent Protectorate interests.

KONDO, Chief of Yoni. The Yoni had for years (roughly from the
1850s) been trying to gain access to the Ribi Bumpe trade, as
their neighbors, the Tyamamendis, had done. Thwarted in this
effort they resorted to pillage, plunder and war. In November
1885, led by one of their war chiefs, Kondo, the Yoni attacked
Songo, in Koya country, a territory within British jurisdiction,
plundered property and took into slavery a number of British
subjects. Governor Rowe hurried to Yoni country to try and
get back the captured British subjects and to punish those responsible for the outrage. Unable to achieve either objective
he consoled himself by arbitrarily arresting some Yoni visiting
Freetown, suspected of having participated in the raid on Songo,
and deporting them to the Gambia.

KONO AND VAI. The Kono and Vai are believed to have immi-
grated into Sierra Leone as one tribe or group possibly in one

of the waves of Mane invasions. Tradition maintains that the Kono settled in approximately their present homeland while their brothers, the Vai, moved southwards towards the coast in search of salt. The story is that salt was scarce in Konosu, the original home of the Kono and Vai somewhere in present-day Guinea. A traveling salesman returned to Konosu and told his countrymen that he had seen a vast expanse of salt water in a distant land. The people decided to set out en masse in search of the salt water. After traveling for many months, some of them got tired and decided to settle in approximately the present Kono homeland. The more adventurous and enterprising continued the journey in search of the salt sea and told the others as they departed "O maa Konoh, Kanii na" ("you wait for us, we will return"). So the group that stayed behind and "waited" became known as Kono, while those that moved towards the sea never returned but called their land Kanina. It has been suggested that Gallinas (the other name for Vai) was given to them by the early Portuguese because of the large number of bush-fowls they saw in Vai country. This is plausible, but the greater possibility is that Gallinas is a corrupt form of Kaninas--i. e., those who will return. The Kono today occupy about 2000 square miles of mountainous territory, covering the entire Kono District with small groups in Guinea and Liberia. The Vai, who are separated from the Kono by the Mende, occupy the southernmost tip of Sierra Leone in an area of about 100 square miles including some 20 and 40 miles of sea coast in Sierra Leone and Liberia respectively.

After moving out of Kono area, the Vai moved towards the coast and settled near the Kife River, where they later participated in the slave trade and provided the Spaniards with one of their largest sources of human cargo in West Africa. They fought a number of trade wars with the neighboring hinterland peoples. The Vai Script, invented around 1850, consists of about 100 characters and is the only indigenous script in this part of Africa. It was recorded by Koelle in 1854 and though not universally used is still known by a few in parts of Vai country. The three major clans among the Vai are the Massaquoi, the Kpaka, and the Rogers and all three are closely interrelated. Unlike their tribesmen in Liberia, among whom the poro is held in high esteem and elaborately stratified, the Vai of Sierra Leone attach minimal importance to the poro, which is confined to certain limited areas of Vai territory. The Vai being a coastal people came into early contact with Europeans and like the Sherbro they also enjoy a reasonably high level of literacy. They are either Muslim or Christian; a non-believer is regarded as an inferior being. The Vai in Sierra Leone have largely been absorbed by the Mende and Mende is spoken by practically all of them.

Kono tradition asserts that the Kono were once a powerful people in present-day Guinea or Mali or both. The helli area of Guinea, regarded as the traditional home of the Kono, contains a hill called Konno Su, believed to be the burial place of early Kono chiefs, and called after the ancient Kono king-

dom. Over-population, soil erosion and attacks by Mende
forced them to seek refuge in large numbers northwards into
Koranko country, returning after a decade or so. Until the
establishment of British rule the Kono were victims of intermittent Mende raids. Farming is the main occupation of the
Kono and the cultivation of cotton and cloth weaving were major
enterprises before the discovery of diamonds in Kono country
in the early 1930s. The Kono believe in patrilineal descent
and are divided into patriclans, or dambi. Although they do
not use clan names as surnames they, too, do associate their
dambi with totems. The major dambi include the Kona, Sawa,
Yawane, Dumbia, Kamala, Gbense, etc. Poro and bundu
(among the Kono Sande) play important roles in the lives of the
people. Other societies and associations are for healing and
dispensing medicines. The Kono are either animist or Christian and a large number are also Mende-speaking.

KONO PROGRESSIVE MOVEMENT. Founded by Tamba S. Mbriwa
in 1955 in protest against the new diamond agreements signed
in that year between the Sierra Leone government and the Sierra Leone Selection Trust (SLST). Exclusively Kono in membership, KPM recruited its members mostly from young men determined to exploit the mineral resources of their district primarily in the interests of Konos and from the ranks of farmers
dispossessed of lands by mining operations--without, they believed, adequate compensation. In 1962, KPM merged with
SLIM to form SLPIM.

KORANKO. A branch of the Mandinka tribe, the Koranko immi-
grated into Sierra Leone from Guinea, probably at the time of
the Mane invasions, possibly in the last waves of invasion. It
has been suggested that the Koranko arrived in Sierra Leone
about 1600, and drove the Limba and Kono out of the Northern
areas of present-day Koinadugu District, only to be pushed
southwards in turn by the Yalunka, who now occupy the north-
ernmost portion of Koinadugu. Today the Koranko occupy the
bulk of Koinadugu District and cover an area of approximately
3000 square miles of thinly populated and mountainous territory. The Koranko are found in large numbers in neighboring
Guinea. They adhere to partriclans or sienu (singular, sie)
analogous to the Temne abuna. The Koranko sienu are also
associated with totems. The major sienu include the Sisi, Fula,
Kuruma, Kagbo, Mara, Toli, Fona, Dau, and others.
Bundu exists in parts of Koranko country, but poro is
little known. There is however a ritual for the initiation of
boys and girls at puberty. The male ritual is known as
birike and the female as biri-mesu. Gbangbani, or kpankpani,
is an exclusively male society among the Koranko; its female
counterpart is known as Kambam. The Kofung is also well
known; other associations include the andomba for males and
the segere for females. The Yelis and Finas form a professional caste of musicians, custodians of oral tradition, and
orators. The Koranko associate these groups with the Kwiate

clan and have developed an attitude of ambivalence towards them. Feared because of their knowledge (they are thought to be the power behind the throne, but because they rely so large-ly upon patronage, at times their status is almost indistinguish-able from utter dependence), they are regarded with contempt as a servile caste. The Koranko have carved a name for themselves as good soldiers in the annals of the Sierra Leone military history. Almost predominantly animist, neither Islam nor Christianity appears to have made much impact among them.

KOROMA, SORIE IBRAHIM. Vice president and prime minister, 1971-1975; vice president and minister of finance 1975. He was educated at the Government Model School, Freetown, and at the Bo Government School, Bo. Koroma worked in the co-operative department (1951-1958) and took a course at the Co-operative College, Ibadan, Nigeria. In 1958 he resigned from government and went into private business and became first secretary-general of the Sierra Leone Motor Transport Union. When the APC was formed in 1960 he became its first national propaganda and organizing secretary. In 1962 he was elected to Parliament as member for Freetown Central I constituency. His parliamentary seat was declared vacant in 1965. In 1967 he was returned to Parliament for the same constituency and, following the return to civilian rule in 1968, he was appointed minister of trade and industry. In a cabinet reshuffle in 1969 he became minister of agriculture and natural resources. In April 1971 he was appointed vice president and prime minis-ter. In a cabinet reshuffle in 1975 he became vice president and minister of finance.

KORTRIGHT, CORNELIUS HENDRIKSON. Governor of Sierra Leone, 1875-1877. Born in 1817, Kortright served in the colonial administration in the West Indies for about 25 years before his appointment as administrator of the Gambia in 1873. He arrived in Freetown on February 14, 1875, and took up of-fice as governor of Sierra Leone. Early in April, Kortright traveled to Sherbro and signed treaties for the maintenance of peace and protection of trade with the chiefs at Bendoo. In June Mamaiah, a town in British Sherbro, was attacked by warriors from Mongerri country. Some factories were plun-dered and a number of British subjects taken into captivity. Kortright suggested a punitive expedition in reprisal, a sug-gestion viewed at the Colonial Office with considerable alarm. In the circumstances a force of armed police strong enough to contain future aggression was posted to Bendoo. He went on leave in July 1875 and returned to the Colony in July 1876. Appointed to the governorship of British Guiana, he left Sierra Leone for good in March 1877.

KOUROUNA OUARA. A powerful Kono chief who, with five other Kono chiefs, signed a treaty with Lt. Maritz, representing the French Government at Waiima on December 1, 1893. De-

scribed in the treaty as "chef du Sewa et grand chef du Kono,"
Kourouna Ouara, by the provisions of the treaty, requested on
behalf of all the Kono chiefs, and was granted, French protection against the Sofas in return for granting exclusive trading
rights to the French in Kono. The chief, on behalf of his colleagues and on his own behalf, also agreed not to enter into
any political or commercial agreements with another power
without the consent of the French Government. The obligations
imposed on the French by the treaty forced Martiz to attack
Pokere and the Sofas believed to be encamped at Waiima on
December 23, 1893. In fact instead of the Sofas, there lay encamped at Waiima a British force under Col. Ellis and Capt.
Lendy. The French and British forces attacked each other in
the mistaken belief that the other was a Sofa force. Lt. Maritz lost his life in the encounter, as did Capt. Lendy and a
number of officers and men on both sides.

Capt. Valentin of the French army wrote a report from
Kissidougou on January 18, 1894, in which he made the following submission: "I endeavored to secure Kourouna Ouara, who
was the sole cause of this incident and who well knowing that
the English were occupying Waiima, arranged to set one force
upon the other and so to join himself with the victors. It was
a favorite method of his and had served him well hitherto.
Thus he had used Porequere's Sofas against the Mende, Lieutenant Martiz against the Sofas and the British against the
French. . . . By dint of patience, I succeeded at last in laying
hands on him. He pretended to have believed in all good faith
that the Sofas had indeed been at Waiima. It is impossible that
a chief such as he, obeyed as he was throughout Kono country,
should not have known immediately of the presence of such a
strong column of troops in his own district." Capt. Valentin
had Kourouna beheaded after finding him guilty of deliberately
provoking the Waiima incident. Another chief, Fatamba, described by Valentin as "our friend," was installed as chief.
With Kourouna's execution all hopes of a French settlement in
Kono faded away.

KRIM. Akin to the Sherbro, the Krim call themselves Kim, or
    Kimi, Krim being a European derivative. The Sherbro call
    them Akima, meaning "these who ran away." The Krim oc-
    cupy an area of about 600 square miles mostly in Pujehun and
    parts of Bonthe districts and are also a coastal people, cover-
    ing some 25 miles of coastline southeast of the Sherbro. They
    form a buffer tribe between the Sherbro and the Gallinas. The
    Krim speak a variant of Sherbro and culturally appear to be
    very close to the Sherbro. They, like the Sherbro, have been
    largely absorbed by the Mende, whose language and cultural
    traits they have adopted. Less than 10 per cent of the Krim
    are said to be Muslims; the bulk are either Christian or
    aminist.

KROO (also Kru). The Kroo, natives of the Coast of Cape Palmas
    in present-day Liberia, started to immigrate into the Colony of

Sierra Leone in the early years of its establishment to work on
the Sierra Leone Company's ships and at the wharf. The first
Kroo arrived in the Colony in 1793. Hard-working, efficient
and enterprising, they had given assistance in the past to slave-
traders, although it is believed that it was impossible to make
slaves of them. After the abolition of the slave trade they rendered valuable service on the British cruisers engaged in the
suppression of the slave traffic. Initially they were transient
workers whose wives and families stayed home in Liberia,
where they returned eventually with their savings--a practice
denounced by their detractors as depriving the Colony of its
wealth. The Kroo were at first encamped at Water Street,
from where they moved westward until in 1816 land was acquired for them near the shore beyond Sanders Brook. This
piece of land, later called Kroo Town, was compulsorily acquired by ordinance from Eli Ackim, a Nova Scotian who was
awarded £62 in reparation. Ackim's protests at being deprived
of land in the interests of aliens were continued by generations
of his descendants until 1906 when another ordinance declared
Kroo Town to be Crown land. In 1808 the Sierra Leone Government had begun a policy of actively encouraging Kroo settlement
on a permanent basis in the Colony.

By 1819 the Kroo population of Freetown numbered more
than 500. There were in addition some 200 Kroo working at
the timber factories up the Sierra Leone River, as well as a
few Kroo fishermen who were settled along the beaches south
of Cape Sierra Leone. The increase in the Kroo population of
the Colony, welcome as a valuable source of labor, introduced
problems relating to discipline and proper conduct. An ordinance, passed to make the Kroo responsible for each other's
crimes, was rejected by the secretary of state. A solution was
found in the appointment of Kroo headmen to assume responsibility for order and to insure good behavior among their tribesmen. The Kroo, if initially reluctant converts to Christianity
(a Methodist Church was opened in Kroo Town in 1840, though
it has been observed few were Christians), are today predominantly Christian. Islam has made virtually no progress
among them in Sierra Leone. Excellent seamen and good ath-
letes, the Kroo are being gradually integrated into the rest of
the Sierra Leone community, and the feeling of being separate
or alien has almost lost its appeal.

KUP, A. P. Pioneer in modern Sierra Leonean historiography and
one of the best known historians of Sierra Leone. Author of
A History of Sierra Leone 1400-1787 (1961) and of Sierra
Leone; A Concise History (1975). Dr. Kup was senior lec-
turer and head, Department of History at Fourah Bay College
(University of Durham), and editor of the journal of the Sierra
Leone Society, Sierra Leone Studies, from 1954 to 1961.

- L -

LAHAI MINAH BAIMBA (also, Lahai Mina Morah). Chief or king
of Maligia (Malaghea) on the River Melakori in the 1850s. He
had grievances against the Sierra Leone Government for prohibiting the slave trade. Outraged, among other things, by the
Sierra Leone Government's seizure of two slave canoes, Lahai
and his fellow chiefs met in December 1854 and demanded redress for the "aggression." When Acting Governor R. Dougan
failed to meet his demands or to give a favorable answer, Lahai ordered all European traders operating within his territories
to leave within ten days. Dougan's reply was an unauthorized
expedition to Melakori, to bully Lahai and his colleagues. The
outcome was a disaster for British arms and for Dougan's career. The expeditionary force suffered 95 casualties, including
four British officers killed and one wounded. Dougan was dismissed from the service. Lahai promised to surrender prisoners and equipment captured during hostilities. European traders, virtually at his mercy, were allowed to return to the Melakori area. (See also MILITARY EXPEDITIONS (2).)

LAHSARU [Lansuru] of Mattru Jong. Lived in the Mattru Jong area
in the 1880s. Described in some texts as a chief, he was most
probably a Muslim fetish priest, who made a living out of the
manufacture of charms and amulets and who performed such
services as "cooking war" (i.e., ensuring victory for his clients against adversaries by exercising supposedly magical and
supernatural powers). Possibly a Susu, he was one of the
organizers of the threatened boycott of Creole trade in the Jong
River area. Lahsaru was one of those arrested and detained
by the Sierra Leone Government authorities for inciting trouble
in the Mattru Jong area in April 1882.

LAING, Capt. GORDON. First European to visit Falaba. Laing
was sent by Governor Sir Charles MacCarthy in 1821 to the
Northern Rivers where he successfully mediated in a war among
the chiefs which obstructed trade to the Colony. He set out
again in 1822 for Falaba where he arrived, the first European
visitor, and was accorded a cordial welcome. His plans to
travel to the source of the Niger were thwarted by the king of
Falaba who refused to grant him permission to proceed further.
In 1825 Laing once more set out, this time from Tripoli, in
search of the source and course of the Niger. He was killed
at Timbuktu.

LANSANA, Brig. DAVID, 1922-1975. First Sierra Leonean to be
commissioned into the RSLMF and first Sierra Leonean brigadier
and force commander of the RSLMF. Born March 27, 1922, at
Baiima, Mandu Chiefdom, Kailahun District. Educated at Central School and Union College, Bunumbu, at Eaton Hall, and at
the Officers Training School at Chester, England. Enlisted in
the army as an officer cadet in 1947, and commissioned in
1952. Appointed brigadier and force commander, RSLMF, on

January 1, 1965. After the general elections of 1967, Brig.
Lansana declared martial law and made the following broadcast
on March 21:

"On Saturday the 18th March, after the elections of the
Ordinary Members were over and the country was waiting for
the elections of the 12 Paramount Chiefs representing the Districts, the state of the Political Parties was All Peoples Congress (APC) 32, Sierra Leone Peoples Party (SLPP) 32 and
Independents 2.

"It appeared that the results of the elections had reflected not political opinions but tribal differences. This meant that
neither the Sierra Leone Peoples Party nor the All Peoples
Congress had a majority because, as I have pointed out, the
number of seats being 78, 32 on either side was less than the
required majority of at least 40. Tension was building up in
the country and as Chief of State Security I interviewed the
Governor-General on the 19th and 20th of March, 1967, that is
to say two days and one day before the other Elections were held,
and informed him that a dangerous situation would be created
if he made any appointment when neither party had a majority
and the Elections had still not been concluded.

"I saw him again on the day of the Chiefs' Elections and
he informed me that despite the fact that neither Party had the
majority and both were 32 : 32 equal, again I repeat 32 : 32,
he proposed to make an appointment of a Prime Minister. I
again informed him that I would not be able to contain any
trouble which might arise if he acted unconstitutionally. Two
hours after my interview with him he decided to make an appointment when neither Party had a majority and Elections were
still in progress.

"I want to make it clear that the Army--and I say this
after consultation with my senior officers--does not, I repeat,
not, intend to impose a Military Government on the people of
Sierra Leone. This country has a record for Constitutional
Government."

Neither the figures of 32 : 32 nor the Constitutional issues raised were quite accurate. Shortly after his broadcast
however, the Brigadier was arrested and detained by his own
senior officers. After the formation of the NRC Government,
Brigadier Lansana was appointed to a diplomatic post in New
York. From New York he moved to Liberia, and thence to
Freetown on extradition orders from the Sierra Leone government. In Sierra Leone he was charged with the assumption and
exercise of certain powers illegally, convicted, and sentenced to
five years' imprisonment in 1968. Released in 1973, he was
again arrested and charged with treason in the case of M. S.
Forna and 14 others. He was convicted and executed at Pademba Road prisons in July 1975.

LARGO EXPEDITION see MILITARY EXPEDITIONS (9)

LAWSON, T. G., 1814-1891. Born in Little Popo on the Bight of
Benin. Sent in 1825 by his father, Chief George Lawson of

Little Popo, to be educated in England, young Lawson broke his journey in Freetown where he spent the rest of his life. In Freetown, as protégé of John MacCormack, the "almost unofficial 'Foreign Secretary' of the Sierra Leone Government," Lawson paid several visits up-country in the company of his patron. He mastered the languages quickly and began to act as interpreter. His relationships with the neighboring chiefs were cordial enough to enable him to marry a granddaughter of Bei Farama of Koya. In 1846 he entered government service as government messenger and in 1852 became government interpreter. His duties as interpreter, which carried with it the status and functions of a police inspector, included visits to the interior to insure that chiefs understood and carried out government policy. More generally he was a kind of public relations officer between government and chiefs. In the performance of these duties Lawson was assisted by an Arabic writer and a few clerks. In 1878 Governor Rowe transformed Lawson's "informal department" into an "Aborigines Branch" of the Secretariat. In 1882 the Aborigines Branch came under the nominal supervision of the assistant colonial secretary while Lawson was in fact effectively in charge. When he retired in 1888 he was given a special award for personal distinction--a silver medal and chain engraved with his name and services. Lawson died in Freetown in June 1891.

LEIGH, LESLIE WILLIAM, 1921- . Commissioner for external affairs (1967-68). Born February 23, 1921. Educated at St. Anthony's Primary School, and at St. Edward's Secondary School, Freetown. Entered Sierra Leone government service in 1941 as third grade clerk in the Public Works Department. Proceeded to Britain in 1942 and joined the Royal Air Force; served at various flying training schools; graduated as sergeant pilot, then became flying sergeant and in 1944 was commissioned an officer in the RAF. Demobilized in February 1947 he joined the Colonial Police Service and was posted to Ghana as assistant superintendent of police; appointed to the same post in the Sierra Leone Police Force in 1948; awarded M.V.O. by Queen Elizabeth II; awarded Colonial Police Medal and the Queen's Police Medal for distinguished service. Appointed commissioner of police in 1963, first Sierra Leonean to hold the post. Deputy chairman and commissioner for external affairs, March 1967 to April 1968 in the NRC regime. Charged with other members of the NRC with treason and sentenced to death; reprieved after serving three years in jail and discharged from the police force.

LENDY, Capt. E. A. W., 1868-1893. In Mendi tradition "Sapi Lendeh" was first assigned in Sierra Leone to the suppression of the slave trade in the territories adjacent to the Colony. Lendy's exploits led to an increase in the number of freed slaves but produced a corresponding resentment from the chiefs, who saw in it all a threat to their source of wealth and to their cherished ways of life. Since the distinction between domestic

slaves and slaves for sale was somewhat blurred, the Colonial
Office had to give a ruling that only slaves actually in transit
could be seized and set free.   A military man bent on achieving
military glory, Lendy looked for opportunities to distinguish
himself on the field of battle.   Reports of frontier misdemean-
ors in the interior he refused to countenance and he was more
often than not at daggers drawn with J. C. E. Parkers, the
civilian superintendent of the Department of Native Affairs which
performed liaison duties between government and the chiefs of
the interior.   Lendy's exaggerated reports of Sofa threats to the
British "sphere of influence" led eventually to the ill-fated
Waiima expedition.   At Waiima on December 23, 1893, British
and French forces sent against the Sofas, opened fire on each
other, each mistaking the other for the Sofas.   In the ensuing
confusion Lendy was shot dead.   (See also MILITARY EXPEDI-
TIONS (12).)

LETTER FROM CHIEFS AT MAMBOLO see MAMBOLO LETTER

LETTER FROM THE RODGERS FAMILY see RODGERS FAMILY
    LETTER

LEWIS, Sir SAMUEL, 1843-1903.   First African to be awarded a
    knighthood by a British monarch.   Born in Freetown on Novem-
    ber 13, 1843.   Educated at Buxton Wesleyan School, Govern-
    ment Boys School and the CMS Grammar School, Freetown.
    Lewis sailed for England to study law in August 1866.   In
    England he studied at Wesley College, Sheffield, enrolled in
    October 1866 at University College, London, as a non-matricu-
    lated student, and in January 1867 was admitted to the Middle
    Temple.   He matriculated in London University in June 1868,
    won an Inns of Court exhibition in 1870 and was called to the
    Bar in 1871.   While a student in England, Lewis went to Paris
    in 1867 as second Sierra Leonean delegate to attend an anti-
    slavery conference sponsored by the British and Foreign Anti-
    Slavery Society and other philanthropic organizations.

         He returned to Sierra Leone in May 1872 and established
    private practice.   His career at the Bar was highly successful
    and his professional reputation along the West Coast almost un-
    rivalled.   He appeared for clients in the Gambia, Lagos and
    Gold Coast courts.   Towards the end of 1872 Governor Hennes-
    sey appointed him acting queen's advocate, a post he held until
    February 1874.   After rejecting an offer to be chief magistrate
    of Lagos, he accepted temporary appointment as police magis-
    trate of Sierra Leone (from April to July 1874) and also served
    for a short while as queen's advocate.   In early 1882 and again
    in August and September 1894 Lewis acted as chief justice and
    for a brief period as queen's advocate in 1895.   On a number
    of occasions he was retained by the Crown to conduct important
    criminal cases.   One such case was the Onitsha murder trial.
    At other times, such as in the Mokassi land dispute, Lewis
    appeared against the Crown.

In November 1872 as acting queen's advocate (the post
carried seats on the Executive and Legislative councils) he took
his seat on the Legislative Council, where though a semi-gov-
ernment official he attacked the Native Pastorate Grant, declaring its inclusion in the estimates "to be wrong in principle
and injurious to the settlement." On March 1, 1882, he became a permanent unofficial member of the Legislative Council
and held his seat until his death in 1903. He had in 1879 submitted "suggestions" for membership, organization, etc., of
the council. He had criticized the existing unofficial members
as lacking in the required knowledge, although he conceded that
they were "persons of exceptional character and considerable
pecuniary means." He suggested that members should not sit
for more than two years and advocated more frequent sessions.
A constitutionalist rather than a democrat, Lewis refrained
from expressing doctrinaire views on the subject.

During his membership in the Council and especially
during Governor Fleming's tenure of office, deliberations of the
Council increasingly assumed the form of parliamentary debates,
while the distinction between "official" and "unofficial" members
became somewhat blurred. The latter development led Lewis
to observe in 1892 that "unlike the Unofficial Members in some
other of Her Majesty's Colonies, those in Sierra Leone do not
study to oppose any and every measure proposed by the government but rather to give it frank support whenever they can
honestly do so," adding however that they reserved the right to
criticize government measures if and when they thought it necessary to do so. Acting on this latter principle Lewis, dis-
agreeing with Governor Rowe's up-country policy, criticized it
in Council as a policy of "going after the chiefs in their own
country to beg them for peace," a policy he stigmatized as humiliating and expensive.

In January 1885 the Sierra Leone Association was formed
and Lewis, away in the Gambia, was elected in absentia as a
member of the Association's council of 19 members. Although
a prominent and active member, he did not share the Association's enthusiasm for armed intervention in the interior. He
preferred instead, "as occasion offers and within certain limits," the system of purchase.

After playing a leading role in the preliminaries for the
establishment of the Freetown municipality, Lewis was elected
its first mayor in 1895 and re-elected in 1896. In 1893 he had
been awarded the CMG and in the New Year Honors of 1896 he
was awarded a knighthood, the first African to be so honored.

When the Hut Tax disturbances broke out in 1898 Cardew
held Lewis and the Creoles generally responsible for fomenting
the insurrection. The Governor believed that Sir David Chalmers, the royal commissioner sent out to investigate and report
on the causes of the disturbances, had been "entirely won over
by Sir Samuel Lewis who I have grounds for supposing has been
getting up the whole case against the government on behalf of
the Chambers of Commerce and the Sierra Leoneans." A leading citizen, and a fervent Methodist, Lewis' interests ranged

from law to politics, journalism and agriculture. He died in
England on July 9, 1903, about four months before his 60th
birthday. He was buried in Acton cemetery. "On the relatively narrow stage of Sierra Leone" wrote his biographer "his
pre-eminence was acknowledged equally by administrators whose
policies he resisted and by Africans whose prejudices he flout-
ed. "

LIBERATED AFRICAN DEPARTMENT (1922-1891). First established about 1811 as the Captured Negroes (i. e. freed slaves)
Department. A commission appointed in 1810 to report on the
state of the West African Settlements recommended that the
second member of the Governor's Council should take care of
captured negroes. Before that date the care and welfare of
captured negroes was entrusted to the collector or chief officer
of customs whose responsibility it was to "receive, protect and
provide for the Captured Negroes. "
      By the recommendations of the 1810 Commission, the
second member of the Governor's Council was enjoined to supervise the "Liberated African Department"; to ensure that the accounts were properly kept and regularly scrutinized by the governor; to be able to state at all times the conditions, disposal
and health of the liberated Africans and to present every week
a report of expenditure on their maintenance. In a dispatch
from the secretary of state for the colonies to Governor Maxwell in 1811, a separate vote was authorized for the maintenance of the captured negroes. It would appear however that,
although the term "Liberated African Department" was in use
roughly from about 1811, it was not until 1822 that the term
acquired its specialized meaning. An official circular of August
15, 1822, was headed "Office of the Liberated African Department" and the official designation of the department as the Liberated African Department came into being from that date.
After a series of reorganizations between 1824 and 1840, the
Department was reduced in 1843 on orders of the Colonial Office and Treasury in London, partly because there was a decline in the number of recaptives or liberated Africans and
partly to save some £12,000 per annum, which was the running
cost of the department. In 1871 further substantial reductions
were made and the department was finally closed in 1891.

LIMBA. The Limba are among the earliest inhabitants of Sierra
Leone. A Limba tradition maintains that the first Limba man
who came to Sierra Leone was called Mansonfundu. He led the
Limba into then Gbande-occupied territory. Recent archaeological discoveries suggest that the Limba may have occupied the
Wara Wara hills as far back as A. D. 600-700s. It is not quite
clear whether the Limba were the first to invade and occupy
areas occupied by the Temne or vice versa. Tribal maps
seem to indicate that the Temne drove a deep wedge into the
areas occupied by the Limba in the north of Sierra Leone.
Today the Limba number probably 750,000 and occupy all the
five districts of the Northern Province and are subdivided into

the following major groups: Wara Wara (subdivided further into Wara Wara Yagala and Wara Wara Bafodea), Safroko, Biriwa, Tonko and Sela Limba. Of these the Wara Wara are believed to be the oldest and the Wara Wara chiefdoms are held to be the traditional home of all Limba. A hill in Wara-Wara country is believed to be inhabited by the guardian spirit of the Limba and the spirits of dead Limba Chiefs are believed to return to it.

The Limba, like the Temne, also have clans. The names, common to the Temne as well, include the Kamara, Kagbo (or Kargbo), Konte (or Conteh), Obloli, Dema, Kemoin, as well as others. Predominantly animist, the Limba appear to have embraced Christianity much more readily than Islam and the evangelical missions, particularly from the USA, have achieved significant successes among them. The most powerful secret societies among them are the Kpankpanie (or Gbangbanie) and the Kofung (or Kofo). An adventurous people, they today are probably more widely spread over Sierra Leone than any other tribal group. They have acquired considerable skill in producing palm wine, a local alcoholic beverage tapped from the oil palm.

LOKO. The Loko occupy some five chiefdoms mainly in the Port Loko and Bombali districts of the Northern Province of Sierra Leone and parts of Moyamba district in the Southern Province around Bradford and Rotifunk. They are akin to the Mende and the Gbande who now inhabit parts of Liberia. Gbande tradition says that their brothers left them at an early date to fight a war in the west. This obviously refers to the Loko whom the Limba today call Gbandin. (The Mende and Loko call each other Njagbe ("nephew"), a mutually unacceptable term.) It would appear that a substantial Mende or Gbande army serving as an advance guard was cut from the main Mende or Gbande group either by the Limba or by the Temne. Thereafter the Loko acquired a distinct Temne influence, in the way of intonation, prefixes and suffixes in addition to an otherwise predominantly Mende dialect. All this occurred, it has been suggested, before or about 1400 but more probably in the 1550s. The Loko thus settled in the north and engaged in commerce with the Temne and, although more often than not the Temne fought the Loko, they were not able to absorb them completely. Os Algoas, an important entrepôt for early Portuguese traders, became known by the end of the 16th century as Port Logo or Port Loko (today a town in Temne country southwest of the Loko chiefdoms, formerly claimed by Susu as well), which presumably derived its name from the Loko slaves shipped from there to the New World. A Loko Kingdom Mitombo was also annexed by the Temne. The Loko are either animist or Christian.

LUCAS, JOHN. Third governor of the Province of Freedom. As governor, John Lucas in June 1788 surrendered five settlers who had robbed a store on Bunce Island to Capt. Bowen, agent for the owners of the store. Although Richard Weaver signed

Capt. Taylor's treaty of August 1788 on behalf of the settlers, John Lucas was described as governor in an additional article repudiating Thompson's treaty of 1787.

LUDLAM, THOMAS. Arrived in Sierra Leone in April 1798, aged 23, to take over the reins of government. He assumed the governorship of the Colony in 1799 and during his first tenure, a new charter was granted to the Settlement on July 5, 1799, constituting Sierra Leone a Colony, authorizing the directors to appoint a governor and Council, but investing them (the directors) with powers normally exercised in other colonies by the secretary of state, and doing away with the experiment of self-government as envisaged by the election of hundredors and tithingmen. The deprivation of any say in their government, coupled with a number of other grievances, led the Nova Scotians to revolt, creating a dangerous situation from which the Company was rescued by the timely arrival of the Maroons. Ludlam planned to settle the Maroons on the land between Pirates' and Whiteman's bays, but changed his mind and decided on Bulom Shore, although this plan did not materialize. It is possible that Leicester Mountain, behind Freetown, may have been so named by Ludlam who had a house there and who came from Leicester in England. Ludlam served as governor of Sierra Leone on three occasions--in 1799; 1803-1805; 1806-1808. He was the last of the Company's governors, an Act for the transfer of the Colony to the Crown having come into effect on January 1, 1808, although he was allowed to stay in office until the arrival of his successor in April of that year. Accused of a number of crimes ranging from immorality to infanticide and encouraging slavery by T. P. Thompson who succeeded him, Ludlam was exonerated. Appointed as one of the commissioners to investigate the British West African Settlements and to report on the slave-trade, he retired from the governorship into a well-paid appointment as commissioner, albeit temporary. In 1810 on his way to Europe Ludlam died at sea, leaving Dawes and Columbine to complete the commission of inquiry.

LUKE, DESMOND EDGAR FASHOLE, 1935- . Minister of foreign affairs (1973-1975). Born on October 6, 1935. Educated at St. Edward's Primary School, the Prince of Wales School, Freetown; King's College Taunton, England, Keble College, Oxford, and at Magdalene College, Cambridge. After qualifying as a barrister he returned to Sierra Leone and set up private practice. In 1964 he received the United Nations Human Rights Fellowship award which enabled him to travel to and do research in India. Sierra Leone's first ambassador to West Germany, 1970-73, he was then elected member of Parliament for Freetown West Ward III constituency in 1973 and appointed foreign minister. He resigned his cabinet office in 1975.

LUKE, the Rev. EDWARD W. F., 1934- . Born December 6, 1934, in Freetown. Educated at the CMS Grammar School, Fourah Bay College (University of Durham), St. John's College,

Durham University, England, and University of Aberdeen, Scotland. Since 1973, organizer and Secretary; West African Association of Theological Institutions, Dean of the Faculty of Arts, senior lecturer and acting head, Department of Theology, Fourah Bay College (University of Sierra Leone). General editor, Aureol Pamphlets (1974-); joint editor with M. E. Glasswell of Essays in Honour of Harry Sawyerr, entitled New Testament Christianity for Africa and the World (1974); author of several articles on religion in Sierra Leone.

LUKE, Sir EMILE FASHOLE, 1895- . Born October 19, 1895, and educated at Wesleyan Boys (later Methodist) Boys High School and at Fourah Bay College (University of Durham). Sir Emile worked in the Sierra Leone Civil Service before proceeding to Britain to study law at Lincoln's Inn. In private practice in Sierra Leone 1926-1944. He was appointed assistant police magistrate, 1944-1945; police magistrate, 1945-1951; acting judge in the Gambia, 1953; acting puisne judge, Sierra Leone, 1951-1954. Chief commissioner of the Boy Scouts Association, Sierra Leone. He was awarded the KBE in 1969 and he became speaker of the Sierra Leone Parliament, 1968-1973. He was chief scout of Sierra Leone, 1969-1971.

- M -

MacCARTHY, Gen. Sir CHARLES. Governor of Sierra Leone, 1814-1824. Scion of the princely family of "MacCarthy Lyragh," MacCarthy was born in 1768 to a French father and an Irish mother. He joined the French army at 18. After the fall of the French monarchy and at the beginning of the Reign of Terror he sought refuge in Ireland. Commissioned into the British army, MacCarthy served in Flanders, the West Indies and Spain. In 1811 he was promoted to the rank of lieutenant colonel and in 1812 was appointed to command the garrison at Senegal and to take charge of the civil administration. In 1814, when Maxwell went on leave, MacCarthy was sent to Freetown as acting governor and when Maxwell resigned in 1815 he became substantive governor of Sierra Leone in 1816. One of his first acts was to restore confidence of the settlers in the government and to create cordial relationships so necessary but so strained before, between governors and governed. Next he addressed himself to the problem of the recaptives, a problem which he saw not in administrative but in human terms, devising the solution in the establishment of well-organized Christian communities. With funds from the British treasury, which proved unable to resist the Governor's financial requests, MacCarthy set about the task of rehabilitating the recaptives. Making use of the alliance between the British government and the CMS, the one providing funds, the other personnel in the form of clergymen and teachers, the Governor divided the Colony into 13 parishes, supervised by CMS clergymen paid by the government, which also agreed to provide funds for building churches, schools and personages.

The Governor concentrated on rural community development, renamed Hogbrook Village, Regent, Cabenda, Wilberforce, and founded some ten more villages in the Colony in
1820. MacCarthy's governorship witnessed an increase in the
quantity and quality of public buildings in Freetown. The jail
was finished in 1816, the foundation stone of St. George's
Church (later Cathedral) was laid in January 1817, a town hall
was built at Water Street, an officers' mess between Fort
Thornton and Pademba Road, a Commissariat store at the
wharf, and other offices and quarters, etc. When he went on
leave to England in 1820, he was awarded a knighthood, the
first governor of Sierra Leone to be so honored. In 1822, he
was promoted to the rank of brigadier general. In 1817 he had
revived the Sierra Leone Gazette, which had ceased publication
in 1810. In an attempt to make the settlers more involved in
the community's affairs and partly to remove barriers of color
in the Colony, MacCarthy appointed a few to municipal office
as mayors and sheriffs. The first, Thomas Carew was appointed mayor in 1818, and John Thorpe was made sheriff. In
1822 MacCarthy invited Marie-Anne Javouhey to Freetown where
she reorganized the liberated African hospital.

In terms of length of tenure, in terms of promoting the
welfare of the recaptives, in terms of establishing cordial relationships between government and governed, his governorship, if somewhat extravagant in expenditure and visionary in
some of its aims, was second to none in 19th-century Sierra
Leone. On January 21, 1824, MacCarthy died at the hands of
the Ashanti in the Gold Coast. His governorship was remem-
bered long afterwards as a golden age.

MACAULEY, BERTHAN, 1929- . Sierra Leone's first queen's
counsel, 1964. Attorney-general, 1963-1967. Born November
12, 1929, at Opobo, Nigeria. Educated at Government Model
School, the CMS Grammar School, Fourah Bay College (University of Durham), Freetown, King's College, London University, and at Gray's Inn London. Author of Questions and
Answers on Contracts. Secretary, International African
Legal Education Committee. Member of the Executive Committee of World Peace through Law Institute. Arrested and
detained by the NRC military government, 1967; charged with
treason, 1968, and convicted, 1969. Sentenced to death, but
reprieved in 1972. Now in private practice in Kingston,
Jamaica.

MACAULEY, KENNETH, 1792-1829. First superintendent of the
Captured Negroes Department (ca. 1811-1815). Relieved of his
duties as superintendent, he went into business as agent of the
firm of Macauley and Babington. He was appointed a member
of the Governor's Council, acting chief justice (1815), and acting governor (1826). A strong supporter of Governor Turner's
vigorous but unauthorized policy of "annexations, treaties,
blockades and wars," Kenneth Macauley as acting governor

pursued a similar policy, motivated more by business interests
than by any vision of spreading the "blessings of civilization"
to the interior.   Macauley was author of The Colony of Sierra
Leone Vindicated from the Misrepresentations of Mr. MacQueen
of Glasgow (1827; reprinted 1968).   Mr. MacQueen had accused
the British government of throwing vast sums of money down
the drain "to keep a useless immoral colony in idleness and en-
rich the Macauleys, observing that the only discernible fruit of
Free Labor was the mulatto population of Freetown."   As one
of those whose "free labor" had contributed in no small measure to the mulatto population of Freetown, Kenneth Macauley
felt constrained to reply.   In particular he tried to show that of
MacQueen's list of 29 officers believed to have died in Sierra
Leone between 1824-1826 only nine had in fact died.   But Macauley himself did not long survive his more accurate statistics.
He died in Freetown in 1829 at the early age of 37, his firm
Macauley and Babington ruined by his over-ambitious projects
and unrestrained spending.

MACAULEY, ZACHARY.   Arrived in Sierra Leone in January 1793
    as second member of the governor's Council.   At the age of 26
    he succeeded William Dawes in April 1794 as governor.   Be-
    fore coming to Sierra Leone, Macauley had had experience of
    a slave population in Jamaica and had in January 1791 paid a
    visit to Sierra Leone.   He served as governor of Sierra Leone
    twice, in 1794-95 and in 1796-99.   All through his tenure of of-
    five as governor the settlers were disaffected, turbulent and re-
    fractory.   On May 6, 1795, at the end of his first term as
    governor, he sailed to Barbados on a slave ship in order to ex-
    pose himself personally to the horrors of the "middle passage,"
    and from Barbados he traveled to England.   He returned to
    Sierra Leone in May 1796 and became governor for a second
    time.   From November 1797 to April 1798 he governed alone
    without a council but registered his decisions as those of gov-
    ernor and council.   During his second term as governor, the
    Sierra Leone Company decided to impose quit rents (q. v.) to
    help defray the costs of running the settlement, a move that
    was vigorously resisted by the settlers.   In order to regularize
    marriages in the Colony, Macauley in 1796 drew up rules which
    recognized as valid and legal only those marriages that were
    performed by the chaplain.   He also added rules making the
    maintenance of bastards obligatory on the fathers.   To secure
    the Colony against attacks, he organized a regular militia.
    When he left for England in April 1799, never to return to
    Sierra Leone, he took with him 25 boys and four girls to be
    educated in England in the hope that they would return to Africa
    as educators and missionaries.

MACDONALD, Col. GEORGE, 1785-1883.   Governor of Sierra
    Leone, 1842-1844.   Born in 1785, joined the Army in 1805
    and served over 20 years in the East Indies.   He fought in
    the French Revolutionary and Napoleonic Wars.   Macdonald ar-
    rived in Freetown on January 31, 1842, and became governor

of Sierra Leone. On November 5, 1842, the Governor entered
into an agreement with Mori Alifa, King of Mellacouri (ceded
to the French by the Anglo-French Convention of 1889), by
which the king undertook to put an end to warfare, to suppress
the slave trade, and to promote trade with the Colony.   In return Mori Alifa was to receive from the British government an
annual payment of 300 bars.   In October 1843, Macdonald dispatched the HMS Soudan with a detachment of troops to Magbele
to remove a prohibition on the timber trade.   On its way back
the Soudan was grounded on rocks.   Macdonald left Sierra Leone
in May 1844 for Dominica.

MACDONALD, NORMAN WILLIAM, 1808-1893. Governor of Sierra
Leone, 1846-1852.   Born in Scotland in 1808 Macdonald joined
the army at an early age and served in India with the Bengal
Cavalry.   Dismissed from the army for misconduct he arrived
in Sierra Leone in 1830, thanks to the good offices of his un-
cle, the adjutant-general, Sir John Macdonald, to take up appointment as second writer in the Colonial Secretary's offices.
Young Macdonald proved to be an intractable subordinate, avidly participating in the squabbles and party strife that characterized Freetown life during the governorships of Findlay and
H. D. Campbell.   In 1840 he was promoted to colonial secretary, and after serving first as lieutenant governor in 1845, he
was appointed governor of Sierra Leone in succession to Fergusson in 1846.   He proved himself as high-handed and over-
bearing in high office as he had been restive and intractable as
a junior officer.
       During his governorship he made attempts to improve
the appearance of Freetown.   Fort Thornton he sought to have
rebuilt, the colonial secretary's office was repaired; so was
the market house at Water Street, now structured to accommodate the police and customs offices.   Extension works were
started on the wharf and a lighthouse was erected at the Cape
near Aberdeen Village.   Macdonald increased the numerical
strength of the police to 100 and had them put in uniform.
Ordinances were passed to control public behavior in Freetown.
Regulations were drawn up to improve sanitation but were apparently not effective enough to prevent an outbreak of yellow
fever in 1847 and of influenza in 1851.   Ordinances reminiscent
of Findlay's days were passed prohibiting the public worship of
thunder, false gods or idols.   When Macdonald went on leave
in 1847 a petition aimed at preventing his return was sent to
the secretary of state, who rejected it.   Another petition pur-
porting to serve the same aim was also rejected.   The Governor made no efforts to conceal his contempt for the men he
ruled.   He convinced himself that Africans were unfit for office and spurned all efforts, official, philanthropic or religious,
to cultivate an indigenous staff.   No mayor was appointed in
1849 and 1850.   In 1851 Thomas Macfoy was chosen, and after
him came none until the 1880s.
       Macdonald entered into a large number of treaties of
peace and friendship with neighboring chiefs.   Some of his

treaties have been described as "the first treaties containing a clause ceding to the Crown jurisdiction over British subjects outside Sierra Leone." His attempts to consolidate and expand British occupation on the Bulom shores were rejected at the Colonial Office. In October 1852, Macdonald retired after serving in Sierra Leone for 22 years.

MACFOY, S. B. A. ("Sherbro Monarch"), 1843-1893. One of the most successful Creole businessmen in Sherbro in the second half of the 19th century. By 1880 Macfoy's imports from a Manchester firm were valued at £40,000 per annum. He exported produce in return. He owned his own cargo steamer, built in England and christened Sherbro Monarch after his nickname. He supported a firm British policy in the Sherbro, although he too demurred at the establishment of British customs posts in the area. By giving loans to chiefs in return for a mortgage on their territories he exerted considerable influence and control over Imperri and surrounding countries. Ruthless and unscrupulous, Macfoy was suspected of instigating a series of ritual murders in Imperri, but could not be brought to trial because of a lack of sufficient evidence. In the 1880s his business was hit by the general world depression but he turned to large-scale farming as a substitute for commerce. In the process he succeeded in retaining his nickname of "Sherbro Monarch." When he visited England in the late 1880s he called at the Colonial Office and met with men like Sydney Webb and Edward Fairfield whom he impressed favorably.

MADDY, PATRICK AMADU, 1936- . Author, broadcaster, actor and journalist. Born in Freetown on December 27, 1936. Educated at Buxton Boys School, St. Edward's Secondary School, Freetown, and at the Rose Bruford College of Speech and Drama in Britain. Artistic director of Pan-African Players, First World Festival of Negro Arts, Dakar; African drama organizer, Danish Radio, and founder/manager, African Theatre, Denmark (1966-68); Acting director of culture and art, Sierra Leone, 1974, and professional head, Sierra Leone National Dance Troup (1975). Pat Maddy's major publications include: Obasai and Other Plays (1971), No Past, No Present, No Future (1973), and Beasts, Bastards and Burdens (1974).

MADOX, the Rev. RICHARD. One of the earliest cartographers of Sierra Leone. In 1582 Madox drew a map of the estuary of the Sierra Leone River, placing Tagrin Point in its present position but describing modern Bunce River as the Sierra Leone River. The estuary--which further up divides into the River Rokel and Port Loko Creek, both of which he did not identify on his maps--he called Tagurine. Madox's interests were wide and varied and covered navigation, the classics, and the social and natural sciences.

MAKAIAH of Largo. Chief of Largo in the present Kenema District in the 1880s. Makaiah was determined to participate in the coastal trade which was bringing so much wealth and prosperity to some of his fellow chiefs. In 1885 he informed Governor Rowe that he had given up war for trade. But his attempts to gain access to the coastal trade proved unsuccessful. So he decided to resort to war. His efforts were not directed against the British, even if his exploits adversely affected British interests. He pointed out that if his warriors invaded territories under British jurisdiction they were not to blame as there were no boundaries clearly delimiting British areas. His activities however diverted trade, particularly produce from the Mano and Moa rivers to the Kittam. Allied to Bokari Gomna, Makaiah continued to obstruct British trade in the Sulima area.

Capt. Copland Crawford was sent to Sulima in 1888 with instructions to defend British interests but not to take the offensive. Crawford traveled to Largo to see Makaiah, who appeared conciliatory and who "agreed to surrender the captives he had brought from Sulima." Crawford however was determined to put an end to Makaiah's activities once and for all. Ignoring his instructions he resorted to the use of force, took the offensive and attacked Makaiah's strongholds around Largo, setting free some 600 of Makaiah's captives. Makaiah, apparently overwhelmed by Crawford's forces, sought refuge with Nyagua of Panguma who after some hesitation surrendered him to the British who deported him to Elmina. Makaiah was allowed to return to Sierra Leone in 1894.

MALAGEAH EXPEDITION see MILITARY EXPEDITIONS (2)

MAMBOLO LETTER, March 1879. A letter written by some chiefs of the Scarcies area who met at Mambolo in March 1879. The letter was a rebuttal of claims made by Governor Rowe after meeting with the Scarcies chiefs at Masama in June 1876. According to Rowe the Scarcies chiefs had asserted at the meeting that they "had always considered the Scarcies River as the Queen's River, that their fathers had told them so long before any treaty existed, that if the Queen wanted any more authority on paper than she had they were very glad to give it to her, only they hoped that their stipends would be increased." Rowe had addressed the chiefs on the need for peace, pointing out that he had "not come to deceive them, that what [he] wanted was peace; that peace could not be had amongst them without someone to whom they could look up to and who would have authority amongst them; that visits such as the one [he] then made could not be carried out without expense to England, and for this reason [he] desired to place their river on the same footing as the Sierra Leone river. They quite agreed to this and signed the agreements...."

Rowe had clearly mistaken platitudes for facts. As these transactions were conducted through interpreters it is impossible to state with any precision whether these were the views held or expressed by the chiefs or whether they were merely attributed to the chiefs by the interpreters. When, in 1879, Rowe tried to implement the 1876 agreements, the Scarcies

chiefs submitted the letter dated March 17, 1879, to Rowe.
The letter, known as the Mambolo Letter, repudiated any suggestions of cession of territory. The Chiefs recalled Governor
Rowe's visit in 1876 but claimed that they had "not the slight-
est remembrance of our having made the offer of any part of
our territory to be under the sovereignty of Her Majesty the
Queen of England.... We understood that your presence here
at that epoch was only as representing England as mediator, and
simply witness to a treaty of peace and friendship between the
Soosoos and ourselves.... ...

"We hereby formally deny having ever signed any act or
treaty which to our knowledge was an offer made by us of any
parts whatever of our territories either land or water, to be
under the sovereignty of Her Majesty the Queen of England, or
giving her any claims or rights to them. ...

"... Though we most sincerely wish to always be on the
most friendly terms with the Gracious Majesty the Queen, we
nevertheless most anxiously desire to keep to ourselves all our
rights in full over all our own territories."

This letter, couched in surprisingly elegant and fluent
language, is of great significance for Sierra Leone's history, in
view of the large number of "treaties of cession of territory"
allegedly signed by chiefs with the British, from the inception
of the Colony in 1787 to the declaration of the Protectorate in
1896. (Cf. RODGERS FAMILY LETTER.)

MANA, Prince of Gendama. Son of King Siaka of Gendama; succeeded his father as king of Gendama in late 1840s. Even before his father's death, Prince Mana, it would appear, had
exercised power in his aged father's name. He it was who
seized Mrs. Try Norman, an Aku woman who had traveled to
Gallinas in search of a French slave-trader Louis, who owed
her wages for service as his washerwoman. Mana captured
Mrs. Norman for debts owed him by a Mrs. Gray to whom she
had been formerly apprenticed. Mrs. Gray on hearing of the
incident appealed to Acting Governor Lt.-Col. Dixon Denham for
redress. Denham traveled to the Gallinas, secured Mrs. Norman's release and made arrangements for the expulsion of
Spanish slave dealers whose conduct towards him he claimed
had been hostile. Mana, acting in his aged father's name,
readily agreed to the destruction of the factories and to the expulsion of the Spanish slave-traders. When questions were
raised by the Foreign Office about the legality of Denham's action the expelled Spaniards claimed over £300,000 in damages.
The Spaniards returned to the Gallinas, but trade was hampered
by a British naval blockade. Threatened with the loss of a
means of livelihood Prince Mana and his fellow chiefs once
more expelled the Spaniards, who eventually sought refuge in
Brazil. In February 1850 the chiefs made a treaty to put an
end to the Gallinas slave trade. W. A. Parker, an Afro-
American, was appointed British consular agent in the Gallinas
where he had formerly been a slave-trader. He was murdered
in 1850 and in reprisal British naval ships destroyed some of

Prince Mana's towns. The prince's enemies took advantage of
his plight to drive him out of the Gallinas area. He returned
later, reestablished his position and appears to have been most
instrumental in thwarting the claims of Liberia to Gallinas
country.

MANO RIVER. Accepted by Liberia in 1886 as the boundary line
between Sierra Leone and Liberia. In 1973 the Mano River
declaration, establishing a customs union and making provision
for cooperation between the two countries in various fields, was
signed by presidents Tolbert of Liberia and Stevens of Sierra
Leone.

MANSFIELD, WILLIAM MURRAY, 1705-1793. Chief justice of
King's Bench (1756); created Earl of Mansfield 1776. His attitude and ruling in two cases involving slaves--Thomas Lewis
in 1771 and James Somerset in 1722--had a tremendous impact
on the history of Sierra Leone. Lord Mansfield had heard
about Jonathan Strong's case in 1765 and of Granville Sharp's
representations on his behalf and could not help feeling uneasy
about the implications--the possible disastrous effects on the
rights of property which it was the business of the law to protect. On the other hand he had begun to convince himself that
Sharp and the abolitionists had a case. In Lewis' case in 1771
he had brought the proceedings to a close on a somewhat am-
bivalent note. "You will see more in this question than you see
at present," said Justice Mansfield. "It is no matter mooting
it now; but if you look into it, there is more than by accident
you are acquainted with. There are a great many opinions
given upon it; I am aware of many of them; but perhaps it is
much better that it should never be discussed or settled. I
don't know what the consequences may be, if the masters were
to lose their property by accidentally bringing their slaves to
England. I hope it never will be finally discussed; for I would
have all masters think them free, and all Negroes think they
were not, because then they would both behave better." In the
circumstances "Lord Mansfield avoided bringing the question to
issue by discharging the Negro on some other pretence."
        When Somerset's case was brought before him in 1772,
he adjourned twice and tried to avoid giving a ruling by suggesting that Somerset's master should set him free. The
master refused. Then Justice Mansfield gave his celebrated decision which in effect asserted that slavery was contrary and
unknown to the laws of England. As a result some 15,000
slaves in England at the time were automatically set free.

MARGAI, Sir ALBERT MICHAEL, 1910-   . Prime minister of
Sierra Leone, 1964-1967. Sir Albert was born on October 10,
1910, at Gbangbatoke, Banta chiefdom, Moyamba District.
He was educated at St. Patrick's School, Bonthe, and at St.
Edward's Secondary School, Freetown. Before proceeding to
Britain to study law at the Inner Temple Inns of Court, Sir
Albert worked as a nurse in the Sierra Leone government

medical service from 1931 to 1944. In 1948, after qualifying
as a barrister he returned home, enrolled as solicitor and advocate in the Supreme Court of Sierra Leone and set up private
practice. His return was well-timed. He came back just in
time to take an active part in the debates on the Stevenson constitution and to play a leading role as one of the chief spokesmen of Protectorate interests. As the first person from the
Protectorate to qualify as a lawyer he had a tremendous initial
advantage for a political career, although his first incursion into the field in the Freetown City Council elections of 1950
proved to be a near disaster. Impressive in appearance and
persuasive in argument, Sir Albert carved for himself a high
reputation for hard work and organizing ability and for getting
things done efficiently and quickly in each of the cabinet positions he held--education, agriculture and natural resources,
finance--between 1951 and 1964. His ebullient nationalism and
his anti-colonialist posture, his age and boundless energy made
him the idol of the angry young men within and without his
party. Although there was a feeling in some quarters that after his reconciliation with his brother, Milton, the latter deliberately groomed Albert for the premiership, there is no
doubt that Sir Albert's own ability and personal qualities did
play a decisive role.

In 1951 he was elected to the Legislative Council as
first Protectorate member and in 1952 was appointed Sierra
Leone's first minister of education, the ablest so far. He was
returned to the House of Representatives in the general election of 1957 as member for Moyamba South constituency.
Elected by the parliamentary caucus as leader of the SLPP
after the 1957 election, Albert was prevailed upon to step
down in favor of his elder brother Milton, the doctor. In the
subsequent allocation of portfolios, Albert rejected cabinet office and went into opposition to form in September 1958 the People's National Party, of which he became leader. Following
the formation of the United Front Coalition he was appointed
minister of agriculture and natural resources in 1959. He was
returned in the 1962 general election as member of Parliament
for Moyamba South constituency and appointed minister of finance. As minister of finance, Sir Albert introduced the decimal currency, established the "leone" as legal tender and created the Bank of Sierra Leone as the country's central and national bank. On April 29, 1964, following the death of Sir
Milton, Sir Albert was appointed prime minister. There was
a storm of protest over the constitutionality of his appointment
and in the ensuing confusion Albert promptly dismissed four
ministers--two of them Karefa-Smart and Mustapha, aspirants
to the throne.

Thereafter Sir Albert settled down to work bringing to
his new office the same brilliance he had displayed in former
positions of power. Within a year however Sir Albert's popularity began to decline. First, he identified himself somewhat
closely with Ghana and Guinea thereby creating the impression
that the style of leadership, if not the political systems, of

those two countries appealed to him and fascinated him. Second, by 1966 he was talking in threatening terms of a republican constitution and of a one-party state. Opponents of both (out of fear and desperation), mostly intellectuals and professionals, joined the ranks of the APC opposition. Third, Sir Albert fell out with a number of able young men in his own party mostly from the provinces, particularly the South and East. In the process he depleted his own ranks. When the 1967 elections were held some of the young men whose candidacies he had so strongly opposed were returned as independents. They in turn refused to support him, a decision which ruined his chances of regaining the premiership. After it became clear that his party had not won the elections, Sir Albert appeared to have hoped, possibly believed, that the army could install him as prime minister against the wishes of the majority of the voters. The army officers had their own views and ambitions. They detained Sir Albert for a few days and imposed a military regime, the NRC, on the country. Had Sir Albert been willing to accept the verdict of the ballot box and to go into opposition, there is little doubt that constitutional government might have been established on a firm basis in Sierra Leone. In 1968 after the overthrow of the NRC and the assumption of power by the APC, Sir Albert went into voluntary exile to Britain, there to beguile his unwelcome leisure by speculating in various business enterprises.

MARGAI, Sir MILTON AUGUSTUS STRIEBY, 1896-1964. First prime minister of Sierra Leone, 1961-1964. Born December 7, 1896, at Gbangbatoke, Banta Chiefdom, Moyamba District. Educated at EUB Primary School, Bonthe, the Albert Academy Secondary School, Freetown, Fourah Bay College (University of Durham), Freetown, and at the Armstrong School of Medicine, King's College (Durham University), Newcastle-Upon-Tyne. Sir Milton was the first person from the Protectorate to obtain a bachelor's degree at Fourah Bay College and the first to qualify in medicine in 1927. He returned home and was appointed a medical officer of Sierra Leone in 1928. From 1928 until his retirement as chief medical officer, Bo, in 1950, Dr. Margai served in almost all government hospitals in the country--a tremendous advantage for his future political career--winning in the process a high and enviable reputation as a surgeon.

      While in government service he was most instrumental in organizing an informal assemblage of leading chiefs which later crystalized into the Protectorate Assembly. As Medical Officer, Pujehun, he organized a midwifery service on modern lines among the native midwives and bundo women in all but one of the chiefdoms of the district. The success of his midwifery service, for which he was awarded the MBE in 1947, was followed up in subsequent stations where he worked as government medical officer until his retirement. He published a simple booklet on midwifery in Mende for the use of illiterate midwives, entitled Mavulo Gbembo Golei ("Cathechism of Mid-

wifery"). He was also able through the midwives to introduce
improvements in bundo initiation rites which ensured less haz-
ardous operations.

He represented Bonthe district as a non-chief in the Protectorate Assembly in 1947. His influence as leading member
of the SOS and PEPU made possible the alliance between Protectorate-educated elite and traditional rulers which found political expression in the SLPP. His high standard of education
and professional competence and his moderate approach to politics encouraged an influential number of Creoles to join the
ranks of the Protectorate-dominated SLPP. He was one of the
moving spirits behind the launching of the first Protectorate
newspaper, the Sierra Leone Observer, in Bo in 1949. He was
elected first president of the SLPP and after the 1951 elections
he became leader of government business, heading six other
party members who were allocated responsibility for some government departments and appointed to the executive council.
Subsequent constitutional developments led to his appointment in
July 1954 as chief minister and towards the end of 1957 as
premier and by the provisions of the independence constitution
of 1961, prime minister. Sir Milton led Sierra Leone to independence in 1961 April 27 with the minimum of conflict; he conducted general elections in 1962 on a multi-party basis without
turmoil and passed away peacefully in his bed on April 28, 1964.

MARIA, Senora (also, Mrs. Monday). Senora Maria or Mrs.
Monday; sister of a king on the Bulom Shore. She married an
employee of the Royal African Company called Monday who was
arrested and executed for plotting to seize the company's factory
at Bunce Island in 1728. Senora Maria however continued to
give devoted service to the Company, performing the functions
of interpreter and intermediary. By 1729 she had built a town
on the north end of Lumley Beach.

MARITZ, Lt. GASTON-MAXIME. In 1893 the French government
sent an expedition into French Guinea to explore the territory
south of Kissidougou and to ascertain what might be the most
suitable natural boundary between the British sphere of influence in Sierra Leone and the French sphere of influence in what
is now Guinea. Accordingly on November 13, Lt. Gaston-
Maxime Maritz, a young French infantry officer, was sent from
Kissidougou to Kono country with orders "to delimit exactly the
English and Liberian boundaries."

On November 15, Maritz received further instructions
from Maj. Richard, Commandant of French Guinea, through
Capt. Valentin in Kissidougou, to settle boundary lines with the
minimum of delay. Maj. Richard added: "... You know that
our British neighbors are not inactive and that they are seeking
to expand towards the southeast. It is therefore essential that
we should be sure of their real rights so as to establish our
own without risk of diplomatic clashes, which Paris wishes to
avoid at any price. Do not allow the English to put you off:
protest energetically against their presence in the Niegueli ...

and demand a formal acknowledgment of your protest.   The validity of our rights is perhaps questionable but we have been appealed to by tribes, who have never acknowledged British protection, and this constitutes a right, at least for the time being. " Capt. Valentin on November 21 urged Maritz to "Try to win over the Kono and Mende chiefs if possible, be consistent in what you tell them, and, if you can, have them sign a treaty placing themselves under our protection. At any rate tell them that under us their land will always remain their own and that we will protect them against the Sofas and the English. "

At Waiima within the British sphere of influence (under the terms of the Anglo-French agreement in Paris on August 10, 1889), but unvisited by British officials, Maritz signed a treaty on December 1, 1893, with six Kono chiefs led by Kouroua Ouara of Soa (i. e. , Sewa).   The others were Maimina of Farandala, Tamba of Waiima, Daguiri, Koumbana and Kontonde.   Famatoro of Sando, Koulibbi and Fashuluku were also represented. With the help of the French, the Kono chiefs attacked Tekuyema and forced Pokere (or, variously, Porokere, Porquere, Poquere) and his Sofas to flee. Maritz then retired to Waiima, thence to Manson, Neya Chiefdom (Koinadugu District), where he hoped to receive fresh orders and reinforcements.   The Kono chiefs then appealed to Maritz for help against Pokere who had once more taken up arms.   Maritz abandoned his original plan and ignored his instructions to set out for Kissidougou and made the fatal decision of returning to Waiima to take on Pokere and the Sofas.   But at Waiima, instead of the Sofas, was encamped a British force commanded by Col. Ellis and Capt. Lendy.

At dawn on December 23, 1893, the British and French forces at Waiima inadvertently or possibly through treachery opened fire on each other, each mistaking the other for the Sofas.   It has now been established that the French troops answered the fire of the British sentries, who on guard duty, had fired at the unidentified armed force, in order to raise the alarm.   The exchange of fire lasted about 40 minutes.   Capt. Lendy and two privates of the Frontier Police were killed; the West India Regiment lost lieutenants Liston and Wroughton, a sergeant-major and 14 privates were severely wounded.   Lt. Maritz was also killed, as were 35 other ranks on the French side.   In 1902 the French government after protracted negotiations agreed to pay the British government £9000 compensation.

MASIMERA EXPEDITION see MILITARY EXPEDITIONS

MASSALLY, A. J. , 1915-1969.   First provincial to be appointed puisne judge (1966).   Born April 20, 1915.   Educated at St. Patrick's School, Bonthe, at St. Edward's Secondary School, Freetown, and at the Middle Temple Inns of Court, London. Elected member of Parliament in 1957; deputy speaker of the House of Representatives and of the Sierra Leone Parliament, 1957-1962.   Appointed magistrate 1962-1965 and puisne judge 1966.   He died in Freetown in 1969 and was buried at Ascension Town Cemetery.

MASSALLY, JAMES CALLAY, 1906-1943. Second Mende and Protectorate person to qualify in medicine. Born December 8,
1906. Educated at St. Patrick's School, Bonthe, St. Edward's
Secondary School, Freetown, and at University College, Dublin.
James Massally returned home in 1939, set up private practice
in Freetown, and then joined government service. He later
served as government medical officer at Kailahun, Bo, Freetown and Pujehun. He died in Pujehun on December 8, 1943.

MATTHEWS, Lt. JOHN. Author of A Voyage to the River Sierra
Leone on the Coast of Africa; Containing an Account of the
Trade and Produce of the Country; And of the Civil and Religious Customs and Manners of the People in a Series of Letters to a Friend in England. The letters were written during
Matthew's residence in Sierra Leone in 1785, 1787 and 1788.
He also included an additional letter on the subject of the African slave trade--an apologia for it. Matthews sketched a map
of Sierra Leone placing the Temne to the east of Port Loko
Creek, the Bullom and the Sherbro eastward of the Rokel river,
the Susu north of the Rokel along the coast, and the Mandingo
inland north of the Rokel.
        Matthews was an agent of a Liverpool firm referred to
in Africa as the Sierra Leone Company. He arrived in Sierra
Leone in September 1785. A former agent of the Company had
been murdered and its property plundered. He however succeeded in getting permission from the chief at Whiteman's Bay
to build stores and other houses. The venture proved quite successful and soon the company became the most prosperous of
the three operating on the river at the time.

MATTURI, S. T., 1925- . Born on October 22, 1925, at Jaiama,
Kono District. Educated at Bo Government School, Prince of
Wales School, Freetown, University of Ibadan, Nigeria and at
the University of Hull, England. First principal of Njala University College (1963). Chairman of National Advisory Committee set up by NRC military regime in 1967. Pro-vice chancellor (1969-1970) and vice chancellor, University of Sierra Leone
(1971-1972). Chairman, West African Examinations Council
(1972).

MAUDE, the Rev. WILLIAM H. Chairman and general superintendent of the Methodist Mission in Sierra Leone (1882-1885
and 1896-1909). The Rev. Maude arrived in Sierra Leone as
a missionary in December 1867. In 1882 he was appointed
chairman and during his first tenure he inaugurated what is
known in English Methodism as the "Worn out Ministers and
Ministers' Widows Auxiliary Fund"--a kind of insurance scheme.
In 1886 Maude left for England but returned in 1896 to become
chairman and general superintendent for a second time. He
retired finally in 1909 after 43 years service in the Methodist
Church, most of them in Sierra Leone.

MAXWELL, Col. CHARLES WILLIAM. Lieutenant governor of

Sierra Leone, 1811-1814. Entered the British army as an ensign in 1795 and saw active service in many areas including Gibraltar, South America and West Africa. After capturing the French fortress of Senegal in 1809, Maxwell was appointed lieutenant governor of Sierra Leone in 1810. He arrived in Freetown on July 1, 1811, to assume his new responsibilities. In Sierra Leone he was faced, among other problems, with the longstanding one of land grants and with the perennial problem of the liberated Africans. He continued Columbine's policy of strict economy in governmental expenditure, reduced public works and salaries and raised revenue from local sources. He passed the first customs ordinance in August, 1812, increased watering dues and issued licenses to foreign ships trading in the Colony. He collected license fees from a number of retail traders in Freetown, reviewed the road tax and levied a horse tax. Authorized to allocate lands that had been promised to the settlers, Maxwell revived quit rents (q.v.). He introduced a new militia ordinance and when the Maroons demurred and grew restive about its provisions, he enlisted support among the recaptives whom he recruited in large numbers in the armed forces. During his governorship Maxwell did more than any of his predecessors--and at times against indifference or opposition from Whitehall--to solve the problem of the liberated Africans. He went on leave in 1814, resigned the governorship of Sierra Leone in 1815 and was appointed governor of Dominica. He died in 1848.

MAY, the Rev. JOSEPH CLAUDIUS, 1845-1902. Born in Freetown in 1845 of a liberated African father, the Rev. J. C. May (as he was known) became a successful Methodist preacher and clergyman. Young May started life as a shop assistant until at age 20 in 1865 it was decided that he too should train for the ministry. He was educated at Borough Road School and Wesley College, Taunton, England, by the London Committee of the Wesleyan Church. He returned to Sierra Leone in 1871 and for three years helped organize and improve Wesleyan village schools in the colony. In 1874 he started the Wesleyan Boys High School and served as its first principal until his death in 1902. With him as principal the school made remarkable progress; it rivaled and some would say even excelled the CMS Grammar School. From 1882-1888 Principal May published The Methodist Herald and in September 1884, assisted by Blyden, founded The Sierra Leone Weekly News, edited and printed by his brother, Cornelius May.

MBAWOLOMEH CHIEF. A powerful Gbandi chief who in 1896, shortly after Kai Lundo's death, attacked Kailahun with a large force of Gbandis, Berris, Sofas and Kissis. In alliance with Kabbah Sei of Gorahun, Mbawolomeh laid waste Fabunde's villages. Captain B. Cave-Browne-Cave was dispatched with a force of Frontier Police to drive him from British-protected territory. Captain Cave-Browne-Cave fell ill and had to return to Freetown. Mbawolomeh meanwhile entrenched his posi-

tion by occupying Balla Vahun, Bomaru and some other towns.
On September 4, 1896, Major Fairtlough attacked Vahun and
dispersed his warriors. The other towns which he had occupied
were also captured but he escaped to Liberia.

M'BAYO, JOSEPH EADRIC, 1923- . Educator and administrator.
Born on December 28, 1923, and educated at the St.
Edward's Primary School, Freetown, EUB School Jaiama, Nimikoro,
Kono District, and Bo Government School, the Prince of Wales
School, Fourah Bay College (University of Durham), and at the
University of Reading, England. Mr. M'bayo was among the
first set of Bo School pupils to obtain a pass in the Cambridge
School Certificate (1943). After acquiring a wide experience in
teaching he was appointed principal, Government Secondary
School, Jimmi Bagbo (1960-1963); Principal, Government Secondary School, Koyema (1964-1966). He then became principal
of the Civil Service Training College, Tower Hill, Freetown
(1966-1969), from where he was appointed permanent secretary,
Ministry of Social Welfare (1969), and secretary to the cabinet
(1969 to the present)--the longest tenure in the country's history. On a number of occasions he has also acted as secretary
to the president.

MEHEUX, JOHN. Born of a French father and a Temne mother,
John Meheux owned considerable property in Freetown. In
Kissy Street he inherited a large estate and Meheux Street
still commemorates it. He was appointed in 1861 as first
permanent sheriff of the Colony, a post tenable during Her
Majesty's pleasure and a post he held until his death. When he
died in 1886, a great deal of his property acquired and inherited
had vanished.

MELVILLE, ELIZABETH HELEN CALLANDER [Mrs. Michael L.
Melville]. Great-granddaughter of a Scottish earl, and the
niece of a British cabinet minister, Miss Callander got married to Michael Linning Melville, registrar of the Mixed Commission Court (Freetown) in 1840 (see following entry). On
returning to Sierra Leone and after the birth of their son, the
Melville's moved from Freetown to "Smith's Hill," above the
town, where she wrote a series of letters published anonymous-
ly in 1849 and entitled A Residence at Sierra Leone, edited by
her cousin the Hon. Caroline Norton and dedicated to Lady
Graham of Netherby. In the preface Mrs. Melville stated that
her work is chiefly compiled from a journal she kept for her
own amusement, and a few of her letters to home friends.
A Residence at Sierra Leone is a substantial work that includes
information on virtually everything in the colony that caught
Mrs. Melville's observant eye. There is an account of the
flora and fauna; notes on the early history of the Colony, the
settlers, Mr. Clarkson, problems of the infant Colony, the
French attack, the Temne rising etc. There is a survey of
the climate, detailed descriptions of storms and tornadoes and
a host of other items. She returned to England for good some

years before her husband's retirement.

MELVILLE, MICHAEL LINNING. Acting governor, 1833. Appointed first to a writership in the Colonial administration in Sierra Leone, Michael Melville returned home, was called to the Bar and came back to Sierra Leone as king's advocate. From July to December 1833 he acted as governor of the Colony having acted as chief justice in 1832. In 1834 he was appointed registrar to the Mixed Commission Court. Six years later he got married to Elizabeth Helen Callander from Scotland and returned with her to Freetown. Melville and his wife moved from their residence at Gloucester Street to "Smith's Hill," above the town on the lower slopes of Mount Aureol. In 1841 he was appointed commissioner of arbitration and in 1842 promoted commissary judge. In his capacity as acting chief justice, he had in 1832 appointed W. H. Savage as counsel for defense of the Aku in the Cobolo War trial. Melville agreed with Defense Counsel Savage (on legal grounds, but partly to spite Governor Findlay) that the Court's jurisdiction in the matter was in fact questionable. At a subsequent trial of the Aku the acting king's advocate Robert Dougan upheld Melville's opinion in favor of the court's lack of jurisdiction. Melville retired in 1848 on £800 a year pension until his death in 1878.

MENDE. A people of Mande speech, probably descendants of the Mane who moved into Sierra Leone in waves of migrations spread over a century or more roughly between A.D. 1450 and 1550. These migrations were at times peaceful, consisting of small bands of hunters slightly more numerous than an immediate family. At other times they appear to have been large military expeditions making their progress through war, plunder and conquest. Today the Mende inhabit an area of about 9000 square miles or roughly one-third of the total surface area of Sierra Leone in the Southern and Eastern provinces and occupy in whole or in part the Moyamba, Bonthe, Bo, Pujehun, Kenema and Kailahun districts. In addition the Mende inhabit the adjacent western corner of Liberia. The Mende in Sierra Leone number slightly over one million and do reside in other parts of the country, particularly in the Western Area, where they are found in the largest numbers outside their territorial districts. They have been described as a nation because "their cultural and linguistic characteristics are sufficiently distinctive to mark them off as a group, and they possess a very definite national consciousness which is supported by traditions, legend and folklore." They can, on the basis of dialect, attitudes toward life and ways of thought, be subdivided into three major groups.

　　(a) Kpa (or Gba) Mende. These inhabit about 16 chiefdoms in the Moyamba, Bo and Kenema districts. They are distinguished particularly by their wholehearted support and membership of the wunde secret society (not found among other Mende), their strong military traditions and, in the case of those in Moyamba and Bo districts, a distinct dialect. Kpa

(or Gba) implies "different." The Kpa Mende account for about
20 per cent of the total Mende population in Sierra Leone.

(b) The Sewa (or "Middle") Mende. These live near and
along the Sewa river, account for about 35 per cent of the
Mende population and inhabit the bulk of Bo and parts of Kenema and Pujehun districts. They occupy a middle position between the Kpa and Ko-Menda and consider themselves as the
purest Mende-speaking group.

(c) The Ko-Mende (or Kolo-Mende). These inhabit the
bulk of Kenema and Kailahun and parts of Pujehun districts and
are predominantly Muslim in religion, although the impact of
Christianity is gaining momentum.

Secret societies, particularly the poro or wunde for men,
sande or bundo for women, and the njayei and humoi for both
sexes, play an important role in the lives of the Mende. Predominantly an agricultural people they supplement their food by
hunting and fishing. They grow rice, their staple food, and
cassava. They also produce coffee, cacao and ginger and exploit the oil palm for oil and kernels. Mostly animist with
strong belief in ancestral worship, in witchcraft and sorcery,
they have over the years become converted in impressive numbers to Islam and Christianity. They have over the decades
absorbed appreciable numbers of smaller neighboring tribes culturally and linguistically and today virtually the entire South
and Eastern provinces are Mende-speaking.

MENDI DEVELOPMENT SYNDICATE. A group of prospectors from
Reading, England, who arrived in the Upper Bagru early in
1898 to look for gold. There were five of them in the party.
One Edward Monger was killed at Bunjema at the outbreak of
the Hut Tax War. Monger was the only non-missionary European victim of the rising.

MENDI MISSION. In 1837 a slave ship with about 200 Mende and
Sherbro slaves sailed from Sherbro for the West Indies. The
ship arrived in Havana, Cuba, where two West Indian slave
dealers bought about 44 of the slaves and put them on a smaller ship, the Amistad, bound possibly for Charleston, South
Carolina, where they hoped to resell them. Enroute from
Cuba the slaves revolted, killed two Cubans and captured three,
while a few escaped by boat. The captive crewmen were
forced by the slaves to steer the Amistad back to Africa and
to Sherbro. Instead the ship arrived at Long Island, New York,
where American officials took the ship and slaves into custody.

The Cubans charged the Africans with murder and piracy. Lewis Tappan, a New York businessman and founder of
the New York Anti-Slavery Society, formed a committee to provide legal aid and other forms of relief for the accused Africans. The trial judge expressed the view that he had no jurisdiction over offenses committed on the high seas in a foreign
vessel. On the instructions of the United States Secretary of
State the district attorney appealed to the Supreme Court.
There Quincy Adams, former President, appeared for the Afri-

cans and secured their release. As the United States government manifested no interest in repatriating them, Tappan's
committee once more took up their cause and made inquiries
about the exact location of their homeland. The trial had lasted some 18 months during which the African slaves had been
introduced to Christianity. In the process, their numbers had
been reduced through death to about 23. Tappan and his committee decided to send the slaves back to Africa accompanied
by missionaries.

In 1842 the survivors, accompanied by the Rev. William
Raymond and family, the Rev. John Steele, and two teachers,
sailed from New York to start what became known as the Mendi
Mission in Sierra Leone. On arrival the missionaries traveled
to Sherbro to negotiate for land with Harry Tucker, who, though
initially uncooperative, subsequently granted the missionaries a
parcel of land near Komende (Kaw Mendi) on a tributary of the
River Jong. Some of the African slaves once home started to
abandon the mission for more familiar pursuits. In 1846 Lewis
Tappan's committee, in association with other missionary
groups, formed the American Missionary Association, a non-
denominational evangelical organization having among its aims
the abolition of slavery. Thomas Garnich, one of the companions of the Rev. Raymond at the Mende Mission, died in
early 1847. Raymond also died later in the same year. Work
at the Mission was continued by George Thompson, who left
New York for Sierra Leone and reached the Mission on July
23, 1848. Anson Carter also arrived at the Mission on July
17, only to die eight days later. Within the first six years of
operation the Mission lost four members of the American Missionary Association--Harndon, Garnick, Raymond and Carter.
Thompson, joined by John S. Brooks, was given land for a
mission station near Tisana. The new place was called Mo
Tappan after Lewis Tappan. Brooks opened Mo Tappan in
1854 and in 1856 Kaw Mendi was abandoned as unhealthy. In
1883 the American Missionary Association handed the Mendi
Mission to the United Brethren in Christ.

MERCANTILE ASSOCIATION. Although the need for a Mercantile
Association in Sierra Leone had been felt in the 1820s, and
Stephen Gabbidon and William Henry Savage had in 1827 actually
proposed its creation, it was not until 1851 that the merchants
in Freetown formed such a group to represent the interests of
a growing business community. C. W. M. Heddle became its
first chairman. The Association had ceased to function effectively by the second half of 1863. It was revived in December 1863 for the purpose of choosing a nominee to represent
mercantile interests in the projected new Legislative Council
constituted by Charter in July of that year. John Ezzidio, a
recaptive, won 23 votes against the European merchant John
Lewis' 13. To discourage any notions of representative government, John Ezzidio's appointment was sanctioned on the clear
understanding that he held office at the queen's, not the merchants' pleasure.

Two years after its formation the Association unsuccessfully petitioned the Colonial Office against new customs tariffs
introduced by Governor Kennedy in 1853. Five years later the
Association petitioned the secretary of state for a new constitution that would, among other things, make provision for a separate Legislative Council. While not accepting the requests of
the petitioners in their entirety, the Colonial Office conceded
the need for a more representative council, and it was subsequently introduced in 1863. The Mercantile Association consistently opposed the claims of the Liberian Republic to Gallinas territory and insisted that the territory be brought under
British influence and protection in the interests of the Colony's
trade.

In 1864 the Mercantile Association was reconstituted as
the Chamber of Commerce. Alexander Walker became its
president, William Lewis its vice president, and W. C. Wal-
cott its paid secretary. The Chamber of Commerce served
among other things as a channel for expressing grievances and
proposing reforms. President Walker advocated a revived
municipal council, a larger Legislative Council and a piped
water supply system for the Colony.

MESSI [Messe] of Massahn. Nominal ruler in the Eastern Kittam.
On June 5, 1883, Queen Messi (Messe) and other chiefs "ceded"
to the British Crown strips of coastal territory embracing parts
of Krim, Massahn, Topan, and other areas, thereby increasing
the territorial area of the Sierra Leone Colony. Thereafter
customs posts were established at Sulima, Mano-Salijah, and
Lavana. In the 1880s Queen Messi also granted Solomon Benjamin Augustus Macfoy.(a successful Creole trader in the Sherbro) concessions to trade duty-free in areas under her jurisdiction. She also used her influence to save some Creole lives
during the 1898 Hut Tax War. At her request the life of Mrs.
Tilley (widow of the catechist Joseph Matthew Tilley, killed in
that war) was spared.

MIGEOD, F. W. H. Colonial civil servant and linguist in Sierra
Leone in the last decade of the 19th and early decades of the
20th century. Author of: The Mende Language, Containing
Useful Phrases, Elementary Grammar, Short Vocabularies,
Reading Materials (1908), "The Syllabic Writing of the Vai
People" (1909), The Languages of West Africa (2 vols.; 1911,
1913), Mende Natural History Vocabulary (1911-1913), West
Africa According to Ptolemy (1915), The Building of the Poro
House and Making of the Image (1916), Mende Songs (1916),
"Some Observations on the Physical Character of the Mende
Nation" (1919) and A View of Sierra Leone (1926).

MILITARY EXPEDITIONS. [This entry is divided into 15 parts,
arranged chronologically.]

(1) Expedition Against the Aku (or, Cobolo War), 1832.
In 1831 a group of dissident Aku, angered by Governor Find-

lay's prohibition of "superstitious practices," and induced by
Thomas Stephen Caulker of the Plantain Islands to support him
against the Temne, left the Colony and encamped at Cobolo on
the Ribi River, east of Waterloo. The people of Waterloo took
alarm and informed the Governor. News reached Freetown towards the end of 1832 that the Aku at Cobolo were plundering
traders on their way to the factories of Sherbro. Volunteers
dispatched to patrol the area suffered one killed and four wounded in an armed confrontation with the Aku. Governor Findlay
mustered all available troops in garrison and sent them to Waterloo where they were joined by a company of the Sierra Leone
Militia and some volunteers. Before the troops reached Cobolo,
the Aku had already suffered reverses and severe casualties at
the hands of the local population. Over 50 were killed or
drowned as they attempted to escape across a creek. Oji Cor-
ri, the leader of the Aku, subsequently lost his life in a final
desperate skirmish with Chief Caulker, who sent captured Aku
prisoners and the ears of their slain leader to Government
Findlay. The troops stayed at Cobolo for four days and then
returned to Freetown.

(2) <u>Malaghea Expedition, 1855</u>. In 1855 an expedition
was sent against King Mina Lahai of Malaghea. A British
trader at Mahala within Lahai's jurisdiction had been robbed of
some £200 worth of goods. The acting-governor, Robert Dougan, asked King Mina Lahai and other chiefs for reparations.
The request was ignored, there was another robbery of a British trader, and to crown it all Lahai gave all traders ten days'
notice to leave their factories in the Mellacouri area. On the
Governor's orders, Captain Haseltine proceeded to the Mellacouri in <u>HMS Prometheus</u> and landed 150 marines with the 1st
and 3rd <u>West India Regiment</u> and 55 police. Overwhelmed by
such a display of force, the Malaghea chiefs agreed to pay
damages and to allow the traders to return--an agreement which
was not fully honored. The Governor then dispatched his private secretary, Eugene Dillett, to Malaghea to demand full payment. Lahai treated Dillett with scant courtesy. As a result,
another expedition was dispatched to Malaghea in May 1855 with
Dillett in the <u>HMS Teazer</u> accompanied by some 200 soldiers to
punish Lahai. The troops arrived on May 21 and partially destroyed the town. The next day the town was again attacked and
this time the troops were suddenly fired upon by the defenders,
who inflicted heavy losses on the troops, killing several.
Retreating under deadly fire the troops tried to get back
to the <u>Teazer</u>. One boat with 40 men capsized and many were
either drowned or dragged from the water and killed. The
<u>Teazer</u> returned to Freetown, leaving behind 95 killed, drowned,
wounded or captured, including four British officers killed and
one wounded. "No such disaster had befallen British arms in
Sierra Leone" wrote a distinguished Sierra Leone historian.
Dougan offered "terms" to Lahai who displayed a magnanimity
in triumph which contrasted sharply with the "violence joined to
infirmity of purpose" displayed by his adversaries. He prom-

ised to return prisoners and captured military equipment and
in return his debts to the traders were written off. In less
than a year he gave up 21 soldiers and allowed trade to go on
as before. Dougan was discharged from the service. He set
up private practice in Freetown until his death in 1871.

(3) Bendu Expedition, October 8-24, 1875. In June
1875 some warboys in the service of the chiefs of Mongray,
adjacent to British Sherbro attacked Mamaiah, a town at the
estuary of the Jong River, plundered some factories and took
into captivity some 33 British subjects, mostly women and children. The rains made it impossible for the Sierra Leone government to send an expedition to the area. Instead a large
force of armed police was dispatched to Bendu to prevent a repetition of the Mamaiah incident. Although some 31 of the 33
captured British subjects had been released, the governor,
Major Rowe on October 8, 1875, left Freetown with one sub-
altern, 40 men of the 1st West India Regiment, and some armed
police in the Colonial steamer Lady of the Lake for Sherbro on
a reprisal mission. When the force arrived at Mongray, the
raiders had escaped, the two remaining captives were surrendered and peace was made with the chiefs. No indemnity was
demanded as an epidemic of smallpox was playing havoc with
the population in the area. The force returned to Freetown on
October 24, 1875.

(4) Bagru Expedition, November 7 to December 21, 1875.
Towards the end of October 1875 a force of Mende attacked and
plundered some areas on the Bagru River and carried off people from villages within British jurisdiction. The civil commandant of Sherbro, Mr. Darnell Davies, accompanied by 19
armed police, left for Bagru to contain the Mende and prevent
further aggression. On November 7 he arrived at Konkonany,
where his force was strengthened by Humpha Rango, chief of
Dodoh, and about 100 of his men. On November 8, Davies'
party reached Kpetegormah, a stockaded town, where they were
repulsed. Davies sustained serious injuries and three of his
policemen were killed. When the news reached Freetown, Governor Rowe on November 15 set out in the Colonial steamer
Sir Arthur Kennedy for Bagru, accompanied by a force of the
1st West India Regiment under the command of Capt. A. C.
Allinson and some armed police. The force encamped at
Tyama Woroo in Bagru and from there advanced and destroyed
en route Gondama and other stockaded towns. At Senehun on
December 21, and on December 30 at Shenge, the Governor
signed treaties with Sherbro and Mende chiefs, who agreed to
submit future disputes to the governor for arbitration, to destroy war stockades and to keep the trade routes open and safe.
They also gave the British the right to collect customs duties
on the seaboard territories under their jurisdiction.

(5) Kikonkeh Expedition, 1879. Kikonkeh Island on the
Great Scarcies River had been "ceded" to the British Crown by

a treaty of November 29, 1847. In 1879 Governor Rowe, determined to avert a loss in customs revenue and to protect British trade and interests in the north of the Colony--where they appeared threatened by French activity--left Freetown with a force of West Indian troops and Sierra Leone police and took possession of the island.

(6) <u>Jong River Expedition, 1882</u>. In May 1882, the acting commandant of Sherbro, Mr. M. W. Laborde, went to Mattru on the Jong River to attend the installation ceremonies of a new king of Jong country. He took with him an escort of four or five constables and presents to the value of £10 for the new king. Due to some misunderstanding the Acting Commandant arrived at Mattru after the installation ceremony. The chiefs however reassembled with the minimum of delay but Laborde insisted on an apology for what he regarded as a slight to his dignity and to his office. In the process the assembly got out of control and some resorted to defiant gestures and insulting language. The Commandant, surrounded by police with fixed bayonets to keep the crowd at bay, was forced to withdraw to his boat. On arriving at the wharf however, he discovered that his boat and its contents had been seized and two of his boatmen flogged. He had to borrow a boat to make his way back to Bonthe. When the news reached Freetown, Governor Capt. Havelock proceeded to the Jong River in a gunboat and with a force of Sierra Leone constabulary. Meanwhile Laborde's boat and its contents had been returned. The Governor, on arrival at Mattru, called on the chiefs and their followers to lay down their weapons. At this point the crowds became noisy, uncontrollable and hostile. In the turmoil a shot was fired which hit a constable on the knee. No sooner had he shouted that he was hit, than the whole escort of police opened fire without orders. The natives fled to the woods and from there fired back without orders. The chief, Lahsaru, was captured and detained, part of Mattru was destroyed by the police, and the expedition returned to Freetown.

(7) <u>Bum Kittam Expedition, 1883</u>. In April 1883 Chief Gbow of Talliah invaded the territory of Chief Tucker in the Bum Kittam River area and captured and destroyed several villages. At Catlin, Gbow and his warriors seized money meant to pay the police detachment at Barmany and treated with contempt and derision attempts by the corporal-in-charge of Barmany to demand an explanation or to seek redress. On April 12, 1883, Acting Governor Pinkett with a force of police left Freetown for Sherbro to put an end to Gbow's activities. The expedition went up the Bum Kittam river, destroyed the towns of Whymah, Hahoon and Senehu, and the war stockades at Catlin, Subu and Mattru, and returned to Freetown on April 20. Soon after, news reached Freetown that a party of warriors had again plundered villages near Bendu and were threatening to attack York Island near Bonthe. On May 16, 1883, Acting Governor Pinkett once more set out for Bonthe with a force of

police under Inspector-General Capt. Jackson. R. A. Pinkett's
force was later joined by a detachment of the 2nd West India
Regiment under Capt. Shelton on May 18, and on May 22 by another detachment of that regiment commanded by Maj. Talbot.

On May 21 the expedition captured and destroyed Momaligi and on the 23rd proceeded to Talliah, Chief Gbow's stronghold, which was attacked on the 25th and captured and destroyed after two hours of fighting. British casualties were put at two
soldiers, one policeman and thirty "friendlies" wounded. The
expedition returned to Freetown via Bonthe on May 26. Gbow
himself escaped but some of his able lieutenants were arrested
and detained as political prisoners in Freetown.

(8) Yoni Expedition, 1887. The Yoni Temne, led by
three warriors, Kondo, Kongo and Kallowah, attacked the government house at Songo in late 1885, wounding several people
and taking others into captivity. Governor Rowe then proceeded
to Robari, the main Yoni town and secured the release of the
captives. On the governor's initiative, peace was arranged between the chiefs of Yoni, Masimera, Quiah and Bompeh, who
became signatories to a treaty of peace signed in Freetown on
May 10, 1886. In February 1887 the Yoni attacked Macourie
near Senehun. In May 1887 they attacked Tungea, killing five
persons and taking over 100 others as captives to Ronietta. In
October 1887 Bauya and Senehun, towns under British jurisdiction and belonging to Madam Yoko, a chief in treaty with the
British, were attacked by the Yoni, who killed three persons
and seriously wounded one policeman. The Yoni next threatened
to attack Rotifunk, another town within British jurisdiction. Yoni
attacks and threats of attack on "British territory" and reprisal
raids by Mende on Yoni country provoked the British War Office into action. Col. Sir Francis de Winton was sent out to
Sierra Leone arriving in Freetown on November 9, 1887, to
take charge of military operations against the Yoni. Accompanied by his staff officers, Maj. Piggott and Capt. Browne,
Sir Francis de Winton had at his disposal a force composed of
18 officers and 1283 men (of whom 953 were carriers or scouts).
Two naval vessels, HMS Acorn and HMS Alecto, were also giv-
en orders to assist the operations. In addition, friendly Bumpe,
Ribi, Mende and Quoya chiefs were asked to supply warriors to
act as subsidiaries to the regular troops during the expedition.
The ships sailed up the Ribi river as far as Mafengbe and with
Mafengbe as a base, a track was cut through the bush to Robari, the main Yoni town, some 12 miles away. Fifteen days'
rations for all ranks were sent to Mafengbe.

One column, commanded by Maj. Piggott and consisting
of five officers and 183 soldiers with a surgeon and carriers,
left Freetown for Mafengbe on November 13, 1887. The rest
of the expedition, commanded by Sir Francis de Winton accompanied by Capt. Hay, deputy governor, and the expedition's political officer, left Freetown on November 15 for Mafengbe.
On November 21, 1887, Robari was attacked by a British force
consisting of 15 petty officers and bluejackets of HMS Acorn

commanded by Lt. Valentine, 200 officers and men of the West
India Regiment commanded by Lt. Nelson, and 45 Sierra Leone
police, under Deputy Governor Hay. The Yoni put up stubborn
resistance but were soon overcome by shells and rockets. Robari was captured in the afternoon and the Yoni surrendered.
British casualties were relatively slight--only 13 wounded. The
force returned to Freetown on December 19, 1887. Sir Francis
de Winton returned to England on January 21, 1888. The Yoni
warriors Kallowah, Kangori and Lela were captured and deported to the Gambia. Other Yoni chiefs involved in raids were
fined a total of £300. A detachment of two officers and 30
soldiers were left at Robari, with police at Momaligi and Rokel
to patrol the roads and prevent further Yoni raids.

(9) Expeditions Against Makaiah of Largo, 1888-1889.
Makaiah of Largo had attacked Sulima in 1887 and in 1888 had
attacked and captured Jehomah, a town belonging to Momoh Kie
Kie (Kai Kai), a treaty chief. An expedition under the command of Capt. R. E. Copland Crawford and a force of police
was sent against Makaiah in late 1888. The force captured
Jehomah on December 2. In the encounter, a large number of
Makaiah's warriors, some 131 it is estimated, were killed and
some 522 of his captives were released. Crawford made use of
a small force of 17 policemen in the attack on Jehomah, only
one of whom was wounded. The expedition then returned to
Sulima. On December 22 Capt. J. S. Hay, the governor, left
Freetown to prevent Makaiah from raiding the Kittam and Bum
districts. Meanwhile Makaiah had heavily fortified Largo, his
main town, which Crawford decided to attack. Reinforced by
a contingent of warriors from Momoh Kie Kie, Momoh Jah and
Gbana Gumbo, and with a detachment of 75 police, Crawford set
out from Bandajuma on January 2, 1889. At Fanima, one of
Makaiah's towns which was captured and burned, 85 bodies of
defenders were recovered from the flames and 665 captives
were released. Casualties on the British side amounted to
three policemen wounded and two "friendlies" killed and ten
wounded. Largo was attacked on January 3 and captured after
about five hours' fighting. Makaiah escaped but was subsequently captured and deported to the Gold Coast.

(10) Tambi Expeditions, 1891-1892. First expedition:
April 22 to May 13, 1891. In December 1890, Mr. G. H.
Garrett, a traveling commissioner, paid a visit to Upper Sanda
country, where warriors commanded by Karimu of Moriah were
fighting against the Upper Sanda. Karimu's forces consisted of
"Muriteis," or rebels, recruited principally from escaped
"slaves" who built fortifications called egois or war camps,
which they used as bases for operations. One such egois had
been built at Tambi, a frontier town between the Susu and Limba countries. Chief Soluku of Bumban, the Limba chief, took
alarm at the nearness of an egois to his territory and appealed
to the British to help him dislodge Karimu's warriors from
Tambi. Garrett's efforts at mediation were unsuccessful and

after encountering further hostility from Karimu, a portion of
one of whose towns he burned, he returned to Freetown. It
was decided to put up a show of force in the area to prevent
future slights or rebuffs to British officials. The force dispatched to Tambi under the command of Maj. Alexander Mc-
Donell Moore, inspector-general of the Frontier Police, was
inadequate for the task. It set out from Freetown on April 22,
1891, and arrived at Tambi on May 5. Attempts to parley with
the warriors at Tambi proved unsuccessful. The police were
fired upon. One constable was killed and four officers and
three men wounded. The force returned to Freetown in dis-
comfiture on May 13, 1891.

Second Tambi expedition: March 14, 1892. After the
first setback at Tambi it was decided to send a larger force,
which set out from Freetown on March 14, 1892, on a punitive
expedition to Tambi. It consisted of four officers and 150 men
under command of Maj. Alexander McDonell Moore, Inspector-
General of the Frontier Police. Once more the British attack
was repulsed and the Frontier Police were forced to retreat,
with Capt. W. H. Robinson killed, four officers wounded, one
policeman killed and 21 wounded.

Third Tambi expedition: March 28 to April 15, 1892.
After the second reverse it was decided to send a full military
expedition against Tambi. A force consisting of 25 officers
and 518 noncommissioned officers and men of the West India
Regiment commanded by Col. A. B. Ellis, four officers and
126 men of the Frontier Police under Maj. Moore, and 380
"friendlies" was dispatched to Tambi. Armed with three
seven-pounder R. M. L. guns and two rocket troughs, the first
two elements of the force set out from Freetown on March 28
and traveled by boat to Robat on the Great Scarcies River.
From Robat they marched to Kukuna and to Kamassassa, where
they were joined by the 380 "friendlies." Tambi was attacked
on April 7 at about 10 a. m. and was captured at about 11:30
a. m. British casualties were assessed at nine wounded; five
"friendlies" were killed and 32 wounded. Karimu's losses were
estimated at 300 killed. Tambi was burned and the force returned to Freetown on April 15.

(11) Expedition to Wondeh Against Ndawa, 1889. In
March 1889 a force of police under the command of Mr. G. H.
Garett, was sent against Ndawa of Wondeh who had threatened
Sulima and Mano Salijah and whose activities were impeding
trade in the Sherbro and Gallinas areas. The force which set
out on the 22, destroyed 13 towns, dispersed Ndawa's warriors
and released some 3000 captives. The police suffered no casualties. This action against Ndawa was the last on record of
the old police force. Early in 1890 on the advice of Col. Sir
Francis de Winton, the Sierra Leone Frontier Police Force was
created.

(12) Expedition Against the Sofas, November 26, 1893,
to January 21, 1894. In the early 1890s, Samory Touré's Sofa

warriors began to make a series of raids into the British
"sphere of influence" in Sierra Leone. In May 1893 the British
government decided to put an end to these incursions and when,
in October 1893, Freetown was informed of Sofa raids into
Bambara Chiefdom in Mende country, an expedition was decided
upon. On November 26, 1893, two officers, 50 NCOs and men
of the West India Regiment, and 200 carriers went by steamer
to Rotombo on the Rokel. This force was sent to form a supply column at Matotoka, block the Freetown-Kuniki road, deceive the Sofas, and give moral support to potential Sofa victims.

The main force, commanded by Col. A. B. Ellis of the
West India Regiment and consisting of 17 officers and 431 men,
was dispatched secretly by night on the 27th and 29th of November, 1893. The force disembarked at Bendu, Sherbro, and
marched to Panguma, arriving on December 13. From Panguma it moved on towards Kerra Yemma, the Sofa stronghold.
On December 23 it encamped at Waiima. Inadvertently or
through treachery a French force consisting of 30 tirailleurs
(skirmishers) and some 1200 native allies, commanded by Lt.
Maritz of the French army, attacked the British camp on Christmas eve, 1893. The British returned the fire and after some
40 minutes of heavy firing British casualties consisted of lieutenants Liston and Wroughton, one sergeant major and four
privates of the West India Regiment, Capt. Lendy, the inspector-
general, and two privates of the Frontier Police Force, all
killed; and one sergeant major and 14 men of the West India
Regiment and three men of the Frontier Police Force, wounded.
Lt. Maritz of the French army and 35 other ranks also lost
their lives. On December 28 the Sofas attacked Tungeah town
and were repulsed with heavy losses by the Frontier Police
under the command of Sub-Inspector Taylor. On January 2,
1894, the Sofas suffered further reverses at Baghema. The
troops began their return march on January 10 and arrived in
Freetown on the 21st.

(13) The Hut Tax War, 1898. Governor Cardew's decision to levy a tax on huts or houses in the Protectorate led to
simultaneous outbreaks of violent resistance over wide areas.
These outbreaks, known as the Hut Tax War, were suppressed
by force. The military operations can be divided as follows:
1. Operations in Karene and Masimera districts aimed
    primarily at defeating Bai Bureh and his allies.
2. Operations in Ronietta district.
3. Operations in Bandajuma and Sherbro districts.
4. The march through the Protectorate in four columns be-
    tween December 1898 and February 1899. Each column
    consisted of one company of the West African Regiment
    and a small detachment of artillery. The columns were
    dispatched as follows: (a) Falaba Column--commanded
    by Lt.-Col. Marshal, West India Regiment; (b) Banda-
    juma Column--commanded by Maj. E. W. Blunt; (c)
    Panguma Column--commanded by Maj. Moore of the

Frontier Police; and (d) Headquarter Column--commanded by Lt.-Col. Cunningham.

The total number of troops engaged in operations 1, 2 and 3 were: European officers (including Frontier Police), 16; Europeans (other ranks), 150; West India troops, 1070; and West African troops (including Frontier Police), 2000. The total number of troops engaged in operation 4 were: officers, 56; and other ranks, troops and police, 995.

British total losses in all four operations were four European officers, 64 NCOs and men, and 92 Carriers killed; 23 European officers, 184 NCOs and men, and 58 Carriers wounded.

(14) Deledugu Expedition, 1923. In June 1923 an outbreak of disturbances was reported in Deledugu Chiefdom, Koinadugu District. A section chief, Bala of Samaindugu, refused to recognize his paramount chief's authority and threatened to destroy Masadugu, PC Dumbalai's headquarters town. When the district commissioner visited the chiefdom, Bala with his supporters withdrew into French territory. It was decided to dispatch a small force commanded by Lt. R. M. Hall consisting of two NCOs and 37 other ranks. The troops arrived after a seven-day march, but as "there seemed little for the troops to do, guards, patrols round the disturbed area, a field-firing exercise in the presence of as many Korankos as possible and the consumption of Bala's maize gardens and some of Dumbalai's cows passed the time until the order came to return by normal march stages. The district commissioner arrived to take over and the platoon reached barracks at Daru nine days later."

(15) Haidara War, 1931. Early in 1930 a Muslim cleric, Idara (or Haidara) Contorfili, entered Sierra Leone from French Guinea and began to preach at Kambia. Initially Haidara's teaching was essentially religious but as his movement gained momentum, his activities assumed an increasingly political flavor. By 1931 Haidara was inciting his followers against the colonial regime by telling them not to pay their taxes. On February 16, 1931, the government decided to move against him. A detachment of the Royal West African Frontier Force commanded by Lt. H. J. Holmes and consisting of 34 men was sent against Haidara's forces at Bubuya. The engagement was brief. Haidara was killed, his forces vanquished; the British officer in charge of the detachment was also killed.

MILITIA. A regular militia in the Colony of Sierra Leone was first organized by Zachary Macaulay between 1794-5. Macaulay's militia was in a sense a people's militia; the rank and file were allowed to elect their own officers. By 1808 it was observed that the militia were without officers and were "more dangerous to themselves than to their ecemy." An ordinance of 1808 making provision for the Colony's defense disbanded all existing military and paramilitary forces and introduced a new militia force recruited from among the able male inhabitants of between 15 and 60 years of age. This ordinance provoked bitter criticism of the government, though no active opposition to it.   Another act of November 1811 relating to the militia also met with strong opposition and in some instances led to emigration from the Colony. There was a popularly-held belief that the provisions of the act--which included drilling under military law and flogging, compulsory taking of the oath of allegiance on penalty of outlawry for failure or refusal--reduced the settlers from free citizens to soldiers, soldiers being regarded in the context as degraded persons. An ordinance of 1829 made further provisions for a militia force to consist of 17 officers and 325 NCOs and men. In a bid to strengthen the Colony's defenses Governor N. W. Macdonald increased the size of the militia in 1846. Governor A. E. Kennedy (1852-4) used the militia as jail guards and once a week allowed the militia band to entertain citizens on the parade grounds at Falconbridge Battery. An 1856 ordinance dated December 5 amended the existing laws relating to the militia of the Colony. The 1856 ordinance enacted that all able male inhabitants of the Colony, not being aliens and being between the ages of 18 and 55 were liable for militia service. The militia force was to consist of one regiment of infantry, cavalry and artillery. Annual service in the militia was limited to 21 days, the times, etc., to be determined by the governor, who also appointed officers and noncommissioned officers. The penalty for refusing to serve as an officer or an NCO or to neglect the required duties was a fine not exceeding £100 or in default a term of imprisonment not exceeding three months. An ordinance of December 29, 1860, established that the force was to be called out once monthly, instead of for 21 days annually. The Koya War of 1861 discredited the militia. When the ordinance of 1860 expired in 1864 the militia force was not revived.

MINAH, FRANCIS MISHECK, 1929- . Born August 19, 1929. Educated at the Methodist Boys High School, Freetown, at King's College, London University, and at Gray's Inn, London. President, Sierra Leone Students' Union of Great Britain and Ireland (1960-1962). UNESCO fellowship to study community development in India and Liberia (1956-1957); Assistant development officer, Social Development Department (1957-1959). Detained under public emergency regulations in 1968 for one month. Minister of foreign affairs since 1975; minister of trade and industry, 1973-1975; member of Parliament for Pujehun South constituency since 1967.

MIXED COMMISSION COURTS. Lord Chief Justice William Murray Mansfield's decision in James Somerset's case in 1772 had given judicial blessing to the activities of the English humanitarian groups against the slave trade. In 1807 and in 1833 the British Parliament passed acts declaring the slave trade illegal in the British Isles and in British overseas possessions respectively. A Vice-Admiralty court was set up in Freetown in 1808 to try the captains of slave ships captured by the British

naval squadron operating along the West Coast of Africa to enforce the abolition acts of the British Parliament. But the
squadron could not legally examine foreign ships for slaves,
unless permitted by treaty with the foreign country involved.
For some three decades the squadron's operations in West
Africa were hampered by these legal difficulties. Between
1815 and 1818 the British government held negotiations and entered into treaties with Portugal, Spain and the Netherlands,
which provided a partial solution to the problem. On July 28,
1817, the treaty with Portugal was signed and on November 27
ratified. The Treaty with Spain was signed on September 23,
1817, and ratified on November 22. On May 4, 1818, the
treaty with the Netherlands was signed; it was ratified on May
25th. In 1826 the government of Brazil signed a similar treaty
with the British government, followed in 1862 by the United
States government. By these treaties the signatories agreed to
declare the slave trade illegal and to enforce its suppression.
Courts of Mixed Commission were set up in Freetown in 1819--
similar courts were established in Portuguese, Spanish and
Dutch ports--to try the captains of captured slave ships. Each
signatory government sent two commissioners, one of whom sat
with a British counterpart on cases involving his own nationals.
To avoid complications that might arise out of the variety of
legal systems and practices a set of stereotype questions was
drawn up which the accused, their representatives and witnesses
answered. The Court of Mixed Commission was under the direct supervision of the Foreign Office and its British members,
the commissariat judge, the commissioner of arbitration, and
the registrar, were paid out of the anti-slave-trade vote. After
the first few years foreign commissionerships were more often
than not unfilled. In the absence of the foreign, the British
commissioners presided alone and when there was no British
commissioner the governor or the most senior official in the
Colony acted as a substitute.

Captured ships were kept in the custody of the marshall
of the Mixed Commission Court. The Court had the authority
to order the ships and non-human cargo to be auctioned by a
court official on behalf of the governments concerned. The
slaves were brought ashore, registered by the Court registrar
and handed over to the Captured Negro Department, renamed
in 1822 the Liberated African Department. Some were apprenticed to masters in Freetown, others were sent to the villages
where superintendents took charge.

The Spanish commissioners left Sierra Leone in 1821
followed by the Portuguese in 1825 and the Dutch in 1828. In
the late 1820s it was proposed to transfer the Mixed Commission Court to Fernando Po but the scheme for the transfer was
dropped in 1832. In 1842 the Portuguese transferred their
court from Sierra Leone. The Netherlands court, which had
not met since 1828, was revived in 1862 when a slave ship
flying Dutch colors was captured and brought to Freetown.
Two American commissioners arrived in Freetown in 1862, but,
as no American slave ships were captured, never sat. The

British treaty with Brazil expired in 1845 and thereafter Brazilian slave ships were captured by Act of Parliament and tried in Vice-Admiralty Courts. So also were Spanish slave vessels, most of which operated without flags or papers and were in the circumstances treated as stateless.

As the Atlantic slave trade lost momentum and declined during the second-half of the 19th century, cases for trial by the Mixed Commission Courts became rarer. By 1865 the Atlantic slave trade had been effectively stamped out. The functions of the Mixed Commission Courts were undertaken by the chief justice who as vice-admiralty judge was empowered in 1871 to try future cases.

MODU, DALA. Son of Fenda Modu of Wonkafong, head of a powerful Mandinka family. Dala Modu a successful businessman, attracted by the set-up in the Colony, settled there with about 50 followers in the mid-1790s. During the Temne attack on the Colony in 1801 and in 1802 Dala Modu remained loyal to the government and was able to persuade some Mandinka and Susu chiefs to surrender Wansey and two other dissidents to Governor Dawes. In 1806, however, Dala Modu, long suspected of dealing in slaves, charged with a number of irregularities and asked out of the Colony by Governor Ludlam, went over to the Bulom Shore with his supporters. At Lungi he was able to persuade other chiefs to "cede" Gambia Island, over which he claimed certain proprietary rights, to the British Crown. In the 1820s he went into the timber trade as agent for Macaulay and Babington, an agency which brought him a handsome commission. In 1826 the Island of Matacong was also "ceded" to the British largely through the good offices of Dala Modu. When, in April 1836, Governor H. D. Campbell formally recognized him as regent of Loko Masama, Dala Modu assumed almost complete control of the Bulom Shore. When later Campbell made him his agent at Magbele, Dala Modu wielded unparalleled powers in the Rokel area. In 1837 Campbell made him chief of Rokon and until his death in 1841 proved himself a useful ally of the British and a skilful mediator between the government and the chiefs.

MOKASSI LAND CASE (1895-1897). Early in 1895 two villages, Mokassi and Bunjema, in the Upper Bagru-Bumpe area, quarreled over a piece of land to which both lay rival claims. The problem was further complicated by the fact that the land "lay near the ill-defined boundary of those tribal districts which since 1861 had nominally formed part of the Colony." Sub-Inspector Charles N. Taylor of the Frontier Police, to whom the matter was referred, upheld the claims of Bunjema. But the Mokassi people suspecting Taylor's motives and believing that his verdict was far from impartial refused to allow their rivals to occupy the land and drove them out. When the case was brought to Freetown, Acting Governor Col. Caulfield also decided in favor of Bunjema. Thereupon the Mokassi people sought legal advice and retained the professional services of

lawyer Samuel Lewis (q.v.). He gave them a written opinion
that "... no policeman has any legal authority to prevent you
from occupying your land or to turn you out of it. Any attempt
by any policeman to do this is unlawful, and you have a right
to resist his interference and if necessary to report it to the
Governor, or to take legal proceedings against him for his unlawful act, should it amount to trespass."

Armed with Lewis' support and advice the Mokassi vil-
lagers returned home and drove their neighbors from the dis-
puted land. Seven Mokassi ringleaders were arrested by the
Frontier Police and sent to Freetown in May 1896 to be detained as "political prisoners." Lewis promptly put in an application on behalf of his clients for a writ of habeas corpus.
Governor Cardew, who had little patience or liking for such
procedures, especially in a matter he considered essentially
administrative, took action to forestall Lewis. The Governor
hastily summoned on the Saturday (the writ had been applied
for on Friday and was not returnable until Monday) a meeting
of the Legislative Council which passed an ordinance to detain
the prisoners in spite of the protests of Lewis and his "unofficial member" colleague, T. C. Bishop. Considerations for
his clients, reverence for the rule of law and professional pride
goaded Lewis on to further action. On behalf of his clients he
brought an action for £15,000 damages against the sergeant who
had effected the arrests. Cardew replied with a Public Officers
Indemnity Ordinance to protect officers acting in good faith and
carrying out orders to keep the peace in the hinterland. In the
debates in the Legislative Council, Cardew stigmatized Lewis's
actions as verging on treason and denounced his motives as
mercenary. Lewis in turn accused the Governor of subverting
the law. Eventually the prisoners were released with a warning against disturbing the peace and with a promise that the matter would be thoroughly investigated.

Lewis, however, was far from satisfied. He pursued
the matter further and it appeared that the Colony Courts might
uphold his contention. To prevent this Cardew on October 16,
1896, introduced a special ordinance which located within the
newly declared Protectorate parts of the Colony "so situated
that they cannot be conveniently governed" from Freetown.
One of its clauses also withdrew jurisdiction over such areas
from the Colony courts even in matters already pending--a clear
reference to the Mokassi case. At this point Lewis sent a petition of protest against the ordinance to the Colonial Office in
London. The petition was unsuccessful. To meet him halfway,
however, another ordinance was passed in May, 1897, "making
costs already incurred in the Colony Courts recoverable in actions transferred to the Protectorate." Lewis had done a great
deal for his clients and for the observance of the rule of law.
But it was clear that he had done enough and there the Mokassi
case ended. Cardew thereafter changed his attitude towards
Lewis whom he had in 1895 recommended for a knighthood and
towards Creoles in general. The conflict between the Governor
and the leading Sierra Leonean is said to have done irreparable

damage to race relations in the Colony.

MOMO JAH of Pujehun. Son of a Fula father and a Mende mother. Under the nominal suzerainty of Chief Zorokong of Messina, Momo Jah in the 1880s exercised effective control over the country around Pujehun. An ally of the British, one of the "friendlies," he provided reinforcements for a number of British military expeditions to disaffected areas, including the expeditions to Largo and to Wonde. In 1898 Momo Jah initially tried to resist the hut tax but was arrested and detained. On his release he refused to take part in the insurrection against the British. Attacks on his towns by "rebels" were repulsed by the Frontier Police, and with his help order was restored to the Gallinas.

MOMO KIE KIE [Kai Kai] of Yoni. Son of a Fula father and a Mende mother. Like Momo Jah, Kai Kai recognized the nominal suzerainty of Chief Zorokong of Messima but was in fact effective ruler of parts of the country around Pujehun in the 1880s. He also recognized the authority of Fawundu, whose sub-chief he was. An ally of the British, one of the "friendlies," he refused to join in the Hut Tax War and helped defend Bandajuma against the "rebels." After restoring order in the Gallinas, Kai Kai took advantage of his British connection to bully neighboring chiefs and to usurp their lands with impunity.

MOMOH, A. J. Distinguished civil servant and prominent public figure. One of the first provincials to make the breakthrough into Freetown society. First vice president of the Sierra Leone People's Party (1951-1957). Member of PEPU and of the SOS. A. J. Momoh also served on a number of commissions of inquiry appointed by the government to investigate and make recommendations on national issues. Member and later chairman of the Public Service Commission until his death in 1968.

MOMOH, Brig. J. S., 1937- . Force commander of the Republic of Sierra Leone Military Forces (RSLMF) and minister of state, government of Sierra Leone. Born on January 26, 1937. Educated at the then Government Rural School, Wilberforce, West African Methodist Collegiate School, Technical Institute, Freetown, the Nigerian Military Academy, Kaduna, where he won the baton of honor as the best cadet in the course in 1962, and the Mons Officer Cadet School in Aldershot, England, where he won the sword of honor for being the best overseas cadet (1963). Commissioned as a second lieutenant (RSLMF), November 1963. Appointed commanding officer of the 1st Battalion (RSLMF), 1969; deputy force commander, 1970; acting force commander, 1971, and force commander, 1972. In a Cabinet reshuffle in 1975 Brigadier Momoh was appointed to the cabinet as minister of state.

MONDAY, MRS. see MARIA, SENORA

MONGER, EDWARD. One of five European gold speculators pros-
pecting for gold in the Upper Bagru at the time of the 1898 Hut
Tax War. He and his four colleagues had escaped the initial
onslaught of the insurgents by making their way through the
bush. Unfortunately he fell ill and was forced to stay put at
Bunjema where Chief Yayi, repudiating his earlier promise of
protection, killed Monger, as soon as his four companions had
gone. Monger was the only European who was not a missionary to be killed in the Mende 1898 massacres. The Yoni allied to the British were sent by Fairtlough to storm Bunjema.
They lost their leader Fula Mansa during the assault but they
captured Bunjema and killed Chief Yayi.

MOORE, ANDREW. One of the early Nova Scotian settlers in the
Colony of Sierra Leone, Moore had been brought up on a plantation in Georgia, USA, and, in Sierra Leone, after the French
attack on the Colony in September 1793, had taken to farming.
One day on his way back from his farm near the present Leicester village, Moore saw a seed on the ground which Afzelius,
the Swedish botanist employed by the Sierra Leone Company,
identified as an indigenous variety of coffee, hitherto unknown.
After his discovery coffee was grown in impressive quantities
on the mountain slopes surrounding Freetown.

MORGAN, Sir ERNEST DUNCAN, 1896- . Born in Freetown on
November 17, 1896. Educated at the Zion Day School, Wilber-
force Street, and at the Methodist Boys High School, Freetown.
Started business in 1921 and in 1938 was elected to the Free-
town City Council under the banner of the West African Youth
League. Served as first nominated member, Sierra Leone
House of Representatives, 1957 to 1961, having been appointed
July to December 1956 as temporary nominated member. A
distinguished citizen and successful businessman, he has served
Sierra Leone in various capacities. He was knighted in Janu-
ary, 1971.

MOURA, JOSE LOPEZ DE. Believed to be a grandson of a Mane
King, de Moura played a dominant role in the trade and politics
of Sierra Leone throughout the first half of the 18th century.
Literate, ostentatiously Christian, but equally attached to his
African charms and amulets, de Moura, a mulatto, has been
described as "an outstanding example of the cultural phenome-
non"--namely the rise of the mulatto traders on the Upper
Guinea Coast in the 17th and 18th centuries. Strongly supported
by other mulattoes and allied to Portuguese traders and local
chieftains, de Moura was powerful enough to cede Sierra Leone
as a doação to the Portuguese Crown. Walter Charles, chief
factor of the Royal African Company in 1727 and 1728, hostile
to mulatto pretensions, was determined not only to stem their
influence but to reduce de Moura's power to manageable pro-
portions. Charles decided to "take effectual care while I stay
in the country that no white black man shall make any figure
here above what the meanest natives do"--in the circumstances

an understandable but quixotic resolution. Aided at first by
de Moura's enemies, and in particular by Moura's sister,
Maria, a loyal ally of the Company, Charles' boast seemed
destined to succeed. But in November 1728 de Moura took the
offensive. De Moura in a few words issued the death warrant
of the Company, scribbled in his own hand and posted at the
watering place. The notice stated that "the ships of all nations
English, French, Dutch, etc., shall have free liberty of trade
in the river and the utmost safety except those belonging to the
Royal African Company of England." The Company's chief ally, the king of Baga, exposed and isolated, was compelled to
eat food at the feet of de Moura--an act symbolizing de Moura's
ascendancy and reinforcing mulatto dominance over African
rulers.

MULCHAHY, the Rev. CORNELIUS, C.S.Sp., 1884-1941. The
most popular and successful Roman Catholic missionary priest
in Sierra Leone in the 20th century. Principal of St. Edward's
Secondary School almost from 1922 until his death in 1941.
One of the best known promoters of sports (particularly cricket
and soccer) in the country's history. Although he died in 1941
Father Mulchahy's name is still a household word in Freetown.

MUSTAPHA, ALHAJI MOHAMED SANUSI, 1903- . Born June
1903; educated at Madrasa Amaria, the Government Model and
the Prince of Wales Schools, Freetown. Joined the Sierra
Leone Civil Service in 1926. Proceeded to Britain to study
law and enrolled at Lincoln's Inn. Returned home and went
into business and founded the firm of Mustapha Brothers (Im-
porters and Exporters and Rice Millers). Elected member of
the Legislative Council for Freetown East Electoral District in
1951. Appointed minister of works and transport, 1953, minister of natural resources, 1957; first Sierra Leonean minister of
finance, 1958; deputy prime minister, 1960. Minister of trade
and industry, 1962, and minister of social welfare, 1963-1964.
Returned to Parliament as member for Bo North constituency
in 1969. Detained under emergency regulations in 1973.

- N -

NAIMBANA, King, ca.1711-1793. A Temne King, living at Robana
and Robaga on the Rokel River; had ruled the Koya Temne
since 1775. He refused to sign Capt. Thompson's treaty of
1787 ceding territory for the rehabilitation of the first settlers
in Sierra Leone. On August 22, 1788, Naimbana signed a
fresh treaty with Capt. John Taylor, repudiating Thompson's
treaty of 1787, but laying the legal foundations of the colony.
As proprietor of Gambia Island, Naimbana, in 1785, had signed
a treaty with the French, leasing part of the Island for a "factory." He then gave them his son Prince Pedro (or Bartholomew) to be educated in France, where he was boarded at a
School in Brest. A second son he entrusted to Muslim clerics

to be brought up as a Muslim, the third, John Frederick (later renamed Henry Granville), he sent to England with Mr. and Mrs. Falconbridge, to be educated at the expense of the Sierra Leone Company. Naimbana maintained reasonably cordial relations with the Sierra Leone Company until his death in February 1793. Mrs. Falconbridge described him in about 1791 in the following words: "The king is rather above common height but meagre withal; the features of his face resemble a European more than any Black I have seen; his teeth are mostly decayed and his hair, or rather wool bespeaks old age, which I judge to be 80; he was seldom without a smile on his countenance, but I think his smiles were suspicious. He gave great attention while Falconbridge was speaking, for though he does not speak our language, he understands a good deal of it; his answers were slow and on the whole tolerably reasonable."

NAIMBANA of Ronietta. The most senior sub-chief to Bai Kompa of Koya in the 1890s. When the hut tax was levied in the Ronietta District, Dr. Hood, the acting district commissioner, reported to Governor Cardew that the majority of chiefs in the district were unwilling to pay the tax, and that the district was in turmoil. Capt. Moore of the Frontier Police was therefore dispatched to Ronietta to take charge of operations on January 21, 1898. His inquiries into the causes of the disturbed state of the district and into the refusal to pay the tax led to the arrest of, among others, Pa Naimbana of Ronietta. The charges against Pa Naimbana were drawn up almost exclusively on the evidence of one Chief Charles Smart, a hostile witness and Pa Naimbana's arch-enemy. On the basis of the evidence so collected Pa Naimbana was charged with intimidating Chief Charles Smart, conspiring with other chiefs to prevent Chief Smart from paying the tax, persuading other chiefs to ignore the notice imposing the tax, and refusing to obey the orders of the district commissioner. Capt. Moore found Pa Naimbana guilty of all the charges and accordingly arbitrarily sentenced him to deprivation of his chieftaincy, 12 months' imprisonment at hard labor, and 36 lashes. Only the corporal punishment was remitted by the Governor.

NAIMBANA, Prince JOHN FREDERICK (later, Henry Granville), ca. 1768-1793. Son of Naimbana, king of the Koya Temne. John Frederick was sent by his father to England with Mr. and Mrs. Falconbridge of the Sierra Leone Company to be educated at the Company's expense. Mrs. Falconbridge, who taught him to read and write on the voyage to England, attested that he was a quick, intelligent pupil. In England, Granville Sharp, proprietor of the Sierra Leone Company, entrusted the "Black Prince's" education to a country clergyman of the Church of England, certified by two bishops as a fit and proper person to be tutor to someone who would be, it was hoped, "as useful in Africa as Alfred and the first Peter were in their respective countries." The young Prince's virtues and diligence were extolled in a tract, "The African Prince," in which he was portrayed on the cover turning away in disdain from an unsuitable book. He returned to Sierra Leone in about June 1793, a few months after his father's death in February, imbued with the hope of preaching the gospel and converting his countrymen to Christianity.

These hopes and aspirations remained unfulfilled. On arrival in Freetown he was taken ashore dying having fallen fatally ill on board. His brother Bartholomew spread the rumor that he had been deliberately done away with. A long palaver between the ship's captain and the family merely assuaged feelings without convincing relatives that the Prince had not been murdered. For generations the imputation of murder to prevent young Naimbana from unraveling the white man's secrets to his countrymen gained currency among the Temne. Fortunately his sad fate did not deter other chiefs from sending their children to be educated abroad. Writing about the Prince in September 1791, Mrs. Falconbridge had this to say. "His person is rather below the ordinary, inclining to grossness, his skin nearly jet-black, eyes keenly intelligent, nose flat, teeth unconnected and filed sharp after the custom of his country, his legs a little bandied, and his deportment easy, manly and confident withal. In his disposition he is surly, but has cunning enough to smother it, where he thinks his interest is concerned; he is pettish and implacable, but I think grateful and attached to those he considers his friends; nature has been bountiful in giving him sound intellects, very capable of improvement and he also possesses a great thirst for knowledge. "

NAIMBANA, Prince PEDRO (also, Bartholomew Naimbana). Son of Naimbana, King of Koya Temne and chieftain of Gambia Island at the estuary of the Sierra Leone river. In January 1785 a French naval officer, De la Jaille, signed a treaty for the lease of part of the island for a "factory." Within a month he had installed a shore battery of 12 cannon. When De la Jaille left the island, he was entrusted with Prince Pedro to be educated in France. The African Prince was boarded at a school in Brest, at £1200 a year in fees. Pedro returned home in 1787, but his father arranged that he should go back to Brest to continue his education. Meanwhile he had been received into the Catholic Church. He returned home for good in 1790. King Naimbana died in February 1793. In about June the same year Prince Pedro's younger brother, Prince John Naimbana, educated in England, returned home to Sierra Leone only to be carried ashore dying. Prince Pedro then put it out that his brother had been deliberately poisoned, lest he unravel the white man's secrets to his black countrymen. That very year, 1793, the French withdrew from Gambia Island, returning in 1794 to bombard and destroy Freetown in reprisal against the British with whom France, become a republic, was at war. After Paris, Brest had been the scene of some of the worst excesses of the Revolution of 1789. Prince Pedro was not only aware of the French attack on Freetown but is actually said to have welcomed his French friends and to have tried to get Bai

Farama, the new king of Koya, to join them against the Colony.

THE NATION (1971-). New name for Unity newspaper; founded
as non-partisan.

NATIONAL CONGRESS OF BRITISH WEST AFRICA [NCBWA].
First conceived in 1913 but actually founded in March 1920 at
Accra in the then Gold Coast, the NCBWA had branches in the
Gambia, Sierra Leone and Nigeria. The members, mostly
drawn from the Western-educated elites and professional class-
es, constituted the first organized articulate group in British
West Africa which sharply and openly criticized the Colonial
political and economic systems. The Accra meeting held from
March 11-29, 1920, was attended by one representative from
the Gambia, three from Sierra Leone (Frederick William Dove
at the time resident in Accra, Leslie Macarthy and Dr. H. C.
Bankole-Bright), six from Nigeria, and 40 from the Gold
Coast. The demands of the Congress were embodied in resolu-
tions and proffered in the form of a memorandum and petition
to the secretary of state for the Colonies. A special delegation with Bankole-Bright as secretary was sent to London with
the memorandum and the petition. Lord Milner, secretary of
state for the Colonies at the time, was influenced by the views
of the governors in West Africa, particularly the governors of
Nigeria and the Gold Coast, who informed him that the NCBWA
was in no way representative of the "native communities on
whose behalf it purports to speak: that its pretensions in this
respect are expressly repudiated by the most authoritative ex-
ponents of native public opinion (including practically all the
chiefs in the Gold Coast), and that the scheme put forward by
the congress would in their opinion be inimical to the best interests of the community."
    Nevertheless, the Congress had only put forward rather
moderate demands, including that: (i) 50 per cent of the seats
in the colonial legislatures of each territory be reserved for
elected African representatives of the people; (ii) a House of
Assembly consisting of the Legislative Council membership plus
six "elected financial representatives" be set up; the functions
of the House of Assembly would include the power to levy taxes
and to debate the annual budget; (iii) municipal councils be created for the major towns and that four-fifths of the councilors
be elected; and (iv) reforms in education (including the establishment of a West African university), commerce, medical
services, the administrative service, and the legal system, be
carried out.
    In effect Congress was asking for a more thorough policy
of Africanization and some of these demands were by no means
new. The secretary of state decided to reject the petition.
Congress members, particularly in Sierra Leone, tried to re-
fute the charges of their detractors. The Sierra Leone Weekly
News of March 12, 1921, pointed out that "the enlightened portion of West Africa is responsible for the unenlightened portion.... It is a right justified by the kinship of Race and

Blood. " To prove that Congress was in fact representative of "native communities," two mass rallies were held at the Wilberforce Memorial Hall in Freetown at which a number of tribal headmen and some Protectorate Africans including a paramount chief sat with members of Congress. The Freetown press was jubilant. In fact, the Congress was not as estranged from the "native communities" as the colonial administrators chose to believe, even if the ties were not as strong as Sierra Leone Congress enthusiasts tried to portray in their newspapers.

A second meeting of the NCBWA was held in Freetown in 1923; a third and a fourth, in the Gambia and in Nigeria respectively in 1930. The achievements of the Congress were far from spectacular, although a few of its demands were partially met. In the Gold Coast and in Nigeria, where it had never really created an impact, the Congress was virtually dead by 1930. In Sierra Leone where the local branch organized itself into a quasi-political party, the NCBWA lingered on in some shape or form into the 1940s. But Wallace-Johnson's Youth League, founded in 1938, had effectively driven the NCBWA off the political stage of Sierra Leone.

NATIONAL COUNCIL OF THE COLONY OF SIERRA LEONE [NCCSL; or, NC]. Founded in August 1950, the NCCSL was virtually a Creole party. For a symbol the National Council had a pair of clasped hands in black outline; above the hands a lighted torch with flame in red outline. The party was formed out of a fusion of a number of political or quasi-political associations. According to the African Standard of August 25, 1950, these groups included the Sierra Leone Democratic Party (National Democratic Party, the West African Youth League, the Sierra Leone Section, the Sierra Leone Socialist Party, the Sierra Leone Political Group, and "The Fourah Bay and Foulah Town Communities"--as well as the African unofficial Colony members of the Executive and Legislative councils. The National Council was also in alliance with the Ratepayers' Association, the Nova Scotian (and) Maroon Descendants Association, the Settlers' Descendants Union, and the Sierra Leone National Council. These groups were exclusively Creole in membership. Other groups in alliance with the National Council--the Artisan and General Workers Union, the Maritime and Waterfront Workers Union, the Sierra Leone Women's Movement--if largely Protectorate in membership, were predominantly Creole in leadership. The leaders of the National Council at the time of its inception were Dr. H. C. Bankole-Bright, president; C. D. Hotoba During, vice-president; and C. M. A. Thompson, general secretary.

The Creoles had fought hard to prevent the implementation of the Stevenson Constitution of 1947, which gave greater representation to the Protectorate in the projected Legislative Council. The abortive attempt to thwart the implementation of the 1947 constitution led to the formation of the National Council, which aimed at stemming protectorate challenge to Creole dominance. The Party's election manifesto for the 1951 Legislative Council elections inveighed against increased Protectorate membership in the legislature and declared, "We object to foreigners [i.e., Protectorate Africans] prepondering in our Legislative Council." After the 1951 elections, Dr. Bankole-Bright introduced a motion (rejected without debate) in the Legislative Council demanding independence for the Colony. He submitted "That this Sierra Leone Government stands impeached by the Creole element of the Colony of Sierra Leone in that it has by its action brought into existence a cleavage between the people of this Colony and Protectorate.... That in consequence of the present existing relationship this Colony through its National Council representatives now ask for its independence to control its own affairs...." The National Council from 1951 to 1957 resorted to violent attacks on the SLPP in the local press, indiscriminately opposed all government measures in the Legislative Council, challenged the validity of the 1951 Constitution, and used obstruction as if it was a virtue. In the general elections in 1957 the party lost all its seats and its candidates, their deposits as well. Dr. Bright died in 1958 and after his death the National Council persisted as a reverred but shadowy party. In May 1960 the party disappeared into the more hopeful ranks of the United Front Coalition.

NATIONAL DEVELOPMENT BANK LTD. [NDB]. In 1965, at the invitation of the Sierra Leone government, a mission from the World Bank and the International Monetary Fund (IMF) visited Sierra Leone and later issued a report recommending the establishment of a development finance institution there. The Sierra Leone Government then set up in July 1966 a steering committee to explore the possibility of establishing a development finance company with special emphasis on the financial, organizational, managerial and legal aspects. At the government's request, a consultant, who became chairman of the steering committee, was provided by the African Development Bank (ADB). As a result of the steering committee's deliberations and on its advice, the National Development Bank Limited was incorporated on March 9, 1968, as a public liability company, under the provisions of the Sierra Leone Companies Act.

The Bank was authorized to invest in (i) the development of medium- and large-scale agriculture (whether corporate or individually sponsored), ranching, forestry and fishing; (ii) the development of manufacturing, assembly and processing industries, including industries engaged in the processing of products of agriculture, forestry and fishing, i.e., agro-based industries; and (iii) the development of engineering, construction, transport, tourist and mining industries. The Bank was also authorized to (i) provide technical assistance and advice for the purpose of promoting agricultural and industrial development; (ii) administer such special funds as may from time to time be placed at the disposal of the Bank; and (iii) undertake such other activities as may be necessary or advantageous for the purpose of furthering the objectives of the Bank.

NATIONAL REFORMATION COUNCIL [NRC], March 1967 to April 1968. Military regime that assumed power in a bloodless coup in Sierra Leone after the general elections of March 1967. The NRC government, consisting of senior army and police officers, was overthrown in April 1968 in a counter-coup organized by the rank and file or army and police units. After the overthrow of the NRC, Sierra Leone reverted to civilian rule.

NATIVE CHURCH PASTORATE. Established on November 1, 1861, as the nucleus of the future Sierra Leone Church, with the handing over by the CMS of nine parishes to the Native Church Pastorate. The pastors in charge of the nine parishes were all Sierra Leoneans, who were no longer agents of the CMS but clergymen of an independent church. The Native Church Pastorate in the initial stages was, however, financed partly from subscriptions of its members and partly from CMS grants. In 1863 the Pastorate's financial problems were to some extent relieved by an annual grant from the Colonial government of £200, increased in 1866 to £600. This government grant remained a source of controversy, political as well as sectarian, until it was abolished in 1876. As the years went by the CMS gradually handed over other parishes to the Pastorate, although the Five Pastors Case did damage relationships between the CMS and the new church in Sierra Leone.

NAVO, S. T. Lawyer and politician. National propaganda secretary (SLPP); Treasurer (PNP). Educated at Bo Government School, the Prince of Wales School, Freetown, and at the Middle Temple Inns of Court, London. Member of the House of Representatives for Bo North constituency (1957-1962); member of Parliament for Bo North (1969-1973). Parliamentary secretary (United Front Coalition) (1960-1962). Detained under public emergency regulations at Mafanta prison, Magburaka 1968. Released in 1969. Member of the SLPP opposition in Parliament until 1973. Appointed puisne judge in 1973.

NDAWA of Wonde. Ndawa was born about 1855 in Majoru or Manjo, a village in the present Kenema District. Sold into slavery as a young man for "woman palaver," Ndawa refused to serve his master and vowed to become a warrior. Subjected to various forms of punishment, Ndawa nevertheless remained faithful to his oath. His master Sellu Tifa decided to sell him to Chief Makavoreh of Tikonko in exchange for a sword. Under Makavoreh's tutelage Ndawa became an accomplished warrior and fought in many campaigns on behalf of his new master. When Makavoreh was threatened by Benya of Blama, Ndawa swore to expel him from Makavoreh's territories. Allied to Kai Lundo of Luawa, another warrior, he embarked on Benya's expulsion. This was the Kpove War of the 1870s (so called because of the practice of decapitating white-livered warriors and storing their heads in a large pot). Together Ndawa and Kai Lundo expelled Benya from Makavoreh's lands. As a sign of gratitude Makavoreh gave Ndawa his freedom.

Thereafter Ndawa embarked on a career of freebooting over most of the present Southern and Eastern provinces of Sierra Leone and as far afield as Liberia. In April 1885, allied to Makaia of Largo, he raided Sulima and Mano-Salijah, whose rulers had signed treaties with the British. In March 1889 as a result of his incessant raids, Governor J. S. Hay dispatched a force of police against him. The force set out on March 22, 1889, for Wondeh, destroyed 13 towns, dispersed Ndawa's warriors and set free some 3000 of his captives. This action against Ndawa was the last on record of the old police force. In 1890, the Sierra Leone Frontier Police Force replaced the old Sierra Leone Police Force. Ndawa rebuilt Wondeh and continued his raids. He waged war against Chief Kutubu of Pendembu, and tried to invade Luawa. In Luawa his moves were thwarted by his former ally and comrade-in-arms Kai Lundo. Ndawa's prowess and successes won for him many enemies. In the end he was ambushed and overpowered. The story goes that one of his assailants, an unknown young man, rushed at Ndawa to kill him, but Ndawa appealed to Jami Lenge, a better-known warrior, saying, "Come Jami Lenge, come and finish me off, lest prosterity should say that a small unknown boy killed the Great Ndawa."

As news of his death (in the early 1890s) spread, incredulous people came to see for themselves. His powerful left arm was cut off and sent to Nongowa, his head was sent to his former foe (Benya of Blama). At Palima, where the Kpove warriors were made to assemble, the rest of his body was cremated and the ashes scattered in the river nearby. Among the Mende, Ndawa is still regarded as one of the greatest Mende warriors of the 19th century.

THE NEGRO (1872-1873). A newspaper founded in Freetown in 1872 and edited by E. W. Blyden, and later by the Rev. G. J. Macaulay. The Negro was sponsored by William Grant, Syble Boyle, G. J. Macaulay, and Thomas Bright and was published by T. J. Sawyerr.

NELSON-WILLIAMS, CLAUDE, 1927- . Medical practitioner and politician. Nelson-Williams was born in Freetown on May 30, 1927. He had his primary school education at Bathurst Street School, Samaria School, and at the Government Model School, Freetown. When his father went to Nigeria to establish legal practice, Claude accompanied him and in Lagos he attended Igbobi College. From Nigeria he went to Britain where he studied at Davis, Lang and Dick, Holland Park, London. He then entered King's College (University of Durham) Medical School, Newcastle-on-Tyne, where he qualified in medicine and became the first African senior house and casualty officer at the Queen Elizabeth Hospital in Gateshead, Newcastle-on-Tyne. When he returned home in 1957, Dr. Nelson-Williams was appointed medical officer, Fourah Bay College Hospital, the first to be appointed on a full-time basis. He revived the S. L. Medical Association and was appointed its president

(1958-59). He took a very active part in national politics and
was one of the foundation members of the PNP. Because of
these activities he resigned his post at FBC, resigned his government appointment, and set up private practice. In 1964-65
Dr. Nelson-Williams was appointed chairman, Committee of
Management, Freetown City Council.

NEW CABENDA see CABENDA

THE NEW ERA (1855-1858; 1858-1859). A weekly newspaper
founded in 1855 in Freetown by William Drape, an Afro-West
Indian printer. The New Era had a slogan--"To consult the
welfare of the people is the first great law." It stopped publication for a few months in 1858 and disappeared finally in 1859.

NEWTON, JOHN. A slavetrader on the Plantain Islands in the middle decades of the 18th century (ca. 1740s-60s), Newton later
became an abolitionist hymn-writer and clergyman. Comment-
ing on the indispensability of liquor in the preliminary negotiations for trade, Newton reported in 1750 that he was unable to
purchase ten slaves in the Sherbro for lack of "the commanding
articles of beer and cider." In his journal he described the
intricacies of trade on the Upper Guinea Coast in the 18th century and the criteria for appraising the quality of slaves for
purchase. He also recorded the methods of dishonesty and deceit used by European traders in their dealings with Africans
as well as African responses and reactions to such chicanery,
pointing out that faced with European debased standards the Africans "in their turn, in proportion to their commerce with the
Europeans ... become jealous, insidious and revengeful." The
entire system was a vicious circle; the Europeans first tam-
pered with goods and indulged in all forms of artifice; the Africans in turn resorted to similar practices in revenge; the Europeans became in turn even more dishonest and the Africans reacted correspondingly.

NICHOLLS, PETER. A Calabar recaptive who served in the Freetown garrison and was the regiment's color-sergeant. He embraced Christianity and became a staunch Wesleyan. After his
discharge from the army, he went into business and opened a
shop at Rawdon Street, Freetown. He then returned to his native Calabar in about 1853. In Calabar he attempted unsuccessfully to break the European monopoly of the oil trade. He came
back to Freetown, engaged in business once more, and became
an active member of the Mercantile Association. He took part
in the elections to the newly constituted Legislative Council in
1863. The candidates were John Ezzidio, a Nupe recaptive, and
John Levi, a European merchant. Levi, who lost to Ezzidio,
was nominated by Peter Nicholls.

NICOL, DAVIDSON S. H., 1924- . Born in Freetown in 1924.
Educated at Government Model and Prince of Wales schools,
Freetown. Studied at the Universities of Cambridge and Lon-

don. Principal of Fourah Bay College, 1960-1967; and vice-
chancellor of the University of Sierra Leone, 1963-7. Chairman, West African Examinations Council 1964-69. In 1969 he
was appointed Sierra Leone's permanent representative at the
United Nations and later Sierra Leone's high commissioner to
the Court of St. James. Deputy secretary general, United Nations. Author of Africa--A Subjective View (1964) as well as
of numerous articles in various journals.

NICOL, GEORGE WILLIAM. Only surviving son of George Nicol
(who was the Sierra Leone Company's carpenter and later private businessman and for whom Nicol Brook is named). Educated in England. He returned to Freetown and entered government service in 1829. He served on the Mixed Commission
Court and was in 1841 transferred to the colonial secretary's
office where he rose to the rank of first writer. In 1859 he
was promoted to the post of colonial secretary, one of the first
Sierra Leoneans to hold such high office. He retired in 1868
and died in Lambeth, England, in 1884.

NICOL-COLE, S. B., 1920- . First Sierra Leonean governor,
Bank of Sierra Leone, 1966. Born on August 8, 1920, at La-
gos, Nigeria. Educated at the CMS Grammar School Freetown,
King's College (Durham University), Newcastle, and at Keble
College, Oxford. Appointed deputy governor, Bank of Sierra
Leone 1964, and governor, 1966. In 1970 he took up appoint-
ment with the International Monetary Fund. Returned home in
1975 and was appointed one of the directors of Barclays Bank,
Sierra Leone, Ltd.

NJALA UNIVERSITY COLLEGE (NUC). Founded in 1963 as a university college with special emphasis on agriculture and education. In September, 1966 NUC became a constituent college of
the University of Sierra Leone.

NORRIS, Maj. RICHARD JOSEPH. In 1891 Norris fought at Tambi
as an ally of Bai Bureh and had been awarded the D. S. O.
Seven years later when Bai Bureh's relations with the British
became strained and hostile, Norris was sent against him. In
command of six officers and 92 men of the 1st West India Regiment, Norris landed at Robat and marched on to Karene. He
played a major role in the campaign against Bai Bureh and
other chiefs in the Karene district during the 1898 Hut Tax War.

NYAGUA of Panguma. A powerful Mende chief and warrior who
ruled in the 1880s over an appreciable area in Bambara Chiefdom, in what is now Kenema District. He was eager to gain
access to the coastal trade, but his route was barred at Wende
(Wonde), where a contingent of warriors from various parts of
the country stopped traders from the interior. In March 1889
G. H. Garrett, after meeting Nyagua and hearing of his handi-
cap, destroyed Wonde, dispersed the warriors, and released a
large number of hostages. On April 25, 1889, Nyagua signed

a treaty of peace with the British Government.   When the Sofas
attacked one of his towns in December 1893, the British sent a
force of 40 Frontier Police to his rescue.   As a treaty, Chief
Nyagua gave up Makaia of Largo to the British in 1894.
        In 1898, although Panguma had been exempted from pay-
ing the hut tax, Nyagua joined other chiefs who opposed the tax
and who resorted to force to prevent its collection.   Nyagua, it
was reported, was determined to drive white men from his
country.   Threatened with arrest, he agreed to persuade his
people to surrender in April 1898.   In May the British, still
suspicious of Nyagua, arrested him.   On June 4th his followers
besieged Panguma with a large force to rescue him.   A British
force arrived to relieve Panguma and Nyagua was taken under
arrest to Kwelu in Ronietta District and thence to Freetown.
In Freetown he and Bai Bureh were removed from prison to a
house in Ascension Town.   He, it was believed, was still sending secret messages to his people at Panguma.   On July 30,
1898, Nyagua, with Bai Bureh and Be Sherbro (Gbana Lewis),
was deported to the then Gold Coast, where he died in 1906.

                            - O -

THE OBSERVER.   A weekly newspaper founded in Freetown in
    April 1975 and published by Sam Short.

O'CONNOR, ANTHONY.   A Popo recaptive who arrived in Freetown
    in 1811 and was sent to school by Chief Justice Edward Fitz-
    gerald.   In 1828, O'Connor became a clerk in the Colonial Sur-
    veyor's Office and was promoted surveyor's clerk in 1845.   As
    a leading recaptive he fought hard to put an end to discrimina-
    tory practices of settlers against recaptives in various aspects
    of the colony's life and particularly in matters of religion.   He
    was the senior recaptive preacher and in 1844, he founded the
    West African Methodist Church, initially and predominantly a re-
    captive separatist movement in Methodism.   He died in 1855.

O'GORMAN, the Rt. Rev. JOHN, C. S. SP., 1866-1935.   Catholic
    bishop of Sierra Leone, 1903-1931.   Born in Ireland in 1866;
    studied for the priesthood in France and at the end of his stud-
    ies was retained in France as professor of philosophy at the In-
    ternational Holy Ghost Seminary.   Soon he was named its direc-
    tor.   He spent some years in the United States, serving first
    as "master of novices" and later taught theology at a college in
    Philadelphia, where he was consecrated bishop in 1903 at the
    early age of 37.   It is a tribute to Bishop O'Gorman's leader-
    ship that he was able to mold a variety of nationalities into one
    heroic missionary band in Sierra Leone--Frenchmen, Poles,
    Austrians, Englishmen, Americans, Germans and Irish.   These
    missionaries were a corps d'élite and yet progress of the mis-
    sion in Sierra Leone was, compared to other regions in West
    Africa, relatively slow.
        In February 1922 Bishop O'Gorman founded St. Edward's

Secondary School, the first Catholic secondary school in all
West Africa and today one of the leading schools in Sierra
Leone. He toured Europe and the United States regularly
soliciting aid for his mission. In 1931, after more than 25
years in Sierra Leone (1903-1931), Bishop O'Gorman was compelled for health reasons to leave Sierra Leone for good. He
died in 1935 in Freiburg, Germany.

ONITSHA MURDER CASE. In September 1880, Lieutenant Governor
T. R. Griffith of Sierra Leone was informed by the secretary
to the CMS at Lagos that a Mr. W. F. John, a Sierra Leonean,
serving as interpreter to the mission at Onitsha, had in 1878
caused to be beaten to death his female ward whom he was said
to have ransomed from slavery. W. F. John, who had by then
returned to Freetown and was teaching at the Wesleyan Boys High
School, was arrested in February 1881 and detained. In May
1882 the assistant colonial secretary, Capt. Richmond, traveled
to the Niger and had arrested and brought to Freetown another
Sierra Leonean, a Mr. Williams and his wife, involved in the
killing of the girl. In all, four persons were charged--Mr.
and Mrs. W. F. John and Mr. and Mrs. Williams. All four
persons and witnesses appeared in court in Freetown. As the
crime had been committed in territory outside British jurisdiction a special court, consisting of the chief justice, the
colonial secretary, the chief magistrate of the Gambia, and the
manager of Waterloo District, was appointed to try the case.
Samuel Lewis was retained by the Crown as counsel for the
prosecution. The case was complex, the procedure somewhat
cumbersome, but Lewis' forensic skill secured the conviction
of the accused. After a trial lasting 15 days the jury found
the accused persons guilty of manslaughter. Two, presumably
Mr. and Mrs. Williams, were sentenced to 20 years' imprisonment; one, Mr. John (who had already been in jail since his
arrest in February 1881), to 18 1/2 years, and the fourth,
presumably Mrs. John, was sentenced to two years' imprisonment. There was considerable public sympathy for the convicted persons and for some years after the trial public petitions were organized for their release. The Onitsha murder
trial necessitated the enactment of an order-in-council in 1885
making provisions for special procedure to try British subjects
accused of crimes committed outside the British settlements in
West Africa.

ORMOND, JOHN. A slave trader in Baga territory for 25 years
(from about 1765-1790). In 1785 Ormond probably leased
Bunce Island from three London partners trading privately and
appeared to have rebuilt the fort towards the end of 1786 to protect his garrison of 17 men against the French on Gambia Island. The magazines, the houses of the governor and clerks,
the docks, halls and warehouses were all rebuilt. Ormond
used his influence to put an end to hostilities on the coast in
order to safeguard the much more lucrative trade in the interior. Described as a notoriously cruel slavetrader Ormond

in the last years of his life is said to have been fond of enter-
taining himself at the expense of the lives and limbs of his
servants. He died in 1790, survived among others by his son
Jack, who committed suicide in 1828.

OWEN, NICHOLAS. An Irishman who after a period of trading up
and down the West Coast of Africa, settled in Sierra Leone in
1754, confining himself mostly to the Sherbro and the River
Jong areas. His brother Blayney concentrated in the northwest
regions of Sierra Leone. Nicholas Owen kept a diary in which
he recorded a lot of useful information not only about trade but
about aspects of Sierra Leone history. From him we learn
that there was a trade depression on the West Coast caused by
the Seven Years' War between Britain and France. In May
1757 he wrote about "such a [seldom known] scarcety of shipping upon this coast ... and such a bad time of trade...."
Owen also commented on the indispensability of liquor in trade
negotiations.

- P -

PALMER, EUSTACE, 1939- . Educationist and author. Born
October 2, 1939. Educated at the Prince of Wales School,
and at the University of Edinburgh. Senior lecturer, Department of English, Fourah Bay College (USL). Author of An
Introduction to the African Novel (1972).

PANDA, G. S., 1911- . First Sierra Leonean commissioner of
labour (1955-59) and first Sierra Leonean secretary to the
cabinet (1961-66). Born on April 13, 1911, at Blama, Kenema
District. Educated at Bo Government School. Joined Sierra
Leone Government Service in 1929 and worked his way up to
permanent secretary, Ministry of Lands, Mines and Labour,
1955-59. Charged with treason in 1968 and convicted 1969.
Reprieved 1972 and now in voluntary exile in London.

PARKES, JAMES CHRISTOPHER ERNEST, 1861-1899. Parkes was
born in 1861. He proceeded to Britain to study law but was
prevented by illness from qualifying as a barrister. He returned to Freetown in 1881 and was appointed a clerk in the
commandant's office at Bonth, a job which gave him considerable insight into the problems of the hinterland. In 1884 he was
transferred to the Aborigines Branch of the Secretariat in
Freetown. He traveled to the Gallinas with governors Rowe
and Hay in 1885 and 1887 respectively. Parkes had assisted
T. G. Lawson, the government interpreter, in compiling a
lengthy memorandum entitled Information regarding the Different Districts and Tribes of Sierra Leone and Its Vicinity
in the early 1880s, which was printed as confidential matter
for official use at the Colonial Office in 1887. In 1894 Parkes
published a small school geography textbook based on the material of the work he and Lawson had compiled.

His vast and intimate knowledge of the interior made his
services invaluable in the Secretariat, whilst his attitude and
approach to the problems of the hinterland made him the chiefs'
most reliable intermediary in their relations with the Colonial
government.   In recognition of his abilities and competence,
Governor Hay removed the Aborigines Branch from the Secretariat, created a separate department, appointed Parkes its
superintendent and renamed it in 1891 the Department of Native
Affairs, directly under the governor's supervision and control.
In 1896 Parkes was promoted secretary for native affairs and
he became in effect the head of the Department of Native Affairs.

His relations with some chiefs of the interior, his approach to its problems, provoked sharp criticisms and at times
mistrust from the military authorities and from the officers of
the Frontier Police Force.   For instance, Samori Touré, whose
defeat by the French was taken too readily for granted by military experts, Parkes was prepared to accept as a friend and to
cultivate as a potential British ally.   Parkes insisted, in spite
of the hostility of his European colleagues, on according a warm
welcome to Samori's Sofa emissaries, encouraging them to give
up war for trade or for more peaceful and productive pursuits.
His pro-Samori posture exposed him to unfair charges of cor-
ruption and double-dealing with the Sofas.   In a number of
memoranda Parkes outlined his own views on British policy for
the interior.   He urged the British government to proclaim a
protectorate over the hinterland of Sierra Leone.   He advocated
a gradual reduction in the size of the Frontier Force and a
general review of their duties and functions, since he envisaged
a peaceful British penetration of the adjacent territories.   He
proposed the appointment of Creoles--about five in number--to
man the Protectorate administration either as political agents
or as district commissioners.   Neither the Governor in Freetown nor the Colonial Office was willing then to entrust the
Protectorate administration to Creoles.   For, according to
Governor Fleming, "we could not depend upon them and they
would be likely to get us all into all sorts of difficulties."
After the declaration of the Protectorate in 1896, Parkes' job
as secretary of the Department of Native affairs ceased to have
relevance.   His health began to deteriorate.   He died on August
10, 1899, at the early age of 38.   His death removed the most
effective and reliable link between Creoles and chiefs and
brought to a premature end all hopes of a Creole/European
partnership in the administration and development of the Protectorate.

PA SANDI VILLAGE.   Named after a local herbalist and native
    doctor, Pa Sandi.   In the 1790s Pa Sandi lived in King Jimmy's
    Town.   When in 1802 the Temne in King Jimmy's Town were
    driven further west of Freetown Pa, Sandi moved southwards
    towards the beach and founded the village called after him.   Pa
    Sandi Village, though still so called by some, was renamed
    Lumley Village after Lt.-Col. Lumley who as acting governor
    of Sierra Leone settled a number of recaptives there in 1827.

PEOPLE (1968-1973). Newspaper founded in Freetown in 1968 and
    edited by Julius Cole as the mouthpiece of the SLPP.

PEOPLE'S NATIONAL PARTY [PNP]. Founded by Mr. (later Sir)
    Albert Margai in September 1958. The origins of the PNP
    could be traced to the events of May 1957 when after the gen-
    eral elections, a split occurred in the SLPP over the question
    of the party's leadership. On May 19, 1957, the parliamentary
    party caucus of the SLPP met to elect a new leader of the
    party. Albert Margai won 21 votes, his brother Dr. Milton
    Margai, 20. To keep the party from disintegrating into two
    almost equal but opposing camps, Albert was prevailed upon to
    step down in favor of the doctor. This he did, with ill-advised
    magnanimity, on certain conditions. The conditions were never
    fulfilled, the promises were quickly dishonored. In the circum-
    stances, Albert rejected a ministerial appointment offered by
    his brother. For over a year all attempts at a rapprochement
    failed. In September 1958 Albert Margai and three other mem-
    bers of the House of Representatives, Arthur Massally, S. T.
    Navo and H. I. Kamara, broke away from the SLPP to form
    the PNP. A few months later Maigore Kallon, then parlia-
    mentary secretary in the SLPP government resigned his ap-
    pointment to join the PNP as national propaganda secretary.
        The first executive or working committee of the PNP
    consisted of Albert Margai, founder (later appointed leader);
    S. P. Stevens, general secretary (later deputy leader), suc-
    ceeded by Y. Sillah as secretary; S. T. Navo, treasurer, and
    M. C. Kallon, national propaganda secretary, as well as A. J.
    Massally, H. I. Kamara, M. S. Turay, Berthan Macauley,
    C. P. Foray, Claude Nelson-Williams, T. J. Ganda, G. B. O.
    Collier, Abu Koroma. The PNP by bringing together the in-
    tellectual and professional groups in both the Colony and the
    Protectorate, and by recruiting particularly its protectorate
    membership from the same sources as the SLPP, was able, if
    only momentarily, to effectively challenge the SLPP political
    monopoly in the provinces. A few months after its inception,
    the PNP in almost dramatic fashion won all the seats in the Bo
    Town Council elections held in 1959. But these electoral suc-
    cesses were never repeated. The SLPP took the PNPs chal-
    lenge seriously and applied the brakes. The PNP put considera-
    ble emphasis on putting an end to the Creole/countryman con-
    frontation, and also succeeded in gaining support in the north,
    particularly in Bombali, Tonkolili and Koinadugu districts. The
    party took as a symbol the elephant, a large but uninspiring
    figure. The party's motto was "Liberty, Freedom."
        In the 1959 district council elections, which the SLPP
    preferred to a general election before independence, the PNP
    put up a poor performance, winning only 29 out of 309 seats.
    The party fared no better in the Freetown City Council elec-
    tions later in the year, winning only ten per cent of the votes
    and no seats. Notwithstanding these electoral setbacks, the
    PNP argued, with some plausibility, that local government

elections, particularly in developing countries, were no clear
evidence of a party's real or potential following. Accordingly,
as the 1960 constitutional talks approached, the party adopted
as a political creed, "general elections before independence."
At the roundtable conference of political parties that preceded
the London talks, the PNP drew closer to the SLPP line until
in the end it too disappeared into the ranks of the United Front
coalition. But before the United Front was formed the PNP
tried to broaden its base by entering into a somewhat uneasy
and shortlived alliance with KPM. It also effected similar arrangements with Mr. I. T. A. Wallace Johnson's "one-man"
Radical Democratic Party (RDP).

Formed in the period between the 1957 general election
and independence in 1961 the PNP attempted to project a future
foreign policy for Sierra Leone. It upheld the principle of non-
alignment, called for an end to the existence of foreign military
and naval bases in the country, and repudiated the preferential
tariff system for British manufactured products. In political
outlook the PNP leaned more towards liberalism with vague professions of socialism. Nicknamed "a lawyers' party" by its
detractors, the PNP adopted an almost superstitious reverence
for the rule of law.

PEREIRA, PACHECO DUARTE. Born in Lisbon in the middle
decades of the 15th century; became governor of Elmina Castle
(at the time Portuguese) between 1520 and 1522. Author of
Esmeraldo de Situ Orbis, --a description of the west coast of
Africa from southern Morocco to Gabon written sometime between 1505 and 1508. From Pereira we learn about the origins
of the name Sierra Leone. "Many people," he wrote, "think
that the name Serra Lyoa was given because many lions were
to be found in that part but that is wrong. It is because Pedro
da Cintra ... when he saw a land so rough and wild, called it
Lyca. That is the only reason and no other explanation is true
because he told me this himself." He also gave a list of words
in Bullom and Temne which later travelers might have found
useful. Pereira's was one of the earliest European descriptions
of the west coast of Africa. At the time he wrote, his impressive knowledge of the new discoveries was a closely guarded
secret. He was in fact censured for divulging so many secrets
in such detail. He died in considerably reduced circumstances
and his maps were not published until 1892.

PETERS, THOMAS. A runaway slave from North Carolina who had
fought in the American War of Independence as a British Loyal-
ist. After the American victory, Peters with others who had
supported the British cause had to seek their fortunes elsewhere. They were sent to Nova Scotia with promises of land
to farm and to settle on. Peters arrived at Annapolis, Nova
Scotia, in 1784. Six years later the promises of land, etc.
were still unfulfilled. In 1791 he decided to travel to Britain
as a spokesman for his stranded comrades in Nova Scotia and
to seek redress. "My people have sent me to inform you

Sirs," he told the directors of the Sierra Leone Company in
London, "that the climate of Nova Scotia has been unfavorable
to them.   The grants of land, contrary to promise have been
withheld from them and we cannot live any longer there.   We
wish to go to the New Settlement in Sierra Leone."   His plea
fell on receptive ears and as a result it was decided to transfer the Nova Scotians to Sierra Leone.

Peters, barely literate, had made his way to London
against tremendous odds.   But his mission had been fruitful.
On his return to Nova Scotia he assumed a position of leadership among the would-be immigrants to Sierra Leone.   When
the Nova Scotians arrived in Sierra Leone in February 1792,
he sought to play a similar role and tried to acquire and wield
power in the new settlement.   This brought him into conflict
with John Clarkson, whom the Sierra Leone Company had appointed as governor.   Peters emerged from the power struggle
with the governor as a defeated and discredited challenger, but
then died on the night of June 25, 1792, a victim of the fever
epidemic that had so decimated the ranks of the Nova Scotians
in Sierra Leone, and of his own overweening selfconfidence.
And yet "without his courage and faith in coming to England,"
writes a leading historian of Sierra Leone, "no Nova Scotians
would have come to Sierra Leone; without the Nova Scotians the
Colony would have failed."

PHILIP, DON see FLANSIRE

PIERCE, EDWARD.   English factor at Bunce Island in the 1670s
and early 1680s.   In the last decades of the 17th century, trade
at Bunce and in Sierra Leone generally was on the decline, and
quite a few traders moved northwards from Sierra Leone in
search of greater profits.   Pierce, who entertained fears that
the French or Dutch might establish a factory on the Isles de
Los and thus intercept ships from Europe before they reached
Sierra Leone, frequently complained of these problems.   When
Pierce died in May 1682, he was succeeded by John Case and
Henry Clark as agents of the English Royal African Company
at Bunce Island.

PIKE, ADOLPHUS.   Pike had served in the Colonial Secretary's
office in Freetown for some two decades since the early 1840s,
but his progress in the service had been delayed and withheld
because of indiscreet and insubordinate behavior.   In 1864 he
was appointed colonial treasurer at a salary of £600 per annum;
this appointment introduced the effective division of the Secretariat into the Colonial Secretary's and Colonial Treasurer's
offices.

PORO.   A powerful male secret society that operates in most parts
of Sierra Leone and in particular among the Sherbro Bullom,
the Mende and the Temne.   No one knows for certain how or
when the society came into being.   Oral tradition refers to its
existence from time immemorial, its origins forgotten or un-

known. There is evidence however that by the beginning of the 17th century, the poro was one of the most important secret societies in Sierra Leone, although at the time it was called pero. Valentin Fernandes made reference to a secret society with a female mascot called pere (which may well have been the poro). Manual Alvares believed that the poro was a Mane organization. Temne oral tradition states that the Temne acquired knowledge of the poro from the Sherbro Bulloms, while the Mende claim to be the original founders of the society. Before the imposition of British rule the poro enjoyed unrivaled power over virtually all spheres of human activity in the parts of the country in which it operated. It was the most important basis of man-made law and governmental authority; it provided the only facilities for educating young males in tribal ways of life and in preparation for manhood. Today its influence, if still widespread, is somewhat on the wane, as its most important functions have been and are being taken over by more efficient competitors--schools, courts of law and the central government.

POROKERRI [POKERE], Chief. Porokerri was one of Samori's able generals. He was involved in a number of exploits, including attacks on Kunike Temne country within the British sphere of influence. Porokerri/Pokere and his Sofas were allies of Foray a Kono chief against Vonjo a Temne Kunike chief. When not fighting for Samori, Pokere and other Sofa generals were wont to offer the services of their troops to any chief who might wish to "buy war." On December 23, 1893, British forces encamped at Waiima in Kono country were attacked by the French in the belief that the British forces were Sofas led by Pokere. Shortly after the Waiima incident, Pokere and his Sofas attacked Tungea near Panguma, in the territory of Nyagua a chief in treaty with the British. The Sofas were repulsed with heavy losses. In this action which took place on December 28, 1893, Chief Pokere/Porokerri was killed.

PORTER, ARTHUR THOMAS, 1834-1908. Born in Freetown in 1834 of an Afro-West Indian father, who was manager at Kent Village in 1831 and the jailer at Freetown in 1833, and a Maroon mother. Porter started life as an artisan, having worked in the 1850s as a mason in the construction of Samaria Church. By the 1880s he had established himself as a successful and prosperous businessman at Gibraltar wharf off Kissy Street, dealing mostly in building materials for military installations. He also served as contractor, shipping laborers to the Congo Free State to work on railways and public works. In 1892 he opened Porter's Royal Hotel in a large stone house built by himself on Wilberforce Street and employed a European manager, Miss Nellie Farrell, to help run it. According to an advertisement in the Sierra Leone Weekly News of December 18, 1893, the Hotel provided among its facilities "excellent cuisine, wine at moderate prices, Bass ale and stout on draught, billiard room and bar, large airy bedrooms."

PORTER, ARTHUR THOMAS, 1924- . Vice chancellor of Univer-

sity of Sierra Leone since 1973. Born in Freetown, educated at
the CMS Grammar School, Fourah Bay College (University of Durham), Selwyn College, Cambridge, Edinburgh University and University of Boston (Mass.). On academic staff of Fourah Bay College 1952 to 1965, lecturer in history, director of the Institute of
African Studies, professor of history and vice-principal. In 1965,
appointed acting-principal, Royal College, Nairobi, Kenya. Author of Creoledom: A Study of the Development of Freetown
Society. (London: Oxford University Press, 1963.)

POST OFFICE SAVINGS BANK. Opened in Freetown on January 1,
1882, under the management and control of the colonial treasurer and initially styled the Treasury Savings Bank. An Ordinance of July 14, 1874, had established a savings bank at the
Post Office but not until January 1882 was the bank actually
opened. The interest rate of the bank was 2 1/2 per cent and
the number of depositors at the end of 1882 was 44. The bank
still operates and the number of depositors is in the thousands.

PRATT, ISAAC BENJAMIN. An Aku from Ife recaptured in about 1825,
Pratt, like so many other recaptives, worked his way up to success
and prosperity. He began in the 1830s to purchase goods at auctions
and to resell at a profit. He made enough to enable him to start a
shop at Gloucester Street. By 1845 he had acquired his own schoon-
er and had in addition to trading begun investing in house property.
He got married to the wealthy widow of another businessman, William Chapman and she enhanced his already impressive fortunes.
His wealth, at the height of his prosperity was estimated at £20,000.
Pratt, with other leading recaptives, following the practice of consolidating ethnic ties by forming companies or societies, founded in
the mid-1850s the Benevolent Society which among other activities
raised funds for the Yoruba mission, inaugurated by Adjai Crowther
in 1845. The Benevolent Society had as its head John Macaulay,
king of the Aku, with Isaac Benjamin Pratt as his deputy. Pratt
was an active member of the Freetown Community and regularly
signed petitions presented to government in protest against unpopular measures--as in 1853 against the abolition of grand juries in
the Colony. Meetings of the Anti-Slavery Society were often held
in his house. After John Macaulay's death in December 1867, Pratt
was appointed to succeed him as king of the Aku. In 1879 Governor
Rowe appointed him to the Legislative Council. When he died in
1880 Pratt's fortunes had declined appreciably. The Aku kingship
lapsed and attempts to revive it in 1891 proved obnoxiously futile.

PRATT, S. A. J. Lawyer and politician. Educated at the CMS
Grammar School, Freetown, Fourah Bay College (University of
Durham), and at London and Oxford universities. Elected to
Parliament as member for Mountain constituency, 1967. Ap-
pointed minister of development, 1968-1969; minister of foreign
affairs, 1971-1973, and attorney general, 1975 to the present.

PRATT, the Rev. W. E. A., 1897- . Chairman and general superintendent of the Methodist Church in Sierra Leone (1960-1967). Born
at York Village on July 6, 1897. Educated at Ebenezer Methodist

School, York, at the United Methodist Collegiate School and at
Fourah Bay College (University of Durham), Freetown. Ordained
a minister of the Methodist Church in 1929. In 1928 the Rev. Pratt
started a Teacher Training College at Tikonko, Bo District, which
later became the Union College, Bunumbu, Kailahun District. He
was president of the first autonomous conference of the Sierra
Leone Methodist Church (1967-1970).

PRATT, WILLIAM HENRY. In 1859 W. H. Pratt was appointed marshall of the Vice-Admiralty Court, the first recaptive to hold such a
high official post. When Governor Kennedy started a Dispensary
Society financed locally to provide free medicine for the poor and
destitute, Pratt was made one of its committee members. When
Ibo recaptives formed the Ibo Association to help, among other activities, the CMS Niger Mission, Pratt was appointed its president.
He made generous contributions to religious bodies irrespective of
differences in religious opinion in an age characterized by bitter
sectarian strife. Listed in 1863 among the 19 largest owners of
houses and land in Freetown, Pratt died in 1865, probably at 60
years of age, without heirs.

PRINCE ALFRED'S DAY. October 10, 1860, was until 1925 commemorated in Freetown as a public holiday and styled officially as "Prince
Alfred's Day." In 1860 HMS Eurylus arrived in Freetown with
Prince Alfred, Queen Victoria's 16-year-old son, serving aboard
as a midshipman. The prince came ashore at Government Wharf and
was driven in a pony carriage by Governor Hill to Government House
where at a reception in the Prince's honor, loyal addresses from
various sections of the community were presented to the royal visitor. Not only was the visit commemorated in the form of a public
holiday, but the uniform of the CMS Grammar School black coat,
white trousers, was based on the midshipman's uniform of the
Prince. HMS Eurylus spent two days in Freetown harbor, but the
Prince because of a sprained knee was able to spend only a few
hours ashore.

PRINCE ALFRED'S TOWN. After the cessation of hostilities in the Koya
War of 1861, a military road was built between Waterloo and Songo
Town. Songo Town was renamed Prince Alfred's Town. It is possible though not definite that the town retained its new name until 1872,
when by the terms of the treaty of retrocession a portion of Koya
declared British in 1861 was returned to the chiefs of Koya.

PRINCESS CHRISTIAN COTTAGE HOSPITAL [PCCH]. Situated in the
east end of Freetown between Fourah Bay Road and the Water Front,
Princess Christian Cottage Hospital, called after a daughter of
Queen Victoria, was opened in 1892 and staffed by a doctor and
three nurses from England. Mrs. Ingham, wife of the Anglican
bishop of Sierra Leone, the Rt. Rev. E. G. Ingham, was most instrumental in raising funds and other forms of support for building
the hospital. She successfully appealed to the trustees of the Colonial Bishopric's fund to surrender a portion of the spacious Bishopscourt grounds for a hospital which could serve not only as a treat-
ment center but also as a training school for nurses. With money

raised from other sources, including £500 donated by R. B. Blaize, an Aku recaptive's son who had prospered in business, the hospital became a going concern. Today with extensions, increased staff and equipment the hospital, now known as the Princess Christian Maternity Hospital, served as a maternity and pediatric center. Originally started by religious bodies the hospital is today run by the Sierra Leone government through its Ministry of Health.

PROTECTORATE EDUCATIONAL PROGRESSIVE UNION [PEPU]. Founded in 1929 by chiefs and non-chiefs of the Protectorate. Its aim was to close the wide gap in development between the Colony and the Protectorate, particularly in the field of education. Accordingly, PEPU provided scholarships for the secondary education of promising youths from the Protectorate. In the 1930s the Union ceased to function effectively. Revived in 1946, it aimed at encouraging "the spread of education in the Protectorate and ... pledged to work for the progress of those parts." Its members included Chief Julius Gulama of Moyamba, Chief Albert Caulker of Rotifunk, and Chief R. B. S. Coker of Jimmi Bagbo, Bo District. The non-chief members were Dr. M. A. S. Margai, Mr. A. J. Momoh, and Mr. Amadu Wurie. One of the first acts of the reconstituted Union was to sponsor Mr. A. M. Margai as a law student in Britain. In April 1951, PEPU joined other political associations to form the SLPP.

PROVINCE OF FREEDOM. The name given by Granville Sharp to the settlement of freed slaves in Sierra Leone between 1787 and 1791.

- Q -

QUAKER, the Rev. James, 1828-1882. Principal, CMS Grammar School 1863-1882. Born at Kent Village in 1828, the son of a disbanded soldier, James Quaker was one of the first pupils enrolled at the CMS Grammar School opened in 1845. From the Grammar School he proceeded to Britain to study at the CMS College at Islington. He returned to his old school as a tutor and on two occasions between 1859 and 1863 acted as principal. Quaker was appointed substantive principal of the Grammar School in 1863 and he held the post until his death in 1882. When Governor Kennedy introduced competitive examinations to recruit staff for the junior ranks of the civil service, Principal Quaker, for the government, conducted the examinations held for the first time in April 1868. The Ethiopian, a monthly journal reporting largely church news, was started in 1876 and edited by Quaker. But it was shortlived and by 1877 had ceased to appear. Principal Quaker acquired a high reputation as a shrewd businessman who carefully supervised the school's finances and sent part of the yearly surplus to England to be invested in an endowment. When he died in May 1882, he left to his successor, the Rev. Obadiah Moore, a school with a healthy financial and academic record.

QUIT RENT. Normally a rent in money or in kind in lieu of services. In 1792 some 1200 freed slaves arrived in Sierra Leone
from Nova Scotia. They had fought as British Loyalists in the
American War of Independence and the outcome had forced them
to seek their fortunes elsewhere. Initially they were sent to
Nova Scotia, where it was hoped they could settle as farmers
owning their land. This scheme did not materialize. Disappointed and aggrieved, they sent a protest mission to Britain
headed by Thomas Peters to seek redress. The Sierra Leone
Company, which had in 1787 already acquired a piece of land in
Sierra Leone for the rehabilitation of victims of the Atlantic
slave trade, manifested considerable interest sympathy for the
Nova Scotians. The directors of the Company sent John Clarkson to Nova Scotia to make arrangements for the transfer, with
the help of the British government, of the Nova Scotians to
Sierra Leone.

     Clarkson, carried away by a wave of emotional enthusi-
asm, made promises to prospective emigrants that were clearly
at variance with his instructions and quite inconsistent with the
Company's declared policy. Asked by the Nova Scotians whether
they had, as was widely rumored, to pay rent for their land in
Sierra Leone, Clarkson assured them, virtually swore, that the
company was offering them land free in Sierra Leone just as
the government had offered them land free in Nova Scotia.
Such charges that they may be asked to pay would not be rents
but rates to defray costs of certain social services. In fact
the directors had decided to offer land to the Nova Scotian settlers "On such terms and subject to such charges and obligations as they themselves [i.e., the Company] should later determine with a view to their general prosperity."

     Land in the new settlement had to be paid for to supple-
ment its finances and the directors regarded quit rents as a
vital and quite reasonable aspect of the Company's income. In
issuing written promises of land to prospective settlers, Clarkson went further to offer lands in Sierra Leone "free of expense." The settlers however did express willingness to repay
gradually the expenses incurred by the Company in establishing
the settlement and did agree to pay taxes to cover some administrative expenses and to provide for the indigent and destitute. They were each promised a grant of 20 acres of land
plus 10 acres for a wife and five acres for each child. These
promises could not be fully honored in Sierra Leone and the
actual grants fell far short of what had been expected. The
Company had decided however "that no quit rent should be
charged till Midsummer 1792; that then, an annual quit rent of
not more than [one shilling] an acre should be payable for two
years, in half-yearly payments; that from that time, i.e. Midsummer, 1794, the rent should be raised to not more than 2
per cent tax on the gross produce of the lands; and that at the
end of three years more, that is Midsummer, 1797, the rent
should again be raised, and fixed at not more than 4 per cent
on the gross produce of the land." It was stipulated further
that failure to clear and cultivate one-third of the allotment in

two years and two-thirds in three years would lead to complete
forfeiture of the land to the Company.   There was considerable
dissatisfaction over the lots allocated to whites and those reserved to the Company.   These measures strengthened the fears
and suspicions of the settlers that the Company had plans to dispossess them of Sierra Leone land in the interests of white settlers.

Between 1794 and 1801 quit rents constituted the most
serious internal problem in the settlement.   Opposition to quit
rents was among the major causes of the Nova Scotian insurrection of 1799.   Nor was it a particularly productive source
of revenue.   In 1796 its estimated revenue yield was about
£200 per annum.   By 1801 it was assessed at less than £100
yearly.   But it remained a source of grievance among the settlers who viewed its imposition as a serious breach of promise
on the part of the Company.   Rather than pay quite rents some
settlers abandoned their grants of land to seek a means of livelihood elsewhere.   In time, "The quit rent issue became fused
with a much wider issue, namely, what amounted to a denial of
sovereignty of the Company government and the asserting of the
settlers' right of self-government, which, to all intents and
purposes, they had enjoyed under Granville Sharp. "

The settlers regarded quit rents as a threat to the value
and security of their lands.   "The most significant long-term effect it has been observed is the legacy of suspicion, insecurity
and uncertainty handed down, as it were, through the inheritance
of tradition from generation to generation.   It must have had a
profound influence on development, particularly agricultural development throughout the history of the colony. "   It has also
been suggested that quit rents may have exacerbated race relations in the Colony by keeping alive the fear, during the Colony's
infancy, that the whites would dispossess the Africans of their
lands.   The difficulties experienced in the collection of quit
rents, the suspicion and hostility it engendered, the small yield
in terms of revenue--all these factors contributed to its abolition first in 1803.   Revived in 1812 quit rents were finally done
away with permanently in 1832.

- R -

RAINY, WILLIAM, 1819/20-1878.   An Afro-West Indian born in
    Dominica in 1819/20, Rainy immigrated to Sierra Leone where
    he worked at the Customs department between 1844-7.   He then
    proceeded to England to study law at the Inner Temple, re-
    turned to Freetown and set up private practice from 1850 to
    1871.   Rainy achieved considerable professional success at the
    bar in Freetown and a great amount of popularity in the com-
    munity at large.   He took up in the Sierra Leone Courts all
    cases that savored of color prejudice.   For instance in Novem-
    ber 1864 he brought an action for assault against the Colonial
    surgeon, Dr. Robert Bradshaw, who had whipped his groom for
    leaving his horse unattended under a rainstorm.   Bradshaw

wisely settled the matter out of court by paying £ 30. Rainy
brought a similar action against the Colonial treasurer, Adolphus
Pike, for hitting his watchman. Some businessmen retained
Rainy only to prevent him from issuing writs against them. Although he appeared on one occasion for the Crown, more often
than not he appeared in opposition to it as in the case of Who-
bay of Imperi, charged with the murder of Patience Peters, a
Popo recaptive. Ostentatiously he assumed the role of champion
of the oppressed. Skillful and able in debate he often ridiculed
his opponents in court and occasionally drove the judges to impose sanctions against him. On one or two occasions he was
charged and fined for contempt of court.

          Rainy was a signatory to practically all petitions to the
Colonial Office representing public protests against Colonial Officers or unpopular government measures. In an age when
petitions provided the most, if not only effective legitimate
avenue for expressing public grievances, Rainy almost became
a professional promoter of petitions. He fell out with successive governors Hill and Blackall and even Kennedy, with whom
he was initially on very cordial terms. Nor did he confine his
legal practice and political agitation to Sierra Leone. He successfully appealed cases on a number of occasions to the Judicial Committee of the Privy Council and appeared in an action
in the Queen's Bench, the first barrister of African descent to
plead in the English Courts. Through his instrumentality a
number of questions were raised in the British Parliament in
relation to issues in Sierra Leone--the jury issue was one, so
also was the professional competence of Judge Horatio Huggins.

          Through a number of newspapers, over some of which
he exercised considerable if not proprietary rights--some local,
like The Sierra Leone Observer, The Interpreter, The West
African Liberator, and others overseas, like The African
Times--William Rainy attacked his detractors, denounced his
adversaries and cowed his potential enemies. In 1867 he attended a meeting of the anti-slavery conference in Paris. As
Sierra Leone's first delegate (the second was Samuel Lewis),
Rainy spoke for all West Africa, drawing attention in a fiery
speech to the imperfect and imprecise political rights of Sierra
Leoneans. The French government in appreciation of professional services rendered to French citizens who were his clients awarded Rainy a gold medal. Back in Sierra Leone Rainy
saw to it that a local branch of the Anti-Slavery Society was
established in Freetown. In July 1871 he left for London, ill
and worn-out, never to return. From London he emigrated to
Australia where he died in 1878.

RAMADAN, Feast of. Ninth month of Islamic year during which
     complete fast from food and drink is observed from sunrise to
     sunset. As the Islamic year is lunar, Ramadan falls succes-
     sively at all seasons of the solar year. In Sierra Leone dur-
     ing the early decades of the 19th century, Islam was regarded
     as a threat to the Christian foundations of the Colony, and its
     adherents were officially treated with suspicion and hostility

and considered on the whole as subversive. In the 1840s however, Muslims started to celebrate the end of Ramadan by holding processions through the streets of Freetown up to Government House, an indication that though still regarded as a separate community, they were no longer considered a threat by the
government. In 1879 Governor Rowe, one of the more reli-
giously tolerant of Colonial Governors, entertained some 700
Muslims at Government House to mark the end of Ramadan.
Today Ramadan is celebrated as a public holiday in Sierra
Leone. The day itself is preceded by a vigil marked by
prayers in mosques and colorful lantern parades in the streets.

RASTON, the Rev. THOMAS, 1815-1896. Chairman and general
superintendent of the Methodist Mission in Sierra Leone (1847-
1849). Raston arrived in Sierra Leone on January 6, 1842,
and for practically all of his time in the country was in charge
of the Methodist Training Institution at King Town. Between
1847-1849 he succeeded the Rev. Badger as chairman and general superintendent. He left Sierra Leone for England in February 1851 and after a short stay sailed for Australia, where he
died.

READE, WILLIAM WINWOOD. Traveled through Freetown in 1861
on his way to the Congo in quest of gorillas. In 1864, Reade
published his Savage Africa, which included a description of
Freetown and its inhabitants with emphasis on their alleged
antipathy towards Europeans and on their unfitness to serve as
jurors because of often prejudiced verdicts. Like some of his
European contemporaries, Reade's earlier experiences in Africa
led him to denounce Christian missionaries and their influence
as harmful and to opine that Islam had far more to offer in the
way of civilizing the African continent. He had no doubt that
by the process of natural selection and the principle of the survival of the fittest, the Negro race would ultimately die out.
      When Reade under the auspices of the Royal Geographical
Society visited Sierra Leone a second time in 1868, he was in
many ways a changed man. He stayed at Regent Village and
admired its similarity to a quiet rural English parish. He got
to know Sierra Leoneans better, became less indiscriminate in
his denunciations and showed himself more ready to applaud
where necessary. His African Sketch-Book, published in 1873,
included a novelette of Sierra Leone--"The Pastor's Daughter"--
in which he made unusually charitable comments about the
Colony.
      By this time the practice of sending diplomatic missions
to the interior begun in 1821 and repeated in 1841 was revived
by Governor Kennedy who sent Reade to Falaba, Solima and the
Niger in 1869. The mission's main purpose was to induce
chiefs to keep open trade routes to the Colony. Reade set out
from Freetown in January 1869 and by way of Port Loko, Bok-
kari, Nedina, Small Boumba, Big Boumba, Kabala and Konkoba
arrived at his destination, the second European (after Maj.
Gordon Laing) to visit Falaba and the Solima countries. He

was not however allowed to proceed to the Niger. He fell ill
and his experiences as he lay brooding and disconcerted were
later published in his <u>Martyrdom of Man.</u> He spent some five
months in the hinterland and was accompanied on his return to
Freetown by a nephew or brother of King Sewa of Falaba, whom
Governor Kennedy sent back with presents for his royal kins-
man.

In June 1869 Reade embarked on a second journey to the
interior. At Falaba, King Sewa, overwhelmed by Kennedy's
generosity, allowed Reade to travel to the Niger, which he
crossed at Bendugu, but unable to find the source ended his
journey at a town called Didi. He returned to Freetown in
October 1869. After his return, he urged the creation of an
office of the interior as a liaison with the chiefs and recommended that the stipend system be extended to Solima and Falaba, arguing as he put it that "the stipend is mightier than the
sword." In 1873 Reade offered to serve as a volunteer in the
Ashanti campaign and died there at the age of 35.

REID, JAMES. Second governor of the Province of Freedom, Reid
succeeded Richard Weaver as governor in 1787. Removed from
office at Weaver's instigation and on charges of improper conduct, Reid was later elected a hundredor and then appointed a
marshal of Granville Town with powers to summon juries and
enforce writs. In about 1802 he became jailer for the Sierra
Leone Company as well as commissary. When he died in 1814
Reid owned three substantial buildings in Freetown.

RENNER, WILLIAM (also, William Awunor-Renner). Renner studied at Liverpool University, University College, London, and
Brussels University, where he obtained an M.D. In 1912 he
took the name Awunor-Renner. In 1884 he was appointed assistant colonial surgeon. His knowledge of mental diseases
enabled him to render great service to the mental asylum at
Kissy, hitherto inadequately supervised and improperly attended
to. In 1898 Governor Cardew appointed him medical officer of
the Volunteer Corps, hastily raised as rumors of an impending
attack on Freetown during the Hut Tax War filtered through the
air. On several occasions Dr. Renner acted as principal medical officer. When the West African Medical Service was
formed in 1902, he was excluded on racial grounds and placed
in a different and inferior category, that of native medical officer. He was however allowed the higher rate of salary in
view of his age and experience. When he retired from government service, he opened a nursing home in a house at Oxford
Street. He became mayor of Freetown in 1916 and died on
March 6, 1917.

ROAD TAX. First enacted by governor and council of the Sierra
Leone Company on October 10, 1795, when provision was made
that "all male Settlers within the said Territory of Sierra
Leone from the age of sixty shall be liable to be called upon
for six days work in the course of a year, for the clearing

and keeping in order the street and roads within the said territory, and in case any person so liable to be called upon shall neglect or refuse to obey summons of the Overseers of Roads (to be hereafter appointed) every person so offending shall be fined in the sum of one Dollar: and all female Settlers being in possession of a Town or Farm lot in the said District shall be liable to be called upon to send a man to work six days in the course of a year and shall be liable to the same fine of one Dollar in case of neglecting or refusing to obey the summons of the Overseer as before mentioned...."

The Road Tax Act or Highways Act was re-enacted in 1801 and amended on September 12, 1812, by an "Act to Amend and Explain an Act for Making and Keeping in Repair the Highways of This Colony." The 1812 Act regularized the administration of the road tax, and substituted for the commissioners of highways, a surveyor of roads (and an assistant surveyor). The 1812 Act laid down that all male residents of the Colony over 16 years of age (and who had resided for not less than three months) and all householders were each to work for six days on the highways. It allowed commutation of either personal labor or the purchase of the necessary implements for money.

In addition to making provision for the maintenance of the highways, the Act also aimed at creating incentives for increased production, particularly agricultural production, as evidenced by the clauses on domestic and other animals used for transport. An amending act of 1818 reimposed the age limit of 60 years, the absence of which in the 1812 act had subjected elderly persons to the same duties as youngsters of 16. The 1818 Act also made provision among other things for the regular appointment of commissioners and surveyors of highways at a fixed date each year. The Highways Act of 1829 stipulated dates for work on the roads--three days in May and June and three days in November and December--"and at such other time or times as may be appointed by the Commissioner or Commissionera of Highways duly nominated under the ... Act."

Another Act of 1856 imposed a road tax of one shilling and six pence per annum per head on all inhabitants between the ages of 16 and 60 with the alternative of working for six days in the year on road maintenance. The penalty for failing to comply with these provisions was a fine of ten shillings or imprisonment at hard labor for not more than ten days. In 1856 re-enactment provoked strong criticism and opposition, which persisted until the road tax was finally abolished in 1872 by Governor Hennessey.

ROBERTS, BARTHOLOMEW. Started as a mate on the _Princess_, London merchantman, Roberts, a Welshman, became a pirate and in 1720 attacked the occupied Bunce Island, destroying warehouses of the Royal African Company. Roberts moved to West Indian Waters but returned to Sierra Leone in 1721, only to be killed at sea a few months later. The trial of his men

in March 1732 virtually put an end to piracy in Sierra Leone
waters. In 1730 French merchants from Nantes and Le Havre
sent out an armed expedition to Sierra Leone waters, burned
the pirates ships and hanged those they captured. Thereafter
Sierra Leone private traders were able to follow their pursuits
in relative peace.

RODGERS FAMILY LETTER (1883). Like the Mambolo Letter
(q.v.) of 1879, the letter from the Rodgers Family of Dibyah
Town, Gallinas, dated April 11, 1883, throws some light on
the so-called treaties of cession of territory which were signed
between the British Government and chiefs of the interior. The
letter was quite clear on the point that no territory had been
sold or ceded and that the signatories regarded themselves as
no more than "mere Friends with the British." The letter,
which follows, was apparently addressed to Governor Havelock
and possibly sent through J. M. Harris.

"I, Malligee Rodgers, Chief of Dibyah Town, together
with the whole of my Families, Do hereby testify this day that
the Amount given to us by Mr. Laboarde, Commandant of British Sherbro, is Ready on hand to be Returned. We had thought
that it was only a Mere Present Given to us by the British Government, As they sometimes does to our late Brother, Prince
Mannah, Kong of Gaindamah and the Gallinas Country, But after
asking the Favour of a friend to Investigate some papers Given
to us by the said Mr. Laborde, Commandant of British Sherbro, we comes to find out That he intends to Buy Our Country.

"Although we are illiterated, our Fore-Parents Never
did sold the Country. We are mere Friends with the British,
and we would Be Ready to do whatever Lies in our Power to
Please the queen of England, But not to sell our Land. Now,
Therefore, we are in perfect Readiness to Return the Said
Money to Prince Jiah of Gaindamah, Say Twenty Pounds."
Signed by 19 Rodgers Family chiefs with their marks X, and
by eight chiefs of Minnah spelling their names "Rogers."

ROGERS-WRIGHT, CYRIL BUNTING, 1905-1971. Minister of foreign affairs, 1964-1965. Barrister and solicitor of the Supreme
Court of Sierra Leone; founder and proprietor of Shekpendeh
newspaper 1956; founder and leader of the United Progressive
Party (UPP); elected member of House of Representatives for
Port Loko East constituency 1957; leader of the opposition,
1957-1960; appointed minister of housing and country planning
in United Front Coalition, 1960-62; re-elected member of Parliament for Wilberforce constituency 1962; appointed minister of
external affairs, 1964-1965; minister of health, 1965-1967; re-
elected member of Parliament as APC member for Wilberforce,
1967; detained by NRC military regime 1967; leading prosecution counsel in treason trials, 1969-70; died in Ireland in 1971
and buried in Freetown.

ROGERS-WRIGHT, CYRUS, 1928- . Lawyer and politician. One
of Sierra Leone's most brilliant barristers. Born at Bonthe,

Sherbro, on February 28, 1928.   Educated at the CMS Grammar School, Fourah Bay College (University of Durham), Freetown, Durham University, England, London University, and the Middle Temple Inns of Court, London.   Arrested and detained under public emergency regulations in 1970.   Released in 1971.

ROWE, Sir SAMUEL. Acting governor of Sierra Leone, 1875-6; governor, 1877-1880, 1885-1888. Born in 1835, studied medicine and entered the army as a military surgeon.   Appointed to West Africa in 1862, Rowe performed professional and administrative duties at Lagos and on the Gold Coast where he served during the Ashanti War of 1873-1874.   He successively administered the governments of Sierra Leone and the Gambia, and governed the West African Settlements in 1877-81 and in 1885-8; the Gold Coast and Lagos in 1881-4.   Between 1875-76 he was acting governor of Sierra Leone.   Because of disturbances in the Sherbro and attacks on British subjects and property, Rowe personally led two expeditions to the area; the first from October 8 to 24, 1875; the second from November 15 to December 30 of the same year.   In the course of the campaigns he signed treaties with chiefs at Sennehoo and at Shenge by which the chiefs agreed to refer disputes to the governor for mediation and arbitration, to promote trade, to destroy war fences and stockades, and to grant to the British government the right to collect customs duties on the seaboard of the territories under their jurisdiction.

In 1877 Rowe was appointed substantive governor of Sierra Leone.   He introduced a number of fiscal and administrative reforms which reduced public expenditure and increased efficiency.   He stopped paying the Native Pastorate Grant, hitherto a cause of sectarian strife and bitterness; curtailed public works, and put an end to school grants and retrenched staff.   He streamlined office procedure, introduced minute papers and spent much time personally supervising details.   As tolerant of Islam as Hennessey, he entertained some 700 Muslims at Government House to mark the end of Ramadan festivities in 1879.   The governor also tried to reconcile the conflicting interests of the Fulah Town, Fourah Bay and immigrant sects, all of whom celebrated Ramadan on different dates.

Rowe pursued a dynamic if at times highhanded policy up-country.   In 1878 he created an Aborigines Branch of the secretariat, responsible for matters relating to the interior.   By February 1879 the Governor had declared the Scarcies area subject to Freetown Customs duties.   In December 1879 he signed treaties of peace with the chiefs of Tikonko, Bumpe and Lugbu districts.   At his invitation a large number of chiefs from various parts of the country assembled in Freetown where on February 6, 1880, he ratified previous treaties with the Tikonko, Bompe and Lugbu districts, and with the chiefs of the Boom and Jong rivers.   Rowe decided to demonitize and to replace by British currency the Spanish, Mexican and South American dollars in circulation in the Colony and valued at four shillings and two pence, but worth far less.   He proposed

to compensate would-be losers in the process with proceeds
from a revived house and land tax. Thwarted in this attempt
by protests, he increased customs duties instead. Awarded a
knighthood and appointed to the Gold Coast, he set sail from
Sierra Leone on May 4, 1880.

At the request of traders and merchants in Sierra
Leone and through pressure from the chambers of commerce
of Manchester and Liverpool, Rowe was reappointed by a reluctant and sceptical Colonial Office to govern Sierra Leone in
1885. During his previous tenure his frequent and pacificatory
visits to the hinterland had won him the confidence, respect
and friendship of chiefs. He had also acquired the reputation
among the inhabitants of the Colony as one who could curb the
warlike propensities of the hinterland tribes and thus promote
and foster the Colony's trade. Rowe was welcomed back by the
Sierra Leone Association as the "courageous supporter of liberty, virtue and right; the true benefactor of the African race
and the powerful protector of the loyal subjects of Her Most
Gracious Majesty Queen Victoria." Such unqualified tribute,
if deserved, raised hopes impossible of fulfillment. He had
recruited three "special service officers" in London to help in
the hinterland where he hoped his old policy of guiding and restraining chiefs would continue to pay dividends. To some extent his hopes were not in vain. The Scarcies area was restored to peace and a number of chiefs elsewhere promised
good behavior. But the mercantile groups in Freetown advocated a stronger, more thorough and effective policy aimed at
establishing a protectorate over the hinterland either by purchase or annexation. On April 14, 1885, the Sierra Leone Association presented a memorandum to the secretary of state
which ascribed the lack of a vigorous interior policy less to
the Governor's unwillingness or indecision than to the prescrip-
tions of the Home government. Far from criticizing the Governor the Association hoped to strengthen his hand. In fact
the Governor and the Association held almost irreconcilable
views on details of interior policy. Their insistence on the
use of military force he considered inexpedient; their advocacy
of a protectorate he thought inadvisable.

The Governor's peace-making missions cost a considerable sum and more often than not implied military expeditions.
Samuel Lewis, a leading spokesman of the Sierra Leone Association, denounced Rowe's policy as expensive, humiliating and
unproductive. The Governor had clearly lost his former reputation and began to experience difficulties with the unofficial
members of the Legislative Council, who had virtually thrown
themselves into the role of official opposition. The Governor's attempts to raise revenue by direct taxation, in particular by reviving the hated house and land tax, were effectively
blocked by Lewis and Sawyerr in Council. In the end, Rowe,
disappointed, worn-out and unwell, withdrew to Madeira on
leave to recuperate and there on August 28, 1888, he died.

- S -

SAMMA, BAI. King of the country on the north side of the Sierra
Leone River, not far from the site of the present town of Kumrabai. In 1678 Jean Barbot referred to Bai Samma as the
principal king of the country, to whom other kings or vassals
paid homage. A certain John Thomas, described in 1668 as a
"mutineer and a rebel," levied and collected tolls in the name
of Bai Samma on ships trading up the River Sierra Leone.
About the same time an entry in the account book at the factory
at Bunce Island showed that some kind of tribute was paid to
Bai Samma. There were probably successive holders of the
title, Bai Samma.

SANUSSI, MOHAMED. An Aku Muslim of Foulah Town educated in
Futa Jalon, Sanussi was an Arabic scholar of high standing who
in addition to owning an Arabic library with a collection of Islamic works by West African authors, also subscribed to a
Constantinople newspaper. In 1872 Governor John Pope Hennessey appointed him government Arabic writer, responsible
among other duties for correspondence between the Sierra Leone
government and those chiefs of the interior like Samori who
sent letters to Freetown written in Arabic. In 1878 Governor
Rowe created an Aborigines Branch of the Secretariat to institute a more formal and organized connection with the interi-
or, and Sanussi, as an assistant to T. G. Lawson, was put on
the staff of the new establishment. Early in 1889 Governor J.
S. Hay separated the Aborigines Branch from the Secretariat
and made it into an independent department directly under the
governor's office. In 1891 the new department was renamed
the Department of Native Affairs. Sanussi retained his post as
government Arabic writer from 1872 until 1901.

SAVAGE, WILLIAM HENRY. Businessman, notary public and legal
practitioner. The first Sierra Leonean to acquire a legal
qualification in England and to practice law in the Colony.
Born in England of an African father and an English mother,
Savage arrived in Sierra Leone in 1808 as a schoolmaster, but
soon became a slave trader in the adjacent territories. He
abandoned the slave trade for legitimate trade, returned to
Freetown in 1820 and became within a few years the most
prosperous trader. When he visited England in 1821 he got
himself appointed a notary public for Sierra Leone at the faculty
office in London. Back in Freetown he set up private practice
appearing mostly in the Court of Recorder and in the Mixed
Commission Court. After the Cobolo War he defended the Cobolo Muslim Aku who had been charged with high treason for
their part in the war. His plea that as Cobolo was beyond
British jurisdiction, his clients could not have committed
treason, was upheld by the Courts. He eventually allowed
some of his Muslim Aku clients to settle on a piece of land he
owned near Fourah Bay called "Savage Square" and this marked
the beginnings of the Fourah Bay Muslim community. Savage

died in 1837 in somewhat reduced circumstances.

SAWYERR, the Rev. Canon H. A. E., 1909- . Clergyman, educationist, author. Born in Freetown, October 16, 1909. Educated at the Prince of Wales School, Fourah Bay College (University of Durham), Freetown, and at St. John's College (Durham University), England, where he read theology. Canon
Sawyerr was a member of the Fourah Bay College academic
staff from 1933 to 1973 and held the following appointments:
tutor (1933-1941); chaplain (1943-1945; 1948-1952); lecturer in
theology (1948-1952); senior lecturer in theology (1952-1962);
professor of theology (1962-1973); vice principal (1956-1958;
1964-1968); dean, Faculty of Theology (1955-1962); dean,
Faculty of Arts (1962-1964); principal (1968-1973); pro-vice
chancellor, University of Sierra Leone (1968-1970), and vice
chancellor, USL, 1970-1972. As a churchman he served as
examining chaplain to the bishop of Sierra Leone (1948-1973)
and as Canon of St. George's Cathedral in Freetown from 1961
to 1974. He edited the Sierra Leone Bulletin of Religion (1962-
1964) and was general editor of Aureol pamphlets from 1960
onwards. Sawyerr was also a member of the World Council of
Churches Commission on Faith and Order and a member of the
Working Committee of the Commission (1963-1971). Canon
Sawyerr is author of Creative Evangelism (1968), The Spring
of Mende Belief and Conduct (1968), and God: Ancestor or
Creator? (1970). He retired from Fourah Bay College in 1973
and took up an appointment at St. John's College, Barbados.

SAWYERR, T. J., 1833-1894. Successful businessman and prominent civic leader. Born at Waterloo in 1833. After saving
some money as a shopkeeper's clerk, T. J., assisted by his
brother Moses, established a bookshop at Rawdon Street in
1856, the first in Freetown. Proprietor of a printing press,
"Sawyerr's Advertising Medium," he published the newspaper
The Negro, founded in 1872 and edited by Blyden. He also
distributed a CMS magazine, Home Words, to which he contributed local news items and which was sent out monthly from
England between 1872 and 1876. Appointed to the Legislative
Council in 1883 until his death in 1894, T. J. Sawyerr was
often a sharp critic of government's measures and a stout de-
fender of local interests.

SCOTT, the Rt. Rev. MOSES N. CHRISTOPHER OMOBIALA, 1911-
. Bishop of Sierra Leone, 1961 to the present, and arch-
bishop of West Africa since 1969. Born August 18, 1911, at
Calabar, Nigeria, and educated at Hastings Elementary School,
Sierra Leone, the CMS Grammar School, Freetown, Fourah
Bay College, Freetown, and the London School of Divinity,
England. From 1937 to 1946 Moses Scott served as a school-
teacher and a missionary in a number of stations in Sierra
Leone. In 1943 he was ordained deacon and in 1945 a priest.
He worked in various parts of the provinces, including Bulom,
Makeni and Bo, where in 1958 he was appointed as archdeacon.

In November 1961 the Rev. Scott was consecrated the twelfth
bishop of Sierra Leone, thereby becoming the first African and
the first Sierra Leonean diocesan bishop. On July 1, 1969, he
became archbishop of the Anglican Province of West Africa,
the first African to hold that high office. Bishop Scott founded
a number of organizations in the Sierra Leone diocese, including
the Diocesan Youth Fellowship, the Diocesan Youth Chaplain,
and the Diocesan Sunday Schools Association.

SEPPEH of Bumpe. One of the signatories to the treaty of peace
and friendships with the British on February 6, 1880. He attacked another treaty chief, Gberri of Gbonge (Imperri), an attack which led to the intervention of Mr. Laborde, acting civil
commandant, Sherbro. Won over by Gberri, Laborde persuaded
other signatories to the treaty to join forces against Seppe.
Overwhelmed by such odds, Seppe gave up war for more peaceful and rewarding pursuits in the form of trade.

SERAPHIM DE LEON, 1586-1657. Among a group of 12 Spanish
Capuchins who set out to found a mission on the "mainland of
Guinea" in 1646. Certain Portuguese officials on the Upper
Guinea Coast viewed the venture with suspicion. Within a year
the Spaniards withdrew to South America. Seraphim, pleading
old age and ill health, remained behind in the company of a yet
older monk, Anthony de Jimena. The latter died within months.
Seraphim then made his way to Sierra Leone, where he labored
for nine years. He took up residence at the "Port of Tombo"
on the River Mitombo, today's Sierra Leone River. In 1656 he
retired to Casheu, a parish center in the present-day Guinea
Bissau where he died in the following year. He acquired a
reputation for heroic sanctity; a contemporary missionary described him as "a Seraph in name, in appearance and in purity
of life." Thanks in part to the great esteem in which Fra
Seraphim was held, his appeal for more missionaries brought
to Sierra Leone other Spanish Capuchins at various intervals
up to the end of the 17th century.

SEVENTEEN NATIONS. An organization formed about 1844 at
Waterloo aimed at providing an avenue for the liberated Africans to settle disputes and other problems amicably. During
Christmas Week, 1843, serious disturbances broke out at Waterloo in which Calabar and Ibo fought against the Yoruba. Casualties were high--six killed and 39 wounded. Troops had to be
sent from Freetown to restore order. Separatist feelings and
national or tribal consciousness among the recaptives or liberated Africans had over the years been fostered and accentuated
through voluntary associations, companies and benefit societies,
organized as they were on tribal or national lines. This development culminated in the Waterloo riots of December 1843.
To prevent a repetition of such large-scale disorders it was
decided that the 17 largest "national" groups in Waterloo should
come together in a more clearly defined organization to settle
disputes which might arise between the various national groups.

The Seventeen Nations was specifically devised to enable the various liberated African groups "to carry on with their judicial and political business at a local level." In a number of other villages the Waterloo model of Seventeen Nations was organized. The system developed into a kind of municipal government by which the liberated Africans tried to administer their own province of freedom until the last decades of the 19th century, when by a gradual process of integration the various national groups had virtually disappeared.

SHARP, GRANVILLE, 1735-1813. Philanthropist and abolitionist, member of the British Parliament, and founder of the Province of Freedom in Sierra Leone for the resettlement of free Negro slaves. Sharp was probably the most persistent British champion of the movement for the abolition of the slave trade. In a series of cases he brought before the English courts--Hyla's Case, 1768, Thomas Lewis's Case, 1770, and Somersett's Case, 1772--he got judicial blessing for his anti-slavery activities. Earlier in 1765 he had succeeded in preventing a Mr. John Kerr, a slave owner, from forcibly taking his slave Jonathan Strong back to Jamaica. Lord Chief Justice Mansfield's decision in the case of Somersett was interpreted by Sharp and his fellow abolitionists to mean that "as soon as any slave sets his foot on English ground he becomes free." From the Old Testament and other ancillary sources Sharp developed his theory of retribution, amplified in his Law of Retribution; Or, A Serious Warning to Great Britain and Her Colonies, Founded on Unquestionable Examples of God's Temporal Vengeance Against Tyrants, Slave-holders and Oppressors--a 350-page tract published in 1776. He had by then convinced himself that slavery was an accursed system and had concluded that only by putting an end to slavery and abolishing the slave trade could Great Britain escape destruction. Sharp was most instrumental in founding Sierra Leone as a home for freed slaves and between 1787 and 1791 the settlement, which he fondly referred to as "my poor little ill-thriven Swarthy Daughter, the unfortunate Colony of Sierra Leone," was virtually his property, until the formation of the St. George's Bay (later the Sierra Leone) Company in 1791.

SHAW COMMISSION OF INQUIRY. A Commission of Inquiry appointed on March 8, 1955, by the governor of Sierra Leone, Sir Robert de Zouche Hall "to enquire into the report on the riots and disruptions of public services in Freetown and its environs in February, 1955 and the underlying causes thereof" and "to enquire into and report on the antecedent strike of the Artisans and Allied Workers Union and of the Transport and General Workers Union in February 1955 and the causes thereof; and to make recommendations." The Commissioners were Sir John Shaw, chairman; the Hon. Mr. Justice C. S. Acolatse, member; Mr. G. G. Honeyman, member; and Mr. J. P. L. Scott, secretary. The commissioners held public meetings from March 11 to April 29 and submitted their report on May 7, 1955.

SHEKPENDEH (1957-1967). Newspaper founded in September 1957
by Mr. C. B. Rogers-Wright as the official organ of the UPP.

SHERBRO   see   BULLOM

SHERBRO BE [BEH] of Yoni (also, Gbana Lewis). Overlord of the
whole of Sherbro; grandson of Kong Kuba, king of Sherbro, who
under the name of Benka (or Banka) signed with other chiefs a
treaty on September 24, 1825 (not ratified but later revived)
with Governor Sir Charles Turner, ceding what is known as
Turner's Peninsula to the British. Kong Kuba's grandson who
had assumed the name Gbana (Kpana) Lewis (possibly derived
from the name of a slave-dealer Louis or Lewis who had lived
in the area in the 1850s) became Be Sherbro of Yoni possibly
in the 1870s. On November 18, 1882, Turner's Treaty of 1825
was revived and Be Sherbro was able to secure a stipend from
the British government, claiming it as successor of his grand-
father. In 1896 Be Sherbro as suzerain of Sherbro, presided
over the installation ceremonies of the new Sokong of Imperri.
After the declaration of the Protectorate in 1896, Be Sherbro
with other chiefs traveled to Freetown in February 1897 to protest to Governor Cardew against the Protectorate ordinance.
Cardew, while insisting that the chiefs had to abide by the provisions of the ordinance, assured Be Sherbro that the ordinance
would not affect him, as his territories were already within the
Colony. On his return home Be Sherbro, far from pleased
with the Governor's assurances, organized a boycott of European and Creole trade by means of the poro. Because of these
activities an ordinance was drafted to detain him if and when
necessary. Another ordinance was passed making the use of
poro to prohibit or obstruct trade a criminal offense. When
the Hut Tax War broke out Be Sherbro was believed to be one
of the moving spirits behind the insurrection. He was summoned to Freetown and jailed on arrival in May 1898 without
there having been any charge proved against him. He, along
with Bai Bureh and Nyagua, was deported to the Gold Coast
on July 30, 1899. Be Sherbro was however allowed to return
home in 1905.

SHERBRO MONARCH   see   MACFOY, S. B. A.

SHERI [SERI]. A Mane king described as king of Sierra Leone at
the time of Hawkins' third visit to the West Coast of Africa in
1567-8. Seri appealed to Hawkins for help to dislodge Sasena
and Seterama, two other Mane kings who had fortified themselves at a place called Bonga on the southern tip of the Sierra
Leone Channel. Hawkins agreed subject to certain conditions
and in the ensuing encounter Hawkins lost some of his men
while "there was slaine of the negros ... our frendes Sheri
Bangi the sonne of King Sheri in the assault."
      Although Hawkins claimed that Sheri did not honor his
obligations, another account of these incidents stated that "the
negro kings [Sheri and the king of the Castros, i.e. the River

Cess] Sente him [Hawkins] words that ... they departed but
nevertheless our general showlde sende to the Castros and there
they wold make readye negros for him...." Hawkins did not
undertake the journey to the Cess to collect his captives.

SHERIFF, SALIA JUSU, 1929- . Leader of the opposition, 1968-
   1973. Born June 1, 1929, at Jojoima in the Kailahun District.
   Educated at Bunumbu Central School, Fourah Bay College (University of Durham), and at King's College, Durham University,
   Newcastle-on-Tyne. Sierra Leone's first indigenous chartered
   accountant. Taught at Bo Government School, 1947-1949, and
   joined the cooperative department, 1949-1951. After qualifying
   as a chartered accountant he returned home and rejoined the
   cooperative department in 1960. He resigned from government
   service and set up a firm of chartered accounts. In the general elections of 1962 he was elected to Parliament as member
   for the Kenema South constituency and appointed minister of
   agriculture and natural resources. In 1963 after a cabinet reshuffle he was appointed minister of trade and industry. Between 1964 and 1967 he served first as minister of education
   and later as minister of health. He retained his parliamentary
   seat in the 1967 general election and after the return to civilian
   rule in 1968 was appointed minister of health in a national government. He resigned his cabinet post and returned to his
   practice as accountant. He was detained under the emergency
   regulations in 1968. He later lost his seat in Parliament after
   an election petition. In the subsequent bye-elections he was returned member of Parliament for Kenema South and became official leader of the opposition in Parliament, until 1973 when he
   and his party, the SLPP, withdrew from the general elections
   held that year.

SHORUNKEH-SAWYERR, A. J., 1861-1929. Bookseller, printer,
   journalist and lawyer, Member of the Legislative Council (1911-
   1924). He changed his name from A. J. Sawyerr to A. J.
   Shorunkeh-Sawyerr following a practice which became fashionable in Freetown circles in the 1880s of adopting African names.
   On August 6, 1885, at one of the meetings of the Sierra Leone
   Association (founded in 1885), Samuel Lewis read a paper in
   which he strongly urged that the hinterland be annexed by purchase as a protectorate. On about August 13 members of the
   Association met to discuss its merits. All except A. J.
   Shorunkeh-Sawyerr accepted Lewis' analysis and proposals.

SIAKA, King of Gendama. King of Gendama, Gallinas country, in
   the early 19th century, and head of the Massaquoi family,
   Siaka sold slaves to French ships operating in the Gallinas
   estuary, through an elaborate system of contracts and sub-
   contracts and made effective use of European employees and
   his own sub-chiefs in the operations. Among King Siaka's best-
   known agents was a Spaniard, Pedro Blanco, resident in the
   Gallinas since 1827 and who on retirement was reputed to be a
   millionaire. These activities of King Siaka led to a blockade

of the Gallinas by Acting Governor Kenneth Macaulay in 1826.
But Sir Neil Campbell, governor in 1826-27, lifted the blockade,
made friends with King Siaka, and sent him a sword and a silver medal as presents. Secured in his well-fortified town of
Gendama, Siaka and his sons lived comfortably in well-furnished
European-style houses. When he died in the late 1840s Siaka
was succeeded by his son, Prince Mana.

SIBTHORPE, A. B. C. (also, Aucandu, prince of Cuccuruku,
Niger), 1829/30?-1916. Educator, historian, geographer,
artist and naturalist. The first Sierra Leonean to produce a
history of the country. Sibthorpe's The History of Sierra Leone,
first published in 1868, has gone through four subsequent edi-
tions (the latest in 1970). It was used as a school textbook
until in about 1886 its use was discontinued largely because of
the author's increasing personal portrayals of himself in the
pages. In addition to the History, Sibthorpe was also author
of a Geography of Sierra Leone (1881).
    A man of many parts he was a naturalist and an artist
(painting and sculpture). He studied herbs, compounded medicines and was a kind of nonprofessional or amateur medical
practitioner. He made incursions into the fields of phrenology,
photography and geology. He sent samples of his geological
and botanical specimens as well as of his paintings to local
and international exhibitions. Sibthorpe, whose origins are
somewhat obscure, was probably a receptive or liberated African from Eastern Nigeria, possibly an Ibo. He attended the
CMS Grammar School, where he enrolled as a pupil on June
21, 1852. He was also a student at the CMS Institution or
College at Fourah Bay. After Fourah Bay he taught at the
CMS Normal Industrial School at Kissy, at Christ Church
School, Pademba Road, Freetown, and at Hastings and Grafton
schools. Sibthorpe died on June 20, 1916, and was buried at
Kissy Village Cemetery.

SIERRA LEONE, REPUBLIC OF, IN BRIEF. Area 27,925 square
miles; population 3.5 million (1974 census). Sierra Leone is
bounded by Guinea to the northwest, north and northeast, and
by Liberia to the east and southeast; capital, Freetown. Formerly a British Colony administered by a chartered Company
(1787-1807) and by the Crown (1808-1961). In 1961 Sierra
Leone became an independent state within the Commonwealth
with a governor-general (representing the British monarch), a
prime minister and a House of Representatives, or Parliament,
elected by universal adult suffrage, except for 12 paramount
chief members, elected by fellow chiefs and chiefdom councilors. In 1971 Sierra Leone adopted a republican form of government. The country is divided into the following administrative areas: Western Area, 256 sq. mi.; Northern Province,
13,925 sq. mi.: Southern Province, 7,868 sq. mi.; and Eastern Province, 5,876 sq. mi. The three provinces are subdivided into districts and the districts into chiefdoms. Agricultural crops include cocoa, coffee, ginger, groundnuts, kola

nuts, palm oil, palm kernels, and rice; the major export is
diamonds. In 1965 Sierra Leone became a signatory to a free
trade agreement with Guinea, Ivory Coast and Liberia, which
did not work as expected. In 1973 Sierra Leone and Liberia
signed the Mano River Union, which makes provision for cooperation in various fields between the two countries.

THE SIERRA LEONE CHURCH TIMES (1884-1886). A newspaper
published under the auspices of the Anglicans and printed on
the CMS Grammar School press.

THE SIERRA LEONE DAILY MAIL (1933-   ). A newspaper founded
in January 1933 and incorporating the West African Mail and
Trade Gazette.

THE SIERRA LEONE FARM AND TRADE REPORT (1886-1887).
A commercial newspaper that also printed general news items,
founded by H. J. Pearce of Little East Street.

SIERRA LEONE FRONTIER POLICE FORCE ["Frontiers"]. By the
1880s both France and Britain had conveniently demarcated, if
somewhat vaguely, their respective spheres of influence in the
areas now covered by the republic of Guinea and of Sierra
Leone. For the British the pursuit of this vigorous policy in
the interior aimed at ensuring peace and stability and at the
protection of trade routes presupposed a military presence and
an effective and organized system of policing the area. Accordingly, on January 15, 1890, the Legislative Council of
Sierra Leone passed an ordinance establishing the Frontier Police Force for service within and outside the Colony. At its
inception the authorized strength of the force was one inspector-
general, three inspectors, four native sub-inspectors, and 280
noncommissioned officers and men. Col. Gerald Fairtlough,
R.A., deputed to raise the new force, embarked on recruitment on May 1, 1890. The Frontier Force was recruited from
practically all tribes and communities in Sierra Leone, and its
hinterland; its efficiency and high standards were further enhanced by the transfer into the new force of some of the most
experienced and able members of the existing civil police force.
In essence the Frontier Police were a paramilitary force.
The first inspector-general was Maj. Alexander C. McDonell
Moore of the Irish Fusiliers who had been and was still in
command of the old police force.
        The uniform was of simple and functional design, con-
sisting of a blue serge tunic and trousers, red fez, and blue
cummerbund, and black leather belts. A snider rifle and
sword a rolled blanket and a haversack completed the equipment. The training of the new force was thorough. Selected
NCOs were sent to Britain to Hythe and to the Guards School
of Instruction at Chelsea. Detachments were stationed over
the protected area, called the "Protectorate" even before 1896--
particularly along the boundaries. In addition to their military functions, the Frontiers were expected to help and advise

chiefs, to keep order, to prevent outbreaks of hostilities, and
to insure and maintain peace. They were not to behave as
rulers or to administer justice or to interfere in any way with
the powers of the chiefs.

By 1893 however barely three years after its formation,
J. C. E. Parkes, superintendent, Department of Native Affairs,
in a July 28 memorandum to the colonial secretary complained
that "during the past few months no less than four serious
charges have been brought against sub-officers of important stations of insulting the chiefs, in one case handcuffing one, and
keeping him in custody for a considerable period, flogging their
people and in other ways taking advantage of them...." Parkes'
views, if in essence factual, were perhaps in detail somewhat
jaundiced, largely because the creation and existence of the
Frontier Force were not in strict conformity with his own plans
for the administration of the proposed protectorate. Nevertheless the fact remains that in many places the Frontiers ignored
their instructions and exceeded their powers and their excesses
contributed in no small measure to the causes of the outbreak
of the Hut Tax War in 1898. In other respects the Frontiers
served the Colonial administration quite admirably, at times
with distinction not only in Sierra Leone but as far afield as
the Gold Coast as they did in the Ashanti Campaign of 1900.

In June 1902 the Sierra Leone Battalion of the West
African Frontier Force (later Royal West African Frontier
Force) came into being. This in effect brought an end to the
Frontier Police Force. Thereafter the titles of inspector-
general, inspector, etc., were abolished, military rank was
given to all officers, and the rank and file resworn.

SIERRA LEONE INDEPENDENCE MOVEMENT [SLIM]. Founded in
November 1956 by Edward Wilmot Blyden III. Blyden, a graduate of Lincoln, Yale, and Harvard universities in the USA and
a member of the Fourah Bay University College Staff, had run
into difficulties at the college and had been involved in a protracted law suit with the college authorities. Deprived of his
post as extramural tutor he launched a political party. The
party, Sierra Leone Independence Movement, was anti-colonial
rather than national, more visionary than practical, and clearly
enjoyed--perhaps even preferred--verbal to active politics. It
chose to call itself a movement because it believed party politics either irrelevant or dangerous or both in a colonial territory. It had strong criticisms for what it regarded as the in-
eptitude of the SLPP and violently denounced what it considered
to be the hobnobbing of the party's leadership with colonialists.
SLIM's invective was particularly directed against the governor
and the colonial administrative hierarchy. It did however put
much emphasis on education and launched a national school
(which did not survive the party). The party attracted mostly
young people--senior secondary school pupils and college stu-
dents--and adopted a tricolor flag of black, red, and green.
In the general election of 1957 SLIM's performance was disappointing. Its four candidates lost their deposits, and there-

after the party merged with another political group, the Kono
Progressive Movement, to form the Sierra Leone Progressive
Independence Movement.

THE SIERRA LEONE JOURNAL. A short-lived newspaper owned by
William Rainny and published in London in about 1865.

SIERRA LEONE LABOUR PARTY. Formed in 1955 in the wake of
the industrial strike in Freetown by Marcus Grant, the most
effective trade union leader at the time and the mastermind behind the 1955 strike. The Labour Party chose as its president
Ronald Beoku Betts, described as an "earnest man of mildly
Fabian views," a lawyer who had appeared as one of the coun-
sels for the union before the Shaw Commission of Inquiry into
the causes of the strike. Grant himself assumed the position
of joint national secretary with Mr. Bankole Sawyerr. The
Labour Party relied on the trade unions for support, but the
unions in Sierra Leone were nonpolitical and their members
were free to belong to any political party that appealed to them.
Although the party was non-Creole, since such members as it
had were largely drawn from Protectorate immigrants into
Freetown, it was a Freetown or Colony party. It had virtually
no attraction for workers in the Protectorate and its attempts
to woo them were far from effective. In the 1957 general election Labour's six candidates, all in the Colony, lost their deposits and thereafter the party gradually disappeared from the
political scene.

THE SIERRA LEONE MESSENGER. Newspaper founded by the CMS
in 1893 for circulation in England to popularize the activities
of the Society.

THE SIERRA LEONE OBSERVER. Newspaper founded in 1949 and
published in Bo and edited by Mr. A. B. Cotay.

SIERRA LEONE ORGANISATION SOCIETY [SOS]. Formed in 1946
ostensibly as an educational and improvement association, the
SOS was in fact a pressure group aimed at providing a base
for the fulfillment of the political aspirations of the Protectorate
elite. The founding members included Dr. John Karefa-Smart,
D. J. Manley, S. P. Stevens, D. L. Sumner, R. B. Kowa,
T. M. Williams and F. S. Anthony. PC Julius Gulama, the
only paramount chief member, was honorary president. It
sponsored "a programme of self development aimed at raising
the standard of living in the country in all its aspects...."
Its political goal was "to tackle ... political subjugation and
discover our hidden resources ... and use them to lay down in
our generation the foundation stones of a united progressive
economically developed and free Sierra Leone." The SOS was
bitterly opposed to the predominant role granted by the Colonial
administration to chiefs in matters pertaining to the Protectorate. The system of local government devised in the post-
World War II period (introducing district councils and a Pro-

tectorate Assembly) as well as provisions for Protectorate representation in the reconstituted central legislature all tended to enhance and buttress the influence and position of chiefs at the expense of the Protectorate-educated elite.

The SOS, in protest against these trends, addressed memoranda to the secretary of state for the Colonies. In the memorandum to the British government in 1947 the SOS rejected "the suggestion ... to confine Protectorate representation [in the reconstituted Legislative Council] to members of the Protectorate Assembly" on the grounds that such a procedure "does not give the franchise to the common people of the Protectorate who are taxpayers and are entitled to even more representation ... than the natural rulers of the country.... That the suggestion under consideration denies the franchise to the literate class of Protectorate people some of whom have had opportunity for higher education...." In another memorandum of November 1948 the SOS accused the Colonial government of deliberately ignoring the Protectorate-educated elite and strongly objected to "the present monopoly over Protectorate representation which chiefs had in the District Councils, the Protectorate Assembly, the Legislative Council and the Executive Council" and recommended "the inclusion of the new progressive and literate element into the membership of the new Legislative Council...."

As the debates between Colony and Protectorate on the implementation of the 1947 proposed constitution gained momentum, the SOS abandoned its seemingly anti-chief stance, thanks to the efforts of Dr. Margai and PC Gulama, adopted a more conciliatory attitude, and threw in its lot with other political groups to form the SLPP in 1951. The Freetown Branch of the SOS in July 1950 adopted a resolution, which after noting that agreement between the Colony and Protectorate was "most unlikely" over constitutional arrangements, asked for the immediate implementation of the projected 1947 constitution. It was resolved "that the British government be called upon forthwith to implement the said Stevenson proposals ... so as to enable the people of the Protectorate to have a say in the management of their affairs and thus end the shameful and undemocratic policy of taxation without representation."

SIERRA LEONE PEOPLE'S PARTY [SLPP]. Founded in April 1951, the outcome of a merger of three political groups; the People's Party (PP), the Protectorate Educational Progressive Union (PEPU), and the Sierra Leone Organisation Society (SOS). The SLPP had as its motto, "One Country One People," as its symbol, the palm tree, and its party colors, bright green. At the time of its inception the following were the office holders and leaders of the party: leader and president, Milton Margai; deputy leader and deputy president, PC Bai Farama Tass II of Kambia; 1st vice president, A. J. Momoh; 2nd vice president, Lamina Sankoh (formerly the Rev. E. N. Jones); national treasurer, Kande Bureh; and national general secretary, H. E. B. John; other leaders included Albert Margai, A. G. Randle, S. P. Stevens and M. S. Mustapha.

The SLPP came into being partly in response to the constitutional developments of the post-World War II era and partly
to represent in more articulate form the mute aspirations of the
Protectorate peoples. In spite of its claims to being a national party,
transcending regional and tribal divisions, and although it had some
Creoles in its hierarchy and among its ranks, it was in a sense
a challenge to Creole dominance and to Creole pretensions.
The bulk of its leadership was recruited from descendants of
traditional ruling families, although as a political party it did
cultivate mass following. But there was always a clear distinction between members and followers. The SLPP was in fact a
patron party, composed of various groups held together in a
somewhat loose association. If it did cultivate the support of the
masses, it rarely mobilized mass following and as a rule es-
chewed mob violence. In the circumstances the party and its
leadership were essentially conservative, an exceptional trend
in third world politics. The party adopted a gradualist approach
to the problems of nation-building, preferring peaceful compromise to open confrontation, bargaining to diktat.
        Because of its ability to accommodate the diversity of
interests within its ranks and since in itself it represented the
variety of interests in the country as a whole, the SLPP was
able for some 15 years to maintain political stability. Committed in principle to the observance of the rule of law, the
SLPP leaders fostered competitive party politics in Sierra Leone
to a degree unparalleled elsewhere in Black Africa. There
were of course aberrations, but these were exceptional. In the
end the party permitted itself to be voted out of power. The
SLPP was in power in Sierra Leone from 1951 to 1967. In the
process it led the country to independence in 1961. It lost its
first leader, Sir Milton Margai, who died in April 1964. Its
second leader, Sir Albert Margai, lost his party and lost power
after the general elections in 1967. Between 1968 and 1973, a
handful of SLPP members of Parliament heroically played the
difficult, if not dangerous, role of official opposition. In 1973
the SLPP, like other opposition parties or groups in Sierra
Leone, was sent off the political stage.

SIERRA LEONE POLICE FORCE. The Sierra Leone Police Force
    owes its origins to the appointment in 1810 of constables in the
    wards of Freetown. By 1826 the number of constables was 26
    and a permanent head constable, Aberdeen Turner, was put in
    charge of the constabulary force, half of whom performed
    duties as a night guard. Governor C. Temple between 1833
    and 1834 provided the night guard with an inspector. Under
    Governor H. D. Campbell, the constables, now called "police,"
    were increased to 60, armed with staves, and offered free
    shoes--but were still without uniforms. Campbell also ap-
    pointed three sub-inspectors under Turner. By 1857 during
    Governor N. W. Macdonald's term of office, the Police Force
    numbered 100 and were provided with uniforms. A police
    ordinance of the same year prohibited the public worship of
    idols and made public appearance without adequate and decent

clothing an offense. In spite of Macdonald's reforms, the performance and appearance of the police force were still unsatisfactory. Governor Kennedy between 1852 and 1854 appointed a
military officer to supervise the force. The men were taught
to use firearms, new uniforms were provided free of charge,
and discipline and morale were considerably improved. The
constables in the villages, till then under orders of managers,
were incorporated into the Freetown Police Force, with a sergeant in charge of each rural police district. In 1861 the force
was reorganized, an army officer was appointed inspector-general, and the men were armed with short carbines.

In 1887 the Force was further enlarged. Between 1887
and 1888 Col. Sir Francis de Winton proposed that the force be
divided and specialized between civilian policing and paramilitary functions to increase efficiency. In addition he recommended that the force, till then a predominantly Creole body,
be recruited from other groups--Mende, Temne, et al. In
1890 the division took place and the Frontier Police, an essentially paramilitary force, was formed. In 1923, police barracks were established in King Tom, Freetown, the first in the
country. During World War II frequent clashes between the
civil population and the armed forces necessitated the organization of a "riot squad" in 1943/44, a highly mobile police unit
dressed in dark brown shirts and trousers and armed with clubs
and shields to deal with outbreaks of violence. In 1954 the
Police Force of the Colony was formally extended into the then
Protectorate, where a court messengers' force attached to district headquarters had performed police and other duties. After
the war a Police Training School was established and subsequently situated at Hastings to train recruits. The Sierra
Leone Police Force, under a commissioner of police, who now
holds cabinet rank in the government, today consists of five
divisions, each subdivided into police districts. There are in
addition a Traffic Section, a Harbour and Immigration Section,
and an Internal Security Unit (ISU). A female branch of the
force, which arose out of the need to guard and care for female prisoners, now numbers a few hundreds and performs all
police duties.

SIERRA LEONE PROGRESSIVE INDEPENDENCE MOVEMENT
[SLPIM]. Formed in September 1959 as a result of a merger
between T. S. Mbriwa's KPM and E. W. Blyden's SLIM. The
merger was made possible through the very close personal ties
between the two leaders (they had grown up together and regarded each other as "brothers") and was dictated by Mbriwa's
desire to broaden the base of support and political activity of
KPM, as well as Blyden's need for political survival. Mbriwa
became president of SLPIM and all SLIM members were asked
to register as members of the new movement. In March 1965
after his recall from exile by the new prime minister, Sir
Albert Margai, Mbriwa announced the dissolution of SLPIM
and declared his membership of the SLPP.

THE SIERRA LEONE RAM. A periodical pamphlet in newspaper
form published by A. J. Sawyerr (later Shorunkeh-Sawyerr) in
1886.

THE SIERRA LEONE SPECTATOR AND WEST AFRICAN INTEL-
LIGENCER. A short-lived newspaper published by Francis
Drape (brother of William Drape) in 1858 in place of The New
Era.

THE SIERRA LEONE TIMES (1890-1912). Newspaper founded in
1890 by the Sierra Leone Printing and Publishing Company and
edited by J. A. Fitzjohn, who also contributed to a special
column entitled "One Thing and Another."

THE SIERRA LEONE WATCHMAN (1842-1846). The first private
newspaper in Sierra Leone founded in 1842 by the Rev. Thomas
Dove of the Methodist mission and printed on the mission press.

THE SIERRA LEONE WEEKLY NEWS (1884-1951). A newspaper
founded and first published on September 6, 1884, by the Rev.
C. May, principal of the Wesleyan Boys High School. The
Weekly News was Sierra Leone's longest-lived newspaper.

SIGNIOR DOMINGO of Royema. Chief of Royema East of Granville
Town II. One of the first local chieftains to send a son to
England to be educated after the establishment of the Sierra
Leone Colony. The son, Antony, returned home and was employed in the accountant's office during Zachary Macaulay's
second term of office as governor. In the final settlement of
boundaries between the Temne and the Colony in July 1807,
Signior Domingo's territories East of Freetown were "ceded"
in return for compensation--to the Colony. Signior Domingo
died later in the year.

SIGNIOR JOSEPH. Originally lived in America but went to School
in England; traveled afterwards to Portugal, where he embraced
Catholicism and took the name of Signior Joseph. Described
traditionally as the first African missionary in Sierra Leone,
Signior Joseph arrived in Freetown in about 1715. He built a
village on the site later occupied by Granville Town, fell out
with his neighbors and quarreled with the English pirate Capt.
Cocklyn, who in 1718 seized his sloop and held him to ransom.
Signior Joseph moved to the site of present Kissy Village where
on April 7, 1721, Surgeon John Atkins, R.N., called on him.
Atkins described him as "a generous and good natured Christian Negro, who had lately removed with his people some miles
up the River. With his old buildings we wooded our ship."
After a long life, tradition has it that Signior Joseph died on
the Banana Islands and was buried in Dublin Village.

SIMERA, Bai. Successive holders of title in the Masimera Chiefdom, Port Loko district. The chiefdom was amalgamated with
Marampa in the 1940s and is now known as Marampa Masimera.

In 1895 under the leadership of Bai Simera, disturbances broke out in Temne country--a continuation of wars which the Yoni started since the 1850s. Lt. Boileau was sent with a small detachment to pacify the area. The disturbances were suppressed with relative ease and a drum (now hanging in the officers' mess at Wilberforce barracks) seized. Fines were imposed on the Masimera and Marampa areas and the Bai Simera was kept in custody until they were paid. When the Hut Tax War broke out in 1898 the Bai Simera was again captured and imprisoned at Kwelu.

SINKER/MOMOH COMMISSION (or Commission on the Civil Service of Sierra Leone), 1952-53. A commission appointed in November 1952 to review and to make recommendations upon the structure, remuneration and conditions of services of the Sierra Leone Civil Service." The report was submitted by the two commissioners, A. P. Sinker and A. J. Momoh, on February 25, 1953.

SINTRA see CINTRA, PEDRO DA

SLATER, Sir ALEXANDER RANSFORD. Governor of Sierra Leone, 1922-1927. After serving as colonial secretary of the Gold Coast, Slater assumed the reins of government in Sierra Leone in May 1922. During Slater's term of office a new constitution was introduced, the first major constitutional development in the Colony since 1863. The 1924, or Slater, Constitution made provision for the first ever elected unofficials (three in number) of the Legislative Council. It also made provision for 11 official members and seven nominated unofficials. Of the seven nominated unofficials, three were paramount chiefs, representing Protectorate interests for the first time in the Colony's legislature. Of the ten unofficials, six were Africans, the three paramount chiefs and the three elected members representing the Protectorate and the Colony respectively.

After the railway strike in 1926, Governor Slater in a dispatch dated April 20, 1926, to the Rt. Hon. L. S. Amery, secretary of state for the Colonies, advocated the deliberate deceleration of the pace of Africanization in all aspects of the Colony's government. After examining and rejecting suggestions for ousting elected members from the Legislative Council, the Governor went on "... I consider that the more dignified course for the Government to adopt is ... to refuse to let that deplorable exhibition of political perversity deflect us ... from our course of seeking patiently to educate public opinion by the means deliberately adopted in 1922. At the same time ... the events of the last four months have supplied Government with abundant reasons for proceeding at a much slower pace with Africanization of the Service and for tightening up control generally by legislative and other measures, while they obviously afford unanswerable arguments against any requests for further constitutional development in the present generation. Already one of the newspapers ... is clamouring for a House of As-

sembly with unofficial control of the purse strings. Even if
the community had behaved with consistently exemplary cor-
rectness during the last few years, such a claim would of
course be preposterous. I have always made it absolutely
clear that there can be no question for many years of conceding
the smallest modicum of self-government--but the 'strike attitude' of so large a proportion of the educated community has
furnished us with an additional and crushing reason for uncompromising rejection of such a demand." Slater retired from
the governorship of Sierra Leone in 1927.

SMART, CHARLES. A member of the Loko Smart family of Mahera. The Smarts were vassals of the Koya Kings who had
originally permitted them to live at Mahera. In the early
1890s, Charles Smart, a young man determined to break away
from the tutelage of the Koya Kings--for long a family ambi-
tion--asked Bai Kompa of Koya to elevate him to the rank and
dignity of chief. When Bai Kompa refused, Smart, previously
educated in Freetown, joined the Frontier Police, subsequently
had himself crowned chief and obtained official recognition.
This was a serious usurpation of the rights of the Koya kings,
an affront to their sovereignty, and a breach of treaty provisions. Thereafter Smart made himself a willing instrument of
British policy and a constant embarrassment to the Koya traditional ruling hierarchy. He was chief prosecution witness
against Pa Naimbana of Ronietta in 1898. He supplied the
British with information about Bai Kompa's alleged anti-tax
activities and joined the British expedition in Ronietta during
the Hut Tax War.

SMART, H. M. JOKO, 1935- . Educator, lawyer and author.
Born on June 26, 1935. Educated at St. Patrick's School,
Bonth, St. Edward's Secondary School, Freetown, Fourah Bay
College (University of Durham), Freetown, Sheffield Univer-
sity, England, Gray's Inn, London, and London University.
Senior lecturer in law, Fourah Bay College (U.S.L.), and
author of several articles on international law and the legal
system of Sierra Leone.

SMART, N. D. J., 1925- . Born on January 8, 1925. Educated at the Government Model School, the CMS Grammar
School, St. Edward's Secondary School, St. Andrew's University, Scotland, the University of Manchester, and the University of London. Associate professor and head, Department of
Education, Fourah Bay College (USL), and one of Sierra
Leone's best-known educationists. First honorary secretary,
Sierra Leone Secondary Teachers Association (subsequently
merged into ATO). Senior Lecturer in English, 1965-68,
acting head, Department of English, 1966, and dean, Faculty
of Arts, 1966-1968, Fourah Bay College (University of Durham). Member of the Editorial Board, West African Journal
of Education, and editor, Sierra Leone Journal of Education,
since 1972. Since 1975, president of the Association for

Teacher Education in Africa (ACTEA), editor and author of
several books and articles.

SMEATHMAN, HENRY. An amateur botanist who between 1771 and
1774 lived on Banana Islands of Sierra Leone collecting specimens for Sir Joseph Banks at Kew Gardens. It was on the
basis of Smeathman's recommendations and of his scheme for
a plantation culture in West Africa that Sierra Leone was chosen
by British philanthropists as a settlement for freed slaves. He
was in fact put in charge of the expedition which was to set out
in late 1786, but he died before the final arrangements were
made. In 1786 Smeathman published his Plan of Settlement to
be made near Sierra Leone on the Grain Coast of Africa, intended more particularly for the service and happy establishment of Blacks and People of Colour, to be shipped as freemen
under the direction of the Committee for Relieving the Black
Poor, and under the protection of the British Government.

SMITH, the Rt. Rev. JOHN TAYLOR, 1860-1938. Canon of St.
George's Cathedral, Freetown, 1890-7; bishop of Sierra Leone,
1897-1901. Appointed a canon of St. George's Cathedral by
Bishop Ingham, the Rev. Smith arrived in Sierra Leone in 1890
with the title "canon missioner." Canon Smith accompanied
Cardew on the Governor's second tour of the hinterland at the
end of January 1895 and later in the year served as chaplain to
the Ashanti expedition. Prince Henry of Battenberg, a grandson of Queen Victoria, on board ship with Canon Smith during
the passage to the Gold Coast, died at sea and the Canon took
the dying man's message to the bereaved royal family. The
Queen made him honorary royal chaplain and in Freetown he
raised funds to build Battenberg Hall in memory of the prince.
     In 1897 Canon Smith was consecrated bishop of Sierra
Leone. He immediately put an end to the unhappy divisions
within the Anglican Church in the Colony caused by the Five
Pastors Case and gave appointments to two of the recalcitrant
pastors, the Rev. Moses Pearce, canon, and the Rev. G. J.
Macaulay, archdeacon. On November 4, 1898, with the revo-
cation of the letters patent of May 22, 1852, and with the
enactment by the Sierra Leone Legislative Council of an act to
incorporate the Cathedral Church of St. George, Freetown, and
to vest the Cathedral in a chapter, the Anglican Church in
Sierra Leone was disestablished. Smith, the first bishop of
the disestablished church, approved of the measure and welcomed it as making the Sierra Leone Church the truly independent institution it had long purported to be. In addition to
raising funds for Battenberg Hall, Bishop Smith rebuilt Bishopscourt and started but left unfinished repairs to the Cathedral.
A champion of Governor Cardew's policies, and a strict but
tactful administrator, Smith introduced a number of changes
at the Cathedral. He returned to England in 1901 and was
appointed chaplain-general of the forces. In 1928 he returned
to Sierra Leone to preach the sermon at the centenary service
at St. George's Cathedral, Freetown.

SMYTHE, JOHN HENRY CLAVELL, Q. C.   Educated at the Government Model School and at the CMS Grammar School, Freetown.
Worked for the Freetown City Council and for the Sierra Leone
Government.   Joined the Sierra Leone Defence Corps and was
commissioned as a bomber pilot officer in the Royal Air Force
in 1943.   Captured and imprisoned in East Germany, he was
released by the Russians at the war's end.   Returned to Britain
and worked at the Colonial Office as liaison officer between
colonial forces in the United Kingdom and the British government.   In July 1947 he enrolled at the Middle Temple Inns of
Court to study law.   Called to the Bar in January 1951.   Returned to Sierra Leone and established private practice in the
same year.   Later in the year he took up appointment in the
law office as Crown counsel.   Awarded the M. B. E. , military
division (1951).   Promoted senior Crown counsel in 1957 and
solicitor-general in 1961 and acted on a number of occasions as
attorney-general.   Retired from government service in 1963 and
went back into private practice.   Appointed chairman, Committee
of Management, Freetown City Council, 1967, and in July 1969
he became the second queen's counsel in Sierra Leone.

SOFA EXPEDITION   see   MILITARY EXPEDITIONS (12)

SOKONG of Imperri.   Successive holders of title in the Imperri
Chiefdom.   One Sokong was elected in 1896 to succeed the last
Sokong who had died in 1870.   T. J. Alldridge, in his A Transformed Colony; Sierra Leone, Chapter 28, "The Making of a
Bai Sherbro and of a Sokong of Imperri," described the 1896
coronation ceremony and photographed the new Sokong surrounded by sub-chiefs and elders.   The new Sokong was hanged
probably at Bonthe along with other leading chiefs accused of
organizing resistance to the hut tax.

STANDARD BANK OF SIERRA LEONE LTD.   First established in
Freetown in 1894 as Bank of British West Africa (BBWA) Ltd.
On July 1, 1957, the Bank was renamed Bank of West Africa
(BWA) Ltd. and on August 24, 1966, as a result of another
change of name, it became known as Standard Bank of West
Africa (SBWA) Ltd.   The Standard Bank of Sierra Leone Ltd.
was incorporated in Sierra Leone on March 18, 1971, and it
acquired the assets and liabilities of the Standard Bank of West
Africa Ltd. in Sierra Leone.

STEVENS, SIAKA PROBYN, 1905-   .   President of Sierra Leone,
1971 to the present.   Born on August 24, 1905, at Moyamba,
Southern Province.   Educated at the Albert Academy, Freetown, and at Ruskin College, Oxford, where he studied trade
unionism.   On leaving school Stevens joined the Sierra Leone
Police Force and rose to the rank of first class sergeant and
musketry instructor.   From 1931 to 1946 he worked on the construction of the Delco (Sierra Leone Development Company) railway, linking the port of Pepel with the iron ore mines at Marampa.   He later became stationmaster and stenographer at

Marampa. A cofounder of the United Mine Workers Union, he
was appointed to the Protectorate Assembly in 1946 to represent the interests of workers. Elected to the Legislative Council in 1951 as second Protectorate member, he was appointed in
1952 as Sierra Leone's first minister of lands, mines and labour. In 1957 he was elected to the House of Representatives
as member for Port Loko East constituency but lost his seat as
a result of an election petition. A member of the PNP, he became its first secretary-general and later its deputy leader.

In 1960 after refusing to be a signatory to the defense
agreements with Britain at the London independence constitutional talks, he returned home and formed the "Elections before independence movement" which later became the APC. In
the 1962 general elections he was returned to Parliament as
member for Freetown West II constituency. In 1964 he was
elected mayor of Freetown and he served the municipality in
that capacity for just about a year. He retained his Freetown
West II constituency seat in the 1967 general elections, after
which he was appointed prime minister. Detained for a few
days by the military regime and deprived of his premiership,
he was reappointed prime minister in 1968 following the overthrow of the NRC. In 1971 he became president of the Republic
of Sierra Leone.

STEVENSON, Sir HUBERT. Governor of Sierra Leone, 1941-1948.
Appointed governor in 1941, Stevenson's tenure witnessed Sierra
Leone's first moves towards self-government. The post-World
War II constitutional changes introduced into British West Africa
affected Sierra Leone and Stevenson was entrusted with the task
of making the necessary proposals for constitutional change in
the country. In 1946, quasi-representative institutions in the
form of district councils and a Protectorate Assembly were introduced into the Protectorate. On October 13, 1947, after
consultations with members of the Legislative Council, the Protectorate Assembly and leading public figures, Sir Hubert submitted his proposals for constitutional change in Sierra Leone
to the secretary of state for the Colonies.

The two salient features of Stevenson's Constitution
were an unofficial African majority in the Legislative Council
and a majority of seats for the Protectorate. The projected
Legislative Council was to consist of 23 members. Of these
seven were officials, two were unofficials nominated by the
governor to represent business interests, four were directly
elected to represent the Colony, and ten were elected by the
Protectorate Assembly from among its own members. Nine of
the Protectorate representatives were to be chosen from among
elected district council members, and one from among the African nominated members. In effect, nine Protectorate members
were to be elected through an indirect process from tribal authority to district council, to Protectorate Assembly to Legislative Council. This process clearly gave paramount chiefs
considerable control, if not a monopoly, of Protectorate representation and evoked the criticism that Protectorate members

were to come to the Legislature through the back door.
  The governor also recommended that for at least the
first three years members of the Legislative Council need not
be literate in English. This proviso was attacked by both
Colony and Protectorate spokesmen, the latter viewing it as a
cynical and sinister move by the Governor to keep the educated
Protectorate elite out of the legislature. Debates over the
Stevenson proposals were heated and protracted. The scheme
was delayed for another four years and finally adopted in modified form in 1951. Sir Hubert had departed from Sierra Leone
in 1948.

SULUKU, (SOLUKU) Chief of Bumban, ca. 1820-1906. In the 1880s,
  Chief Suluku ruled over the Biriwa Limba with headquarters at
  Bumban. He was an uneasy ally of the Sofas, whom he did not
  fully trust; he therefore made overtures to the British, with
  whom he signed a treaty of friendship on February 4, 1888.
  When the Hut Tax War broke out in 1898, Suluku, at the outset
  reported hostile to the British, offered his services as mediator between Bai Bureh and the British. In Koinadugu District
  the 1898 rising made little progress because of the loyalty of
  Chief Suluku to the British government.

SUMNER, D. L., 1907- . Educator, politician and author. Born
  on February 19, 1907, at Shenge, Kagboro Chiefdom, Moyamba
  District. Educated at the Albert Academy, Freetown, and at
  Lincoln University, USA. Founding member and president of
  the Amalgamated Teachers Organisation, 1948-1957. Formerly
  lecturer at Union College, Bunumbu, and education secretary,
  Eastern Province. Author of Education in Sierra Leone (1963).
  Elected member of Parliament for Kenema East constituency in
  1957 and between 1957 and 1967 appointed minister of communication, minister of health and minister of trade and industry.

SUPHULO. Bullom King of Baga on the Rokelle in the 1720s. His
  relationships with Don José Lopez de Moura were strained. In
  1728 he took sides with Walter Charles, the Royal African
  Company's chief agent in Sierra Leone, in a quarrel between
  Charles and the mulattoes and in particular Lopez. When the
  Company lost face in the ensuing encounter and wound up its
  business, Suphulo found himself in an untenable position deprived of the support of his ally and at the mercy of his great
  adversary. He was compelled in the circumstances not only to
  eat his own words but with cruel contempt to eat food placed
  at the feet of Lopez--a gesture which pronounced and reinforced
  the incontestable dominance of the Afro-Portuguese at the time.

SUSU AND YALUNKA. The bulk of the Susu (also, Soussou or
  Soosoo) people are to be found in Guinea, where they constitute
  one of the oldest tribal groups. In Sierra Leone they are confined to five chiefdoms, and parts of two others. It has been
  suggested that the Susu and Yalunka are a branch of the same
  people, the names signifying little more than a geographical

distinction. In Sierra Leone the Susu and Yalunka occupy parts
of Kambia, Port Loko and Koinadugu districts, and are kept
apart in Koinadugu district by a small wedge of Limba.

Susu and Yalunka tradition maintains that they arrived in
Futa Jalon some time after the Temne and Baga and created a
powerful state in Sulima and Sankaran, east and south of Futa,
and in the process intermingled with Fula and other tribes.
There were intermittent clashes between the agricultural Susu
and Yalunka and the pastoral Fula culminating in the subjugation
of the Yalunka by the Fula until the early decades of the 17th
century, when led by a blacksmith they threw off the Fula yoke
and moved south to their present territory. Peace between the
Yalunka and Fula was concluded at Falaba ("palaver town"),
now the headquarters of the Sulima Chiefdom, Koinadugu District. In 1784 the first Yalunka chief was installed at Falaba
and his four sons opened up the country. In the 1890s Yalunka
development experienced a setback after the attack on Falaba by
the Sofas. When the British established a sphere of influence
over the hinterland of Sierra Leone in the 1880s, Susu territory was included. In 1889 by the terms of the Anglo-French
agreement the larger and more northerly portion of Susu country was ceded to the French.

Susu and Yalunka cultivate rice and millet as major
crops. Subsidiary crops include groundnuts, yams, cocoa yam,
sweet potatoes and cassava. The Yalunka, possibly as a result of Fula tutelage, have also acquired pastoral traits, and
each family generally has one or two cows, with some sheep
and goats. Children herd the cattle and women do the milking
and butter-making. The Yalunka are also well-known as black-
smiths, goldsmiths, and leather-workers. The Susu and Yalunka have patriclans known as siya. The important Yalunka
clans include the Kamara, Dumbwia (Dumbuya), Sisi, and
Kwiate (Kuyate), and the Susu major clans include the Bangura,
Fofana, Dumbwia (Dumbuya), and Kaba. The Susu are predominantly Muslim and it is estimated that some 80 per cent
profess that faith. The Yalunka by contrast are about 40 per
cent Muslim.

- T -

TAMBI EXPEDITIONS see MILITARY EXPEDITIONS (10)

TAQI, IBRAHIM BASH, 1931-1975. Journalist and politician.
    Minister of information and broadcasting, 1969-1970. Born at
    Ropolo, Tane Chiefdom, Tonkolili District, on September 18,
    1931. Educated at the Prince of Wales School, Freetown,
    Ibadan University, Nigeria, and at Heidelberg University, West
    Germany. Mr. Taqi's effective journalism, particularly as a
    columnist of We Yone, the APC mouthpiece, contributed in no
    small measure to the discomfiture of the SLPP at the polls in
    the 1967 general elections. Elected to Parliament in March
    1967 as member for Freetown East I constituency. He was

sworn in as minister of information but civilian rule was inter-
rupted by the NRC military regime. On the return to civilian
rule in 1968 Mr. Taqi became a government back bencher until
his appointment in April 1969 as minister of information and
broadcasting. In September 1970 he was arrested and detained
under public emergency regulations. Released in 1973 he was
again arrested in 1974 and along with 14 others charged with
treason. He was convicted and executed at Pademba Road
Prisons in July 1975.

TAYLOR, Sub-Inspector CHARLES N. An African sub-inspector in
command of the Frontier Force at Mongeri in 1893, Taylor
with a force of 40 Frontier Police routed Pokeri [Porokerri]
and his Sofas at Tungea near Panguma in December 1893.
Pokere was killed in the action and two years later Taylor was
awarded the D.C.M. for his skill and bravery against the Sofas.
In 1895 Sub-Inspector Taylor mediated in a land dispute between
Mokassi and Bunjema villages in the Upper Bagru-Bumpe area.
He decided in favor of Bunjema. The Mokassi people appealed
to the acting governor, Lt.-Col. Caulfield, who upheld Taylor's
verdict. The matter was finally referred to the courts in Freetown where Samuel Lewis appeared for the appellants.

TAYLOR, DANIEL PETER HUGHES. Educated at the CMS Grammar School, Freetown, Wesley College, Taunton, England, and
King's College, London, where he became a member of the
Royal College of Surgeons in 1874. He was for most of his
professional career engaged in private practice in England,
Freetown, and Bathurst, Gambia. He served for a short while
as assistant surgeon at Bonthe and acted as coroner in Bathurst
in 1883 and 1884. He was the father of the composer and mu-
sician Samuel Coleridge-Taylor born in London of an English
mother. Dr. D. P. H. Taylor died in 1904.

TAYLOR, JAMES, 1842-1901. A devoted Wesleyan of Aku parentage, Taylor had in his younger days served a prison sentence
for theft. Undaunted but sobered by the experience, he prospered in business, owned "Taylor Square" at Water Street, and
cultivated a coffee farm at Fourah Bay. With the help of the
Rev. Benjamin Tregaskis, Taylor in about 1872 or 3 began publishing a newspaper, The Independent, a persistent and effective
counterblast to The Negro, edited by Blyden and later by the
Rev. G. J. Macaulay. By the end of 1873 Taylor had put The
Negro out of business and thereafter his Independent was between 1873 and 1875 the only newspaper in Freetown. It ran
essay competitions and raised the standard of journalism but it
too stopped publication in 1878. In January 1880 the Wesleyans
opened a Female Institution which was in fact virtually owned
by James Taylor, its manager. Elected mayor of Freetown in
1897, Cardew appointed Taylor honorary captain of the Volunteer Corps, formed in 1898 to defend Freetown during the Hut
Tax War. A public-spirited man who spent a great deal of his
time and money in the interests of the community, Taylor died
in 1901.

TAYLOR, Capt. JOHN. Owner and master of the Myro, a brig
hired by Sharp to transport new emigrants and supplies to the
Sierra Leone settlement in 1788. The Myro arrived in August.
Taylor, though not in government service and without authority
to act on behalf of the British Government, signed a treaty on
August 22 with the chiefs. Taylor's treaty repudiated Thompson's of 1787 and is regarded as the legal beginning of the
Colony. On his return to England he claimed over £85 from
the British government as the cost of the treaty goods, plus
over £50 as entertainment for chiefs and followers in Sierra
Leone. He was reimbursed for the treaty but the claim for
entertainment was rejected.

TAYLOR-CUMMINGS, E. H., 1890-1967. Medical practitioner and
prominent political and public figure. Born on December 7,
1890. Educated at the Wesleyan Boys High School, Fourah Bay
College (University of Durham), Freetown, and at Liverpool
University in England. Medical officer, Sierra Leone government, 1920; retired from government service in 1947 having
risen to the post of senior medical officer. Re-engaged in government service, 1955-1957. Nominated member of the Freetown City Council, 1936-1947; mayor of Freetown, 1948-1954.
Member of Commission on Higher Education in West Africa,
appointed by the British Government, 1943. President of Fourah
Bay College Council, 1950-1953.

TEJAN-SIE, Sir BANJA, 1917-   . Governor-general of Sierra
Leone, 1970-71. Born August 7, 1917. Educated at Bo Government School and Prince of Wales School, Freetown. Worked
as a station clerk, Sierra Leone Government Railway, 1938-39,
and as a nurse in the Medical Department 1940 to 1946. Studied at the London School of Economics and at Lincoln's Inn,
where he was called to the Bar in 1951. He returned home
and set up private practice. In 1953 he was elected vice president of the Sierra Leone Peoples' Party. In 1958 he was appointed police magistrate. In April 1967 he was appointed chief
justice and in April 1968 appointed officer performing the functions of governor-general. In September 1970 he was appointed
governor-general, a position he held until April 1971, when
Sierra Leone adopted a Republican Constitution.

TEMNE. According to oral tradition, the Temne occupied Futa in
what is now the Republic of Guinea for generations before they
were driven south by the Susu and other Mande-speaking peoples. Thereafter the Temne built up an empire in the coastal
forest regions which by the early 17th century enjoyed considerable power and wealth, derived mostly from trade. Again
the Temne empire was destroyed by a Mande-speaking people
who established themselves as suzerains over Temne country--
hence the prevalence of Mande surnames among the Temne.
Another tradition maintains that the Temne arrived in Sierra
Leone from the northeast (possibly in the late 1400s), cut off
the Loko from the Mende, moved west and drove a deep wedge

into Limba-held territory.

Certainly by the early 16th century the Temne had pushed
their way to the coast. Valentin Fernandes wrote in 1507, admittedly from secondary sources, that Sierra Leone was inhabited by Buloms and Temne and that each village was ruled
by a chief or bee (modern Temne bai). By late 18th century
the Sierra Leone Peninsula was in Temne hands and was ceded
by Temne chiefs in 1787 to the British for the resettlement of
freed slaves. Today the Temne occupy an area of about 8000
square miles in the Northern Province, mostly in Tonkolili,
Bombali, Port Loko and Kambia districts and number probably
one million.

The Temne are subdivided into two major groups. The
Sanda Temne in the north and the Yoni Temne in the south.
The latter are believed to belong to an older stock. There are
also the smaller groupings of the Kholifa and Kunike Temne.
The Temne are an agricultural people, although a few do raise
cattle, but over the decades they have taken increasingly to
trade. They cultivate rice, groundnuts, cassava and millet;
cash crops include palm kernels and kola nuts. Before the
imposition of colonial rule, they acquired considerable notoriety
for military ventures.

They have a highly developed political system, although
as a rule they do not have female chiefs. The paramount chief
or bai, once elected, cannot be removed from office; for the
Temne "the Chief is priest as well as king. He who has been
consecrated and annointed embodies the community soul; he
cannot abdicate or be de jure deposed, for, in a sense, he and
the country are one and by the mystic chain binding him to
predecessors and successors alike he is as immortal as our
race. When his hour strikes he will return to Futa whence he
came...."

Apart from the bai the Temne have a hierarchy of
chiefs: the oboma or deputy chief acts on behalf of the chief
(bai) during the latter's illness and until the official announce-
ment of his death; the orok or pa rok acts as regent in the in-
terval between the death of the bai and the installation of a new
bai; the kapr masim (often the same person as the orok)
guards the sacred box containing the bai's insignia of office;
and the kumrabai operates as the bai's principal adviser (formerly the title of bai (pa) suba, which has fallen into desuetude,
was used in Masimera for instance to denote the same person
as the kumrabai). The alimami and alikali--Islamic titles
meaning, respectively,--the leader in prayer and judge were
borrowed and adapted for political ends. These titles, whose
holders retain office irrespective of the death of a bai, refer
to certain categories of sub-chiefs or chiefs of sections of the
chiefdom. The kaprs--these correspond roughly to magistrates,
the chief of whom is the kapr masim (see above). It has been
observed that the office of kapr exists only in chiefdoms with
the poro. The kaprs are appointed by the new bai and they
cease to hold office at his death. Kapr gbobora is the bai's
hunter and commissariat officer, and the kapr loya, the chief's

legal adviser. The santigis, selected from the leading men in
the chiefdom, perform a wide variety of functions, ranging from
constables and messengers, to minor judges and chiefs of small
towns, etc.

Islam enjoys considerable following among the Temne,
although Christianity is making impressive inroads. The main
secret societies for men are the poro and the Ragbenle, the
latter is regarded as the more decisively political where both
exist. The Bundo is exclusively for women. The Kofung or
Kofo is prevalent among the Sanda Temne and the Limba.
Other societies or associations include, for men, the Katokodo
(in many ways similar to the Kofung) and the Jumunko and
Kaloko; for women, the Baruba, Kure, Ramena and Kinki societies.

The Temne claim descent from some 25 patrilineal
clans, each possessing an eponymous ancestor. The major
clans, or abuna, include Kamara (with Mela, Soya, Kabia,
etc., as alternative names), Bangura (with Konte or Conteh or
Konde, Samura, Mara, Kalma, Dema, etc., as alternatives),
Kanu (with Keita, Kagbo or Kargbo, Kalu, Mansare, etc., as
alternatives), Kuroma or Koroma (with Fofana, Sanko or San-
coh, Fona or Fornah, Tula, etc., as alternatives), Ture or
Turay (with Toli, Toronko, Kuri, Numu, etc., as alternatives),
Sanho or Sanoh (with Munu, Sanko, Seki, etc., as alternatives).
Each abuna or clan is associated with a symbol or totem (tana)
often an animal, bird or plant, which members of the clan may
not see, touch, use or kill. The form of prohibition differs
and varies with each abuna and the penalty for non-observance
or for breach of the prohibition also varies. A particular tana
may be associated with more than one abuna.

TEMPLE, Maj. OCTAVIUS. Lieutenant Governor of Sierra Leone,
1833-1834. Had served in the army 1799-1828. On December
8, 1833, Temple arrived in Sierra Leone to take office; unwilling to be embroiled in the wars of the interior he concentrated his efforts on reorganizing the Liberated African Department. But these efforts were short-lived. Temple died
on August 13, 1834, after being in office for only eight months.

THOMAS, JAMES JONATHAN. Successful businessman and leading
public figure. Born in Wellington Village, J. J. Thomas began life as a printer's apprentice. In 1867 he went to Lagos
as a merchant's clerk, prospered in business, and married his
master's daughter. From Lagos he made handsome contributions to public charities in Freetown. In 1896 he came back
home and got married for a second time, to Rhoda Hebron.
In 1900 he settled for good at Wilberforce House Gloucester
Street. He continued to contribute generously to charities and
endowed a public library. In 1901 he was appointed to the
Legislative Council and was awarded a C. M. G. in 1908.

THOMAS, JOHN H. MALAMAH. Prosperous businessman and
prominent public figure. Born at Hastings of Aku recaptive

parentage and educated at the village school. John Thomas,
at the early age of fourteen went to the Northern Rivers as a
trader's clerk. Twelve years later he was on his own and assisted by a loan from Dr. Robert Smith, assistant colonial surgeon, he established a factory at Malama ("Malama Factory"),
Sierra Leone River. There he acquired considerable wealth,
moved to Freetown and became known as Malamah Thomas.
He built a house at Little East Street, "Malamah House," dec-
orated with carved heads and so he became known also as
"Head-Head" Thomas. Dealing mainly in cottons, Malamah invented his own brand, "Malamah Baft," patented in England.
Between 1904 and 1914 he was elected mayor of Freetown eight
times, missing the office of first citizen only in 1908 and 1909.
A public-spirited man who gave generously to the poor, he also
served on the Legislative Council.

THOMAS, M. E. KOSONIKE, 1932- . Educator, engineer and
artist (painting). Born on March 7, 1932. Educated at the
Methodist Boys High School, Freetown, the University of St.
Andrews, Scotland, and at the University of Leeds, England.
Dean, Faculty of Pure and Applied Science (1968-70); professor
in engineering and head of department (1969-); vice principal,
Fourah Bay College, University of Sierra Leone (1970-74);
(1975-). Visiting scientist, Structural Division, Department
of Civil Engineering, University of Illinois, USA (1964-65);
visiting reader in civil engineering, University of East Africa
at Nairobi (1967); external examiner in civil engineering, universities of Zambia and Makerere (1976). Designer and de-
tailer with Ove Arup and Partners, Manchester, England; bridge
engineer with Leonard Fairclough & Co. and with the West
Riding Country Council, England (1961-62); structural designer
with Chadwick O'Leocha and Partners, Manchester (1963-64).
Consultant to the UN Commission for Africa at Addis Ababa,
Ethiopia, on the application of science and technology to development (1971). Materials and structures consultant for Tech-
sult & Co., 26 Percival Street, Freetown, one of the leading
indigenous engineering firms of consultants. Author of several
technical reports and papers on the behavior of concrete, plain
and reinforced, as well as the behavior of sandcrete and sta-
bilized laterite building blocks and lateritic concrete. Author
also of a number of articles on scientific and technical education in Africa. Member of the Advisory Committee on Engineering Education in Middle Africa (1967-); president of the Sierra
Leone Science Association (1971-74); president, Sierra Leone
Institution of Engineers (1972-74); president of the West African
Science Association (1974-76).

THOMPSON, MAXIMILIAN AND FREDERICK AUGUSTUS. Two
eldest sons of Moses Thompson of Kissy, a financial genius,
who died prematurely in 1877. In 1885 the two started business
in the Sherbro as Thompson Brothers with headquarters in
Bonthe. In 1892 their younger brothers, Gauzevoort, Maitland
and Columbus, joined the firm. In 1895 Thompson Brothers

established a branch in Manchester, the first indigenous Sierra Leonean firm to open a branch in England. In Freetown the firm owned a wharf and warehouses at Cline Town and a store at Wilberforce Street. The firm gave strong financial support to the Anglican Church in the Sherbro and contributed generously to charity in Freetown and Kissy, the home village. During the 1898 Hut Tax War, Thompson Brothers suffered severe losses and 12 of their factories were destroyed. Concessions obtained by the firm procured to compensate for the 1898 losses proved worthless. The name of the firm was revived later and it continued to do business in Sierra Leone into the middle decades of the 20th Century.

THOMPSON, the Rev. Canon P. E. S., 1931- . Educator and theologian. Born on January 8, 1931. Educated at the Government Model School, the CMS Grammar School, Fourah Bay College (University of Durham) and at St. John's College, Durham University, England. Canon of St. George's Cathedral, Freetown, since 1975. Senior lecturer in theology and chaplain at Fourah Bay College (USL). Coauthor of school textbook, How the Christian Faith Began (1973). Author of "The approach to the Old Testament in an African Setting," Ghana Bulletin of Theology (1962), and several other articles on religious themes.

THOMPSON, Capt. THOMAS BOULDON. Commanded the fleet of three ships, the Atlantic, the Belisarius and the Nautilus, which brought the first settlers from England to Sierra Leone in May 1787. Thompson was instructed to transport the settlers to Sierra Leone, make arrangements with the chiefs for land to settle the colonists, and stay in Sierra Leone as long as was necessary. Should the chiefs in Sierra Leone prove refractory, Thompson was to proceed further down the Coast until he could find more amenable chiefs. On landing he negotiated with the local chiefs in May 1787 and made a treaty which authorized the founding of the Province of Freedom. In return for £59 worth of goods, the chiefs "ceded" the shore from the watering-place to Gambia Island some 10 miles in length and to a depth of 20 miles. Thompson's treaty was repudiated and superseded by another treaty of August 22, 1788, which is regarded as the legal foundation of the Colony. Thompson stayed until September 16, when, after giving the settlers arms and ammunition and sending King Tom a present, he sailed back to England.

THOMPSON, Lt. THOMAS PERRONET. Governor of Sierra Leone, 1808-1810. Born in 1783 at Hull in Yorkshire. Educated at Queen's College, Cambridge, where he graduated B.A. in 1802. In 1803 he joined the navy as midshipman but left in 1806 to join the army as a lieutenant in the 95th Rifles; he saw active service in Latin America. In 1808 he was appointed, at 25, governor of Sierra Leone, the first to be appointed by the Crown, an appointment that was secured largely through the good offices of William Wilberforce. Thompson embarked on

his new duties with a great deal of enthusiasm and zeal for reform and a determination to introduce order and discipline in
the community. Shortly after taking office he disbanded the
Volunteer Forces established by Day and introduced a new
trained militia recruited from all males between the ages of 15
and 60. Convinced that the name Freetown had been "perverted
to the Purposes of Insubordination and Rebellion," he changed
it to Georgetown. He issued new currency in pounds, shillings,
and pence in place of the dollar and cents hitherto used by the
company, on the grounds that the dollar tended to revive revolutionary American ideas among the settlers. Public buildings,
Thompson believed, were part of his new order. Accordingly
he requested a government house, a court house, barracks, a
hospital and a church. The chapels set up by the settlers he
regarded as no more than places of amusement. In any event,
in the new scheme of things, there was no place for dissenting
chapels. Thompson's criticisms of the existing situation in the
Colony were directed against the Sierra Leone Company and
particularly its last governor, Thomas Ludlam. He denounced
the apprenticeship system as a disguised form of slavery, released apprenticed liberated Africans and threatened Ludlam
with persecution under the Abolition Act. In place of the apprenticeship system, he proposed to rehabilitate liberated Africans in rural communities around Freetown. Such violent denunciations of a powerful company and its servants were bound
to offend people in high places. In the end Thompson was recalled in a manner that seemed close to dismissal, in just the
second year of his governorship.

THORNTON, HENRY. A rich banker, member of the Black Poor
   Committee formed in 1786, shareholder of the St. George's
   Bay (later Sierra Leone) Company, and chairman of its board
   of directors. The bill to incorporate the Company was sponsored in the House of Commons by Thornton, who, to mollify
   its opponents, agreed to allow British ships free trade, except
   in slaves within the Company's territories. The Bill passed
   the House of Commons by 87 votes to 9 and became law on
   June 6, 1791. As chairman of the Sierra Leone Company,
   Henry Thornton had more to do with the Sierra Leone Settlement at its inception than any of his colleagues. Although an
   avowed abolitionist and a generous patron, his relationships
   with the settlement remained all through essentially businesslike.
   He treated the settlers "more as employees cooperating to advance the Company's good than as equals in need of assistance."
   Distrustful of a "bar" currency, he insisted on silver and copper coinage in dollars, cents and pennies for the Company. At
   the settlement in Sierra Leone, St. George's Hill (renamed
   Thornton Hill after Henry Thornton) was chosen as a site for a
   fort, called Fort Thornton, which later became the official
   residence of the governor. It was largely through the efforts
   of Thornton that the British Government agreed to assume responsibility for Sierra Leone, the transfer being effected in
   Freetown in January 1808. In 1799 Thornton and other evan-

gelical churchmen founded the Church Missionary Society (as it became known in 1813) to sponsor missions and to convert the indigenous population. Sierra Leone was among its first fields of labor.

THORPE, ROBERT. Chief justice of Sierra Leone, 1811-1815. Thorpe was the first chief justice to be appointed by the Crown Colony to Sierra Leone. Although his appointment had taken effect from 1808 he did not arrive in Sierra Leone until July 1811. He was dismissed from the justiceship in 1815 and back in England he resorted to pamphlet warfare against the Colony and its administrators.

THE TIMES. A weekly newspaper founded in August 1975 and edited by Mr. Laminah Rogers.

TIMOTHY, EMANUEL BANKOLE, 1923- . Journalist and author. Born in Freetown on July 3, 1923. Educated at the Buxton Amalgamated School, the Methodist Boys High School, Freetown, and at University Tutorial College, London. Worked as a reporter for Express Newspapers, London, and as assistant editor of Commonwealth Today, Central Office of Information, London. Deputy editor, Ghana Daily Graphic, Accra. Chief information officer, Ministry of Information, Freetown. Awarded the honor of Member of the Royal Victorian Order in 1961. Public relations officer of Dicorwaf (Diamond Corporation West Africa Ltd.), London. Author of Kwame Nkrumah, a biography (1955). Bankole Timothy became one of the first victims of "deportation orders" in emergent Africa, when in 1958, he was repatriated to Sierra Leone on orders of the Ghana government.

TOM I, King. A Temne sub-chief under King Naimbana who lived at Robana and Robaga on the Rokel. King Tom signed a treaty with Capt. Bouldon Thompson in 1787 which authorized the founding of the Province of Freedom for the rehabilitation of victims of the Atlantic slave trade. The treaty of 1787, rejected by King Tom's superior, King Naimbana, was repudiated on August 22, 1788, and superseded by Capt. John Taylor's treaty with Naimbana of that date. King Tom died in about June 1788.

TOM II, King. A Temne chief from the Bunce River area who as Pa Kokelly succeeded King Jimmy in 1796 as king of the "watering-place" and assumed the old title of King Tom. His son Henry pursued a course of study in England at the expense of the Sierra Leone Company. After King Jimmy's death, King Tom II was appointed by Bai Farama, his suzerain, to act as "landlord" of the Sierra Leone Company. Upset by the Company's unwillingness to observe the traditional rules binding landlord/tenant relationships, King Tom II refused to comply with treaties made by his predecessors. Representatives of the Sierra Leone Company vainly tried to convince him that by the provisions of the 1788 August treaty, the piece of territory

"ceded" and paid for had been alienated. King Tom insisted
that land was inalienable. Disputes also arose between the
King and the Company over boundary lines, particularly on the
West end limit of the Colony.

Towards the end of 1799, the Nova Scotians, aggrieved
among other things by the imposition of quit rents (q.v.), rebelled against the Company and found in the refractory King
Tom a ready ally. On November 18, 1801, encouraged by
refugee rebels, Temne forces of King Tom and Bai Farama attacked Fort Thornton, Freetown, killing an officer, two soldiers
and a number of civilians. On December 2, 1801, the Colony
took the offensive by attacking and burning King Tom's towns
between Freetown and the Cape. Overwhelmed by the Colony's
display of force, King Tom sought refuge in the Northern rivers,
where the Mandinka chiefs, assuming a neutral posture, attempted to mediate between the Temne and the Colony. But
Fatima Fodi, the Mandinka chiefs' envoy, encouraged King Tom
to continue the fight. Attempts to sue for peace by Capt.
Charles Bullen of the HMS Wasp, whose sailors had taken part
in the attack on King Tom's towns in December, proved equally
unsuccessful. When Bullen sailed away on April 1, 1802, the
Temne chiefs, who had promised peace, decided to strike again.

On Sunday, April 11, the Temne, with some refugee
rebels reinforced by Susus attacked Fort Thornton again. Repulsed within half an hour, they were driven out of the Colony.
But King Tom, supported by a Bullom war-chief held out in
sullen hostility and encamped threateningly on the Bulom Shore.
King Tom's Bullom ally however soon lost his authority and
was expelled from his dominions. Left virtually alone, King
Tom returned to his domains east of the Colony until, in 1807,
a final settlement was arranged at Robis between him and the
Colony. The new treaty signed on July 10, 1807, acknowledged
the Colony's right by conquest to the lands west of Freetown.
The Temne chiefs also "ceded" parcels of territory in the east
of the Colony and "thus the Colony's original right to the peninsula, cession" by means of purchase, "was superseded by conquest."

TOURE, SAMORI [SAMADU], 1830-1900. A Madinka warrior from
Bissandugu, who rejecting the title of king or sultan styled himself "Samori son of Lafla, African of the Negro Race, Prince
of Believers." In the 1870s, Samori and his armed horsemen
known as Sofas carved for themselves an empire on the Upper
Niger by means of war in the name of Islam. Samori's exploits won him additional territory in Kissi, Kono, Limba and
Koranko countries and he even threatened the Temne. His em-
pire-building propensity brought him into conflict with the
French and into an unesay alliance with the British. He signed
three treaties with the French in 1885, 1887 and in 1888. Of
these perhaps the most important for Sierra Leone's future was
the treaty of March 1887 by which Samori recognized the Niger
as the boundary between his territories and the French sphere
of influence and put his empire under French protection--a

move which deprived Sierra Leone of the bulk of its hinterland.
Samori effectively played the two imperial powers against
each other. By 1890, after repudiating the French treaties, he
showed himself willing to accept British protection. He made
official contacts with the British through a number of agents:
Edward Wilmot Blyden; Maj. Augustus Morton Festing, who
visited him in 1887 and 1888 and who, exceeding or ignoring
his instructions, wrung from Samori a promise of a treaty,
as well as a railway concession; George H. Garrett, a traveling
commissioner. Samori, distrustful of the French, welcomed
Garrett and once more offered his country to the British--an
offer acceptable to Governor Hay but rejected by the Foreign
Office. At the unofficial level Samori was courted by Alfred
Lewis Jones, a Welshman who controlled the Sierra Leone
Coaling Company. Jones provided arms for Samori's Sofas
and sent one of his agents, Capt. Williams, to Samori in January 1892. Samori readily granted Jones wide concessions including the right to levy taxes and to coin money in his territories. He also gave a black ostrich as a gift which Jones
presented to Queen Victoria. The Colonial Office however was
unwilling to get embroiled with the French through the initiative
of a private businessman and Jones was prevented from pursuing
the matter further.
Samori continued his exploits and in 1893 caused British
and French forces to open fire on each other at Waiima in Kono
country, where both forces had been sent to contain the Sofas
and to prevent them from ravaging territories within the spheres
of influence of either power. The French continued to fight
Samori until 1898 when he was captured and deported to Libre-
ville, Gabon, where he died in 1900.

THE TRADER. A short-lived monthly newspaper founded and published in Freetown by S. H. A. Case in 1891.

TREGASKIS, the Rev. BENJAMIN, 1814-1885. Chairman and general superintendent of the Sierra Leone Methodist Church
(1864-1874). Born in 1814, ordained a Wesleyan Methodist
Minister in 1836, Tregaskis served in the West Indies 1836-64.
In 1864 he was appointed superintendent of the Wesleyan Missions in Sierra Leone and the Gambia. His tenure of office in
Sierra Leone from 1864 to 1874 introduced sectarian strife and
almost destroyed the peaceful and friendly relationships among
the various churches in the Colony. To Tregaskis, brought up
on English nonconformist hatred of the privileges of the established church, interdenominational cooperation was at best
cowardice or at worst a cynical surrender of Wesleyan principles. Devoted, able and ruthless, he aimed at developing a
well-organized, highly disciplined, Wesleyan Church in Sierra
Leone and under his authoritarian superintendency, Methodism
in the Colony assumed a new and uncompromising militancy.
Numbers dwindled but Tregaskis undismayed, preferred quality
to mere numbers.
Determined to break the monopoly on higher education

held and enjoyed by the Anglicans, he sponsored two Sierra
Leone youths, J. C. May, to train in England in 1865 to work
in his projected Wesleyan Boys Secondary School to rival the
CMS Grammar School, and Samuel Lewis, to study law in England in 1866. May was educated at Borough Road School and
Wesley College Taunton at the expense of the London Committee. Tregaskis gave Lewis letters of introduction to prominent
Methodists and wrote to the Missionary Society in London "urg-
ing them to 'build up influence' with this young man by attention, advice and friendship."

The government annual grant to the Native Church Pastorate, raised to £500 in 1867 and which most Sierra Leoneans
irrespective of denominational differences wished to see continued, Tregaskis was determined to abolish. The grant was
strongly supported by the newspaper The Negro, edited by Blyden
and later by the Rev. G. J. Macaulay. In alliance with James
Taylor, a prosperous shopkeeper, Tregaskis launched a rival
paper, The Independent, to discredit and vilify The Negro, its
publishers and proprietors. Within a year The Negro was effectively silenced.

Tregaskis' attack on the Pastorate grant and House and
Land Tax found support among members of the English Wesleyan
Methodist Committee who proved a pliable instrument in the execution of the superintendent's wishes. They petitioned the secretary of state combining sectarian grievances with complaints
against the House and Land Tax in Sierra Leone. When the tax
was abolished by Governor Hennessy on August 22, 1872, Tregaskis held a religious service in thanksgiving. The Pastorate
grant was swept away in 1875. John Ezzidio, at whose request
and insistence Tregaskis had been sent to Sierra Leone, had by
so doing unwittingly conjured up an unrelenting rival. The Superintendent literally sent Ezzidio to a premature grave and re-
joiced openly at his death in 1872. Wesley Church, Ezzidio's
dream, still under construction, Tregaskis was determined to
prevent from completion. It was however finished and opened
in 1886, eleven years after Tregaskis' departure.

In 1871, J. C. May returned from England, but Tregaskis, jealous of his own protégé, delayed his ordination and
only in 1874 agreed to open the Wesleyan Boys High School.
In the same year, Tregaskis, on leave in England, was replaced as Superintendent, by the Rev. Charles Knight, the first
African to be so appointed. Tregaskis returned to Sierra Leone
on the pretext of supervising the rebuilding of Rawdon Street
Church (later known as "College Chapel") which he had earlier
vested in himself by special ordinance. Finally in September
1875 he took leave of Sierra Leone for good, gloomily predict-
ing the end of Methodism in the Colony. He died in 1885.

TUBOKU-METZGER, ALBERT EMERICH. An Aku descendant from
    Kissy village. One of the first graduates (in 1881) of Fourah
    Bay College after its affiliation to Durham University in 1876,
    A. E. Metzger studied theology. For a few years he served on
    the Niger Mission and in 1885 joined the government service,

where interest in academic qualifications was minimal, and carried neither status nor salary. Metzger was given an extra treasury clerkship. In 1891 however he was appointed to the substantive post of chief clerk to the master and registrar. In 1887 he had added the name Tuboku, his father's Yoruba name, to that of his father's German missionary pastor at Kissy. The urge to assume African names, inspired by Blyden, had become fashionable among Creoles at the time and its aim was to emphasize their Africanness and infuse in them a self-conscious pride.

TUBOKU-METZGER, F. C., 1928- . Educator, lawyer and author. Born May 10, 1928. Educated at the Prince of Wales School, Freetown, Kings College (Durham University), England, the University of Pennsylvania, USA, and at the Middle Temple Inns of Court, London. Since 1969, associate professor and head, Department of Law, Fourah Bay College (USL); author with A. Milner, et al., of Leading Cases in Sierra Leone (1975). Chairman, Tuboku-Metzger Committee on Secondary Schools' Fees.

TUCKER, P. L. Educator, administrator and lawyer. Born at Bonthe, Sherbro. Educated at St. Patrick's School, Bonthe, Catholic School, Blama, St. Edward's Secondary School, Freetown, Fourah Bay College (University of Durham), Freetown, Oxford University and Gray's Inn, London. Secretary to the prime minister, 1966-1967, and secretary general I, National Reformation Council government, 1967. Establishment secretary, 1964-1966. Principal, Kenema Secondary School and Principal Magburaka Secondary School (1955-1962). In voluntary exile in Britain since 1967.

TURNER, Maj.-Gen. Sir CHARLES. Governor of Sierra Leone, 1825-1826. Enlisted in the British Army as ensign in 1795, rose to the rank of captain in 1803 in the Royal African Corps, was promoted to major in 1804 and lieutenant colonel in 1807 in the Royal West India Rangers. In 1814 he was promoted to colonel and in 1821, major general. Disabled by the loss of an arm in 1812, he retired on half pay in 1818. Holder of the honors, Order of the Bath, Commander of the Portuguese Order of the Tower, Commander of the Turkish Order of the Crescent, Turner arrived in Sierra Leone on February 5, 1825, and took the oath of office as governor.

During his short governorship, Turner concentrated on reducing government expenditure. He retrenched laborers from civilian public works and used those he could on constructing barracks. He reorganized the Liberated African Department and reduced its cost by some £17,000 annually. On July 29, 1915, he passed an ordinance to regulate and control labor, to determine periods of engagement and to impose penalties for neglect of work. The cooperation between the government and the CMS in the rural communities was abandoned and a new agreement substituted government managers for missionary superintendents in the villages. Turner put emphasis not on fostering orderₗᵧ Christian communities but on increasing productivity of agricultural crops. With the parish plan virtually abandoned, the recaptives fell back on their own resources. In the process their spirit of independence was strengthened and this made possible the evolution of a new society which by the middle decades of the 19th century effectively challenged the dominance of the early settlers.

Eager to put an end to the slave trade and to promote legitimate trade, Turner embarked on treaty-making with the adjacent territories. On September 24, 1825, he signed treaties with the chiefs of Sherbro country by which what is known as Turner's Peninsula was "ceded" to Great Britain. This treaty was not ratified by the Crown but it was revived in 1882 by fresh agreements between the British Government and the chiefs. On December 12, 1825, Turner entered into similar arrangements with the chiefs of Bacca Lokkoh country to the north of the Colony. By this treaty the Governor accepted the sovereignty of the territories offered by the chiefs to the British Government. Early in 1826 Governor Turner led an expedition to Sherbro to suppress slave traders. After taking part in a few engagements he returned to Freetown towards the end of February. On March 7, 1826, he died at Government House, a little after a year in office.

- U -

UNITED DEMOCRATIC PARTY [UDP]. A short-lived political party formed in September 1970. Its leaders maintained that the UDP came into existence in protest partly against certain provisions of a projected constitution, partly against certain governmental policies and measures, and partly against the increasing tendency towards personal rule. The UDP was in fact a breakaway movement from the ruling APC and its leaders hoped, it appeared, to wrest political power from the ruling party by "forcing the issue." The UDP was formed as a sequel to the resignation from government of two senior ministers--Minister of Finance Dr. M. S. Forna and Minister of Development Mr. M. O. B. Taqi. The leaders of the party included Dr. John Karefa-Smart, Dr. M. S. Forna, Mr. I. B. Taqi, Mr. M. O. B. Taqi, Dr. Hamid Taqi and former PC N'Silk. Feared because of its excesses and feared more so because of its great potential, particularly in parts of the Northern Province, the UDP was proscribed less than a month after its formation. The government made use of its emergency powers to arrest and detain the leaders of the party and a number of prominent citizens believed either to have been members of or to have had sympathies with the party.

UNITED SIERRA LEONE PROGRESSIVE PARTY [UPP]. Formed in June 1954 by Mr. C. B. Rogers-Wright and by Mr. I. T. A. Wallace Johnson, the latter a member of the Legislative Council

who had resigned membership of the National Council in 1952.
The formation of the UPP almost coincided with the arrival of
the Keith-Lucas Commission, which may well have provided
the initial impetus for its formation.   The UPP declared as one
of its major aims the integration of Colony and Protectorate by
removal of existing barriers, real or imaginary, between the
two communities.   The UPP argued that the existing two major
parties, the SLPP and the NC, were unsatisfactory--almost ir-
relevant--in the political stresses of the period, the one too
concerned with matters relating to the Protectorate, the other
ultra-Creole.   The party appeared willing to recruit into its
ranks the more moderate Creoles and radical Protectorate
elements, potential rebels against the traditional power structure.   It supported demands for universal adult sufferage but
made proposals for a second chamber particularly for chiefs.
It attempted a "grass roots" approach by sending teams of
speakers to tour the Protectorate, though it failed to buttress
its position by establishing effective branches up-country.

   Although its role in inciting anti-tax demonstrators in
parts of the Northern Province in 1956 may have been minimal,
the UPP did exploit the riots for political ends to the full.   Its
leader Mr. C. B. Rogers-Wright in bye-elections held in 1957
to the central legislature won a seat in Port Loko East, a remarkable feat--the first Creole to win a seat in the Protectorate, more impressively against a very distinguished opponent.
The UPP in the same bye-elections won the Moyamba North
seat when Valesius Neal-Caulker, one of the few Protectorate
members of the party hierarchy was returned.   But the party's
electoral successes were short-lived.   First in August 1956 its
National Propaganda Secretary, Mr. M. A. Tarasid, a "Protectorate boy," resigned to join the SLPP, accusing the UPP's
executive of discriminating against him in favor of a Creole.
Earlier, two prominent northerners, whose membership the
party claimed, had resigned.   So also had the party's vice-
president for the Northern Province.   By the second half of
1959 the party had disintegrated further.   The general-secretary,
Mr. John Nelson Williams, then a member of the legislature,
resigned in protest against a decision of the executive (in the
UPP political practice the executive was synonymous with the
leader, Mr. Wright).   The rump of the UPP members of Parliament severed relations with the party, on the grounds that
Mr. Wright's leadership was no longer tolerable.   They formed
a new group, the Independent Progressive Party (IPP), with
Mr. Valesius Neal-Caulker as leader and Mr. Gideon Thomas
as secretary.   The UPP finally disappeared into the United
Front Coalition, its erstwhile leader and general secretary both
accepting responsible positions in the SLPP-led United Front
government.

UNITY (1965-1971).   Newspaper founded in October 1965 as the official organ of the SLPP.

UNIVERSITY OF SIERRA LEONE.   Founded by the University of

Sierra Leone Act, 1967. USL has two constituent colleges, Fourah Bay College and Njala University College.

- V -

VAI [or Gallinas] see KONO AND VAI

VAI [Vei] SCRIPT. A syllabic phonetic script with 215 characters invented by the Vai people probably in the early 19th century or earlier. The Vai Script, with characters quite distinct from the Roman or Arabic, is the oldest indigenous form of writing yet discovered in this part of Africa. Initially codified by Momodu Doalu Boakai, a Vai, it was studied by the Rev. Koelle who used it as a basis for a Vai grammar book which he published in 1853.

THE VANGUARD. Founded and published by Laminah Sankoh, who in 1951 surrendered to the SLPP his proprietary rights over the paper. The Vanguard ceased circulation in 1962.

VASSA GUSTAVUS see EQUIANO, OLAUDAH

VENN, the Rev. HENRY. Honorary secretary of the Church Missionary Society in Sierra Leone 1841-1873. Conscious of the criticisms against the educational system in mission schools, with its emphasis on academic rather than on vocational or technical education, Venn did all he could to remedy the defect. He encouraged agricultural pursuits and promoted the export of African produce. He was also one of the moving spirits behind the opening of the Industrial School and a Normal School to train teachers by the CMS in 1850. "His declared policy was to foster self-reliance among converts, to encourage them to take an active part in their mission and in time to take it over as their own church freed from alien missionary control. He felt his Society's task was building independent churches then withdrawing to new fields." Venn died in 1873.

VIDAL, the Rt. Rev. EMERIC OWEN. Bishop of Sierra Leone, 1852-1854. Vicar of an Anglican parish in Sussex, England, and a linguist of some standing who had helped Ajayi Crowther with his Yoruba Grammar. When in 1852 by letters patent an Anglican diocese for all the British possessions in West Africa between 20° North and 20° South latitude was created, the Rev. Vidal was, on the recommendation of the Church Missionary Society, appointed its first bishop. Consecrated by the Archbishop of Canterbury on Whitsunday 1852 as bishop of the new West African Anglican Diocese, Bishop Vidal arrived in Freetown on the mail steamer Propontis on December 27, 1852.
     In 1854 Bishop Vidal visited the Yoruba mission, then part of his diocese and ordained T. B. Macaulay and Thomas King--the first West Africans to be ordained by a bishop. On his way back to Freetown, the bishop fell ill and died at sea

on December 24, 1854, and was buried in Freetown on the 26th. In his short two-year term, Vidal laid a solid foundation for the future Sierra Leone Anglican Church. He drafted a church constitution which his untimely death prevented from being ratified. In an age when most Christians, particularly missionaries, regarded Islam as an evil and corrupt religion, Vidal was exceptional in his attempts to treat Islam with seriousness, sympathy and understanding.

VOLUNTEER CORPS (FORCE). When Sierra Leone was selected to resettle persons displaced by the Atlantic slave trade, prospective settlers were made to sign an agreement with a clause by the terms of which each "binds and obliges himself or herself to the other settlers for the Protection and Preservation of their common Freedom." In practice this obligation proved quite inadequate for the defense of the settlement. Attacks by neighboring tribes, an invasion by a French squadron, and a host of other problems made it impossible for the settlement to prosper as a commercial venture. By 1800 the Sierra Leone Company was compelled to request financial support from the British government to help defray the costs of maintaining the Colony. On July 9, 1804, the British Parliament voted for the Colony of Sierra Leone the sum of £14,000, including £4000 for the Volunteer Force which Capt. William Day, R.N., governor of Sierra Leone (in 1803 and again in 1805), had brought into being by enlisting in a Corps of Volunteers in 1803 the Nova Scotian and Maroon inhabitants of the Colony.

The Volunteer Corps in spite of its name was handsomely paid. Between 1804 and its dissolution by Governor Thompson in 1808, the Volunteer Corps, dressed in blue and scarlet uniform, cost the Colony an average of £3000 a year in pay and accoutrements. In 1831 during Governor Findlay's tenure, a separate force, the Sierra Leone Loyal Volunteers, attired in red jackets with blue collars and cuffs, was created in the villages of the Colony. In 1898 during the Hut Tax War the Creoles, fearful of an attack on Freetown, petitioned Governor Cardew to be allowed to form a Volunteer Corps for the defense of the city. Cardew agreed. On May 4, 1898, a Volunteer Force was raised by ordinance. The governor was empowered to make rules for the discipline of the force whose members were required to take an oath to serve until "incapacitated by age, infirmity or otherwise, unless they should sooner resign, be discharged or quit the Colony." Some 100 volunteers enlisted and for about four months rendered useful service guarding Freetown at night. On September 15, 1898, after the suppression of the Protectorate rising, the force was disbanded by proclamation.

- W -

WAIIMA INCIDENT see MILITARY EXPEDITIONS (12)

WALL, THOMAS ALFRED. A young European clerk from Manchester recruited into government service by Governor Kennedy
without making him take the Civil Service entrance examination.
This irregularity, which involved Kennedy in a breach of promise to fill the junior ranks of the service by competitive examinations, provoked public discontent and criticism. In 1876
Wall was appointed commandant and posted to the Sherbro. In
1881 a chief of Brama on the Bumpe River attacked some Creoles for seducing his wife. Other chiefs who presided over the
case found both chief and Creoles equally at fault and imposed
fines accordingly. The Creoles appealed to Wall who sent three
policemen to arrest the chief of Brama, an area he believed to
be under British jurisdiction by the provisions of Turner's
treaty of 1825. The three policemen were repulsed. Wall then
took a force of policemen to the area and arrested several people for alleged complicity in the attack on his emissaries.
        The Commandant's unauthorized reprisal raid raised a
public furor. The government in Freetown and the Colonial
Office were equally dismayed at the implications of exercising
British authority in an ill-defined area outside recognized limits.
Subsequently Wall was dismissed from the service for sending
policemen to capture children in villages in British Sherbro,
transporting them to Freetown, having them condemned (fully
aware of the fact they they were not slaves), and receiving
£200 bounty money. He argued with persuasion that he had not
acted illegally. The case dragged on for five years and thanks
to inadequate and faulty evidence, as well as some powerful support at the Colonial Office, Wall got away with his offense.
Eventually he was transferred to another colony.

WALLACE-JOHNSON, ISAAC THEOPHILUS AKUNNA, 1895-1965.
        Born in Wilberforce village (Freetown) in 1895, educated at the
village school, Wilberforce, at the Centenary Tabernacle School,
Freetown, and at the People's University of Moscow, USSR.
At 18, Wallace, as he was popularly known, joined the Sierra
Leone government service as an outdoor officer of the Customs
Department. Soon he persuaded his colleagues to go on strike
for better wages and he, with some of the leading strikers,
was promptly dismissed. Reinstated, he again agitated for
higher wages and better conditions of service. Transferred to
the army as record and confidential clerk he saw service in
East Africa, the Cameroons and the Middle East. He was
demobilized in 1920 and thereafter worked briefly at the United
African Company (UAC) and then at the Freetown City Council,
where he rose to the position of chief clerk of the Water-Works
Department. Discharged from the City Council for organizing
his fellow employees to demand more pay and better conditions
of service, he decided to become a seaman and for five years
visited European, Asian and African seaports. He found time
to publish The Seafarer, a periodical devoted to promoting the
welfare of seamen.
        By 1930 Wallace was back in Sierra Leone and in that
year using an alias, E. Richards, was the unofficial repre-

sentative of the Sierra Leone Railroad Workers' Union to the First International Conference of Negro Workers in Hamburg, Germany, where he was elected to the presidium, after making an impressive and impassioned speech. By 1931 he was in Nigeria, where he founded that country's first labor union, the African Workers Union, in 1931. In the same year he was invited to the International Labor Defense Congress in Moscow where using another pseudonym, W. Daniels, he enrolled as a student at the People's University. Wallace-Johnson returned to Freetown in February 1933, but moved on to Nigeria where under a number of pen names--e.g., W. Daniels, E. Richards, and Abdul Mohamed Afric--he became editor of The Nigerian Daily Telegraph and contributed to The Negro Worker. Virtually harassed out of Nigeria for his militant journalism and labor union activities, he went to the Gold Coast, where in association with Bankole, Awunor-Renner, and Wata Ofei, he organized the West Coast Youth League and contributed articles to The Gold Coast Spectator and to The African Morning Post, both published in Accra.

In 1936, as Mussolini's troops attacked Abyssinia, Wallace published an article in the African Morning Post entitled "Has the African a God?" "Personally," he wrote, "I believe the European has a God in whom he believes and whom he is representing in his churches all over Africa. He believes in the god whose name is Deceit. He believes in the god whose law is 'Ye strong, you must weaken still further the weak.' Ye 'civilized' Europeans you must 'civilize' the 'barbarous' Africans with machine-guns. Ye 'Christian' Europeans you must 'Christianize' the 'pagan' Africans with bombs, poison gases, etc."

For publishing this article Wallace was arrested and charged with seditious libel. The Gold Coast Supreme Court found him guilty and sentenced him to a fine of £50 or three months' imprisonment. Wallace paid the fine, appealed and lost, and finally took the matter to the Judicial Committee of the Privy Council, which, while it did not find the article seditious, upheld the conviction on the grounds that under the Gold Coast criminal code such an attack on religion reflected on the government of the colony. While in England, Wallace worked at the newly established International African Service Bureau as general secretary and with the help of George Padmore, Jomo Kenyetta, and others, established the Pan-African Federation, aimed at promoting the welfare of African workers. He also founded two magazines, The African Sentinel and Africa and the World. Two thousand copies of the former were seized and confiscated by the comptroller of customs in Freetown, when Wallace returned to Sierra Leone from Britain in April 1938.

Shortly after his arrival he formed the West African Youth League--Sierra Leone Branch, with its official organ, The African Standard, a newspaper, founded in January 1939. Within a year Wallace had organized in addition to the West African Civil Liberties and National Defence League and the

West African Youth League, eight labor unions throughout
Sierra Leone.   These were the Public Works Workers' Union,
the Mabella Coaling Company Workers' Union, the King Tom
Docks Workers' Union, the All Seamen's Union, the Bonthe
Amalgamated Workers' Union, the Pepel and Marampa Miners
Workers' Union, and the Motorists' Union.   Colonial authorities
in Sierra Leone took alarm and did everything to stop Wallace-
Johnson's labor union activities.   In September 1939, he was
arrested and detained under the emergency Colonial Defense
Regulations.   While in detention he was charged with criminal
libel for publishing an article in The African Standard earlier
in August 1939 entitled "Who Killed Fonnie?"   Fonnie had died
tied to a post after being flogged on the orders of Mr. John
Henry de Burgh, district commissioner of Bonthe, Sherbro, who
had encountered some opposition on a tax collection mission in
the area.   The article suggested that the DC had in effect killed
Fonnie.   Wallace was found guilty of criminal libel by a judge
and three assessors and sentenced to a year's imprisonment.
He wrote poems in prison, later published under the title,
Prison in the Muse, describing the shocking conditions in the
Central Prison at Pademba Road Freetown.   These poems provoked an official investigation which led to some administrative
and other changes.

On March 19, 1942, Wallace, still detained under the
emergency defense regulations, was sent on exile to Bonthe,
where he made use of his unwelcome leisure by teaching adults
to read and write.   He was released from detention in the latter part of 1944 and on his return to Freetown was elected to
represent Sierra Leone at the World Trade Union Congress,
held in London in February 1945.   In September 1945, at a
meeting held in Paris, Wallace was elected to the Executive
Committee of the World Federation of Trade Unions Congress.
He was with Nkrumah, Padmore and others, one of the organizers of the Pan-Africanist Congress held in Manchester,
England, in 1945.

In 1951 Wallace successfully contested the Wilberforce
and York electoral district seat on the Legislative Council as
a member of the NCCSL.   He broke away from the NCCSL to
join the UPP and retained his seat in the 1957 elections to the
Sierra Leone House of Representatives.   By 1959 he had severed ties with the UPP and had formed his own party, the
Radical Democratic Party (RDP), largely a one-man band.   By
then Wallace was a spent force, although he was a delegate to
the constitutional talks in London in 1960 which finalized arrangements for independence in 1961.   Fearless and indomitable,
hard-working and austere, Wallace rejected all attempts to control his crusading zeal by the attractions of office, even though
in his last days he was far from well-off or comfortable.   He
died in Ghana in an automobile accident in May 1965 and was
buried in Freetown, accompanied by probably the greatest
funeral turn-out in the country's history.

WALLIS, Capt. C. B.   One of the British officers who took part

in operations during the 1898 Hut Tax War.   Although Wallis
fought mostly in the South, in Bandajuma District, among the
Mende and Sherbro, he did also describe the campaign in the
North, in Karene District, among the Temne and other northern
tribes.   In 1903 he published The Advance of Our West African
Empire, in which he gave a vivid and detailed account of his
experiences in the war, paid a warm tribute to Bai Bureh's
organizing ability, military tactics and strategy, and contrasted
Bai Bureh's conduct of the war with the rising in Mendeland.
Wallis was also author of, among other works, West African
Warfare (1903), The Poro of the Mendi (1905), and In the
Court of the Native Chiefs in Mendi-Land (1905).

WALMSLEY, the Rt. Rev. JOHN.   Bishop of Sierra Leone 1910-
1923.   Educated at Brasenose College, Oxford, Walmsley was
ordained an Anglican priest in 1891.   Between 1894-98 he was
vice-principal of Wycliffe Hall, Oxford, and then became Vicar
of Normandy-by-Derby and chaplain to the forces, Normanton
Barracks, 1898-1904.   On June 24, 1910, he was consecrated
bishop of Sierra Leone.   Bishop Walmsley, unmarried all his
life, arrived in Freetown in 1910 accompanied by his sister,
Miss Edith Walmsley.   A zealous missionary, he concentrated
his efforts on the missions in the Protectorate, which he visited often.
        His extensive tours of the hinterland, conducted on foot,
were unmatched by any of his predecessors.   His interest in
the Protectorate missions led to the appointment of an archdeacon, the first Anglican archdeacon of the Protectorate, the
Rev. Canon E. T. Cole.   In 1908 Bishop Walmsley received
the sum of £3000 raised from contributions at the Pan-Anglican
Conference held in London in that year to be used at the bishop's discretion in the diocese of Sierra Leone.   He donated the
money to Fourah Bay College to finance the training of Anglican
clergymen.   When the College was threatened with closure because of lack of funds, Bishop Walmsley effected a scheme of
cooperation between the CMS and the Methodist Missionary Society to finance and administer the College, an arrangement
which ensured its survival.   He died in 1923 and was buried
in Freetown at Kissy Road Cemetery.

WALPOLE, GEORGE.   Commander of Jamaican government troops
against Maroons who had rebelled and had resorted to guerrilla
warfare in the mountains in Jamaica.   When it was decided to
hunt them out with dogs, the Maroons, assured by Gen. Walpole
against further reprisals, agreed to surrender.   But as soon as
they capitulated, the Jamaican legislature deported them to
Halifax Nova Scotia and passed an act making it a capital offense for them to return to the Island.   The assembly also
made financial provision for their maintenance.   The British
and Nova Scotian governments yielded to the circumstances.
Walpole, repudiated by the Jamaican legislature, sent back a
gift of £500 guineas the Assembly had voted him, went home
to England, resigned his commission and went into opposition

politics. The Maroons, some 550 of whom had emigrated to
Sierra Leone in 1800, still looked to Walpole as champion of
their cause and continued to send petitions of protest to him
against conditions in their new home. Walpole Street in
Maroons' Town in Freetown was called after him.

WANSEY, NATHANIEL. A Nova Scotian immigrant who in 1799
   was elected deputy chairman by the Tithingmen of the Colony.
   Wansey and a number of Nova Scotian dissidents tried to capture and exercise power illegally and refused to obey the authority of the governor and council. When summoned by Governor Ludlam to explain their conduct, Wansey and his associates resorted to the use of force. The Nova Scotian rebellion
   of 1799 in protest against quit rents (q.v.) and a number of
   other grievances was to a large extent inspired by Wansey.
   He escaped capture once or twice but eventually his Mandinka
   and Susu allies surrendered him to the Colony government.

THE WARDER. Newspaper published in 1868 (only once) by the
   Rev. Benjamin Tregaskis in which he indirectly warned against
   the dangers of an established church in Sierra Leone.

THE WATCHMAN AND WEST AFRICAN RECORD (1875-1886). A
   newspaper founded and published by M. H. Davies.

WE YONE. Newspaper founded in 1964 as the official organ of the
   APC party.

WEATHERSTON, the Rev. JOHN. Chairman and general superintendent of the Methodist Mission in Sierra Leone (1856-1858).
   Weatherston arrived in Freetown on November 27, 1856. His
   tenure was plagued by ill-health and personal misfortune. His
   wife died in Freetown on August 31, 1857. A year later on
   August 19, 1858, he returned to England.

WEAVER, RICHARD. First chief in command or governor of the
   first Province of Freedom established by the settlers in Sierra
   Leone in 1787. He fell ill in September and was succeeded by
   James Reid as governor. On recovery, Weaver accused his successor of pilfering the provisions and was reinstated as governor. On August 22, 1788, when Capt. John Taylor signed a new
   treaty invalidating Thompson's treaty of 1787, Richard Weaver,
   with Capt. Taylor, Dr. Thomas Peall and Benjamin Elliott,
   signed on behalf of the settlers. This treaty of August 1788 is
   regarded as the legal beginning of the Colony of Sierra Leone.

WEEKS, the Rt. Rev. JOHN WILLIAM. Bishop of Sierra Leone,
   1855-1857. Came out to Sierra Leone as a CMS missionary
   on November 3, 1824, worked in the mountain villages of Regent and Gloucester, and also at Hastings. Weeks taught his
   schoolboys carpentry while his wife taught the girls to spin.
   In the mountain villages he experienced considerable difficulty
   with church benefit and welfare societies or church relief com-

panies whose initial goals were the fostering among other
things, of brotherly love and harmony between their members.
They were in fact cooperative societies which provided assistance in happiness or in distress for their members. Soon the
societies got out of hand and Weeks in 1842 blamed the companies for a break-down in church discipline and religious observance. Unable to suppress them he sensibly came to terms
with the societies, playing the role of nominal overseer. At
Hastings, in the early 1830s, he was confronted with another
and less assimilable phenomenom--the worship of idols, particularly those of Shango, the god of thunder. When Weeks in
the late 1840s decided to return home to England to work in a
parish in Lambeth, the people of Wellington Village, his former
parishioners, sent him small financial assistance as a mark of
sympathy with "the sad state in which his countrymen are at
present." In 1855 he returned to Sierra Leone as the second
Anglican bishop. Hailed with popular enthusiasm by former
pupils and old converts, he set about his episcopal duties with
a corresponding zeal. In June 1856 he ordained eight deacons,
six of them educated and trained exclusively in the Colony, laying the basis for a future Sierra Leone pastorate. He visited
the Yoruba mission only to die on his return to Freetown on
March 25, 1857.

WELLESLEY-COLE, ROBERT BENJAMIN AGEH, 1907- . Born
in Freetown on March 11, 1907. Educated at the Government
Model School, the CMS Grammar School, Fourah Bay College
(University of Durham), King's College (Durham University),
Newcastle-on-Tyne, where he qualified in medicine in 1935;
member, Ophthalmological Congress of Oxford; fellow, West
African Association of Surgeons; fellow and vice-president, West
African Association of Physicians. In private practice in the
United Kingdom mostly in Newcastle and in Nottingham until the
late 1960s when he returned home to Freetown and went into
government service as a consultant. Author of Kosso Town
Boy (1960), an autobiographical novel.

WEST, the Rev. WILLIAM, 1811-1898. Chairman and general superintendent of the Methodist Mission in Sierra Leone (1860-
1862). After the death of the Rev. John Bridgart in 1859 no
resident chairman and superintendent of the Methodist Mission
in Sierra Leone was appointed. Instead the Rev. William West,
chairman and general superintendent of the Gold Coast since
1857, was put in charge of the Sierra Leone District. For
three years he commuted between Cape Coast and Freetown.
When he returned to England in 1872 after 15 years in West
Africa he was already a sick man. In 1873 he went completely
and permanently blind. He died on April 17, 1898.

THE WEST AFRICAN HERALD (1868-1870?). A newspaper pub-
lished in Freetown by Charles Bannerman from the Gold Coast.
After about two years, Bannerman removed it to the Gold
Coast.

THE WEST AFRICAN LIBERATOR (1869-1870?). Newspaper founded and published by William Rainy.

THE WEST AFRICAN MAIL AND TRADE GAZETTE (1920-1932).
A commercial newspaper published in Freetown; incorporated by
The Sierra Leone Daily Mail in 1933.

THE WEST AFRICAN REPORTER (1876-1877, 1879-1884). Newspaper founded by William Grant.

THE WEST AFRICAN TEMPERANCE RECORD (1878). A newspaper published from time to time by a lodge of the Order of
Good Templars.

WEST AFRICAN YOUTH LEAGUE. Founded in May 1938 by I. T.
A. Wallace-Johnson, who became its organizing secretary.
The West African Youth League was the "offspring" of the West
African Civil Liberties and National Defence League which it
immediately supplanted. With its bi-weekly meetings held on
Sunday and Thursday afternoons, its sincere appeal to all sections of the Sierra Leone population, its militant rhetoric, its
ardent fraternity (all members addressed each other as com-
rade), its relentless attacks on the economic, political and
social ills of the country, the Youth League injected for the
first time in Sierra Leone's history a sense of national consciousness based on mass support.
          The League's political objectives included increased
representation in the Legislative Council, adequate representation on the Executive Council, emancipation of women, and
universal adult suffrage. If these goals exasperated local
colonial administrators who did everything they could to destroy
the League, they were by no means irreconcilably opposed to
British colonial policy. Because of the organizing secretary's
antecedents, the League was suspected by its detractors of being Communist-inspired. In November 1938 it successfully
contested the Freetown City Council elections and captured all
the four seats--and made history by securing among the four
the first woman to hold elective office in British West Africa.
          In the process the League introduced for the first time
in Sierra Leone the element of competitive party politics.
These successes were short-lived. The Colonial authorities
adopted high-handed repressive measures against the League,
imprisoned practically all its leaders during the war, and drove
fear into the rank and file. By the end of World War II it had
ceased to be a formidable force. The league's demise brought
to an end the first truly nationalist movement in the country's
history.

WILBERFORCE, WILLIAM, 1759-1833. British philanthropist and
orator; leading figure in the movement for the abolition of the
slave trade and the movement's chief spokesman in the House
of Commons. Member of the African Association, founded in
1788 to sponsor the exploration of the unknown interior of the

African continent.   Member also of the Clapham Sect, which
had much to do with the formation of the CMS.   Wilberforce,
with Granville Sharp and Henry Thornton, was most instrumental in the establishment of a home for freed slaves in
Sierra Leone.   He continued to manifest considerable interest
in the Colony until his death in 1833.

WILLIAMS, E. J. A., 1932-   .   Mathematician and educator.
Born November 29, 1932.   Educated at the Prince of Wales
School, Freetown, and at Queen's University, Belfast, Ireland.
Purser Student, 1955-1957.   Sloan Post-doctoral fellow at the
Massachusetts Institute of Technology, USA, 1961-1962.   Ap-
pointed lecturer, 1958, senior lecturer, 1962, and professor
(1970) and head, department of mathematics, Fourah Bay Col-
lege, USL.

WILLIAMS, E. J. B., 1897-1961.   Educator and administrator.
Born on August 19, 1897.   Educated at the CMS Grammar
School and at Fourah Bay College (University of Durham).
First Sierra Leonean to obtain a pass in the Oversea Cam-
bridge School Certificate examination (1914).   Supervising
teacher and inspector of schools (1934-1948).   Acting principal,
Bo Government School, 1943-1948.   Education officer, Sierra
Leone Government (1945-1953).   Retired from government ser-
vice in 1953 and joined the Freetown City Council as education
officer (1953-1961).

WILLIAMS, G. L. V., 1922-   .   Civil servant and administrator.
Born on May 31, 1922.   Educated at Hastings Primary School,
the CMS Grammar School, Freetown and at Balliol College,
Oxford.   Secretary to the president and administrative head of
the civil service.   Entered the civil service in 1940 and worked
his way up to permanent secretary, 1963; provincial secretary,
1966; secretary-general, NRC Secretariat, 1968; secretary to
the prime minister, 1968, and secretary to the president, 1971.

WILLIAMS, M. O., 1929-   .   Dean of the Faculty of Pure and Applied Science, professor and head of the Department of Zoology
at Fourah Bay College (USL).   Born on December 6, 1929.
Educated at the Prince of Wales School, Freetown, Trinity
College, Dublin and at the University of Glasgow.   Author of
several articles in scientific journals--for example, Experimental Parasitology, Journal of the West African Science Association, Journal of Helminthology, Bulletin de l'Institute
Fondamentale d'Afrique Noire, and Bulletin du Museum National
d'Histoire Naturelle.   Founder and president of the Sierra
Leone Biology Teachers Association (1968-1971); leader,
Permanent Study Group in Sierra Leone for UNESCO pilot
project for the development of new techniques and methods in
biology teaching in Africa.

WILLIAMS, the Rev. P. A. J., 1906-1975.   Chairman and general
superintendent of the Methodist Church in Sierra Leone (1967-

1975). Synod secretary, Methodist Church in Sierra Leone, 1956-1964. Born at Kissy Village (Freetown) on August 4, 1906. Educated at Buxton Methodist School, Wesleyan Boys High School and at Fourah Bay College. Ordained as a minister of the Methodist Church in 1948. He died in Freetown in December 1975.

WILLIAMS, P. J. Prominent public figure and politician. Founding member of the SLPP and from 1953-1958 the party's national vice-chairman. One of the four independents who after the 1967 general election wrote a letter to the governor general to make it clear that they wished to remain as independents in parliament. (See KAI SAMBA, K. I.). P. J. Williams was first chairman of the Bo Town Council (1959-1963). He represented the Bo Town II constituency in Parliament from 1962-1972. He was deputy speaker of Parliament, 1962-1963, and resident minister, Southern Province, 1969-70. He died in a road accident in March 1972.

WILSON, JOHN MACAULAY. He became King George II of Kafu Bullom in 1826 and the first Sierra Leonean to have been referred to as a surgeon and to have practiced medicine in the Colony. Son of King George I, Bai Sherbro of Kafu Bullom, Wilson was among the young Africans sent to England by the Sierra Leone Company for further training either in 1794 or in 1799. When he returned home, after studying possibly at Edinburgh, he was appointed apothecary by the Company. In 1808 when Sierra Leone became a Crown Colony, Wilson became government apothecary, a post that was abolished in 1815. In 1817 Governor Sir Charles MacCarthy sent him to Regent as acting surgeon and by 1822 he was referred to in the Sierra Leone Almanac as colonial surgeon at Leicester. When his father died in 1826, Wilson, who had lost his job as a result of the closure of his hospital, succeeded as King George II, Bai [Bey] Sherbro of Kafu Bullom. He set on foot negotiations for the "cession" of the Kafu Bulom Shore to the British Crown, but died before the actual transfer was effected in March 1827.

WINTERBOTTOM, THOMAS. Arrived in Sierra Leone in July 1792 as surgeon to the Sierra Leone Company and stayed in the Colony until April 1796. Author of An Account of the Native Africans in the Neighbourhood of Sierra Leone; To Which Is Added an Account of the Present State of Medicine Among Them (2 vols.; 1803).

WONDEH EXPEDITION see MILITARY EXPEDITIONS (11)

WRIGHT, E. H., 1935- . Born November 27, 1935. Educated at the Prince of Wales School, Freetown, and at the University of Hull, England. Professor and head, Department of Chemistry (1971-), Dean, Faculty of Pure and Applied Science (1970-1974), Fourah Bay College, University of Sierra Leone. Fellow of the Chemical Society, London; fellow of the Royal

Institute of Chemists, London, and member of the Faraday Society, London. Royal Society and Nuffield Foundation Commonwealth fellow at the University of Bristol (1963); Carnegie Corporation visiting fellow to the United States and Canada (1967). Sierra Leone's representative to the Scientific Council of Africa (OAU), (1970 to the present). External examiner in chemistry, University of Ife (1974 to the present). External examiner in chemistry, Universities of Benin and Cape Coast (1975 to the present). Author of several scientific articles in learned journals--e.g., Journal of the Chemical Society, Transactions of the Faraday Society, and Journal of Physical Chemistry.

WRIGHT, the Rt. Rev. GEORGE WILLIAM. Bishop of Sierra Leone, 1923-36. Consecrated bishop of Sierra Leone on November 1, 1923, and installed in St. George's Cathedral on November 30 of the same year. A shrewd and energetic administrator, his tenure of office as bishop of Sierra Leone saw important changes in the diocese. Shortly after taking office, a revised version of the Sierra Leone Church Constitution of 1890 was adopted and received clerical assent at a service held in St. George's Cathedral. Bishop Wright also launched a 100,000 shilling appeal fund to alleviate the Church's financial problems. The fund did go some way towards the solution of the problem. In 1936 the Pongas and Gambia severed ties with the Sierra Leone Church and were made a separate diocese with the consecration of Bishop Daly as the first bishop of the Gambia. In the same year Bishop Wright was transferred to the newly created Diocese of North Africa.

WURIE, AHMAD, 1898-   . Educator and politician. Born at Gbinti on August 27, 1898, and educated at Bo School--a foundation pupil and one of the school's most distinguished alumni. First Sierra Leonean acting principal of Bo School, 1933-34; 1936; 1947-48; headmaster, Koyeima School, 1935. Mr. Wurie was appointed inspector of schools, 1942, education officer, 1952, first principal of Kenema Secondary School, 1952, and education secretary, Northern Province, 1955. He was returned as member of Parliament for Port Loko North constituency in the 1962 general election and appointed minister of education (1962-65) and minister of the interior (1965-67).

- Y - Z -

YALUNKA see SUSU AND YALUNKA

YOKO, Madam. Born in a small village near Taiama, Moyamba District in about 1850 (her age was estimated in 1885 at about 35 years). Her family subsequently moved to Taiama where she was initiated into the Sande (bundu) society, through which she acquired fame as a great and beautiful dancer. She then married the chief of Taiama Gbenje, who was very friendly with Chief Gbanya of Senehun on the Bumpe River southwest of

Taiama. When her husband died, Yoko married Gbanya, and moved to Senehun, her new husband's home. There she established her own "Sande Bush," to which she attracted girls from all over Kpa Mende country. At the height of her fame, initiation into Yoko's "Sande" was, it has been suggested, equivalent to being "presented at court." Young girls from most ruling houses were trained by Yoko, who then ensured their marriage to the leading and great contemporary chiefs and warriors, thereby procuring the friendship and gratitude of those who mattered.

As chiefs thought it unwise and unsafe in those days to travel out of their chiefdoms, Gbanya sent his favorite Yoko on a number of missions including those to high government officials in Freetown. In the process she became well known over a wide area in the country and in official circles as well. Gbanya died in July 1878. Before his death he had asked Governor Rowe to help Yoko to succeed him. Rowe willingly did so. After Gbanya's death Yoko became more involved with British officialdom. She exploited this connection to extend and consolidate her power. Her chiefdom, described as the largest in the hinterland, extended at the height of her power from Bauya in the west to Tabe in the East and from the Temne chiefdoms in the north to the Banta and Sherbro chiefdoms in the south and southwest--an area roughly equivalent in territory to the present Moyamba District. She had other consorts after Gbanya's death, one of the most powerful being Thomas B. Caulker of the Bompe branch of the Caulker family. After the declaration of the Protectorate in 1896 and during the 1898 Hut Tax War Madam Yoko remained a strong and loyal ally of the British. She was occasionally mentioned in dispatches by a number of governors with whom she came in contact--Rowe, Havelock, Hay, Fleming, Cardew, King-Harman, and Probyn. After the Hut Tax War and because Senehun had been attacked and sacked by Yonis, Yoko moved her capital in 1899 to Moyamba, where she died in 1906. She was succeeded as chief of Moyamba by her brother, Lamboi.

YONI EXPEDITION see MILITARY EXPEDITIONS (8)

ZIZER, J. C. Lawyer and publicist. Mr. Zizer, a descendant of a family well known for public spiritedness and political protest, returned home to Freetown after a distinguished career at the Lagos bar. He spent much of his time in Freetown writing on the political, economic and social problems of his day, including town planning and fair employment. He died July 21, 1959, aged 68.

ZOROKONG of Messima. Chief of Messimah, Krim country, in the 1880s. Zorokong exercised a kind of vague overlordship over the country around Pujehun (or Gombu), the river head of the Wanje. This piece of territory was under the effective control of Momo Kai Kai and Momo Jah, sons of Mende fathers and Fula mothers. On October 21, 1883, Zorokong and other chiefs signed a treaty with the governor, Sir A. E. Havelock, "ceding" parts of the Krim and Messimah-Manoh countries to the British.

ZOUCHE HALL, Sir ROBERT DE. Governor of Sierra Leone, 1953-1956. Sir Robert's tenure was marred by outbreaks of social unrest in many parts of the country. In 1955 a very serious general strike of daily wage workers nearly wrecked Freetown. Troops had to be called out to restore order. In 1956 a series of risings against chiefs in parts of the Northern and Southern provinces taxed the government's resources to the utmost.

BIBLIOGRAPHY

Introductory Note

There are already in existence two comprehensive bibliographical works on Sierra Leone. One is by Harry Luke: Bibliography of Sierra Leone, first published in 1910, followed by a second edition (London: Oxford University Press, 1925), 230p. A new edition was published in 1969 by Negro Universities Press, New York. Luke's bibliography lists 1103 items and covers the period 1505 to 1924. The second is by G. J. Williams: A Bibliography of Sierra Leone, 1925-1967 (New York: Africana Pub. Corp., 1970), 209p. William's bibliography lists 3047 items. In addition a number of attempts have been made to supplement either of these two major bibliographies or both of them.

P. E. H. Hair in 1958 and 1960 wrote two articles. The first, "A Bibliographical Guide to Sierra Leone, 1460-1650," was published in Sierra Leone Studies, new series, X, 1958, pp. 62-72. The second, "A Bibliographical Guide to Sierra Leone, 1650-1800," appeared in Sierra Leone Studies, new series, XIII, 1960, pp. 5-49. Hair in the two articles listed about 147 items. In 1958 Ruth Jones, under the auspices of the International African Institute, London, produced a bibliography entitled "West Africa: General, Ethnography/Sociology, Linguistics." Under the heading Sierra Leone some 221 items are listed. Other important contributions to the bibliographical study of Sierra Leone include:

Helen F. Conover--"Africa South of the Sahara; A Selected Annotated List of Writings." (Washington, D.C.: Library of Congress, 1963); 28 items.

Hans Zell--"A Bibliography of Non-Periodical Literature on Sierra Leone" (excluding Sierra Leone Government publications; 1966).

A. A. Walker--"Official Publications of Sierra Leone and the Gambia" (Washington, D.C.: Library of Congress, 1963).

"Sierra Leone Library Publications"--published by the Sierra Leone Library Board since 1962.

J. P. Switzer--"A Bibliography of Sierra Leone 1968-1970" (Njala University College Library, 1971).

J. S. T. Thompson--Sierra Leone's Past; Books, Periodicals, Pamphlets and Microfilms in Fourah Bay College Library, 1971. (This is a subject catalog of the Sierra Leone Collection, a special collection containing materials on Sierra Leone and her immediate neighbors, Guinea, Liberia and the Gambia.)

BOOKS

Alldridge, T. J. The Sherbro and Its Hinterland. London: Macmillan and Co., 1901. 356p.

_____. A Transformed Colony: Sierra Leone As It Was and As It Is; Its Progress, Peoples, Native Customs and Undeveloped Wealth. London: Seeley & Co., 1910. 368p. (Reprinted by Negro Universities Press, New York, 1970.)

Awooner-Renner, M. A Visual Geography of Sierra Leone. London: Evans, 1971. 48p.

Ayandele, E. A. Holy Johnson; Pioneer of African Nationalism, 1836-1917. London: Frank Cass, 1970. 417p. (Cass Library of African Studies; African Modern Library, no. 13.)

Banbury, G. A. Lethbridge. Sierra Leone; or, The White Man's Grave. London: Sonnenschein & Co., 1888. 296p.

Banton, M. P. West African City: A Study of Tribal Life in Freetown. London: Oxford University Press for the International African Institute, 1957. 288p.

Bart-Williams, P. J. The Story of St. George's Cathedral. Freetown: Government Printer, 1970. 77p.

Bebler, Anton, ed. Military Rule in Africa; Dahomey, Ghana, Sierra Leone and Mali, edited for the Center of International Studies, Princeton University. New York: Praeger, 1973. 259p.

Bishop, W. L. Three West African Nations; Liberia, Ghana, Sierra Leone; A Comparative Study. New York: American-African Affairs Assoc., 1969. 22p.

Bowers, H.; Marsh, S. E.; and Showers, M. D. Yalunka Kharan Fanyi Kitabuna; Reading Book in the Yalunka Language. London: S. P. C. K., 1907. 41p.

Cartwright, John R. Politics in Sierra Leone, 1964-1967. Toronto: University of Toronto Press, 1970. 296p.

_____. Directory of Scholars in the Social Sciences Who Have Done Field Work or Had Other Research Experience in Sierra Leone. London, Ontario: Department of Political Science, University of Western Ontario, 1970. 30p.

Charlesworth, Maria. Africa's Mountain Valley; or, The Church in Regent's Town (Regent Village, Sierra Leone), West Africa. London, 1856. 272p.

Clarke, J. I. Sierra Leone in Maps, 2d. ed. London: University of London Press, 1969. 120p.

Clifford, Marie Louise. The Land and People of Sierra Leone. Philadelphia: J. B. Lippincott, 1974. 159p.

Cole, N. H. A. The Vegetation of Sierra Leone. Njala, Njala University College, 1968. 198p.

Collier, Gershon B. Sierra Leone; Experiment in Democracy in an African Nation. New York: New York University Press, 1970. 143p.

Correspondence and Other Papers Concerning Sierra Leone and Adjacent Territories, 1863-1886. Shannon: Irish University Press, 1971. 514p., plates, col. maps (British parliamentary papers, colonies, Africa, 53). (Facsimile reprint. of 1st. ed. --London: HMSO, 1863-1886.)

Cox-George, N. A. Finance and Development in West Africa: The Sierra Leone Experience. London: Denis Dobson, 1961. 333p.

Cronise, Florence, and Ward, H. W. Cunnie Rabbit, Mr. Spider and the Other Beef: West African Folk Tales, a Collection of Folk Tales Told by Natives of the Sierra Leone Protectorate, Mainly Mendes and Temnes in Their Dialect of Pidgin English. London: Swan Sonnenschein, 1903. 330p.

Crooks, J. J. Historical Records of the Royal African Corps. Dublin: Browne and Nolan, 1925. 137p.

_____. A History of the Colony of Sierra Leone, Western Africa. London: Frank Cass, 1972. 375p. (Cass Library of African studies; general studies no. 101). (Facsimile reprint of 1st. ed.--Dublin: Browne and Nolan; London: Simpkin, Marshall, Hamilton, Kent, 1903.)

Crowder, M. Pagans and Politicians. London: Hutchinson, 1959. 224p.

_____. West Africa Under Colonial Rule. London: Hutchinson, 1968. 540p.

Dallas, R. C. History of the Maroons from their Origin to the Establishment of Their Chief Tribe in Sierra Leone; With a History of Jamaica. London, 1803. 2 vols.

Dalton, K. G. A Geography of Sierra Leone. London: Cambridge University Press, 1965. 63p.

Dalziel, J. M.   The Useful Plants of West Tropical Africa; Being an Appendix to the Flora of West Tropical Africa by Hutchinson and Dalziel.   London: Crown Agents, 1937.   612p.

Davies, R. P. M.   History of the Sierra Leone Battalion of the Royal West African Frontier Forces.   London: The Author, 1930.   147p.

Elias, T. O.   Ghana and Sierra Leone; The Development of Their Laws and Constitutions.   London: Stevens and Sons, 1962. 334p.

Falconbridge, A. M.   Narrative of Two Voyages to the River Sierra Leone During the Years 1791-1793, new impression.   London: Frank Cass, 1967, 287p.   First published 1794.

Field, G. D.   Birds of Freetown Peninsula.   Freetown: Fourah Bay College Bookshop, 1974.   76p.

Findlay, G. S., and Holdsworth, W. W.   The History of the Wesleyan Methodist Missionary Society.   London: Epworth Press, 1921-24.   5 vols.   (Vol. IV [1924] gives a full account of the Wesleyan Mission in Sierra Leone on pp. 71-117.)

Fitzjohn, William Henry.   Ambassador of Christ and Caesar. Ibadan: Daystar Press, 1975.   154p.

_____.   Chief Gbondo; A Sierra Leone Story.   Ibadan: Daystar Press, 1975.   79p.

Fyfe, Christopher.   Africanus Horton: West African Scientist and Patriot.   1835-1883.   London: Oxford University Press, 1972. 169p.

_____.   A History of Sierra Leone.   London: Oxford University Press, 1962.   773p.

_____.   A Short History of Sierra Leone.   London: Longmans, 1962.   194p.

_____.   Sierra Leone Inheritance (West African History Series). London: Oxford University Press, 1964.   352p.

_____ and Jones, Eldred, eds.   Freetown; A Symposium.   Freetown: Sierra Leone University Press, 1968.   232p.

George, Claude [Esu Buji].   The Rise of British West Africa; Comprising the Early History of the Colony of Sierra Leone, new impression.   (Originally published by Houlston and Sons, London, 1904.)   London: Frank Cass & Co., 1968.   468p.

Gervis, P.   The Sierra Leone Story, new ed.   London: Cassell, 1956.   240p.

Goddard, T. N. The Handbook of Sierra Leone. London: Grant Richards for Sierra Leone Government, 1925. 336p. (Reprinted by Negro Universities Press, New York, 1969.)

Gorvie, M. Old and New in Sierra Leone. London: Butterworth Press, 1945. 80p. (Africa's Own Library, 9.)

_____. Our People of the Sierra Leone Protectorate. London: Butterworth Press, 1944. 65p. (Africa's Own Library, 6.)

Great Britain. Parliament. House of Commons. Select Committee on Free Labourers from the East. Reports from Select Committees on Free Labourers from the East, on the Slave Trade at Mauritius and on the Settlements of Sierra Leone and Fernando Po. Dublin: Irish University Press, 1968. 2, 89, 137 (10)p., plates (British Parliamentary Papers, slave trade, 1; 1810/11 [225] vol. 2; 1826 [430] vol. 3; 1826/27 [90] vol. 6; 1830 [661] vol. 10). (Facsimile reprint of 1st. ed., London.)

Griggs, E. L. Thomas Clarkson, The Friend of Slaves. London: Allen and Unwin, 1936. 210p.

Hailey, Lord. Native Administration in the British African Territories. Part III. West Africa; Nigeria, Gold Coast, Sierra Leone, Gambia. London: H. M. S. O., 1951. 350p.

Hakluyt, Richard. The Principall Navigations, Voiages and Discoveries of the English Nation, Made by Sea or Over to the Most Remote and Farthest Distant Quarters of the Earth at Any Time Without Compasse of These 1500 Yeeres. Imprinted at London by George Bishop and Ralph Newberie, Deputies to Christopher Barker ..., 1589. (2d. ed., London, 1598-1600, 3 vols.; 3d. ed., London, 1869-1812, 5 vols.; 4th ed., James Maclehose & Sons, Glasgow, 1904-5, 12 vols.)

Hall, P. K. The Diamond Fields of Sierra Leone. Freetown: Geological Survey of Sierra Leone, 1969. (Geological Survey of Sierra Leone, bulletin no. 5.)

Hanson, J. W., et al. Report on the Supply of Secondary-Level Teachers. Country Study No. 11, Sierra Leone. East Lansing: Michigan State University for Overseas Liaison Committee, American Council on Education, 1970. 85p.

Hargrave, G. G. African Primitive Life as I Saw It in Sierra Leone, British West Africa. Wilmington, N.C.: The Author, 1945. 115p.

Hargreaves, J. D. A Life of Sir Samuel Lewis. London: Oxford University Press, 1958. 112p. (West African History Series.)

Harris, J. M. Annexations to Sierra Leone. London, 1883. 66p. (Reprinted by Commercial Printers Co., Freetown, 1975.)

Harris, W. T., and Sawyerr, H. A. E. The Springs of Mende Belief and Conduct; A Discussion of the Influence of the Belief in the Supernatural Among the Mende. Freetown: Sierra Leone University Press, 1968. 152p.

Hilliard, F. H. A Short History of Education in British West Africa. London: Nelson, 1957.

Hirst, E., and Kamara, I. Benga. London: University of London Press, 1958. 80p.

Holmes, H. J. Behind Mount Lion: Treks and Tours in Sierra Leone. Andover: Advertiser Printing Works, n.d. [193?]. 93p.

Huxley, E. Four Guineas; A Journey Through West Africa. London, Chatto and Windus, 1954. 303p. (Sierra Leone, pp. 37-74.)

Ijagbemi, E. A. Gbanka of Yoni. Freetown: Sierra Leone University Press, 1973. 41p.

Ingham, E. G. Sierra Leone After a Hundred Years, new impression. London: Frank Cass and Company Ltd., 1968. (Cass Library of African Studies.) (First ed., 1894.

Institut Fondamental d'Afrique Noire. Le Massif des monts Loma (Sierra Leone). Fasc. 1. Dakar: Ifan, 1971. 417p. (Memoires de l'Institut Fondamental d'Afrique Noire, No. 86.)

Jack, D. T. Economic Survey of Sierra Leone. Freetown: Government Printer, 1958. 74p.

Jarrett, H. R. A Geography of Sierra Leone and Gambia. London: Longmans, 1964. 115p.

Johnson, L. G. General T. Perronet Thompson, 1783-1869: His Military, Literary and Political Campaigns. London: George Allen and Unwin, 1957. 294p.

Johnson, T. S. The Story of a Mission: The Sierra Leone Church, First Daughter of the CMS. London: S.P.C.K., 1953. 149p.

Kalous, Milan. Cannibals and Tongo Players in Sierra Leone. Auckland: The Author, 1974. 320p.

Kessen, J. M. Report on Sierra Leone Railways [mimeographed]. 1965. 103p.

Kilham, Hannah. Specimens of African Languages Spoken in the Colony of Sierra Leone. London: Printed for a Committee of the Society of Friends for Promoting African Instruction, 1828.

Kilson, M. L., Jr. Political Change in a West African State;
    A Study of the Modernization Process in Sierra Leone. Cam-
    bridge, Mass.: Harvard University Press, 1966. 301p.

Kingsley, Mary H. Travels in West Africa. London: Macmillan
    & Co., 1897. 743p. (2d. ed., abridged, 541p.)

_____. West African Studies, 2d. edition. London: Macmillan
    & Co., 1901. 507p.

Kirsop, Joseph. The Life of Thomas Truscott, Missionary to
    Sierra Leone. London: Andrew Crombie, 1890. 165p.

Kopytoff, J. H. A Preface to Modern Nigeria: The Sierra
    Leoneans in Yoruba 1830-1890. Madison, Wisc.: University
    of Wisconsin Press, 1965. 440p.

Kreutzinger, Helga. The Picture of Krio Life; Freetown 1910-
    1920. Vienna: Ferdinand Berger and Sohne, OHG, Hohn, N.O.,
    1968. 100p. (Acta ethnologica et linguistica, no. 11, 1968.)

Kup, A. P. A History of Sierra Leone 1400-1787. London: Cam-
    bridge University Press, 1961. 212p.

_____. Sierra Leone; A Concise History. Newton Abbot, Eng-
    land: David and Charles, 1975. 272p.

Labor, A. B. C. Merriman. Handbook of Sierra Leone 1901.
    Manchester. 206p.

_____. Handbook of Sierra Leone 1904-5. Manchester.

Laing, Alexander Gordon. Travels in the Timannee, Kooranko and
    Soolima Countries in Western Africa. London: John Murray,
    1825. 456p.

Lardner, H. H. Manual on Cultivation of the Commercial Products
    in Sierra Leone. London: Davies, Roblin and Pearce, 1890.
    109p.

Lewis, Arthur J. Higher Education in Sierra Leone. Washington,
    D.C.: American Council on Education Liaison Committee, 1968.

Lewis, Roy. Sierra Leone. London: H. M. S. O. for Colonial Of-
    fice (Corona Library), 1954. 263p.

Linstead, E. P. B. Morning at Mount Aureol. London: Laurie,
    1948. 173p.

Little, K. L. The Mende of Sierra Leone: A West African People
    in Transition, rev. ed. London: Routledge and Kegan Paul,
    1967. 308p. (First pub., 1951.)

_____. West African Urbanization: A Study of Voluntary Associations in Social Change. London: Cambridge University Press, 1965. 179p.

Lucan, T. A. Civics for Sierra Leone Book I. London: Longmans, 1970. 47p.

_____. _____. Book II. London: Longmans, 1970. 79p.

Luke, H. C. A Bibliography of Sierra Leone. With an Introductory Essay on the Origin, Character and Peoples of the Colony. Oxford: Clarendon Press, 1910. 144p. (2d. ed., London: Oxford University Press, 1925. 230p. Reprinted by Negro Universities Press, New York, 1969.)

_____. Cities and Men: An Autobiography. London: Bles, 1953-1956. 3 vols.

Lynch, H. R. Edward Wilmot Blyden. London: Oxford University Press, 1967. 272p.

Macaulay, Kenneth. The Colony of Sierra Leone Vindicated from the Misrepresentations of Mr. McQueen of Glasgow, new impression. London: Frank Cass & Co., Ltd., 1968. 127p. (Orig. pub., Edinburgh, 1827.)

Macbrair, R. M. Grammar of the Madingo Language with Vocabularies. London, 1837. 74p.

McCulloch, M. "Peoples of Sierrs Leone," in Forde, D., ed., Ethnographic Survey of Africa. Western Africa. Part II. London: International Institute, 1950. 102p. (Reprinted with new bibliography, 1964.)

McDonnell, M. F. J. The Laws of the Colony and Protectorate of Sierra Leone. London: Waterlow & Sons, Ltd., 1925. 3 vols.

Marke, C. Origins of Wesleyan Methodism in Sierra Leone. London: C. H. Kelly, 1913. 240p.

Martin, E. C. The British West African Settlements, 1750-1821: A Study in Local Administration. London: Oxford University Press, 1927.

Michell, H. An Introduction to the Geography of Sierra Leone. With a Chapter on the Geology of Sierra Leone by F. Dixey. London: Waterlow & Sons, 1919. 128p.

Migeod, F. W. H. The Languages of West Africa. London: Kegan Paul, Trench, Trubner & Co., 1911-1913. 2 vols.

_____. The Mende Language, Containing Useful Phrases, Elementary Grammar, Short Vocabularies, Reading Materials.

London: Kegan Paul, Trench, Trubner & Co., 1908.   271p.

_____. A View of Sierra Leone. London: Kegan Paul, 1926.
   351p.   Reprinted by Negro Universities Press, New York, 1970.

Milner, A., et al. Leading Cases in Sierra Leone. Oxford:
   African Law Reports, 1975. 647p. (African legal casebooks
   3.)

Milton Margai Teachers' College (1960-1970): Ten Years of Service. Njala: Njala University College Publications Centre,
   1970. 50p.

Montagu, Algernon. The Ordinances of the Colony of Sierra Leone.
   London: H.M.S.O., 1857-1881. 6 vols.

Newland, H. O. Sierra Leone; Its Peoples, Products and Secret
   Societies: A Journey by Canoe, Rail and Hammock Through a
   Land of Kernels, Coconuts and Cacao. London: John Bale,
   Sons and Danielson, 1916. 251p. (Reprinted by Negro Univer-
   sities Press, New York, 1969.)

Newbury, C. W. British Policy Towards West Africa. Select
   Documents. Vol. I, 1786-1874; Vol. II, 1875-1914. London:
   Oxford University Press, 1965. 656p.

Nicol, Davidson. Africanus Horton; The Dawn of Nationalism in
   Modern Africa; Extracts from the Political, Educational and
   Scientific Writings of J. A. B. Horton, M.D., 1835-1883.
   London: Longmans, 1969. 185p.

Nylander, G. R. Grammar and Vocabulary of the Bullom Language. London, 1814. 159p.

Olson, G. W. Church Growth in Sierra Leone; A Study of Church
   Growth in Africa's Oldest Protestant Mission Field. Grand
   Rapids, Mich.: Eerdmans, 1969. 222p. (Church growth
   series.)

Peaslee, A. J. "Constitutions of Nations." In vol. I, Africa
   (The Hague: Nijhoff, 1965). (1961 Constitution of Sierra
   Leone, pp. 715-771.)

Peterson, John. Province of Freedom; A History of Sierra Leone
   1787-1870. London: Faber, 1969. 354p., plates, maps.

Poole, C. E. Lane. A List of Trees, Shrubs, Herbs and Climbers
   of Sierra Leone. Freetown: Government Printing Office, 1916.
   159p.

Poole, T. E. Life, Scenery and Customs in Sierra Leone and the
   Gambia. London: Richard Bentley, 1850. 2 vols.

Porter, A. T. Creoledom; A Study of the Development of Freetown Society. London: Oxford University Press, 1963. 151p.

Pratt, W. E. A. An Autobiography. Sierra Leone: Government
Printing Department, 1973.

Rankin, F. Harrison. The White Man's Grave; A Visit to Sierra
Leone in 1834. London: Richard Bentley, 1836. 2 vols.

Ranson, B. H. A. A Social Study of Moyamba Town, Sierra Leone.
Zaria: Institute of Administration, Amadu Bello University,
1968. 110p.

Republican Sierra Leone. Freetown: Government Information Services, 1973. 58p.

Riddell, J. B. The Spatial Dynamics of Modernization in Sierra
Leone. Evanston, Ill.: Northwestern University Press, 1970.
142p.

Rodney, Walter. A History of the Upper Guinea Coast, 1545-1800.
Oxford: Clarendon Press, 1970. 283p.

Sawyerr, H. A. E. God: Ancestor or Creator? Aspects of Belief in Ghana, Nigeria and Sierra Leone. London: Longmans,
1970. 118p.

Schon, J. F. Grammar of the Mende Language. London:
S. P. C. K. , 1882. 99p.

_____. Mende-English and English-Mende Vocabulary. London:
S. P. C. K. , 1884. 255p.

Scott, D. J. R. "The Sierra Leone Election of May, 1957," in
Mackenzie, W. J. M. , and Robinson, K. E. , eds. , Five
Elections in Africa. London: Oxford University Press, 1960.
(pp. 168-280.)

Seddall, Henry. The Missionary History of Sierra Leone. London:
Hatchard & Co. , 1874. 246p.

Shields, L. Mende Manual of Prayers, Catechism and Hymns.
Sherbro, Sierra Leone, 1912. 116p.

Shreeve, W. W. Sierra Leone; The Principal British Colony on the
Western Coast of Africa. 1847.

Sibthorpe, A. B. C. The History of Sierra Leone, 4th ed. With
an introduction by Robert W. July. London: Frank Cass, 1970.
228p. (Cass Library of African Studies: African modern library, no. 9.)

Sierra Leone. Commission on Higher Education. Report. Freetown: Government Printer, 1970. 50p.

Sierra Leone Education Review, draft final report, May, 1974. Freetown: Government Printer. 260p.

Smith, Robert A. The All Peoples Congress: A Contemporary Political History of Sierra Leone. Monrovia, Liberia: Providence Publications, 1972. 131p.

Smith, William. A New Voyage to Guinea Descriptive of the Customs, Manners, Soil, Climate, Habits, Buildings, Education, Manual Arts, Agriculture, Trade, Employment, Languages, Ranks of Distruction, Diversions, Marriages, and Whatever Else is Memorable Among the Inhabitants. With an Account of Their Animals, etc. London, 1744.

Snelgrave, William. A New Account of Some Parts of Guinea and the Slave Trade. London: J. J. & P. Knapton, 1734. 288p. (Reprinted with a map, 1754.)

Spitzer, Leo. The Creoles of Sierra Leone; Responses to Colonialism, 1870-1945. Madison: University of Wisconsin Press, 1974. 260p.

Steel, Robert Walter. The Human Geography of Sierra Leone [mimeographed]. Freetown: Fourah Bay College, 1968. 349p.

Sumner, A. T. A Handbook of the Mende Language. Freetown: Government Printing Office, 1917. 191p.

_____. A Handbook of the Sherbro Language. Published by the Crown Agents for the Colonies for the Government of Sierra Leone, 1921. 132p.

_____. A Handbook of the Temne Language. Freetown: Government Printing Office, 1922.

Sumner, D. L. Education in Sierra Leone. Freetown: Sierra Leone Government, 1963. 475p.

Thomas, N. W. An Anthropological Report on Sierra Leone. Part I. Law & Custom of the Temne and Other Tribes. London: Harrison and Sons, 1916. 196p.

_____. _____. Part II. Timne-English Dictionary. London: Harrison & Sons, 1916. 139p.

_____. _____. Part III. Timne Grammar and Stories. London: Harrison & Sons, 1916. 86p.

_____. Specimens of Languages from Sierra Leone. London: Harrison & Sons, 1916. 62p.

Thompson, George. The Palm Land; or, West Africa Illustrated; Being a History of Missionary Labours and Travels, With Descriptions of Men and Things in Western Africa; Also a Synopsis of All the Missionary Work on That Continent, 2d. ed. London: Dawsons, 1969. 456p. (Orig. pub. , Cincinnati: Moore, Wilstach, Kays, 1858.)

Thompson-Clewry, Pamela. Foods and Nutrition Laboratory Handbook. Njala: Njala University College, 1970. 201p.

Thorpe, Robert. A Letter to W. Wilberforce, Esq. , M. P. , Vice-President of the African Institution etc. , Containing Remarks on the Reports of the Sierra Leone Company and African Institution: With Hints Respecting the Means by Which an Universal Abolition of the Slave Trade Might be Carried into Effect. London: F. C. & J. Rivington, 1815. 84p.

Trevelyan, G. O. Life and Letters of Lord Macaulay. London, 1876. (Gives a detailed account of the sack of Freetown by French revolutionary sailors in September 1794 during the governorship of Zachary Macaulay, father of Lord Macaulay.) (Reprinted 1881 and 1908.)

Trimingham, J. S. Islam in West Africa. London: Oxford University Press, 1959. 262p.

Trotter, J. K. The Niger Sources and the Borders of the New Sierra Leone Protectorate.... With Four Full-Page Illustrations & a Map. London: Methuen & Co. , 1898. 238p.

Unwin, A. H. Report on the Forests and Forestry Problems in Sierra Leone. London: Waterlow & Sons, 1909. 54p.

Utting, F. A. J. The History of Sierra Leone. London: Longmans, 1931. 178p.

Van Der Laan, H. L. The Lebanese of Sierra Leone. The Hague: Mouton, 1975. 385p.

_____. The Sierra Leone Diamonds: An Economic Study Covering the Years 1952-1961. London: Oxford University Press for Fourah Bay College, 1965. 228p.

Vergette, E. D. Certain Marriage Customs of Some of the Tribes in the Protectorate of Sierra Leone, 2d ed. Freetown: Government Printing Office, 1919. (First pub. , 1919.)

Villelume, Baron de. Au coeur de l'Afrique. Paris: Beauchesne et Die. , 1910. 275p. (Describes a visit to Freetown.)

Wadström, C. B. Adresse au Corps législatif et au directoire exécutif de la république française (au sujet des colonies de Sierra Leona et Boulama). Paris, 1795.

_____. An Essay on Colonization, Particularly Applied to the Western Coast of Africa, With Some Free Thoughts on Cultivation and Commerce; Also Brief Descriptions of the Colonies Already Formed or Attempted ... in Africa, Including Those of Sierra Leone and Bulama. London: Darton and Barvey, 1794.

Walckenaer, C. A. Collection des relations de voyages par mer et par terre en différentes parties de l'Afrique depuis 1400 jusqu'à nos jours. Paris: Chez l'éditeur, 1842. (Contains the voyages of Finch, Villaut, Barbot, Atkins, Labat, La Jaille, Matthews, Golberry, Beaver, Winterbottom, Laing, et al.)

Walker, Samuel A. Missions in Western Africa Among the Soosoos, Bulloms, etc. Dublin, 1845. 572p.

_____. The Church of England Mission in Sierra Leone, Including an Introductory Account of That Colony and a Comprehensive Sketch of the Niger Expedition in the Year 1841. London, 1847.

Wallis, C. Braithwaite. The Advance of Our West African Empire. London: T. Fisher Unwin, 1903. 318p. (Reprinted by Negro Universities Press, New York, 1969.)

_____. West African Warfare. London: T. Fisher Unwin, 1903.

West, Richard. Back to Africa; A History of Sierra Leone and Liberia. London: Cape, 1970. 357p.

Wilson. Notes on Malaria in Connection with Meteorological Conditions at Sierra Leone. London: H. K. Lewis, 1899.

Winterbotom, Thomas. An Account of the Native Africans in the Neighbourhood of Sierra Leone to Which is Added an Account of the Present State of Medicine Among Them, 2d. ed., with a new introduction by J. D. Hargreaves and E. M. Backett. London: Frank Cass, 1969. 2 vols. (Cass Library of African Studies: travels and narratives, no. 52). (Facsimile reprint of 1st. ed., London: J. Hatchard & J. Mawman, 1803.)

Yassin, M. Tales From Sierra Leone Retold by Mohamed Yassin. London: Oxford University Press, 1967. 55p.

Young, R. A First Geography of Sierra Leone (Brought Up to Date by Adams S.A.S.), 2d ed. London: Longmans, 1963. 88p.

Zell, H. M., ed., with Williams, G. J. The Freetown Vademecum. Freetown: Fourah Bay College Bookshop, 1966. 80p.

_____. _____. Supplement No. 1 [mimeographed]. 1967. 29p.

ARTICLES AND PAMPHLETS

Adams, S. A. S. "Some Thoughts on Teacher Education in a Developing Country." Sierra Leone Journal of Education, 2/2,
1967, pp. 19-23.

Adande, A., and Savounet, G. "Un Métier a tisser en pays Kono
(Sierra Leone) [a weaving trade in Kono country]." Notes
Africaines (Dakar), no. 61, 1954, pp. 21-22.

Addison, W. "The Nomori of Sierra Leone." African World (London), supplement, July 2, 1930.

_____. "Steatite Figures from Moyamba, Sierra Leone." Man,
XXIII, 1923.

Adler, S. "Malaria in a Chimpanzee in Sierra Leone." Annals of
the Liverpool School of Tropical Medicine and Parasitology,
vol. XVII, no. 1, 1923.

_____, and Cummings, E. H. T. "Malignant Growths in Natives
of Sierra Leone." Annals of the Liverpool School of Tropical
Medicine and Parasitology, vol. XVII, no. 4, 1923.

Akar, J. J. "The Arts in Sierra Leone." African Forum (New
York), 1, 1965, pp. 87-91.

Al-Harazim, S. D. "The Origin and Progress of Islam in Sierra
Leone." Sierra Leone Studies, o.s., no. 21, 1939, pp. 12-26.

Archibald, Adams G. "Story of the Deportation of Negroes from
Nova Scotia to Sierra Leone." Collections of the Nova Scotia
Historical Society, VII, 1891.

Armstrong, R. L. "The Road System of Sierra Leone." Sierra
Leone Trade Journal, 1, 1961, pp. 56-59.

Aubert, M. "Kissi Customs" (extracts from the book, Coutumiers
indigènes de la Guinée). Sierra Leone Studies, o.s., no. 20,
1936, pp. 88-95.

Avery, T. L. "An Analysis Over 8 Years of Children Admitted
with Measles to a Hospital in Sierra Leone, West Africa."
West African Medical Journal (Lagos etc.), 12, 1963, pp. 61-
63.

Awooner-Renner, M. "Our Educational Needs." Journal of Edu-

251

cation (Freetown), 2/2, 1967, pp. 11-14.

Bailey, L. F. "Teaching Through Trial and Error; NEA Teach Corps in Sierra Leone." Senior Scholastic, 84, April 17, 1964, 10T-11T.

Bakshi, T. S. "Bananas of Southern Sierra Leone." Economic Botany (Lancaster, Pa.), 17, 1963, pp. 252-262.

Bangura, J. S. "The Co-operative Movement in Sierra Leone." Economic Review, (Freetown), 2/1, 1967, pp. 1-9.

Bannerman, D. A. "A New Race of Sheppardia from Sierra Leone." Bulletin of the British Ornithologists' Club (London), 1931, pp. 128-129.

Banton, M. P. "Economic Development and Social Change in Sierra Leone." Economic Development and Cultural Change (Chicago), 2, 1953, pp. 136-138.

_____. "An Independent African Church in Sierra Leone." Hibbert Journal; A Quarterly Review of Religion, Theology and Philosophy (London), 55, 1956-57, pp. 57-63.

_____. "The Origins of Tribal Administration in Freetown." Sierra Leone Studies, n.s., no. 2, 1954, pp. 109-119.

Bassir, O. "The Food Habits of the Mendes." Africana (Newcastle-upon-Tyne), 1/2, 1949, pp. 23-24.

_____. "Marriage Rites Among the Aku (Yoruba) of Freetown." Africa, 24, 1954, pp. 251-256.

Bates, G. L. "Sierra Leone As a Winter Resort for Birds." Sierra Leone Studies, o.s., no. 16, 1930, pp. 18-20.

Beetham, T. A. "A Sierra Leone Missionary to Kenya." Sierra Leone Bulletin of Religion, no. 1, 1959, pp. 56-57.

Benjamin, E. "The Sierra Leone Census, 1963." Bulletin, Journal of the Sierra Leone Geographical Association, no. 9, 1965, pp. 63-71.

Beresford-Stooke, G. "Sierra Leone's Potential Riches." New Commonwealth, Aug. 17, 1953, p. 169.

Berry, J. W. "Creole as a Language." West Africa, no. 2207, Sept. 1959, p. 745.

_____. "The Structure of the Noun in Kissi." Sierra Leone Studies, n.s., no. 12, 1959, pp. 308-315.

Betts, V. O. "The Home Development Programme--Sierra Leone."
Women Today, 6/3, 1964, pp. 49-53.

Birch, J. P. "The Geography of Sierra Leone and Its Influence on
Communications" (substance of a lecture). Bulletin, Journal
of the Sierra Leone Geographical Association, no. 2, 1957, pp.
3-5.

Birkett, J. D. "Two Sierra Leone Tarpon." West African Review,
26/338, Nov. 1955, pp. 985-986.

Blacklock, B. "Breeding Places of Anopheline Mosquitoes in Freetown." Annals of the Liverpool School of Tropical Medicine
and Parasitology, vol. XV, no. 4, 1921.

Bockari, J. "The Derivation of Mende Names for the Months of
the Year." Sierra Leone Studies, n.s., no. 4, 1955, pp. 208-
210.

_____. "Some Funeral and Other Ceremonies Among the
Mendis." School Notes (Department of Education, Freetown),
no. 9, 1945, pp. 40-43.

Bradshaw, A. T. von S. "Vestiges of Portuguese in the Languages
of Sierra Leone." Sierra Leone Language Review, 4, 1965,
pp. 5-37.

Brown, C. V. "Banking in Sierra Leone: A Comparative Survey."
Bankers' Magazine (London), 201, 1066, pp. 193-199.

Brown, G. W. "The Poro in Modern Business, A Preliminary Report on Field Work." Man, 37, 1937, pp. 8-9.

Burgess, R. C. "Sierra Leone and the Surveyor." Journal of the
Royal Institution of Chartered Surveyors (London), 29, 1950,
821-830.

Burney-Nicol, S. "How Hydroelectricity Can Reduce the Price of
Current in Sierra Leone." Sierra Leone Science Bulletin
(Freetown), 1/1, 1962, pp. 31-33.

Byrne, J. "Sierra Leone: Trade and Communications." Journal
of the African Society (London), 29, 1929, pp. 1-6.

Calcott, D. "Factors Relating to Erosion and Soil Conservation
in Sierra Leone." Bulletin, Journal of the Sierra Leone Geographical Association, no. 1, 1956, pp. 8-10.

Campbell, W. A. "Colonial Geological Abstracts, Part XI, Sierra
Leone." Colonial Geology and Mineral Resources (London), 6,
1956, pp. 217-225.

Cardew, F. "Railway Schemes: Sierra Leone." Liverpool Chamber of Commerce. African Trade Section, 1895.

Carney, D. E. "The Economics of Health in Conditions of Low Population Growth: The Example of Sierra Leone." International Social Science Journal (UNESCO, New York), 17/2, 1965, pp. 277-283. (Published also in French in Revue Internationale des Sciences Sociales, 17/2, 1965, pp. 296-303.)

_____. "The Integration of Social Development Plans and Overall Development Planning in Sierra Leone." Overseas Quarterly (London), 4, 1965, pp. 141-143. (Published in French in Revue Internationale des Sciences Sociales, 16, 1964, pp. 387-408.)

Carpenter, A. J. "Objectives and Methods in Rice Breeding and Selection in Sierra Leone." Agronomie Tropicale (Noget-sur-Marne), 18, 1963, pp. 783-785.

Carter, M. "Professional Women of Sierra Leone." African Women (London), 3, 1959, pp. 57-59.

Caulker, D. H. "A Short Account of the Origin of Kono E. U. B. Mission Work." Sierra Leone Outlook, 48/1, Jan. 1961, pp. 10-13.

Chalmers, Lady. "In Defence of Sir David Chalmers." Nineteenth Century and After, March 1900.

Charles, N. "Educational Problems in Sierra Leone." West African Review, 31/397, 1960, pp. 41-47.

Chaytor, D. E. B., and Williams, M. O. "The Freshwater Fishes of the Freetown Peninsula." Bulletin de l'Institut Française d'Afrique Noire (Paris, Dakar), A, 28, 1966, pp. 1041-1063.

Clarke, A. "The View from Freetown." African Development, 1/10, 1967, 3.

Clarke, J. I. "Letter from Freetown." Journal of the Durham University Geographical Society (Durham), 6, 1963-1964, pp. 8-13.

_____. "The Population of Sierra Leone." Sierra Leone Science Bulletin (Freetown), 1/2, 1963, pp. 14-16.

_____. "Sex Ratios in Sierra Leone." Bulletin Journal of Sierra Leone Geographical Association, no. 9, 1965, pp. 72-77.

Clarke, W. R. E. "The Foundation of the Luawa Chiefdom" (the story of Kailahun and Ndawa). Sierra Leone Studies, n.s., no. 8, pp. 245-251.

Colbeck, E. M. "Annie Walsh Memorial School, Freetown, Sierra Leone." East and West Review (London), 22, 1956, pp. 116-122.

Cole, I. E. "Two Spider Stories from the Temne." Sierra Leone Studies, o.s., no. 21, 1939, pp. 106-109.

Cole, J. Abayomi. "Trees, Herbs and Roots in West Africa." Journal of the Royal Society of Arts, Sept. 22, 1906.

Cole, N. H. A. "Ecology of the Montane Community at the Tingi Hills in Sierra Leone." Bulletin de l'Institut Française d'Afrique Noire (Paris, Dakar), A, 29, 1967, pp. 904-924.

Coleson, E. P. "The Colony of Sierra Leone; An Experiment in Tropical Development." The Social Studies (Brooklawn, N.J.), 50, 1959, pp. 12-19.

Conton, W. F. "The Content of West African Education; A View from Sierra Leone." West African Journal of Education, 7/21, 1963, pp. 74-76.

_____. "The Educational System of Sierra Leone." Journal of Education (Freetown), 1/1, 1966, pp. 3-7; 1/2, 1966, pp. 5-10.

Cookson, C. E. "Haidara's Rebellion" (letter). Sierra Leone Studies, n.s., no. 4, 1955, p. 229.

Coomber, H. E., and Coombs, T. J. "Ginger from Sierra Leone." Colonial Plant and Animal Products (London), 1, 1950, pp. 140-143.

Cotay, A. B. "Sierra Leone in the Post-War World." African Affairs, 58, 1959, pp. 210-220.

Couper, Leslie. "Some Notes on West African Currency." Colonial Office Journal, vol. III, no. 2, 1909.

Cox-George, N. A. "Direct Taxation in the Early History of Sierra Leone." Sierra Leone Studies, n.s., no. 5, 1955, pp. 20-35.

_____. "Sierra Leone Needs Stability." New Commonwealth, July 1959.

_____. "Some Problems of Financing Developments in Sierra Leone, West Africa." Public Finance (The Hague), 8, 1953, pp. 115-145.

Creighton, T. R. M. "Sierra Leone at the Polls." Spectator, 208, May 25, 1962, pp. 673-674.

Crosby, K. H. "Polygamy in Mende Country." Africa, 10, 1937, pp. 249-264.

Crossley, E. M. "Sierra Leone--Diamond Country." African Trade and Development (London), 4/12, Dec. 1962, pp. 16-17.

Crowder, M. "An African Aristocracy." Geographical Magazine (London), 31/4, 1958, pp. 183-190.

_____. "Sierra Leone: £20 Million for Iron Ore." New Commonwealth, June 1958, pp. 564-566.

Cuthbert, J. M. "A Comparison Between Bloods of Some Non-Malarial and Malarial European Soldiers in Sierra Leone." Journal of the Royal Army Medical Corps, vol. XVII, no. 1, 1911.

Dalby, T. D. P. "Banta and Mabanta." Sierra Leone Language Review, no. 2, 1963, pp. 23-25.

_____. "The Extinct Language of Dama." Sierra Leone Language Review, no. 2, 1963, pp. 50-54.

_____. "An Investigation into the Mende Syllabary of Kisimi Kamara." Sierra Leone Studies, n.s., no. 19, 1966, pp. 119-123.

_____. "Language Distribution in Sierra Leone, 1961-1962." Sierra Leone Language Review, no. 1, 1962, pp. 62-67.

Dalton, K. G. "A Fula Settlement in Mendeland." Bulletin, Journal of the Sierra Leone Geographical Association, no. 6, 1962, pp. 4-5.

_____. "Recent Development in Sierra Leone." Bulletin of the Ghana Geographical Association (Accra), 6/2, 1961, pp. 3-12.

_____. "Rice from the Scarcies River." Bulletin, Journal of the Sierra Leone Geographical Association, no. 5, 1961, pp. 9-10.

Daveau, S. "The Loma Mountains." Bulletin, Journal of the Sierra Leone Geographical Association, no. 9, 1965, pp. 2-11.

_____. "Ruissellement et soutirages dans la haute vallée du Denkale (Montes Loma, Sierra Leone) [drainage and river capture in the upper Denkale Valley (Loma Mountains, Sierra Leone)]." Bulletin de l'Association des Geographes Francais (Paris), nos. 330/331, 1965, pp. 20-27.

Davies, A. P. "Church Teacher Training in Sierra Leone." East and West Review, July 1951, pp. 90-94.

Davies, E. J. "Some Problems of Design and Maintenance of Water Supplies in Sierra Leone." Journal of the Institution of Water Engineers (London), 15, 1961, pp. 57-69.

_____; Garber, N. J.; and Harleston, A. E. "Design Storm Hyetographs from Studies of Rainfall in the Western Area of Sierra Leone." Journal of the Institution of Water Engineers (London), 20, 1966, pp. 67-74.

D'Azevedo, W. L. "Uses of the Past in Gola Discourse." Journal of African History, 3, 1962, pp. 11-34.

Decker, T. "Jubilee of the Sierra Leone Protectorate." West African Review, 17, Sept. 1946, pp. 992-993.

_____. "The Krios of Sierra Leone: The Youngest British West African Tribal Group." African World, July 1947, 21 and Africa (London), 1/2, 1949, pp. 9-10.

Deighton, F. C. "Origins of Creole Plant Names." Sierra Leone Studies, o.s., no. 22, 1939, pp. 29-32.

_____. "Pasture and Fodder Plants of Sierra Leone." Sierra Leone Agricultural Notes (Njala, Freetown), no. 6, 1944.

_____. "Preliminary List of Fungi and Diseases of Plants in Sierra Leone." Kew Bulletin (London), 1936, pp. 397-424.

Dent, J. M. "Sierra Leone Measures." Sierra Leone Agricultural Notes, no. 24, 1956, 2p. (mimeo.).

_____. "Some Soil Problems of Empoldered Rice Lands to Sierra Leone." Empire Journal of Experimental Agriculture (Oxford), 15, 1947, pp. 206-212.

Despight, S. M. "A Short History of the Gallinas Chiefdoms." Sierra Leone Studies, o.s., no. 21, 1939, pp. 5-12.

Dewdney, J. C. "The Distribution of Employment in Sierra Leone." Sierra Leone Geographical Journal (Freetown), no. 11, pp. 51-59.

Dixey, F. "The Geology of Sierra Leone." Quarterly Journal of the Geological Society of London (London), 81, 1925, pp. 195-222.

_____. "The Physiography of Sierra Leone." Journal of the Royal Geographic Society, Nov. 1921.

Dixon-Fyle, S. R. "Economic Structure and Short Period Behaviour of the Sierra Leone Economy." Economic Review (Bank of Sierra Leone, Freetown), 2/3, 1967, pp. 1-27.

Djoume, C.   "La Cérémonie funéraire dans le Kissi; funérailles et succession d'un chef" [the funeral ceremony of the Kissi: funerals and succession of a chief].   Education Africaine; Bulletin de l'Enseignement de l'Afrique Occidentale Française (Goree), 32/108, 1934, pp. 21-27.

Donovan, C. E.   "Educational Development in the Protectorate." Education Bulletin (Education Department, Sierra Leone [Bo]), 1/1, 1951, pp. 8-12.

Dorjahn, V. R., and Hogg, T. C.   "Job Satisfactions, Dissatis-factions and Aspirations in the Wage Labour Force of Mag-buraka, a Sierra Leone Town."   Journal of Asian and African Studies (Leiden), 1, 1966.

Drummond, D. B.   "The Stick and Sand Game."   Sierra Leone Studies, o.s., no. 16, 1930, pp. 67-68.

_____, and Kamara, K.   "Some Koranko Place Names." Sierra Leone Studies, o.s., no. 16, pp. 27-34.

Earthy, E. D.   "Short Note on the Kissi Smith."   Man, 34/180, 1943, pp. 158-161.

Easmon, M. C. F.   "Bunce Island."   West African Review, 22, 1951, pp. 1257-1260.

_____.   "Conditions of Medical Work in a West African Bush Station."   Journal of Tropical Medicine and Hygiene, 28, 1925, pp. 128-131.

_____.   "The Massaquoi Crown."   Sierra Leone Studies, o.s., no. 22, pp. 83-89.

_____.   "Sierra Leone Doctors."   Sierra Leone Studies, n.s., no. 6, 1956, pp. 81-96.

Easmon, R. S.   "Tuberculosis in Sierra Leone."   NAPT Bulletin (London), 65, 1945, pp. 260-263.

Eddy, T. P.   "Tuberculin Testing in Sierra Leone."   West African Medical Journal (Lagos), no. 6, 1957, pp. 1-9.

Edwards, D. C.   "Cotton in Sierra Leone: An Attempt to Improve the Native Type."   Empire Cotton Growing Review (London), 7, 1930, pp. 91-97.

Edwards, F. A.   "The French and Sierra Leone."   Gentleman's Magazine, 1898.

Everett, M.   "Sierra Leone (Strategic Importance."   Journal of the Royal United Service Institution (London), 86, Aug. 1936, pp. 501-504.

Fenton, J. S. "Characters in Mendi Stories." Sierra Leone Studies, o.s., no. 15, 1929, pp. 34-51.

Ferron, P. M. "Early Environmental Stimulation Among Freetown Creoles, a Comparative Study." Educational Research (London), 8, 1966, pp. 217-222.

_____. "Some Thoughts Concerning the Establishment of an Institute of Education in Sierra Leone." Teacher Education (London), 7/3, 1967, pp. 201-210.

Finnegan, R. H. "Limba Religious Vocabulary." Sierra Leone Language Review, no. 2, 1963, pp. 11-15.

_____. "The Traditional Concept of Chiefship Among the Limba." Sierra Leone Studies, n.s., no. 17, 1963, pp. 241-253.

Fisher, H. J. "Ahmadiyya in Sierra Leone." West Africa, no. 2329, Jan. 1962, p. 73.

Fitch-Jones, B. W. "An Inscribed Rock at Sierra Leone." Journal of the Royal Geographic Society, vol. LXIV, no. 2, 1924.

Fox Bourne, H. R. "Sierra Leone Troubles." Fortnightly Review, LXIV, 1898.

Freeman, H. "Vai and Their Kinsfolk." Negro History Bulletin (Washington), 16, 1952, pp. 51-63.

Frere, N. G. "The Cultivation of Swamp Rice in the Scarcies Delta." Sierra Leone Studies, o.s., no. 7, 1925, pp. 39-42.

_____. "Notes on the History of Port Loko and Its Neighbourhood." Sierra Leone Studies, o.s., no. 2, 1919, pp. 45-51. (Reprinted, April 1926, pp. 63-69.)

Fyfe, C. H. "The Countess of Huntingdon's Connexion in Nineteenth Century Sierra Leone." Sierra Leone Bulletin of Religion, 4, 1962, pp. 53-61.

_____. "The Life and Times of John Ezzidio." Sierra Leone Studies, n.s., no. 4, 1955, pp. 213-223.

_____. "Royal Charter for Fourah Bay College." West African Review, 31/388, 1960, pp. 18-21.

_____. "A Royal Visit in 1860." Sierra Leone Studies, n.s., no. 12, 1959, pp. 259-272.

Gaillard, J. "Un Français, roi du Fouta-Djallon." Bulletin du Comité d'Etudes Historiques et Scientifiques de l'Afrique Occidentale Française, vol. VIII, no. 2, 1924.

Gamble, D. P. "The Population of Kenema." Sierra Leone Geographical Journal (Freetown), no. 11, 1967, pp. 15-24.

Garrett, G. H. "Sierra Leone and the Interior to the Upper Waters of the Niger." Journal of the Royal Geographic Society, vol. XIV (new series), 1892, p. 433.

Glanville, R. R. "The Game Birds of the Northern Province." Sierra Leone Studies, o. s., no. 21, 1939, pp. 35-43.

Gledhill, D. "Additions to the Grass Flora of Sierra Leone." Boletim da Sociedade Broteriana (Coimbra), 41, 1967, pp. 57-62.

_____. "Ecology of the Aberdeen Creek Mangrove Swamp." Journal of Applied Ecology (Oxford), 51, 1963, pp. 693-703.

Gordon, W. T. "A Note on Some Large Diamonds Recently Recovered from the Gravels of the Woyie River, Sierra Leone." Bulletin of the Imperial Institute (London), 43, 1945, pp. 111-120.

Griffeth, T. R. "Races Inhabiting Sierra Leone." Journal of the Anthropological Institute, XVI, 1886.

Gutteridge, W. F. "Sierra Leone and Her Army." British Army Review (London), 1961, 7p.

Gwynne-Jones, D. R. G. "Rubber Production in Sierra Leone." Bulletin Journal of the Sierra Leone Geographical Association, no. 9, 1965, pp. 23-26.

Gyasi-Twum, K. "Sierra Leone Students Leaving Fourah Bay College Between 1944 and 1956." Sierra Leone Studies, n.s., no. 10, 1958, pp. 85-98.

Hair, P. E. H. "A Check-List of British Parliamentary Papers on Sierra Leone." Sierra Leone Studies, n.s., no. 19, 1966, pp. 146-150.

_____. "Creole Endeavour and Self Criticism in Sierra Leone Church Missions, 1900-1920." Sierra Leone Bulletin of Religion, 8, 1966, pp. 6-18.

_____. "Ethnolinguistic Continuity on the Guinea Coast." Journal of African History, 8, 1967, pp. 247-268.

_____. "The Spelling and Connotation of the Toponym 'Sierra Leone' Since 1461." Sierra Leone Studies, n.s., no. 18, 1966, pp. 43-58.

Hall, H. U. "Secret Societies of Sierra Leone" (abstract). Nature (London), 143, Feb. 25, 1939, 338.

Hall, R. "Nineteenth Century Chief's Medals." Sierra Leone Studies, n.s., no. 12, 1959, pp. 201-210.

Hambly, W. D. "A Trident from Sierra Leone in the Collections of the Field Museum of Natural History (Chicago)." Man, 31/44, 1931, 42.

Hamelberg, E. "The Jesuits in Sierra Leone 1605-1617. A Whirlwind of Grace." Sierra Leone Bulletin of Religion, 6, 1964, pp. 1-8.

Hamilton-Hazeley, L. E. A. "The Education of Women and Girls in the Provinces." Journal of Education (Freetown), 1/1, 1966, pp. 20-23.

Hargreaves, E. "Garden Pests and Diseases in Sierra Leone." Pamphlets, Lands and Forests Department, Sierra Leone (Freetown), no. 14, 1929, 38p.

Hargreaves, J. D. "Constitutional Change in Sierra Leone." Colonial Review (London), June 1957, pp. 50-51.

_____. "End of an Era." West African Review, 32/401, May 1961, pp. 53-60.

_____. "Sir Samuel Lewis and the Legislative Council." Sierra Leone Studies, n.s., no. 1, 1953, pp. 40-52.

Harnetty, E. A. "A Few Notes on the Yalunka Country and an Outline of Its History." Sierra Leone Studies, o.s., no. 21, 1939, pp. 75-78.

_____. "A Sierra Leone Sidelight on the European Crisis. Sept. 1938." Sierra Leone Studies, o.s., no. 22, 1939, pp. 49-51.

Harris, S. H. "American's Impressions of Sierra Leone in 1811" (with text of Paul Cuffee's letters). Journal of Negro History (Lancaster, Pa.), 47, 1962, pp. 35-41.

Harris, W. T. "Ceremonies and Stories Connected with Trees, Rivers and Hills in the Protectorate of Sierra Leone." Sierra Leone Studies, n.s., no. 2, 1954, pp. 91-97.

_____. "How the Mende People First Started to Pray to Ngewo." Sierra Leone Bulletin of Religion, 5, 1963, pp. 61-63.

Hatch, J. "Election Without Issue." New Statesman, 63, June 8, 1962, 820.

Hawkes, D. D. "The Freetown Layered Complex" (abstract). Journal of the West African Science Association, 10, 1965, 68.

Heiser, F. B. "Fourah Bay College." Church Missionary Review, 77, 1926, pp. 60-72.

Herskovits, M. J. "Kru Proverbs." Journal of American Folklore, 43, 1930, pp. 225-293.

Hill, O. M. "Sierra Leone: New African Nation." Foreign Trade, 115, May 6, 1961, pp. 16-17.

Hilliard, F. H. "Fourah Bay College. Anglican Religious Training College Looks Forward." East and West Review (London), Oct. 1950, pp. 11-116.

Hirst, E. "An Attempt at Reconstructing the History of the Loko People from About 1700 to the Present Day." Sierra Leone Studies, n.s., no. 9, 1957, pp. 26-39.

_____. "Some Religious Practices of the Lokos of Kalangba (Northern Province Sierra Leone)." Ghana Bulletin of Theology (Achimota), 1, 1958, pp. 4-8.

Hofstra, S. "Personality and Differentiation in the Political Life of the Mende." Africa, 10, 1937, pp. 436-457.

_____. "The Social Significance of the Oil Palm in the Life of the Mende." International Archives of Ethnography (Leiden), 34, 1937, pp. 105-117.

Holas, B. "La Circomcision dans le pays Kissi [circumcision in Kissi country]." Acta tropica (Basel), 6, 1949, pp. 350-379.

_____. "Dènkongo, dieu de la foudre des Kissiens [Denkongo, god of the founder of the Kissis]." Notes Africaines (Dakar), no. 36, Oct. 1947, pp. 12-13.

_____. "Echantillons due folklore Kono [charms in Kono folklore]." Etudes Guinéennes (Conakry), no. 9, 1952, pp. 3-90.

_____. "Sur la présence de la pensée totémique en Afrique noire: position theorique de la question, exèmple des Kono [on the presence of totem belief in black Africa: the theoretical position; the Kono example]." Garcia de Orto (Lisbon), 3, 1955, pp. 427-443.

Holden, C. L. "Education Officer in Sierra Leone." Corona, 11/8, 1959, pp. 300-302.

Hollins, N. C. "Mende Law." Sierra Leone Studies, o.s., no. 12, 1928, pp. 25-44; o.s., no. 13, 1928, pp. 29-33; o.s., no. 15, 1929, pp. 57-58.

_____. "A Note on the History of the Court Messenger Force." Sierra Leone Studies, o.s., no. 18, 1932, pp. 72-80.

_____. "Precis of Events in the Safroko Limba Chiefdom."
Sierra Leone Studies, o.s., no. 7, 1925, pp. 35-38.

Hornell, J. "Kru Canoes of Sierra Leone." Mariner's Mirror,
15, 1929, pp. 233-237.

_____. "The String Games and Tricks of Sierra Leone."
Sierra Leone Studies, o.s., no. 13, 1928, pp. 3-9.

_____. "The Tuntu Society of Dema Chiefdom (with an addition-
al note by P. Hamblin-Smith)." Sierra Leone Studies, o.s.,
no. 13, 1928, pp. 17-21.

Horstead, J. L. C. "Towards an Indigenous Church in Sierra
Leone." East and West Review, April 1946, pp. 41-46.

Houis, M. "Le Minorités ethniques de la Guinée côtière: situation
linguistique (Baga, Temne, etc.) [ethnic minorities of the
Guinea Coast; linguistic situation (Baga, Temne, etc.)]."
Etudes Guinéennes (Conakry), 4, 1950, pp. 25-48.

_____. "Que sont les Soso? [who are the Susu?]." Etudes
Guinéennes (Conakry), 6, pp. 77-79.

Hudson, Arthur. "The Missionary in West Africa." Journal of the
African Society, no. 8, 1903. (Deals with the Missionary question in its bearing on the Sierra Leone Rebellion of 1898.)

Hutton, J. Arthur. "West African Finances." Journal of the African Society, no. 2, 1902.

Ijagbemi, A. "The Writing of Temne History." Proceedings, Njala
Geographical Association (Njala), no. 3, June 1967, pp. 8-10.

Inga, B. "Ceremonies on the Death and Crowning of a Paramount
Chief in Temne Country." Sierra Leone Studies, o.s., no. 2,
1919, pp. 57-61. (Reprinted, April 1926, pp. 71-76.)

Innes, G. "A Note on Consonant Mutation in Bandi." Sierra Leone
Studies, n.s., no. 14, 1960, pp. 90-92.

_____. "A Note on Mende and Kono Personal Names." Sierra
Leone Language Review, 5, 1966, pp. 34-38.

_____. "An Outline Grammar of Loko with Texts." African
Language Studies (London), 5, 1964, pp. 115-173.

Jabati, S. A. "Agricultural Development in Sierra Leone." Sierra
Leone Trade Journal, 7, 1967, pp. 7-11.

_____. "Industrial Development in Sierra Leone." Sierra Leone
Trade Journal, 5, 1965, pp. 118-119.

Jacobs, K. C. "Economy and Development in Sierra Leone."
Corona, 12, 1960, pp. 370-373.

Jaeger, P. "La case kouranko (Guinée française et Sierra Leone)
[the Koranko house (French Guinea and Sierra Leone)]." Notes
Africaines, no. 31, 1946, pp. 16-19.

_____. "Contribution a l'étude du modelé de la Dorsale Loma-
Man (Sierra Leone) [contribution to the study of the Loma-Man
Range (Sierra Leone)]." Revue de Geomorphologie Dynamique
(Paris), 3, 1953, pp. 105-113.

James, G. W. "A Brief Account of the Temne Constitutional Law,
with Special Reference to the History and Customs of the Koia
Chiefdoms, with Notes by R. S. Hooker." Sierra Leone Studies, o.s., no. 22, 1939, pp. 112-119.

Jarrett, H. R. "Lunsar: A Study of an Iron Ore Mining Centre in
Sierra Leone." Economic Geography (Worcester, Mass.), 32,
1956, pp. 153-161.

_____. "Mineral Developments in Sierra Leone." Geography
(Sheffield), 42, 1957, pp. 258-260.

_____. "Some Aspects of the Urban Geography of Freetown,
Sierra Leone." Geographical Review (New York, etc.), 46,
1956, pp. 334-354.

_____. "Weather in Sierra Leone." Geographical Journal (Lon-
don), 120, 1954, pp. 124-127.

Jellico, M. R. "Women's Groups in Sierra Leone." African
Women (London), 1, 1955, pp. 35-43.

Johnson, C. E. O. "The Impact of Mining in Sierra Leone."
Journal of King's College Geographical Society, 13, 1962, pp.
17-23.

_____. "The Problem of Rural Depopulation in the Sierra Leone
Peninsula." Journal of King's College Geographical Society
(Newcastle-upon-Tyne), 14, 1963, pp. 36-41.

Johnson, H. M. A. "The Vocational Outlook of the Sierra Leone
'Creole'." Sierra Leone Studies, o.s., no. 22, 1939, pp. 52-
57.

Jones, E. D. "Krio in Sierra Leone Journalism." Sierra Leone
Language Review, 3, 1964, pp. 24-31.

_____. "Sierra Leone and the English Language; The Results
of an Investigation into the Use of English by Adults in Sierra
Leone." West African Journal of Education, 6, 1960, pp. 10-
18.

_____. "Some Aspects of the Sierra Leone Patois of Krio."
Sierra Leone Studies, n.s., no. 6, 1956, pp. 97-100.

Jones, T. S. "Notes on Monkeys of Sierra Leone." Sierra Leone
Agricultural Notes (Njala, Freetown), no. 22, 1950, 7p. mimeo.

_____, and Cansdale, G. S. "Notes on the Commoner Sierra
Leone Mammals." Nigerian Field (London, etc.), 31, 1966,
pp. 4-17.

_____, and Cave, A. J. E. "Diet, Longevity and Dental Disease
in the Sierra Leone Chimpanzee." Proceedings of the Zoological
Society of London (London), 135, 1960, pp. 147-155.

Jones, W. D. "Blyden, Gladstone and the War." Journal of Negro
History (Lancaster, Pa.), 49, 1964, pp. 56-61.

Jones-Quartey, K. A. B. "Sierra Leone After the 'Non Coups'."
(1). Legon Observer, 2/26, Dec. 1967, pp. 8-10.

_____. "Sierra Leone and Ghana: Nineteenth Century Pioneers
in West African Journalism." Sierra Leone Studies, n.s., no.
12, 1959, pp. 230-244.

_____. "Sierra Leone's Role in the Development of Ghana, 1820-
1930." Sierra Leone Studies, n.s., no. 10, 1955, pp. 73-84.

Jordan, H. D. "The Development of Rice Research in Sierra
Leone." Tropical Agriculture (Trinidad), 31, 1954, pp. 27-32.

_____. "Some Notes on a Collection of Native Rice Varieties at
Rokupr Together with a Key for their Identification." Sierra
Leone Agricultural Notes (Njala, Freetown), no. 21, 1950, 17p.
mimeo.

Juby, L. W. "Land of Interminable Bush. The Church in Mendeland." World Dominion (London), Sept.-Oct. 1951, pp. 307-
313.

July, R. W. "Africanus Horton and the Idea of Independence in
West Africa." Sierra Leone Studies, n.s., no. 18, 1966, pp.
2-17.

_____. "Nineteenth-Century Negritude: Edward W. Blyden."
Journal of African History, 5, 1964, pp. 78-86.

Jusu, B. M. "The Haidara Rebellion of 1931." Sierra Leone
Studies, n.s., no. 3, 1954, pp. 147-153.

Kaim-Caudle, P. R. "Review of Economic Changes in Sierra
Leone 1930-1955." Durham University Journal, 1957, pp. 34-
41.

_____. "Sierra Leone--Hopes and Prospects." Durham University Journal, 54, 1961, pp. 21-31.

Kamara, K. "Notes on Some Customs of the Kurankos." Sierra Leone Studies, o.s., no. 17, 1932, pp. 94-101.

Karefa-Smart, J. "Africa in World Affairs." [Mainly on Sierra Leone.] African Studies Bulletin (New York), 6, no. 1, March 1963, pp. 4-13.

_____. "The Challenge of Sierra Leone's New Status." Optima (Johannesburg), 2, 1961, pp. 93-97.

Keith-Lucas, B. "Electoral Reform in Sierra Leone." Political Studies (Oxford), 3, 1955, pp. 97-108.

_____. "Sierra Leone: Problems of Independence." University of Toronto Quarterly (Toronto), 31, 1961, pp. 96-109. (Reprinted in Maclure, M., and Anglin, D., eds., Africa: The Political Pattern, Toronto: University of Toronto Press, 1967.)

Kershaw, R. "What Happened in Sierra Leone." New Statesman, 31, March 1967, 428.

Khuri, F. I. "Kinship, Emigration and Trade Partnership Among the Lebanese of West Africa." Africa, 35, 1965, pp. 385-395. (Based on work carried out in Magburaka, Sierra Leone and Quadougou, Upper Volta.)

Kilson, M. de B. "Mende Folk Tales." West African Review, 31/397, 1960, pp. 87-91; 32/398, 1961, pp. 45-48.

_____. "Social Relationships in Mende Domeisia." Sierra Leone Studies, n.s., no. 15, 1961, pp. 168-172.

Kilson, M. L., Jr. "Grass Roots Politics in Africa: Local Government in Sierra Leone." Political Studies (Oxford), 12, 1964, pp. 47-66.

_____. "Sierra Leone Politics--The Approach to Independence. Parts I-IV." West Africa, 18, June 25, 2, July 9, 1960, 688-689; 709, 744-745; 773-774.

King, V. E. "Future Trends in Education in Sierra Leone." Proceedings of the Njala Geographical Association, no. 2, April 1967, pp. 10-11.

Kirby, D. "Ballots in the Bush: A Case Study of Local Elections in the Bo District of Sierra Leone." Journal of African Administration (London), 9, 1957, pp. 174-182.

Konte, K. A. "A Few Notes on the History of the Karene District Lokos." Sierra Leone Studies, o.s., no. 22, 1939, pp. 120-127.

Koroma, U. H. "The Bronze Statuettes of Ro-Ponka, Kafu Bulum."
Sierra Leone Studies, o.s., no. 22, 1939, pp. 25-28.

Kreutzinger, H. "The Eri Devils in Freetown, Sierra Leone."
Acta Enthnologica et Linguistica (Wien), no. 9, 1966, 73p.

_____. "Die Markte von Freetown [the markets of Freetown]."
Mitteilungen der Anthropologischen Gesellschaft in Wien (Vienna),
93/94, 1964, pp. 40-61.

Kup, A. P. "Early Portuguese Trade in the Sierra Leone and
Great Scarcies Rivers." Boletin Cultural da Guine Portuguesa,
18, 1963, pp. 107-124.

_____. "Instructions to the Royal African Company's Factor at
Bunce, 1702." Sierra Leone Studies, n.s., no. 5, 1955, pp.
44-53; no. 6, 1956, pp. 71-80.

_____. "Islam in Sierra Leone." West Africa, no. 2214, 1959,
941; no. 2215, 1959, 969.

_____. "Jesuit and Capuchin Missions of the 17th Century."
Sierra Leone Bulletin of Religion, 5, 1963, pp. 27-34.

Lambert, S. "Ghana, Nigeria and Sierra Leone." Architectural
Design (London), 32, 1962, pp. 328-342.

Langley, E. R. "Marriage Customs Amongst the Temnes." Sierra
Leone Studies, o.s., no. 13, 1928, pp. 54-59.

_____. "A Tale of Nimi Koro Chiefdom, Kono District." Sierra
Leone Studies, o.s., no. 15, 1929, pp. 29-33.

Little, K. L. "The Changing Position of Women in Sierra Leone
Protectorate." Africa, 18, 1938, pp. 1-17.

_____. "The Mende Farming Household." Sociological Review
(Ledbury), 40/4, 1948, pp. 1-20.

_____. "The Political Function of the Poro. Part I." Africa,
35, 1965, pp. 349-365.

_____. "The Political Functions of the Poro. Part II. The Re-
lation of the Chief to the Poro." Africa, 36, 1966, pp. 62-71.

_____. "Social Change and Social Class in the Sierra Leone
Protectorate." American Journal of Sociology (Chicago), 54,
1948, pp. 10-21.

Littlejohn, J. "The Temne 'Ansasa'." Sierra Leone Studies, n.s.,
no. 13, 1960, pp. 32-35.

_____. "Temne Space." Anthropological Quarterly, 36, 1963,
pp. 1-17.

Loveridge, A. J. "The Present Position of the Temne Chiefs of Sierra Leone." Journal of African Administration (London), 9, 1957, pp. 115-120.

Lucan, T. A. "Review of Education in Sierra Leone in the Last Five Years." Journal of Education (Freetown), 1/1, 1966, pp. 12-19.

Luke, T. C. "Some Notes on the Creoles and Their Land." Sierra Leone Studies, o. s., no. 21, 1939, pp. 53-66.

Lynch, H. R. "The Attitude of Edward W. Blyden to European Imperialism in Africa." Journal of the Historical Society of Nigeria (Ibadan), 3, 1965, pp. 249-260.

_____. "Edward Wilmot Blyden: Africa's First Ambassador to Europe." Presence Africaine (Paris), 31, 1966, pp. 141-148.

_____. "The Native Pastorate Controversy and Cultural Ethno-Centrism in Sierra Leone." Journal of African History, 5, 1964, pp. 395-414.

Macgregor, W. D. "The Forest Production Programme in Sierra Leone." Farm and Forest (Ibadan), 3, 1942, pp. 116-119.

_____. "Forestry in Sierra Leone." Journal of Forestry (Washington), 46, 1948, pp. 184-187.

Malcolm, J. M. "Mende Warfare." Sierra Leone Studies, o. s., no. 21, 1939, pp. 47-52.

Maplestone, P. A. "A Survey of the Parasites Found in Natives of Sierra Leone." Annals of the Liverpool School of Tropical Medicine and Parasitology, vol. XVIII, no. 2, 1924.

Margai, A. M. "Sierra Leone." New Commonwealth Trade and Commerce, no. 12, 1966, 553.

_____, and Anthony, F. S. "Memorandum to the Secretary of State for the Colonies on the New Constitution." Sessional paper no. 48 of 1948 (typescript).

Margai, M. A. S. "Music in the Protectorate of Sierra Leone." Magazine of West African Students Union of Great Britain, 2, 1926, pp. 38-40.

_____. "Welfare Work in a Secret Society." African Affairs, 47, 1948, pp. 227-230.

Mason, A. E. W. "Making Good." Cornhill Magazine, Jan. 1910. (A story, based on fact, of the Human Leopard Society in the Sherbro District, Sierra Leone.)

Mauny, R.   "Masques Mendé de la société Bundu (Sierra Leone)
[Mende masks of the Bundu society (Sierra Leone)]."   Notes
Africaines, no. 18, 1959, pp. 8-13.

McBurney, D. A.   "Teko Livestock Farm."   Sierra Leone Agricultural Notes (Njala), no. 11, 1944, 11p. mimeo.

Meecham, K.   "A Survey of the Pelagic Fishing and Fisheries of
the West African Seaboard."   Sierra Leone Science Bulletin
(Freetown), 1/2, 1963, pp. 33-42.

Mekeel, H. S.   "Social Administration of the Kru."   Africa, 10,
1937, pp. 75-96; 12, 1939, pp. 460-468.

Mengot, A. D. A.   "The Challenge from Mount Aureol."   West
African Review, 26/333, June 1955, pp. 521-525.

_____.   "Convocation on Mount Aureol."   West African Review
27/342, 1956, pp. 217-221.

Menzies, A.   "Exploratory Expedition to the Mende Country."
Church Missionary Intelligencer, 1868.

Mercer, Roy.   "Banking in West Africa."   Colonial Office Journal,
vol. III, no. 3, 1910.

Migeod, F. W. H.   "The Building of the Poro House and Making
of the Image, Sierra Leone."   Man, XVI, 1916.

_____.   "Mende Songs."   Man, XVI, 1916.

Milburn, S.   "Kisimi Kamara and the Mende Script."   Sierra Leone
Language Review, 3, 1964, pp. 20-23.

Mintenko, G. P.   "Sierra Leone; A One-Product Market."   Foreign
Trade (Toronto), 121, June 13, 1964, pp. 20-21.

Mitchell, P. K.   "Irrigation in Sierra Leone: Possibilities and
Prospects."   United Nations conference on the application of
science and technology for the benefit of the less developed
areas, Sept. 21, 1962.   (mimeographed paper.)

_____.   "Matotoka: A Sierra Leone Chiefdom Town."   Sierra
Leone Studies, n.s., no. 17, 1963, pp. 269-277.   (An expanded
and revised version appeared in Bulletin, Journal of the Sierra
Leone Geographical Association, no. 7, 1964, pp. 18-24.)

_____.   "Notes on Land Tenure Systems in Sierra Leone."
Bulletin, Journal of the Sierra Leone Geographical Association
(Freetown), no. 7/8, 1964, pp. 39-43.

Morrison, C. R.   "The Vai Speaking Peoples of the Southern
Province."   Sierra Leone Studies, o.s., no. 22, 1939, pp.
104-107.

Mould, P. S. "Rural Improvement by Communal Labour in the Bombali District of Sierra Leone; A Case Study." Journal of Local Administration Overseas (London), 5, 1966, pp. 29-46.

Mudge-Paris, D. B. "Tales and Riddles From Freetown, Sierra Leone." Journal of American Folklore (Lancaster, Pa.), 43, 1930, pp. 317-321.

Ndanema, I. M. "The Martha Davies Confidential Benevolent Association." Sierra Leone Bulletin of Religion, 3, 1961, pp. 64-67.

_____. "The Rationale of Mende 'Swears'." Sierra Leone Bulletin of Religion, 6, 1964, pp. 21-25.

N'diaye, S. "Masques d'ancêtres de la société Poro de Sierra Leone [ancestral masks of the Poro Society of Sierra Leone]." Notes Africaines, no. 103, 1964, pp. 73-81.

Neustadt, I. "Sierra Leone; Sociology at the University College of Sierra Leone." Nov.-Dec. 1965, Paris, UNESCO, 1966, 64p.

Newland, C. H. "Problems Associated with Development in Sierra Leone." Farm and Forest, 5, 1944, pp. 21-24.

_____. "The Sofa Invasion of Sierra Leone (With a note on the Waiima incident by Hancock, G. C.)." Sierra Leone Studies, o.s., no. 19, 1933, pp. 162-171.

Newman, T. M. "Archaeological Survey of Sierra Leone." West African Archaeological Newsletter, (Legon), no. 4, March 1966, pp. 19-22.

Newns, F. "Bird Watching Around Freetown." Nigerian Field (London, etc.), 28, 1963, pp. 172-183.

Nicholls, E. H. O. "Report on the Administration of the Public Works Department, Sierra Leone." Freetown, Government Printer, 1928, 38p.

Nicol, D. S. H. W. "Fourah Bay College." Times, Supplement on Sierra Leone, April 27, 1961.

_____. "Politics, Nationalism and Universities in Africa." African Affairs, 62/246, Jan. 1963, pp. 20-28.

_____. "West Indians in West Africa." Sierra Leone Studies, n.s., no. 13, 1960, pp. 14-23.

Nicol-Cole, S. B. "The Colony-Protectorate Gap in Sierra Leone." Africana, the Magazine of the West African Society (London), 1/2, April 1949, pp. 27-28.

Olakanpo, J. O. W.   "The Loynes Report and Banking in Sierra
Leone." Bankers' Magazine (London), 194, 1962, pp. 19-27.

Olu-Wright, R. J.   "The Physical Growth of Freetown."   Paper
presented at the Freetown Symposium, Fourah Bay College,
Dec. 1966, 8p. mimeo.

O'Reilly, J.   "From a College at Bo: Teacher Training." West
African Review, 22, 1951, pp. 37-39.

Orestov, O. V.   "Strane i'Vinykh gor [in the country of the Lion
Mountains]." Ogonek (Moscow), no. 34, 1961, pp. 22-23.
(Comments on independence celebrations with particular refer-
ence to the arrest of members of the opposition party.)

Orr, G. B.   "A Biographical Note on the Rt. Hon. Sir Matthew
Nathan, P.C., G.C.M.G. (1862-1929)." Sierra Leone Studies,
n.s., no. 8, 1957, pp. 252-254.

Osipov, V.   "S'yerra Leone: obstoyatel'stva i lyudi [Sierra Leone:
conditions and peoples]." Aziya i Afrika Segodnya (Moscow),
no. 11, 1961, pp. 34-35.

Ozanne, P.   "A Preliminary Archaeological Survey of Sierra Leone."
West African Archaeological Newsletter (Legon), no. 5, 1966,
pp. 31-36.

_____.   "Sierra Leone Archaeology." Research Review (Institute
of African Studies, University of Ghana, Legon), 2/2, 1966,
pp. 39-41.

Padmore, G.   "Democratic Advance in Sierra Leone." Crisis, 64,
1957, pp. 149-153.

Panda, G. S.   "Report of the Board of Inquiry into the Docks Dispute." Freetown, Government Printer, 1967, 25p.

Parsons, R. T.   "Death and Burial in Kono Religion." Sierra
Leone Bulletin of Religion, 3, 1961, pp. 55-64.

_____.   "Religion in Kono Village Life." Sierra Leone Bulletin
of Religion, 1, 1959, pp. 36-47.

Pastor.   "Le Langue soso [the Susu language]. Voix de Notre-
Dame, Dec. 4, 1931, pp. 406-409.

Paulme, D.   "L'Excision en pays kissi [excision in Kissi country]."
Comptes Rendu de l'Institut Francais d'Anthropologie (Paris),
no. 3, Jan. 1947-Dec. 1949, 5.

_____.   "La Notion de sacrifice chez un peuple 'fétichiste' [the
idea of sacrifice among a fetish people]." Revue de l'Histoire
des Religions (Paris), 132, 1946, pp. 48-66.

Peaslee, A. J. "Constitutions of Nations." Vol. I, Africa (Constitution of Sierra Leone, April 27, 1961, pp. 715-771). The Hague: Nijhoff, 1965.

Perowne, L. "The Sierra Leone Broadcasting Service." Corona, 13, 1961, pp. 134-135.

Person, Y. "L'Aventure de Porèkeré et le drame de Waiima [the Porekore adventure and the Waiima affair]." Cahiers d'Etudes Africaines (Paris), 2, 1965, pp. 248-316.

_____. "Les Kissi et leurs statuettes de pierre dans le cadre de l'histoire Ouest africaine [the Kissi and their stone carvings in the framework of West African history]." Bulletin de l'Institut Française d'Afrique Noire (Paris, Dakar), B, 23, 1961, pp. 1-59.

_____. "Samori et la Sierra Leone [Samori and Sierra Leone]." Cahiers d'Etudes Africaines, 7, 1976, pp. 5-26.

Petch, G. A. "Economic Planning in Sierra Leone, 1945-1953." West Africa Institute of Social and Economic Research, annual conference, Ibadan, 1953, pp. 25-38.

_____. "Report on the Oil Palm Industry of Sierra Leone." Sierra Leone Government, 1955. 233p. (mimeo.).

_____. "Social Problems at Marampa." West Africa, April 1954, 367.

Piggott, C. J. "The Maintenance of Soil Fertility in Sierra Leone." Transactions of the Sixth International Congress of Soil Science, Paris, 1956, vol. D.

Pollett, J. D. "The Diamond Deposits of Sierra Leone." Bulletin of the Imperial Institute (London), 35, 1937, pp. 333-348.

_____. "The Geology and Mineral Resources of Sierra Leone." Colonial Geology and Mineral Resources (London), 2, 1951, pp. 3-28. (Reprinted for Geological Survey Department, Sierra Leone, by H. M. S. O., 1951, 28p.)

Porter, A. T. "Ethnic Relations in Sierra Leone." Institute of Race Relations Newsletter, April 1961, supplement, 4p.

_____. "Family Histories and West African Social Development: The Role of the Creole in Nineteenth Century Sierra Leone." In Historians in Tropical Africa; Proceedings of the Leverhulme Inter-Collegiate History Conference, Salisbury, Southern Rhodesia, 1962, pp. 305-315.

_____. "Religious Affiliation in Freetown, Sierra Leone." Africa, 23, 1953, pp. 3-14.

Probyn, Leslie. "Alcohol and the African: The Experiment in Sierra Leone." Nineteenth Century and After, no. 400, June 1910.

_____. "Sierra Leone and the Natives of West Africa." Journal of the African Society, no. 23, 1907.

Proudfoot, L. "Ahmed Alhadi and the Ahmadiyyah in Sierra Leone." Sierra Leone Bulletin of Religion, 2, 1960, pp. 66-68.

_____. "Mosque-Building and Tribal Separatism in Freetown East." Africa, 29, 1959, pp. 405-416.

_____, and Wilson, H. S. "Muslim Attitudes to Education in Sierra Leone." Muslim World (Hartford, Conn.), 50/2, 1960, pp. 86-98.

Quilliam, Abdallah. "A Chapter in the History of Sierra Leone." Journal of the African Society, no. 9, 1903. (Deals with Islam in Sierra Leone; see also under Vivian, W.)

Reichman, S. "Domestic Air Transport in Sierra Leone." Bulletin, Journal of the Sierra Leone Geographical Association, no. 9, 1965, pp. 27-33.

Renner, G. T. "Geographic Regions of Sierra Leone." Economic Geography (Worcester, Mass.), 7, 1931, pp. 41-49.

Renner, W. "Management of Labour by Native Midwives." Journal of Tropical Medicine and Hygiene, Dec. 21, 1908.

_____. "The Spread of Cancer Among the Descendants of the Liberated Africans or Creoles of Sierra Leone." Journal of Tropical Medicine and Hygiene, July 15, 1910.

Renner, W. A. "Germany's Development Aid to Sierra Leone." Afrika (Bonn), 5, 1964, pp. 211-212.

Rivers, D. G. "Variations of the Earth's Magnetic Field in Sierra Leone." Sierra Leone Science Bulletin (Freetown), 1/1, 1962, pp. 20-25.

Roberts, G. E. P. "The First Gold." Sierra Leone Studies, o.s., no. 22, 1939, pp. 9-14.

Robertson, S. D. M. "The Sierra Leone Railway." Corona, 13, 1961, pp. 109-113.

Rodney, W. A. "A Reconsideration of the Mane Invasions of Sierra Leone." Journal of African History, 8, 1967, pp. 219-246.

Root, J. W. "British Trade with West Africa." Journal of the African Society, no. 1, 1901.

Ruete, T. "Sierra Leone's Straw Cloths." African World, 28, Feb. 1929, supplement.

Rydings, H. A. "Prince Naimbana in England." Sierra Leone Studies, n.s., no. 8, 1957, pp. 200-208.

Samba, K. "Soil Conservation in Sierra Leone." Farm and Forest (Ibadan), 8, 1947, p. 83.

Sanceau, V. E. H. "The Sierra Leone Topographical Survey." Empire Survey, Review (London), 2, 1933, pp. 163-166.

Sankoh, L. "The Fourah Bay College Fund: The Alternative." Freetown: The author, 1948, 24p.

_____. "The Significance of Our Acceptance of the Municipality Ordinance...." Freetown: The Author, 1947.

Sawyerr, H. A. E. "The African Adventure." East and West Review, 14/4, 1948, pp. 110-113.

_____. "Ancestor Worship." Sierra Leone Bulletin of Religion, 6, 1964, pp. 25-33.

_____. "Origins of the Mende Concept of God." Sierra Leone Bulletin of Religion, 9, 1967, pp. 66-73.

_____. "Postpositions and Prepositions in the Mende Language." Sierra Leone Studies, n.s., no. 8, 1957, pp. 209-220.

_____. "The Role of a University of Sierra Leone--A Projection." Journal of Education (Freetown), 1/1, 1966, pp. 11-16.

Scanlon, D. G. "The Bush School." Phi Delta Kappan, 4/1, Jan. 4, 1960, pp. 148-150.

Schlenker, C. F. "Temne Customs." Church Missionary Record, June 1851.

Senior, M. M. "Woman in the African Village Church." International Review of Missions (London), 37, 1948, pp. 403-409.

Serle, W. "Birds of Sierra Leone, Parts I-IV." Ostrich, 1948, pp. 129-141; 187-199; 1949, 70-85; 114-126.

Sesay, S. I. "Koranic Schools in the Provinces." Journal of Education, Freetown, 1/1, 1966, pp. 24-26.

Sesay, S. M. "Drivers in the Transport Industry: A Case Study of Road Transport in Sierra Leone." Sierra Leone Studies, n.s., no. 19, 1966, pp. 86-97.

Shelford, F. "The Railways of British West Africa." Board of

Trade Journal, no. 175, 1900.

Shuffrey, P.   "The Poro; An African Initiation Society."   Life and
Letters, autumn 1937, pp. 43-47.

_____.   "West African Careers for Young Men: Opportunities
on the Gold Coast and in Sierra Leone."   Field, 6, Dec. 1930,
826.

Simpson, A. G.   "Report on the Sierra Leone General Election,
1957."   Freetown (Government Printer), 1957.

Simpson, D.   "A Preliminary Political History of the Kenema Area."
Sierra Leone Studies, n.s., no. 21, 1967, pp. 52-61.

Skuse, T.   "The Mapping of Sierra Leone."   Bulletin, Journal of
the Sierra Leone Geographical Association, no. 7/8, 1964, pp.
29-32.

Songo-Davies, J. A.   "The Annexation of Sulima, Lavana and Mano
Salija."   Sierra Leone Studies, o.s., no. 17, 1932, pp. 34-39.

_____.   "Jawi Chiefdom."   Sierra Leone Studies, o.s., no. 15,
1929, pp. 63-66.

_____.   "The Origin of the Masimera Chiefdom."   Sierra Leone
Studies, o.s., no. 13, 1928, pp. 22-24.

Spears, R. A.   "Tone in Mende."   Journal of African Languages,
6, 1967, pp. 231-244.

Spencer, D.   "Cassava Marketing in Sierra Leone."   Proceedings
of the Njala Geographical Association, no. 3, June 1967, pp. 1-
7.

_____.   "Operating of Small Rice Mills in Sierra Leone."
Njala: Njala University College, 1967.   16p. (mimeo.).

Spitzer.   "Creole Attitudes Toward Krio--An Historical Survey."
Sierra Leone Language Review, 5, 1966, pp. 39-49.

_____.   "Maledictions and African Glories: Freetown Intellec-
tuals and the Negro Past."   Paper presented at the Freetown
Symposium, Fourah Bay College, Dec. 1966.   7p. (mimeo.).

Stanley, Lord.   "Narrative of Mr. W. C. Thompson's Journey from
Sierra Leone to Timbo, Capital of Futah Jallo in Western
Africa."   Journal of the Royal Geographical Society, vol. XVI
(old series) 1846, pp. 106-138.

Stevens, S. P.   "Trade Unionism in Sierra Leone."   Empire Review and Journal of British Trade (London), 1948, p. 5.

Stone, G. E.   "Tobacco, Its Growth and Production in Sierra
    Leone." Sierra Leone Science Bulletin, 1/3, 1966, pp. 17-19.

Sumner, A. T.   "The Derivation of Certain Place Names in the
    Protectorate of Sierra Leone." Sierra Leone Studies, o.s.,
    no. 15, 1929, pp. 4-15.

_____. "The Kunkubé." (A peculiarly constructed canoe made
    and used in some parts of the Protectorate by members of the
    "Aligator Society"--Mende and Sherbro.) Sierra Leone Studies,
    o.s., no. 12, 1928, pp. 23-24.

_____. "Mendi Writing." Sierra Leone Studies, o.s., no. 17,
    1932, pp. 29-33.

Swindell, K.   "Diamond Mining in Sierra Leone." Tijdskrift voor
    Economische en Sociale Geografie (Den Haag), 57, 1966, pp.
    96-104.

_____. "Iron Ore Mining in West Africa: Some Recent De-
    velopments in Guinea, Sierra Leone and Liberia." Economic
    Geography (Worcester, Mass.), 43, 1967, pp. 333-346.

Terrier, Auguste. "La Frontière franco-libérienne." Bulletin
    Mensuel Du Comité De L'Afrique Française, XIX, no. 4,
    April 1910. (Deals in part with the northeastern boundary of
    Sierra Leone.)

Thomas, A. H.   "The Pre-School Child in Sierra Leone." West
    African Medical Journal, n.s., 10, 1961, pp. 314-319.

Thomas, T. C. E.   "Notes on the Mosquitoes and Mosquito-Borne
    Infections of Sierra Leone." Parts I and II. West African
    Medical Journal, n.s., 9, 1960, pp. 163-171.

Thompson, W. R.   "Field Notes on the Birds of Sierra Leone."
    Ibis, 1925, pp. 47-70.

Thorne, E. M. F.   "Some Notes on Industrial Development in
    Sierra Leone." Sierra Leone Studies, n.s., no. 20, 1967,
    pp. 201-205.

Timothy, E. B.   "The Deeds of Bokari, A Temne Folk-Tale,
    Freely Retold." African Affairs, 1952, pp. 61-72.

Turay, A. K.   "Temne Supernatural Terminology." Sierra Leone
    Bulletin of Religion, 9, 1967, pp. 50-55.

_____. "A Vocabulary of Temne Musical Instruments." Sierra
    Leone Language Review, 5, 1966, pp. 27-33.

Ture, A. B.   "Notes on the Customs and Ceremonies Attending
    the Selection and Crowning of a Bombali Temne Chief." Sierra

Leone Studies, o.s., no. 22, 1939, pp. 95-103.

Turner, H. W. "The Church of the Lord: The Expansion of a Nigerian Independent Church in Sierra Leone and Ghana." Journal of African History, 3, 1962, pp. 91-110.

Urquhart, D. H. "Report on the Cocoa Industry in Sierra Leone and Notes on the Cocoa Industry of the Gold Coast." Bournville: Cadbury Bros., Ltd., 1955. 43p.

Van dercook, J. W. "Devil-Bush of the Golas, A Secret Society that Dominates Tribal Life." Asia, 27, Jan. 1927, pp. 32-37.

Van der Laan, H. L. "Notes on the Statistical Documentation of the Economy of Sierra Leone." Sierra Leone Studies, n.s., no. 18, 1966, pp. 62-68.

Vivian, William. "Mendi Country, and Some of the Customs and Characteristics of Its People." Journal of the Anthropological Institute, XII, 1896.

_____. "The Missionary in West Africa." Journal of the African Society, no. 9, 1903. (A reply to no. 8, 1903--see Quilliam.)

Wallis, C. Braithwaite. "The Poro of the Mendi." Journal of the African Society, no. 14, 1905.

Wapensky, B. A. "Devaluation of the Leone and Sierra Leone." Economic Trends. Bank of Sierra Leone (Freetown), n.s., no. 2, 1967, pp. 17-21.

Warren, H. G. "The Arrest of Bai Forki After the 1898 Rising." (Publication of contemporary report with foreword by Frere, N. G.) Sierra Leone Studies, o.s., no. 20, 1936, pp. 129-132.

_____. "The History of the Chiefs of Tambakha Yobanji." Sierra Leone Studies, o.s., no. 15, 1929, pp. 67-71.

_____. "Notes on the Yalunka Country." Sierra Leone Studies, o.s., no. 13, 1928, pp. 25-28.

Watts, J. C. D. "The Chemical Composition of the Bottom Deposits from the Sierra Leone River Estuary." Bulletin de l'Institut Française d'Afrique Noire (Paris, Dakar), A, 19, 1957, pp. 1020-1029.

_____. "The Saw Fish of Sierra Leone." Nature (London), 182, 1958, pp. 961-962.

_____. "Seasonal and Tidal Fluctuations in the Trawl Catches from the Sierra Leone River Estuary." Nature (London), 183, 1959, pp. 1748-1849.

White, H. P.   "The Railways of Sierra Leone."   Railway Magazine (London), 106, 1960, pp. 231-237.

White, P. F.   "The Sierra Leone Survey."   Royal Engineers' Journal (Chatham), 46, 1932, pp. 303-309.

Wilkinson, J. L.   "Child Malnutrition in Sierra Leone."   Scottish Medical Journal, 9, 1965, pp. 64-67.

Williams, G. J.   "The Guma Valley Scheme, Sierra Leone." Geography (Sheffield), 50, 1965, pp. 163-166.

_____ .   "Quaternary Studies in Sierra Leone: A Review." Bulletin de l'Institut Française d'Afrique Noire, A, 28, 1966, pp. 427-430.

_____ .   "A Relative Relief Map of Sierra Leone."   Sierra Leone Geographical Journal, no. 11, 1967, pp. 11-14.

_____ .   "Some Observations on the Rainfall of the Freetown Peninsula."   Journal of the West African Science Association, 9, 1964, pp. 140-150.

Williams, R. H. K.   "The Konnoh People."   Journal of the African Society, Part I, no. 30, 1909; Part II, no. 31, 1909.

Williams, V.   "Some Aspects of Local Leadership in Relation to Population Movements in the Northern Region of Sierra Leone." Antropolog-nytt.   Organ for Antropolog-forenurgen, Stockholms Universitet (Stockholm), no. 6, 1965, pp. 8-16.

_____ .   "Social Change Among the Pastoral and Non-Pastoral Fulbe-Speaking Peoples of the Northern Region of Sierra Leone, 1964-1965."   Field report, University of Stockholm, 1966.

Wilson, H. S.   "The Changing Image of the Sierra Leone Colony in the Works of E. W. Blyden."   Sierra Leone Studies, n.s., no. 11, 1958, pp. 136-148.

_____ .   "E. W. Blyden on Religion in Africa."   Sierra Leone Bulletin of Religion, 2, 1960, pp. 58-66.

Wood, C. T.   "A Crowther Manuscript in Cape Town."   Bulletin of the Society of African Church History, 1, 1964, pp. 99-100.

Wood, J. Y.   "Prevention Measures Against Insect-Borne Disease." Report, Medical Department, Sierra Leone, 1925, pp. 15-18.

Woodhead, N., and Tweed, R. D.   "A Consideration of Freshwater Algae of Sierra Leone."   Proceedings of the Linnean Society of London (London), 166, 1956, pp. 82-86.

Wurie, A. "The Bundukas of Sierra Leone." Sierra Leone Studies, n.s., no. 1, 1953, pp. 14-25.

Young, R. R. "An Adult Literacy Campaign in Sierra Leone." Overseas Education (London), 15, 1944, pp. 97-100.

Young, W. C. E. "An Analysis of the 1965-66 West African Examinations Council General Certificate of Education Advanced and Ordinary Level Results and a Comparison with the 1964-65 Results in Sierra Leone." Research Bulletin, Department of Education, Fourah Bay College, no. 3, 1967, 74p.

_____. "Statistics of Education, 1964-1965." Research Bulletin, Department of Education, Fourah Bay College, no. 2, 1966, 64p.

Yudkin, J. "Riboflavin Deficiency in the West African Soldier." Journal of Tropical Medicine and Hygiene, 49, 1946, pp. 83-87. (Investigation of some 1050 troops in Sierra Leone.)

Zouche-Hall, R. de. "A Museum for Sierra Leone?" Sierra Leone Studies, n.s., no. 3, 1954, pp. 130-135.

Zwernemann, J. "Zum Gottesbegriff der Vai [the Vai concept of God]." Afrika und Ubersee (Hamburg), 43, 1959, pp. 127-132.